T0311881

Human Ecology Economics

This book presents "human ecology economics" as a new and more comprehensive interdisciplinary framework for understanding "world conditions and human systems." Global concerns addressed by this framework include climate change, poverty and inequality, resource scarcity, social conflict, financial instability, and governance crises – all of which threaten the sustainability of the global system. The book helps economists rethink the boundaries and methods of their discipline – so that they can participate more fully in debates over humankind's present problems and the ways that they can be solved.

Authors contributing to this book agree that human ecology economics is a superior framework for responding to global sustainability concerns because, unlike traditional economics and other social sciences, it allows a long run-time perspective, encourages use of the humanities, and effectively juxtaposes "sustainability" and other interdisciplinary issues alongside traditional economic issues. The contributors explore the following types of questions: What drives innovation and evolution in the world economy? What allows the U.S. one-third of the world's wealth and a leadership role going into the twenty-first century? How can we better understand and address the causes of poverty, inequality, social conflict, and inadequate food and energy supplies? Will responding to climate change and other concerns require changes in our ways of being? The book is written for the non-specialist as well as the professional economist in order to advance shared understanding of these "challenges to humankind."

This book is relevant to courses in Economics, International Relations, Environmental Science and Studies, Ecology and Political Economy among others, and will also benefit any professional audience interested in world conditions and global concerns, including business people, non-profit organisations and governments.

Roy E. Allen is Dean and Professor of Economics at the School of Economics and Business Administration, Saint Mary's College of California, U.S.A.

Routledge frontiers of political economy

1 Equilibrium Versus Understanding
   Towards the rehumanization of
   economics within social theory
   Mark Addleson

2 Evolution, Order and Complexity
   Edited by Elias L. Khalil and
   Kenneth E. Boulding

3 Interactions in Political Economy
   Malvern after ten years
   Edited by Steven Pressman

4 The End of Economics
   Michael Perelman

5 Probability in Economics
   Omar F. Hamouda and Robin Rowley

6 Capital Controversy, Post
   Keynesian Economics and the
   History of Economics
   Essays in honour of Geoff Harcourt,
   volume one
   Edited by Philip Arestis,
   Gabriel Palma and Malcolm Sawyer

7 Markets, Unemployment and
   Economic Policy
   Essays in honour of Geoff Harcourt,
   volume two
   Edited by Philip Arestis,
   Gabriel Palma and Malcolm Sawyer

8 Social Economy
   The logic of capitalist development
   Clark Everling

9 New Keynesian Economics/Post
   Keynesian Alternatives
   Edited by Roy J. Rotheim

10 The Representative Agent in
    Macroeconomics
    James E. Hartley

11 Borderlands of Economics
    Essays in honour of Daniel R. Fusfeld
    Edited by Nahid Aslanbeigui and
    Young Back Choi

12 Value, Distribution and Capital
    Essays in honour of Pierangelo
    Garegnani
    Edited by Gary Mongiovi and
    Fabio Petri

13 The Economics of Science
    Methodology and epistemology as if
    economics really mattered
    James R. Wible

14 Competitiveness, Localised
    Learning and Regional
    Development
    Specialisation and prosperity in small
    open economies
    Peter Maskell, Heikki Eskelinen,
    Ingjaldur Hannibalsson,
    Anders Malmberg and Eirik Vatne

15 Labour Market Theory
    A constructive reassessment
    Ben J. Fine

16 Women and European
    Employment
    Jill Rubery, Mark Smith, Colette Faga
    and Damian Grimshaw

17 **Explorations in Economic Methodology**
From Lakatos to empirical philosophy of science
Roger Backhouse

18 **Subjectivity in Political Economy**
Essays on wanting and choosing
David P. Levine

19 **The Political Economy of Middle East Peace**
The impact of competing trade agendas
Edited by J. W. Wright, Jnr

20 **The Active Consumer**
Novelty and surprise in consumer choice
Edited by Marina Bianchi

21 **Subjectivism and Economic Analysis**
Essays in memory of Ludwig Lachmann
Edited by Roger Koppl and Gary Mongiovi

22 **Themes in Post-Keynesian Economics**
Essays in honour of Geoff Harcourt, volume three
Edited by Claudio Sardoni and Peter Kriesler

23 **The Dynamics of Technological Knowledge**
Cristiano Antonelli

24 **The Political Economy of Diet, Health and Food Policy**
Ben J. Fine

25 **The End of Finance**
Capital market inflation, financial derivatives and pension fund capitalism
Jan Toporowski

26 **Political Economy and the New Capitalism**
Edited by Jan Toporowski

27 **Growth Theory**
A philosophical perspective
Patricia Northover

28 **The Political Economy of the Small Firm**
Edited by Charlie Dannreuther

29 **Hahn and Economic Methodology**
Edited by Thomas Boylan and Paschal F. O'Gorman

30 **Gender, Growth and Trade**
The miracle economies of the postwar years
David Kucera

31 **Normative Political Economy**
Subjective freedom, the market and the state
David P. Levine

32 **Economist with a Public Purpose**
Essays in honour of John Kenneth Galbraith
Edited by Michael Keaney

33 **Involuntary Unemployment**
The elusive quest for a theory
Michel De Vroey

34 **The Fundamental Institutions of Capitalism**
Ernesto Screpanti

35 **Transcending Transaction**
The search for self-generating markets
Alan Shipman

36 **Power in Business and the State**
An historical analysis of its concentration
Frank Bealey

37 **Editing Economics**
Essays in honour of Mark Perlman
Hank Lim, Ungsuh K. Park and Geoff Harcourt

38 **Money, Macroeconomics and Keynes**
Essays in honour of Victoria Chick, volume one
Philip Arestis, Meghnad Desai and Sheila Dow

39 **Methodology, Microeconomics and Keynes**
Essays in honour of Victoria Chick, volume two
Philip Arestis, Meghnad Desai and Sheila Dow

40 **Market Drive and Governance**
Reexamining the rules for economic and commercial contest
Ralf Boscheck

41 **The Value of Marx**
Political economy for contemporary capitalism
Alfredo Saad-Filho

42 **Issues in Positive Political Economy**
S. Mansoob Murshed

43 **The Enigma of Globalisation**
A journey to a new stage of capitalism
Robert Went

44 **The Market**
Equilibrium, stability, mythology
S. N. Afriat

45 **The Political Economy of Rule Evasion and Policy Reform**
Jim Leitzel

46 **Unpaid Work and the Economy**
Edited by Antonella Picchio

47 **Distributional Justice**
Theory and measurement
Hilde Bojer

48 **Cognitive Developments in Economics**
Edited by Salvatore Rizzello

49 **Social Foundations of Markets, Money and Credit**
Costas Lapavitsas

50 **Rethinking Capitalist Development**
Essays on the economics of Josef Steindl
Edited by Tracy Mott and Nina Shapiro

51 **An Evolutionary Approach to Social Welfare**
Christian Sartorius

52 **Kalecki's Economics Today**
Edited by Zdzislaw L. Sadowski and Adam Szeworski

53 **Fiscal Policy from Reagan to Blair**
The left veers right
Ravi K. Roy and Arthur T. Denzau

54 **The Cognitive Mechanics of Economic Development and Institutional Change**
Bertin Martens

55 **Individualism and the Social Order**
The social element in liberal thought
Charles R. McCann Jnr

56 **Affirmative Action in the United States and India**
A comparative perspective
Thomas E. Weisskopf

57 **Global Political Economy and the Wealth of Nations**
Performance, institutions, problems and policies
Edited by Phillip Anthony O'Hara

58 **Structural Economics**
Thijs ten Raa

59 **Macroeconomic Theory and Economic Policy**
Essays in honour of Jean-Paul Fitoussi
Edited by K. Vela Velupillai

60 **The Struggle Over Work**
The "end of work" and employment alternatives in post-industrial societies
Shaun Wilson

61 **The Political Economy of Global Sporting Organisations**
John Forster and Nigel Pope

62 **The Flawed Foundations of General Equilibrium Theory**
Critical essays on economic theory
Frank Ackerman and Alejandro Nadal

63 **Uncertainty in Economic Theory**
Essays in honor of David Schmeidler's 65th birthday
Edited by Itzhak Gilboa

64 **The New Institutional Economics of Corruption**
Edited by Johann Graf Lambsdorff, Markus Taube and Matthias Schramm

65 **The Price Index and its Extension**
A chapter in economic measurement
S. N. Afriat

66 **Reduction, Rationality and Game Theory in Marxian Economics**
Bruce Philp

67 **Culture and Politics in Economic Development**
Volker Bornschier

68 **Modern Applications of Austrian Thought**
Edited by Jürgen G. Backhaus

69 **Ordinary Choices**
Individuals, incommensurability, and democracy
Robert Urquhart

70 **Labour Theory of Value**
Peter C. Dooley

71 **Capitalism**
Victor D. Lippit

72 **Macroeconomic Foundations of Macroeconomics**
Alvaro Cencini

73 **Marx for the 21st Century**
Edited by Hiroshi Uchida

74 **Growth and Development in the Global Political Economy**
Social structures of accumulation and modes of regulation
Phillip Anthony O'Hara

75 **The New Economy and Macroeconomic Stability**
A neo-modern perspective drawing on the complexity approach and Keynesian economics
Teodoro Dario Togati

76 **The Future of Social Security Policy**
Women, work and a citizen's basic income
Ailsa McKay

77 **Clinton and Blair**
The political economy of the third way
Flavio Romano

78 **Marxian Reproduction Schema**
Money and aggregate demand in a capitalist economy
A. B. Trigg

79 **The Core Theory in Economics**
Problems and solutions
Lester G. Telser

80 **Economics, Ethics and the Market**
Introduction and applications
Johan J. Graafland

81 **Social Costs and Public Action in Modern Capitalism**
Essays inspired by Karl William Kapp's theory of social costs
Edited by Wolfram Elsner, Pietro Frigato and Paolo Ramazzotti

82 **Globalization and the Myths of Free Trade**
History, theory and empirical evidence
Edited by Anwar Shaikh

83 **Equilibrium in Economics**
Scope and limits
Edited by Valeria Mosini

84 **Globalization**
State of the art and perspectives
Edited by Stefan A. Schirm

85 **Neoliberalism**
National and regional experiments with global ideas
Edited by Ravi K. Roy, Arthur T. Denzau and Thomas D. Willett

86 **Post-Keynesian Macroeconomics**
Essays in honour of Ingrid Rima
Edited by Mathew Forstater, Gary Mongiovi and Steven Pressman

87 **Consumer Capitalism**
Anastasios S. Korkotsides

88 **Remapping Gender in the New Global Order**
    Edited by Marjorie Griffin Cohen and Janine Brodie

89 **Hayek and Natural Law**
    Eric Angner

90 **Race and Economic Opportunity in the Twenty-First Century**
    Edited by Marlene Kim

91 **Renaissance in Behavioral Economics**
    Harvey Leibenstein's impact on contemporary economic analysis
    Edited by Roger Frantz

92 **Human Ecology Economics**
    A new framework for global sustainability
    Edited by Roy E. Allen

Human Ecology Economics

A new framework for global
sustainability

Edited by Roy E. Allen

Routledge
Taylor & Francis Group

LONDON AND NEW YORK

First published 2008
by Routledge
2 Park Square, Milton Park, Abingdon, Oxon OX14 4RN

Simultaneously published in the USA and Canada
by Routledge
605 Third Avenue, New York, NY 10017

Routledge is an imprint of the Taylor & Francis Group, an informa business

Typeset in Times by Wearset Ltd, Boldon, Tyne and Wear

British Library Cataloguing in Publication Data
A catalogue record for this book is available from the British Library

Library of Congress Cataloging in Publication Data
A catalog record for this book has been requested

ISBN 13: 978-0-415-56939-2 (pbk)
ISBN 13: 978-0-415-77091-0 (hbk)

Contents

List of illustrations   xii
Preface and acknowledgments   xiv

PART I
The human ecology economics framework   1

1   A human ecology approach to economics   3
    ROY E. ALLEN

    Introduction 3
    A structural overview of human ecology 4
    Human ecology economics applied to various issues
        and problems 10

2   Innovation and evolution in the world economy   21
    GEORGE MODELSKI

    Introduction 21
    Evolution and change in the world economy 22
    Co-evolution 24
    The evolutionary paradigm 27
    World economic history 28
    K-waves and economic evolution 32
    K-waves and global political leadership 37
    The information economy 40
    Some implications for world politics 43

PART II
Globalization and development   47

3   Strange priors: understanding globalization   49
    DONALD SNYDER

Introduction 49
A human ecology approach to globalization 50
Economic globalization and belief systems 52
Globalization and development 69
Why is globalization so controversial? 78
Summary and conclusions 86
Appendix 87

**4   The peasant betrayed: a human ecology approach to
land reform in Nepal**   97
RAVI BHANDARI

Introduction 97
Underlying belief systems behind land reform 99
*Underlying situation of land markets and land reform in
    Nepal 102*
*What is to be done? Current proposals from Maoists and the
    World Bank 112*
Earlier land reforms in Nepal 115
Current and proposed legislation 117
Conclusions 123

**PART III
Money, capital, and wealth in the human ecology**   141

**5   Money and wealth in the human ecology: recent U.S.
"money mercantilism"**   143
ROY E. ALLEN

Introduction 143
Recent developments and instabilities in financial markets 145
A human ecology understanding of "wealth" 150
U.S. money mercantilism 155
Conclusions 160

**6   Money and capital in the human ecology: rethinking
mercantilism and eighteenth-century France**   163
GUILLAUME DAUDIN

Introduction 163
*On the importance of the invisible for the development of the
    visible French economy 166*
*On the role of external trade in accumulating circulating
    financial capital 174*
Conclusion 182

PART IV
Global concerns, ways of being, and the future 187

7 The role of economics in climate policy 189
ASBJORN MOSEIDJORD

Introduction 189
The climate challenge 190
The challenge to the human ecology 193
The economic traditions and beliefs 195
Building cost-effective institutions 201
Finding the best mitigation path 207
Conclusions 217
Appendix 218

8 Re-adjusting what we know with what we imagine 230
ANTONIO CASSELLA

Introduction 230
Population growth 235
The increase of poverty and affluence 237
Food and water shortages 238
The sixth extinction 240
The myth of green energy 242
Toward human-level artificial intelligence (HLAI) 246
The meeting of the self and the other 248
Concluding remarks: the slaying of the dragon and the return
  of Quetzalcoatl 251
Appendix A: definitions of key concepts 253
Appendix B: the growth of the world population, economy, and
  energy demand (2003–2060) 257

9 "Ways of being" in the economic system 265
ROY E. ALLEN

Introduction 265
Reconciling opposition between ways of being 269
Hierarchy (which ways of being are "dominant?") 283
Good versus bad, and freedom 284

Index 297

Illustrations

Figures

1.1	Structural conditions in the human ecology	7
1.2	Structural conditions in the human ecology: a bank	8
1.3	Structural conditions in the human ecology: the economic system	9
2.1	Growth in the number of internet hosts (Internet Domain Survey) fitted to a logistic curve	43
3.1	The four elements of a human ecology	51
3.2	Attitudes towards globalization	54
3.3	Eliminating poverty through growth	70
3.4	Eliminating poverty through redistribution	70
6.1	Gross physical product and population	167
6.2	Different types of capital	173
6.3	Evolution of french trade	179
7.1	Global CO_2 emissions and atmospheric concentrations, 1800–2001	191
7.2	Global warming process: a simplified description	192
7.3	Present value of $1 million to be received at different times in the future, at 5 and 1 percent discount rates	213
7.4	The power of decision frameworks: cost–benefit versus sustainability	215
7.A1	The fossil fuel market and the corresponding CO_2 emissions	219
7.A2	Emission reductions supply and demand	222
7.A3	Fossil fuel market surplus under three policy scenarios	223
8.1	Siege of Troy: growth of the poor	236
8.2	Chimæra: growth of the rich	237
8.3	The deterioration of the commons of the Earth	238
8.4	The effects of human encroachment on biodiversity	241
8.5	An assessment of fossil-fuel resources	242
8.6	Siege of Troy: growth in per-capita and world energy consumption	243

8.7   Chimæra: growth in per-capita and world energy
        consumption   243
8.8   Energy surplus by source, 2005–2060   245
8.9   To go and to come back   250
9.1   Ways of being (gods) as structural conditions of the
        human ecology   266
9.2   A mandala for the human ecology   267

Tables

2.1   Rational choice and evolutionary approaches compared   28
2.2   Evolution of the world economy   29
2.3   Evolution of the silk roads 100 BC to AD 1500   31
2.4   Evolution of the global economy   31
2.5   K-waves: the sequence of global leading sectors   34
2.6   Clustering of major innovations   37
2.7   The co-evolution of global economies and politics   38
2.8   K-waves and the attainment of global leadership   39
2.9   World microprocessor market shares   42
7.1   World primary energy use and reserves, 2001   198
7.2   Present-value equivalents   213
8.1   Per-capita income and energy consumption in the AE
        compared with sub-Saharan Africa and Southern Asia at
        the turn of the twentieth century   237
8.A1 Global population growth 2005–2060   257
8.A2 Global GDP growth in Siege of Troy   258
8.A3 Global GDP growth in Chimæra   258
8.A4 Global GDP per capita   259
8.A5 Global energy demand   260
8.A6 Global energy intensity   260
8.A7 Global energy per capita   261
9.1   Examples of ways of being (gods) within the global
        economy   266

Preface and acknowledgments

Dr. Kenneth Watt, Professor of Evolution and Ecology at the University of California, Davis, drew various interdisciplinary scholars together in the mid-1990s to produce an "Encyclopedia of Human Ecology." I was asked to coordinate the section on economics and integrate it with other sections on resources, demographics, systems theory, and so on. The encyclopedia remains unpublished, but this book stems from that initial effort. The goal was to understand what is happening to humankind – an ambitious goal that was driven by various concerns for the future.

Leading up to publication of this book, the economics group has presented its research twice at the annual meetings of the Allied Social Science Association, first in January 2000 in a session titled "A Human Ecology Approach to Economics," sponsored by the Association for the Study of the Grants Economy (ASGE), and second in 2007 in a session titled Sustainability of the Global System: New Insights from "Human Ecology Economics," sponsored by the Association for Social Economics (ASE).

Human Ecology Economics has thus been supported from the beginning by other heterodox approaches to economics. From their websites, "ASGE is devoted to the use of economic methodology to study non-market forms of reciprocity, linking economics to philosophy, psychology, sociology, and other social sciences," and ASE was formed

> to advance scholarly research and writing about the great questions of economics, human dignity, ethics, and philosophy. Its members seek to explore the ethical foundations and implications of economic analysis, along with the individual and social dimensions of economic problems, and to help shape economic policy that is consistent with the integral values of the person and a humane community.

Saint Mary's College of California should also be acknowledged as an excellent environment for interdisciplinary work of this kind that respects human values. The four contributing authors from Saint Mary's College – myself, Ravi Bhandari, Asbjorn Moseidjord, and Donald Snyder – have long studied and taught economics, but also important for this book, we have been encouraged by our college environment to consider various liberal arts approaches that ask fundamental questions about the human condition. In my own case, participation in the college's Collegiate Seminar program, especially its Greek Thought seminar, led to insights about "deep mythic structures" underlying contemporary thoughts and values, including about how the economic system works. It was also a pleasure to design and teach an upper division undergraduate course titled "Human Ecology Economics" in the fall of 2007, based upon this project, and to see how interdisciplinary students, especially coming from the college's departments of Economics, Environmental Science and Studies, etc., react to the material. I thank them for their patience and insights.

Linking economics to philosophy, psychology, sociology, and other social, human, and earth sciences – always careful to understand boundaries but willing to incorporate other ways of thinking – has been necessary for this project. The other contributing authors, Guillaume Daudin, George Modelski, and Antonio Cassella, have been open to that process, and in the case of Modelski and Cassella, expertise has been added more directly from political science and psychology, respectively.

All the authors have rich and diverse international backgrounds, and it has been delightful to learn from them informally, as well as through their written contributions. I am sure that, as editor, I have not done sufficient justice to their work. The building of a coherent sustainable ecology of thought, e.g. this book, seems to be just as difficult as building and maintaining a physical ecology. As editor I accept full responsibility for any mistakes or errors of judgment in that regard.

Roy Allen, 2008

Part I

The human ecology economics framework

Part I, comprising Chapters 1 and 2, provides a structural breakdown of "the human ecology" (see Figure 1.1); it argues for the new field of "human ecology economics"; and, as an introduction to the rest of this book, it discusses various topics that are addressed by this framework. In the editor's view, human ecology can be defined as both (a) the interrelated world conditions and human systems, and (b) an interdisciplinary field or perspective that studies world conditions and human systems. "The economic system" is seen as a subsystem of "the human ecology." Therefore, "economics" or "human ecology economics" (the study of the economic system) can be seen as a sub-field of "human ecology" (the study of the human ecology).

This approach is proposed to give economists maximum conceptual freedom to rethink the boundaries and methods of their discipline – so that they can participate more effectively in debates over humankind's present problems and on the ways that they can be solved. Current global concerns addressed by this book include climate change, poverty and inequality, challenges of economic growth and development, resource scarcity, social strife, effectiveness of global institutions, financial crises, and governance crises. These interrelated risks threaten the sustainability of the global system as we currently know it.

Authors contributing to this volume are in general agreement that human ecology economics is a new framework to effectively respond to these global sustainability concerns, because, unlike other economic analysis:

1   a very long run-time perspective is allowed;
2   it allows use of the humanities and other social sciences including a formal role for belief systems, "ways of being," and social agreements in the economic system;
3   everything varies – including belief systems, ways of being, and social agreements – and is dependent on everything else in complex, coevolutionary feedback processes;
4   global systems are emphasized; and
5   sustainability and other interdisciplinary issues are effectively juxtaposed with more traditional economic issues.

Part I also elaborates the various dynamic and evolutionary perspectives that "give life" to this human ecology economics structure. In this evolutionary process, clusters of new technologies, leading industrial and commercial sectors (currently the post-1973 information-industries), and supporting institutions allow "long-waves" of economic growth, which coincide with political leadership by the successful nation or nations (currently the U.S. and others). Periodic "clashes of civilizations," as well as the rise and fall of economies, are explained by these processes. While involving all structural components of the human ecology (as per Figure 1.1) in his analysis, in Chapter 2 George Modelski develops the dynamics of this human ecology approach, including Darwinian "human species" processes of search, selection, cooperation, innovation, reinforcement, etc. The reader is allowed a more comprehensive and long-run understanding of economic change compared to the growth and development models found in contemporary literature.

1 A human ecology approach to economics

Roy E. Allen

Introduction

A search for "human ecology" on the Google search engine produces an overwhelming 55 million results. A more traditional academic search, at the University of California, Berkeley library produces 903 references, which are scattered in various libraries ranging from Bioscience to Business and Economics and Environmental Design. Textbooks proposing to summarize this field include the early environmental-conservationist effort *Human Ecology: Problems and Solutions* (Ehrlich *et al.*, 1973), and the recent *Fundamentals of Human Ecology* (Kormondy and Brown, 1998). The former focuses on "the biological and physical aspects of man's present problems and on the ways that they can be solved," (p. v) and the goal of the latter "is to present the fundamentals of ecology and their application to humans through an integrated approach to human ecology, blending biological ecology with social science approaches," (p. xvii).

Much of this literature arose out of the environmental movement of the 1960s and 1970s, and gained breadth through recent explosions of interdisciplinary activity within academic institutions. At the College of the Atlantic, Maine, founded in 1969, the only degree offered to students is in human ecology, "which indicates that students understand the relationships between the philosophical and fundamental principles of science, humanities, and the arts."

Discussions of "human ecology" often include an important role for culture – as when anthropologists such as Brown (ibid.) handle the subject. In *Human Ecology as Human Behavior: Essays in Environmental and Developmental Anthropology* (Bennett, 1996) the author finds that:

> "human ecology" is simply the human proclivity to expand the use of physical substances and to convert these substances into resources – to transform Nature into Culture, for better or worse. ... Humans exploit and degrade, but they also conserve and protect. Their "stewardship" refers to constructive management of Nature, not cultural determinism.

The author's use of the term, as developed in this book, allows for most of these approaches, including a major role for the humanities and the interdisciplinary social sciences. The "structural overview of human ecology" developed in this chapter can be used to sort out various perspectives, rather than limit the reader to one or the other. Subsequently in this chapter, the author proposes a definition of "the economic system" as a subsystem of "the human ecology." Therefore, "economics" (the study of the economic system) can be seen as a sub-field of "human ecology" (the study of the human ecology).

This approach is proposed to give economists maximum conceptual freedom to rethink the boundaries and methods of their discipline – so that they can participate more fully in debates over "humankind's present problems and on the ways that they can be solved." Contributing authors in this book both identify problems in our economic system, and help to find solutions. Along the way, a "human ecology approach to economics," or "human ecology economics" seems to find its justification.

The human ecology approach to economics developed by the author is similar to the relatively recent field of "ecological economics." The latter has been given its impetus by the 1989 journal of the International Society for Ecological Economics, *Ecological Economics*, and various publications including the first real textbook, *An Introduction to Ecological Economics* (Costanza *et al.*, 1997). Earlier origins of this field are discussed by Juan Martinez-Aler in *Ecological Economics* (Martinez-Aler, 1987).

The emphasis on *human* ecology combined with economics brings the "*human*ities" as well as the physical science-based field of ecology to the study of economics, and the framework is thus broader than ecological economics. For example, as argued in Chapter 9, ideologies and "ways of being" (as defined through fields such as philosophy, psychology, sociology, religious studies, literature, etc.) are important structural components of the economic system, and they are not given sufficient attention within the fields of ecology, economics, or ecological economics – although a recent article in *Ecological Economics* did call for greater attention to the role of ideology and values (Söderbaum, 1999). Clearly the field of ecological economics could give greater importance to the role of intangible beliefs, values, various social constructs, etc., and how these intangible conditions co-evolve with tangible resources and populations, as per Norgaard (1994), but then, what we would seem to have is "a human ecology approach to economics," or "human ecology economics" rather than ecological economics.

A structural overview of human ecology

None of the 903 references to "human ecology" at the University of California, Berkeley, library cites the famous science fiction writer and social commentator H.G. Wells. Wells was one of the first to propose and develop this area of studies, and his articulation probably comes closest to the approach used here – given its emphasis on global economic and political processes. In an article in *Harper's Monthly Magazine* in 1937 he notes:

But in view of the number of able and distinguished people we have in the world professing and teaching economic, sociological, financial science and the admittedly unsatisfactory nature of the world's financial, economic, and political affairs, it is to me an immensely disconcerting fact that [Wells'] *Work, Wealth and Happiness of Mankind*, which was first published in 1932, remains – practically uncriticized, unstudied, and largely unread – the only attempt to bring human ecology into one correlated survey.

(Wells, 1937, p. 472)

Well's emphasis on a more interdisciplinary political economic approach responding to global concerns was complemented, before World War II, by various other earlier uses of "human ecology," as nicely summarized in the free electronic encyclopedia, Wikipedia (see http://en.wikipedia.org/wiki/Human_ ecology):

In the USA, human ecology was established as a sociological field in the 1920's, although geographers were using the term much earlier. Amos H. Hawley published *Human Ecology – A Theory of Community Structure* in 1950. He dedicated the book to one of the pioneers in the field who had begun writing the work with Hawley, R.D. McKenzie. Hawley contributed other works to the development of the field. In 1961, an important reader, Studies in Human Ecology, was published.

(edited by George A. Theodorson)

The issues that were important to H.G. Wells concerned "what is happening to mankind," and he used "human ecology" to describe the interdisciplinary framework or field that might provide a forum for scholars to investigate these issues. In *World Brain* (1938), he noted that knowledge was becoming so fragmented, so intradisciplinary, so disconnected from the major problems of humanity, that it was proving less useful to policymakers. Speaking of the people in the League of Nations and Roosevelt's "brain trust," he thought they had "uncoordinated bits of quite good knowledge," but they "knew collectively hardly anything of the formative forces of history...[nor of the] processes in which they were obliged to mingle and interfere." His solution to this problem was the development of an encyclopedia as

the means whereby we can solve the problem of that jig-saw puzzle and bring all the scattered and ineffective mental wealth of our world into something like a common understanding, and into effective reaction upon our vulgar everyday political, social and economic life.

Wells thought that human ecology should bring together various bodies of scholarship: "flowing into the problem of human society [would be] a continually more acute analysis of its population movements, of its economic processes, of the relation of its activities to the actual resources available."

Based upon these issues raised by Wells, and based upon subsequent, similar writings of economists such as Kenneth Boulding, this book proposes "a human ecology approach to economics." Boulding is acknowledged here especially for his work in the area of General Systems Theory, including the Society for General Systems Research. His essays in this area are collected in a 1974 volume (Boulding, 1974) and elaborate on many of the issues raised in this book, especially notions of what constitutes a social system. This book can be thought of as an update to Boulding's work – it reconstitutes some of the systems terminology of his 1974 volume as well as *Ecodynamics: A New Theory of Societal Evolution* (Boulding, 1978), and applies its framework to a host of contemporary issues: economic globalization and development; world energy resources and climate change; population trends and food challenges; money, capital, and wealth creation, transfer, and destruction; ideologies, mythologies, and "ways of being" in the economic system; evolution and innovation in the economic system including the role of institution and organizations; the rise of the "new economy"; and so on.

Human ecology can be defined as both (a) the interrelated world conditions and human systems, and (b) an interdisciplinary field or perspective which studies world conditions and human systems. As a body of studies, it seeks to coordinate previously disconnected knowledge, and make that knowledge available for a wide variety of practical purposes. If "interdisciplinary" means "activities taking place between well-identified disciplines," then human ecology is also transdisciplinary or non-disciplinary, because it does not assume that established disciplines are sufficiently comprehensive building blocks to frame the analysis. Phenomena-based and issue-based approaches are used as well as discipline-based approaches. Human ecology is also multidisciplinary, because it uses elements of various disciplines to build realistic models.

I propose various structural components or building blocks of human ecology. Perhaps the most fundamental components are human populations, belief systems, social agreements, and physical environments and resources. From these basic structural conditions other structural conditions emerge, such as organizations, institutions, and for the purpose of this book, economic systems. This structural identification or taxonomy is not meant to be the only way to characterize the human ecology, but rather a helpful starting point for discussion.

Figure 1.1 organizes the four basic structural conditions into quadrants. "Belief systems" is shown in the upper left quadrant, which can be defined as "ways of organizing alleged truths and convictions." Examples include, but are not limited to mythologies, religions, faiths, ideologies, philosophies, mathematics, science, and various academic fields. Social agreements, shown in the upper right quadrant, can be defined as "the structure that humans impose on their interaction." Social agreements usually reduce uncertainty; they are the formal and informal "rules of the game." Examples include, but are not limited to: politics; law; use of money; communications; and norms of culture and etiquette. In the lower right quadrant is "human populations" with characteristics that include birth, fertility, death rates, population age structure, migration, and spatial

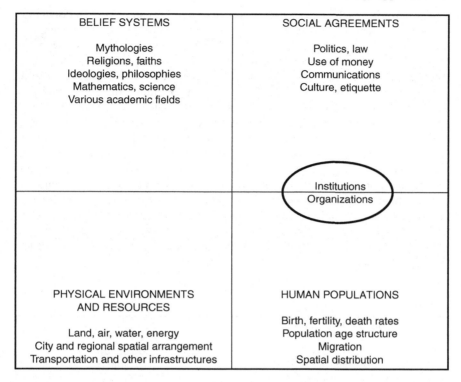

BELIEF SYSTEMS	SOCIAL AGREEMENTS
Mythologies Religions, faiths Ideologies, philosophies Mathematics, science Various academic fields	Politics, law Use of money Communications Culture, etiquette
PHYSICAL ENVIRONMENTS AND RESOURCES Land, air, water, energy City and regional spatial arrangement Transportation and other infrastructures	HUMAN POPULATIONS Birth, fertility, death rates Population age structure Migration Spatial distribution

Figure 1.1 Structural conditions in the human ecology.

distribution. In the lower left quadrant is "physical environments and resources," which includes land, air, water, energy, city and regional spatial arrangement, transportation and other infrastructures – both natural endowments as well as human-built.

The four basic structural conditions in the human ecology can also be more directly combined with each other to form new structural conditions. For example, as shown in Table I, "organizations" can be defined as *human populations* bound together by common *social agreements* – examples include firms, trade unions, political parties, and regulatory bodies. Of course, organizations use, and interact with, *belief systems* and *physical environments and resources*, but these interactions are not generally necessary in order for organizations to exist as legal entities. In common usage, "institutions" are sometimes closely synonymous with "organizations," and sometimes more synonymous with "social agreements." A useful definition for human ecology (similar to social agreements) from Douglass North is: Institutions are the rules of the game – both formal rules and informal constraints (conventions, norms of behavior, and self-imposed codes of conduct) – and their enforcement characteristics (North, 1997, p. 225).

Furthermore, each of the sub-elements in Figure 1.1 can be broken down into sub-sub-elements. For example, maybe we want to understand what a commercial bank is. With regard to belief systems, perhaps a bank relies upon the mathematics of exponential growth (such as the law of compound interest) and stock-and-flow-variable models, rather than the entire field of mathematics; and, maybe there is mostly an ideology of making money rather than other faiths or belief-system orientations. In Figure 1.2, these sub-sub-elements of belief systems are shown separately in the belief systems quadrant within the circle called "a bank." From the physical environment and resources, perhaps a bank requires commercial office space and utility infrastructures, which are therefore shown separately in that quadrant. Sub-sub-elements from social agreements and human populations are also identified, and when all sub-sub-elements are bundled together, we have the structure of "a bank." And what type of organization (human population bound by social agreements) is a bank? As shown in Figure 1.2, when the bank-structural-elements from human populations are bundled together with the bank-structural-elements from social agreements, then the new bundle is what we commonly call "a firm."

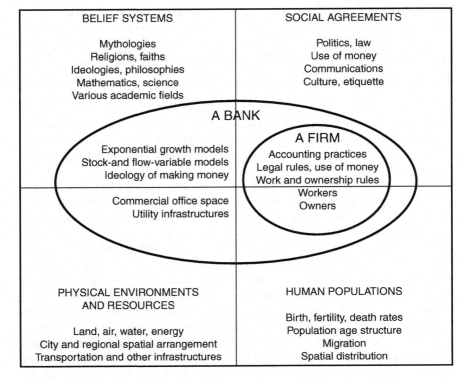

Figure 1.2 Structural conditions in the human ecology: a bank.

Based upon these structural components of the human ecology, Figure 1.3 shows a possible bundle of structural elements that might be used to describe the economic system. In this scheme, economic systems are shown to have important elements from each of the four basic structural conditions. Regarding belief systems, the human ecology approach proposes that the economic system relies heavily on mathematics, science, (traditional textbook) economics, ideal, faith, and myth among other factors. The types of social agreements, which are important in the economic system, include, but are not limited to, the use of money, policy, regulation, networks, and culture. From human populations there are workers, entrepreneurs, consumers, and policymakers, among others, and from physical environments and resources there are commodities, infrastructures, and natural resources among other tangible goods and structures.

Compared to most economics literature, which minimizes the importance of belief systems, social agreements, institutional change, and the integrity of physical environments and resources, the human ecology framework might allow for a more comprehensive identification and explanation of economic processes. Also in contrast to much of the economics literature, these structural components are assumed to interact with each other "endogenously" over time. That is, each

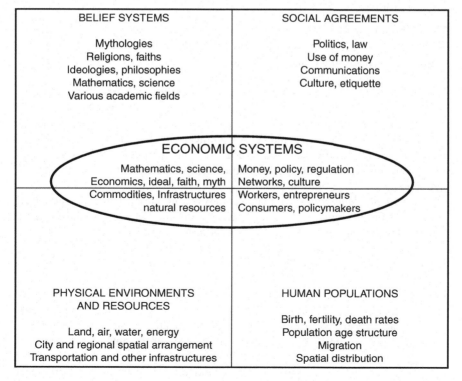

BELIEF SYSTEMS	SOCIAL AGREEMENTS
Mythologies Religions, faiths Ideologies, philosophies Mathematics, science Various academic fields	Politics, law Use of money Communications Culture, etiquette

ECONOMIC SYSTEMS

Mathematics, science, Economics, ideal, faith, myth	Money, policy, regulation Networks, culture
Commodities, Infrastructures natural resources	Workers, entrepreneurs Consumers, policymakers

PHYSICAL ENVIRONMENTS AND RESOURCES	HUMAN POPULATIONS
Land, air, water, energy City and regional spatial arrangement Transportation and other infrastructures	Birth, fertility, death rates Population age structure Migration Spatial distribution

Figure 1.3 Structural conditions in the human ecology: the economic system.

structural condition, defined broadly as per Figure 1.1, co-evolves with each of the others in complicated feedback processes, and all structures change. Broadly defined, no structural condition is absolutely fixed or "exogenous" or serves as a "global controller" of the others. Of course, human populations cannot exist without physical environments and resources, but human populations rearrange, destroy, and create new physical environments and resources.

Within "physical environments and resources," the laws of thermodynamics and other laws of natural science might serve as global controllers, as continually debated within the literature. However, the reader should note that "physical environments and resources" also includes the built environment and what human populations arbitrarily identify as "resources," which is partly based upon belief systems, the evolution of technology and social agreements, what organizations do, etc. Similarly, within "human populations," a certain amount of biological "hard wiring" might serve as a global controller, as debated in the literature, but clearly birth, fertility, death rates, migration and other characteristics of "human populations" are affected by what goes on in the other quadrants.

Human ecology economics applied to various issues and problems

The authors contributing to this volume are in general agreement that *Human Ecology Economics* is, indeed, as per the subtitle of the volume, a "new framework for global sustainability" as follows:

- *Long run-time perspective.* Unlike most economic analysis, the "world conditions and human systems" studied in this volume require perspectives and analysis for case studies stretching hundreds and thousands of years, such as climate change, the rise and fall of political and economic powers, assessments of mercantilism versus free trade, capitalism versus socialism, long-run resource availability, population-carrying capacity of the planet, long-run innovation and evolution, etc.
- *Use of the humanities.* Human ecology economics, to differentiate itself even from ecological economics, draws from the humanities, and formally incorporates into economic analysis the role of faiths, ideals, mythologies, belief systems, ways of being, etc. These "intangible components" of the economic system correlate with, and mutually impact, the tangible components.
- *Everything varies and is dependent on everything else.* Given the long run-time perspective of human ecology economics, all structural components of that human ecology – belief systems, social agreements, institutions, organizations, human populations, physical environments and resources – are allowed to change and co-determine changes in everything else. Most other frameworks within economics and related disciplines assume that some of these structures are constant.

- *Global systems emphasized.* The "world conditions and human systems" examined in this volume involve and impact most regions of the world. Unlike many other perspectives, the human ecology economics framework thus starts with broader and more comprehensive global perspectives, and treats smaller regional situations as "sub-ecologies" of the global system.
- *"Sustainability" and other interdisciplinary issues juxtaposed with "economic" issues.* As per the challenge of H.G. Wells, this more comprehensive human ecology approach is designed to help economists and others rethink the boundaries and methods of their discipline so that they can participate more fully in debates over humankind's present problems and on the ways that they can be solved. The four-quadrant diagram of Figure 1.1 – literally a framework – has proved useful among contributing authors to define "economics" (as per the use of Figure 1.3) and "sustainability." Regarding "sustainability," given the diversity of approaches to this topic, this book suggests the following: *In order to define sustainability, please indicate which structural elements within the four quadrant diagram of Figure 1.1 are being "sustained" and which are allowed (or required in many cases) to change, so that an ecology is defined as "sustainable."*

In Chapter 2, George Modelski correlates elements from the four quadrants of Figure 1.1 in order to explain technological innovation, economic growth, and global political leadership over the long history of economic development. Modelski identifies an evolutionary process whereby clusters of new technologies, leading industrial and commercial sectors (currently the post-1973 information-industries), and supporting institutions allow "long-waves" of economic growth, which coincide with political leadership by the successful nation or nations (currently the U.S. and others). Periodic "clashes of civilizations," as well as the rise and fall of economies, are explained by these processes. While involving all structural components of the human ecology as per Figure 1.1 in his analysis, Modelski develops the dynamics of this human ecology approach, including Darwinian "human species" processes of search, selection, cooperation, innovation, reinforcement, etc. The reader is allowed a more comprehensive interdisciplinary understanding of economic change compared to the growth models found in contemporary economics literature. The long-term formation of "the world market," as well as the recent "information economy" are seen as evolutionary stages of the human ecology. The processes of evolution and change in the economic system identified by Modelski are used by other authors throughout the book.

Modelski examines the interaction and "coevolution" of economic and political processes in the evolution of the world economy and world politics, and he "reacquaints" economics with politics. Back in 1776, when Adam Smith published *An Inquiry into the Nature and Causes of the Wealth of Nations*, the field of political economy was in its beginning stages as a sub-field within "moral philosophy." Adam Smith, sometimes called "the father of market capitalism," was a Professor of Moral Philosophy. Economics did not break free from political economy and try to escape from politics, ethics, and various other fields until much later – notably through the writings of Alfred Marshall (1890), among others.

One disadvantage, as the author mentioned earlier, of separating economics from moral philosophy, is that typical economic research now fails to identify the *belief systems* that are embedded in the analysis, which therefore results in severe "missing variables" and "incoherent specification" problems and difficulties in comparing literature. In the language of Douglass North:

> it is the belief systems of societies and the way they evolve that is the underlying determinant of institutions and their evolution... [furthermore] contrary to both the economic history literature and the economic growth literature – old and new – the primary source of economic growth is the institutional/ organizational structure of a political economy and until we focus on that subject we shall not advance knowledge on economic growth.
>
> (North, 1997, pp. 224–225)

Modelski's Chapter 2, along with this chapter, thus establishes Part I of this book. This chapter provides a structural identification of "the human ecology" along with the scope of economics topics and interdisciplinary methodologies to be allowed, and Chapter 2 elaborates various dynamic and evolutionary perspectives that "give life" to this human ecology economics structure.

Chapters 3 and 4 comprise Part II of this book, which applies the human ecology economics framework to a more in-depth understanding of the global economic system and the factors that are currently influencing growth and development within that system.

Chapter 3 by Donald Snyder uses the human ecology framework to identify and critique belief systems within the economics literature surrounding the controversial and important topic of recent "globalization." Through this literature, one can identify whatever common understanding of the global human ecology is currently available, including an understanding of what might be needed to sustain the system. Identifying these competing beliefs, and reconciling and verifying them where possible, constitutes a response to H.G. Wells' challenge and to the challenge of this book.

Snyder's thesis is that disagreements about globalization processes are primarily due to differences in *belief systems* and *social agreements* (Basic structural components of the human ecology economics framework of Figure 1.1 are italicized here for emphasis).

Specifically, the *physical environment and resources* factors (natural resources, transportation, communications) and *human population* factors (migration, spatial distribution) that are relevant to globalization have been widely discussed elsewhere. Though vastly important, they do not play much of a causal role in disagreements about globalization, so Snyder's chapter treats them as given and focuses on belief systems and social agreements.

Different observers, each viewing globalization through the lens of his or her own belief system, see different "globalization realities." Evidence which is persuasive to one group is deemed irrelevant by another. Concepts crucial to one organization's world view (fairness, for example) play a secondary role in the world view of others. These belief-system differences affect opinions about globalization-related *social agreements*, and thus about the *institutions* and *organizations* of globalization (e.g. the proper role of the IMF).

In Chapter 3 Snyder describes the belief systems of those who are for and against globalization. It starts with Kanbur's (2001) rough distinction between "finance ministry" types and "civil society" types, from which a more detailed set of groupings is developed. Globalization manifests itself in a multitude of ways. The chapter focuses on two areas where the disagreements have been intense: the relationship between openness and growth; and linkages from globalization to poverty and inequality. The chapter concludes with an assessment of reasons for differences in views, and prospects for greater agreement in the future.

Chapter 4, by Ravi Bhandari, examines in greater detail several of the "strange priors" mentioned by Donald Snyder that have to do with economic development in less developed countries. What is generally examined by Bhandari is the current call for land reform in many developing countries, and what is specifically examined is the use of land reform as a key intervention for sustainable agricultural systems in Nepal. The author argues that present problems in Nepal are a result of external needs and their alliances in Kathmandu, rather than the factual conditions on the ground.

Chapter 4 draws upon Bhandari's experience as a World Bank consultant in Nepal and employs the human ecology framework to uncover the curiously persistent and unanimous support for various kinds of land reform by both the far right and left. On the right, market-assisted land reforms are led chiefly by the World Bank, policymakers, and government officials, and a plethora of NGOs; and on the left, radical land reforms are led by the state and supported by civil society groups such as members of the "People's War" in Nepal today. These are curiously persistent positions given that nearly all land reforms throughout the entire Third World (with the notable exception of East Asia) have failed miserably. In fact, the welfare of the very same people the reforms were designed to protect (namely, the poor tenant-cum-borrower) have more often than not declined. An assessment of past land reforms confirms this view. A history of sustained regressive ecological distribution, in which the economic policies of the monarchy and Government of Nepal overwhelmingly favored the feudal aristocracy and political elite at the expense of the poor, are shown to have contributed to ecologically unsustainable practices also disproportionately affecting the latter.

In particular, a human ecology approach challenges the established *belief system* in economics where formal titled ownership of land, no matter how small is assumed to be generally more efficient than the diverse "pre-capitalist" *social arrangements* and contractual agreements that prevail in developing country agriculture. At the core of this dominant belief system is the long-term pursuit of individual property rights, small proprietorship as a goal, a depoliticization of the rural population where political actors are equated with economic ones, and where potential sources of conflict and inequality are best approached through market mechanisms and minimal state intervention.

Moreover, a human ecology perspective towards land reform, as applied to the case study of present Nepal whose future hangs in the balance, weakens the case for all types of land reform considerably. Unlike competing belief systems in the current global debates on land reform and tenure security that suffer from key 'omitted variables,' all four quadrants of Figure 1.1 are explicitly taken into consideration including:

1   an adverse macroeconomic environment that induces increasing economic inequality, political instability and conflict;
2   how rural markets actually work with respect to existing social arrangements;
3   economic deprivation and related grievances of the poor; and
4   the pressure of modern forms of property rights on the natural, physical, and social environment.

This chapter suggests, based on the experience of Nepal, that the highly unequal and unegalitarian land distribution may be the *result* of these structural conditions rather than a cause. In parallel with Snyder's chapter on the debates on globalization, a human ecology of land reform is a telling example of how strong "politically correct" beliefs from each opposing side are ideologically based, and as such, can lead to dangerous policy conclusions.

Part III of this book moves the analysis from the more tangible and physical growth and development processes discussed in Part II to the more intangible and symbolic financial processes of the global system. In this regard, *belief systems* are found to be especially important determinants of financial outcomes. For example, financial crises can occur if the *belief system* of debtors and creditors is not compatible with the ability of *the human population* working with *the physical environment and resources* to produce wealth. Invisible belief systems have supported a money economy based on the transcendental "law of compound interest" and an easing of lending restrictions. The acceptance and growth of "offshore finance" is an example of how belief systems – in this case free-market capitalist ideology – drive changes in institutions, *social agreements*, and ultimately, *physical environments and resources*. Offshore market institutions, such as the Bangkok International Banking Facility, encouraged unsustainable over-lending, excessive unprofitable construction of real estate, etc., and ultimately contributed to the risk of crisis, recession and misery throughout Asia in 1997. "The logic of global finance," with its interest-rate-parities and other formal and informal rules, can be thought of largely as an "institution" as per North's definition above. And, this *institution*, for much of the world economy, now seems to serve as a *global controller*. In the language of human ecology discussed above, *human populations*, their *belief systems*, their *social agreements*, and their relationship with *the physical environment and resources* are increasingly impacted by, and are conforming to or reacting against the logic of global finance.

These issues are addressed in Chapter 5. The author suggests that the new global economy, especially its financial side, has evolved over time to become the "infrastructure of the infrastructure" – largely as a result of advances in information-processing technology, other innovations, and changing *social agreements* and *belief systems* such as government deregulation based upon free-market capitalist ideology. In his 1944 book, *The Great Transformation*, Karl Polanyi argued that during the industrial revolution "self-regulating market economy" became dominant over most other social systems and even constrained what nation-states could do – the late nineteenth century, often called a period of "British hegemony," was actually a period of transnational market hegemony which was only centered in London. Chapter 5 argues that a new great transformation is now occurring within self-regulating transnational market economy: global financial markets are now becoming more autonomous and controlling than non-financial markets.

The human ecology approach, with its emphasis on belief systems and institutions, can be used to reinterpret economic history as well as current trends. Many of the financial processes identified in Chapter 5 to explain recent U.S. prosperity are used by Guillaume Daudin in Chapter 6 to explain early European history. Chapter 6 elaborates the importance of financial processes in the *ancien régime* of France during the early industrial revolution period, and it provides insights into these "great transformations." Then, as now, the ability of *the human population* working with *the physical environment and resources* to produce wealth can be significantly affected by *social agreements* regarding the use of money and by financial *institutions*. In particular, both the *ancien régime* of the eighteenth century, and the U.S. in recent decades benefited from the inflow of foreign monetary wealth, which was used to expand domestic money, credit, economic growth, and wealth. This process allowed economic activity to be better coordinated and more efficient on a large scale, and it encouraged more intensive production and consumption activities.

Compared to typical literature, the human ecology approach to economics might allow for better modeling of both the successful *ancien régime* and recent U.S. prosperity. Typical literature has been puzzled by these two epochs, because it looks for the source of new economic growth more narrowly in technology, physical resources, and inherent labor productivity while assuming incorrectly that the impact of money, changing institutions, and international political power is fairly neutral. This new framework of Allen and Daudin is supported by other researchers including Clark (1998), whose work indicates that the Industrial Revolution was more of an "industrious revolution" resulting from new workforce participation and coordination, rather than a breakthrough in technology and inherent skills of the average worker as per the emphasis of common economics literature.

England, like France, supported its economic growth in the early industrial revolution period with massive amounts of imports and appropriation of wealth from its empire. The "Malthusian Trap" of overpopulation and poverty was avoided, and *human populations* grew fast, as aided by new political-economic *institutions* and *organizations*, and by *belief systems* regarding work and exploitation of *the physical environment and resources*. Enhanced money transaction systems brought, especially, under-utilized rural labor into the formal economy in Britain as well as France. Exploitation of coal, and thus railroads, steam engines, and other changes in *the physical environment and resources* all co-evolved with these other structural conditions in the human ecology.

In the human ecology approach used by Daudin and Allen to arrive at these conclusions, as in any natural science ecology approach, intraspecies negotiations and transactions are exploratory, adaptive, often individualized, and the outcomes are not known to all members of the species. This belief system has different consequences than the belief system of neoclassical economics in which transactions costs (a catch-all category for a variety of intraspecies activities) are assumed to be either trivial or not worth exploring except as a general constraint on the otherwise superior "efficiency" of markets. For example, if full information, to all, on intraspecies transactions, is not available, as per the human ecology approach, the evolution of prices is not as straightforward, because prices cannot be changed by spontaneous unanimous social agreement. Thus, as Daudin and Allen find, money is not simply a veil on the real economies, but can actually play a major role, in the eighteenth century as well as nowadays, in determining the comparative and absolute prosperity of nations. Money, as an invisible element of the human ecology or "social agreement," as well as related notions of "capital," within a complicated process of intraspecies negotiation and transaction, are shown to be system drivers.

An important component of this process Allen calls, in Chapter 5, "money-mercantilism."

Historically, "mercantilism" is the use of restrictive trade policies and colonial empires, especially by the European *ancien régime* of the seventeenth and eighteenth centuries, in order to accumulate monetary wealth such as gold and silver. The institutional advantage used by powerful European states to appropriate unequal gains from international commerce was recognized by the German Historical School in the nineteenth century as an important determinant of "the wealth of nations" – perhaps a more important determinant than the decentralized "invisible hand" interactions and efficiencies of supply and demand which Adam Smith described in *An Inquiry into the Nature and Causes of the Wealth of Nations*. What Allen adds to the historical mercantilist perspective, in order to make it "money-mercantilism," is the notion that extraction of money-wealth from other regions, through institutional advantage, does not require trade in merchandise and services, but instead it only requires dominance in financial affairs. Elaboration of these issues provides new insights into the historic free-trade versus mercantilism/nationalism debate.

Through the issues raised by Part I, II, and III of this book, the human ecology approach might thus shed light on economic growth, development, financial stability and wealth debates. While these issues are not new, a framework such as Figure 1.1 might at least help clarify the debates and increase the coherence of various models. One well-known model that has been around for decades is the effort by Herman Daly and others to describe a "steady-state" economy as an antithesis to the "growth economy." By "steady state" Daly means that "two basic physical magnitudes are to be held constant: the population of human bodies and population of artifacts (stock of physical wealth)" (Daly, 1991, p. 16). In the framework of Figure 1.1, the lower two quadrants – human populations and physical environments and resources – would have stationary magnitudes (although their composition would change). Daly and others then proceed to identify coherent belief systems and social agreements, and hence organizations and institutions, which would be compatible with a steady state.

A "steady state" economy or ecology is an older notion that is increasingly replaced by notions of a "sustainable" economy or ecology. Part IV of this book – Chapters 7, 8, and 9 – applies the human ecology framework to, as per the H.G. Wells challenge, "coming challenges to humankind." Most of these challenges have to do with challenges to the "sustainability" of what we know and value.

Chapter 7 by Asbjorn Moseidjord helps define notions of sustainability while at the same time contrasting "sustainability analysis" with the "cost–benefit analysis" typically applied by economists. Moseidjord applies both frameworks to one of the most important (depending on your belief system) sustainability issue and global concern of our generation: climate change.

Sustainable development is currently defined by the Intergovernmental Panel on Climate Change in the same way that it was defined earlier by The World Commission on Environment and Development (1987) as: "Development that meets the needs of the present without compromising the ability of future generations to meet their own needs." As elaborated by Moseidjord in Chapter 7, this popular and general notion of sustainability integrates "three sets of values: economic well-being, social justice, and environmental quality in a limitless time perspective." To make this notion of sustainability useful, contributing authors agree that it needs to be broken down more carefully in the four quadrant diagram of Figure 1.1 – an exercise that also requires identification of the "belief system" used to define these vague concepts of well-being, justice, and quality. In other words, which structural elements within the four quadrant diagram of Figure 1.1 are being "sustained" and which are allowed (or required) to change, so that an ecology is defined as "sustainable?" Furthermore, not only structural but also dynamic cause-effect linkages between the three core values need to be identified. Some may argue that there are trade-offs between the core values; others that environmental quality is just a means to realizing the other two values. In particular situations, controversies may arise over the criteria to judge the degree to which the values are realized.

In terms of climate change, as discussed by Moseidjord, the U.N. has begun to clarify its position on what needs to be held constant or sustained: partly in response to the IPCC's findings since its establishment in 1988, the U.N. entered into the United Nations Framework Convention on Climate Change (1992) with the essential objective being "…stabilization of greenhouse gas concentrations in the atmosphere at a level that would prevent dangerous anthropogenic interference with the climate system." Given this starting point, and a new consensus that potentially dangerous (however defined) global warming as caused by humans is happening, Moseidjord turns his attention to mitigation policy and the role of economics and other frameworks in identifying solutions. His general conclusion is that global warming results from a specific failure of human institutions and its solution requires appropriate institutional change. Within certain limits (in order to maintain its integrity) economics can help with peaceful and cost-effective ways to accomplish that institutional change in response to climate change and other global concerns.

And how does appropriate institutional change happen in response to global concerns? As quoted above from Douglass North, "it is the belief systems of societies and the way they evolve that is the underlying determinant of institutions and their evolution..." Chapters 8 and 9 by Cassella and Allen, respectively, delve further into the belief system roots of personal, cultural, and institutional change. The notion of "belief system" is expanded to encompass personality traits, social behaviors, physical energies, etc. – all of which might need to change or evolve in response to the global sustainability concerns raised by this book.

A list of major interrelated global sustainability concerns is discussed by Cassella in Chapter 8, and it includes climate change catastrophes, abject poverty, starvation, scarcity of energy, food, water, shelter, pandemics, use of weapons of mass destruction, loss of the support of communication and other infrastructures, social strife and violence, failure of global institutions, financial crises, and governance crises.

In order to better identify the risk of these global concerns over the next fifty years, in Chapter 8 Antonio Casella provides two hypothetical long-term scenarios (actually "drifts") that constitute a challenging paradox: the history-based "Siege of Troy" (in which the gap between the wealthy and the poor becomes socially intolerable) and the imaginary "Chimæra" (in which that gap is decreased). Both drifts prove to be untenable. However, considering them is useful in a quest for global sustainability within the framework of the dilemmas posed by population growth, intolerable poverty, reduced biodiversity, imperiled quality of the atmosphere, potential food restrictions, and increased competition for space-energy resources.

Although no definitive solutions for overcoming these dilemmas are presented, the issues discussed by Casella point to an urgent need to "re-imagine" methods of planning that link respect for tradition with new, inter-subjective educational schemata that might reconcile human social growth with the global environment at large. Ultimately then, examination of our belief systems, and resulting social agreements, and modification of our "invisible conditions" might be the only way that human populations can sustain themselves with limited physical environments and resources. Maybe new, more environmentally sound ways to achieve psychic wants, perhaps allowed by new, low-fuel-using communications technologies, is a way out of the Malthusian dilemma. The emphasis within human ecology economics, on the systematic understanding of the role of belief systems and other intra-species relations, might then prove to be propitious indeed.

Drawing upon his research on the social limitations of autistic individuals, as well as other understandings of creativity and social change, Cassella explores ways that the human ecology might avoid less sustainable "ways of being" in the like of self-importance, hatred, fear, greed, and ambition, in favor of more sustainable ways of being that nurture the human ecology toward understanding, seeking and displaying altruism, humility, motherly love, serenity, sobriety, responsibility, etc.

In various authors' views, less tangible beliefs and ways of being change along with, and mutually impact, the more tangible conditions – productive resources, human populations, commodities, etc. Thus, to exclude the less tangible conditions results in what economists call "missing variable problems," and what others might call incoherence, confusion, misunderstanding, or narrow-mindedness. For example, if economic analysts or decision-makers are operating under different hidden ideologies, or if they are not aware of the "deep mythic structures" that drive them, then shared understanding and effective problem solving are difficult. In this situation people often do not know when they agree with each other, or when it is necessary to "agree to disagree."

In Chapter 9, the author struggles further with questions such as these, and broadens ethical frameworks to include "ideologies, mythologies, and ways of being in the economic system." From the four basic components of the human ecology proposed in this chapter – belief systems, social agreements, human populations, and physical environments and resources – the author constructs "ways of being" as "bundles of faiths, beliefs, social behaviors, personality traits, and physical energies." Six specific examples (many more can be posited) of ways of being are discussed which the author believes to be "at play" in the economic system.

Economic decision-makers, policymakers, business groups, environment or social movements etc., might all be, at certain times, "in the grip" of one or more of these ways of being. The advantage of "holding at arms length" and contemplating these ways of being is that one might then be in a better position to "chose" a way of being, or at least be aware of its consequences. Also, the author demonstrates that economic history, including developments in capitalism, socialism, technology, environmentalism, etc., can be better understood when the "deep mythic structures" underlying these developments are exposed and discussed.

In the author's view, at the root of many economic problems, in addition to misunderstood, ignored, or dysfunctional "*invisible* conditions" – belief systems, ethical frameworks, ways of being, social agreements, etc. – there is also misunderstanding of complex feedback processes between the *visible* conditions – human populations and physical environments and resources. In many cases, perhaps misunderstanding of the feedback processes between the *visible* conditions is due to ignorance of an intermediary role played by *invisible* conditions. In the human ecology approach, allowing for the possibility that each of the structural conditions in the four quadrants of Figure 1.1 might be dependent on the others, in complex ways, might result in better descriptions, modeling, and predictions of a variety of economic processes.

References

Bennett, John W. (1996), *Human Ecology as Human Behavior: Essays in Environmental and Developmental Anthropology*, Transaction Publishers: New Jersey.

Boulding, Kenneth E. (1974), *Collected Papers, Volume Four: Toward a General Social Science*, Colorado Associated University Press: Boulder.

Boulding, Kenneth E. (1978), *Ecodynamics: A New Theory of Societal Evolution*, Sage Publications: Beverly Hills.

Clark, Gregory (1998), "Too much revolution: agriculture and the industrial revolution, 1700–1860," paper presented at the 38th Annual Cliometrics Conference, Washington University in St. Louis, May 8–10.

Costanza, Robert, John Cumberland, Herman Daly, Robert Goodland, Richard Norgaard (1997), *An Introduction to Ecological Economics*, St. Lucie Press: Florida.

Daly, Herman E. (1991), *Steady-State Economics, Second Edition with New Essays*, Island Press: Washington, D.C.

Ehrlich, Paul R., Anne H. Ehrlich, and John P. Holdren (1973), *Human Ecology: Problems and Solutions*, W.H. Freeman and Company: San Francisco.

Kanbur, Ravi (2001) "Economic Policy, Distribution, and Poverty: the Nature of Disagreements," *World Development*, 29 (6), pp. 1083–1094.

Kormondy, Edward J. and Daniel E. Brown (1998), *Fundamentals of Human Ecology*, Prentice Hall: New Jersey.

Marshall, Alfred (1890), *Principles of Economics*, Eighth Edition 1920, Macmillan Company: New York.

Martinez-Aler, Juan (1987), *Ecological Economics*, Basil Blackwell: Oxford.

Norgaard, Richard B. (1994), *Development Betrayed: the End of Progress and a Coevolutionary Revisioning of the Future*, Routledge: London.

North, Douglass C. (1997), "Some fundamental puzzles in economic development," in W.B. Arthur, S. Durlauf, and D. Lane (eds.) *The Economy as a Complex Evolving System II*, Addison-Wesley: New York.

Polanyi, Karl (1944), *The Great Transformation*, Beacon Press: Boston, MA.

Smith, Adam (1776), *An Inquiry into the Nature and Causes of the Wealth of Nations*, c.1965, Random House: New York.

Söderbaum, Peter (1999), "Values, Ideology, and Politics in Ecological Economics," *Ecological Economics*, 28, pp. 161–170.

Wells, H.G. (1937), "The Idea of a World Encyclopedia," *Harper's Monthly Magazine*, April, pp. 472–482.

Wells, H.G. (1938), *World Brain*, Doubleday, Doran & Co.: New York.

World Commission on Environment and Development (1987) *Our Common Future*, Oxford University Press: New York.

2 Innovation and evolution in the world economy

George Modelski

Introduction

The author's recent work (Modelski and Thompson, 1996) indicates that today's students of economics pay less than appropriate attention to three problem areas:

1 the very long-range analysis of the world economy;
2 the all-pervasive role of innovation; and
3 the "human ecology" links between the economy, politics, society, and culture.

This chapter explores these expansive questions in a systematic manner. The manner is systematic because it is grounded in an evolutionary perspective. The notions of evolution and systemic change that are discussed in the next section are basic to the "human ecology approach" used throughout this book, and are therefore explored thoroughly before they are applied to the study of long-run political-economic processes. That is why, after setting out the essentials of the evolutionary perspective, this chapter goes on to:

1 sketch out a long term view of economic history;
2 highlight the role of innovation and evolution in that process; and
3 delineate the links between economics and politics at the global level over the millennium now past.

This account specifies the dynamic processes driving the structural components of human ecology elucidated by the four-quadrant diagram Roy Allen presents in Chapter 1 (Figure 1.1): belief systems, social agreements, human populations, and physical environments and resources. As for Douglass North's distinction, this account concerns both *institutions*: "formal rules and informal constraints, such as conventions, norms of behavior, self-imposed codes of conduct, and their enforcement," as well as *organizations*: the agents whose policies and interactions animate evolution at the most basic level, in all dimensions of the world system. The institutional level is seen as basic, and changes at a millennial pace, and concerns, for the world economy of the modern era, the market economy (Table 2.2). Organizations, on the other hand, change at a faster clip all through the modern era (Table 2.4), with, for example, banks prominent in the Italian Renaissance; trading companies in the Dutch era; industrial enterprise in the British; and multinational corporations in the American periods.

The principal assignment for this chapter is to trace long-term patterns in the evolution of economic and political structures. Particular interest focuses on the modern era and the interactions, in that time span, of these two sets of processes. But to put such large-scale developments in context, it is necessary to clarify the nature of this evolutionary approach, and the broad outlines of the evolution of the world economy over the long span of what we know as history.

Evolution and change in the world economy

The approach adopted here is best described as "evolutionary" because it centers on the problem of understanding social change as the product of learning processes involving the mechanisms of innovation, selection, cooperation, and reinforcement. It seeks to clarify how and why the economic organization of the human species has reached the degree of complexity and productivity it exhibits today, and how and why the world political system exhibits the degree of global reach and effectiveness it has today, and how both of these sets of structures might change over the foreseeable future.

The distinctive characteristic of this approach is its "human species" and "human ecology" focus, that is, its conception of social evolution as a set of continuing and interlinked processes of change involving the entire human species. It might be contrasted with accounts that place the emphasis on the "evolution" of individual societies and on the questions of "why do societies differ, and how do they change over time" – questions that have preoccupied many social scientists attracted by evolutionary theories. By contrast, the present approach adopts a planetary species outlook, and focuses on the world as a whole.

Social change, in and of itself, is not really surprising. We might postulate that humans continuously search for ways of bettering their conditions, and will change their behavior as the situation requires. Travelers between *A* and *B* will seek out the best route between these points – one that is shortest, safest, or the most economical – and they will change the routing arrangements according to the relevant circumstances guided by considerations of rational choice. In the economy, too, both producers and consumers are always on the lookout for improved performance.

What is not so easy to account for are patterns of change over long periods with pronounced directionality. These involve questions of a different order – not just how to get from *A* to *B*, but why not go to *C* or *D* instead, and in the process invent new ways that take us to *F*. When shifts in preferences come to the foreground, and the constraints on action are loosened, different modes of explanation usually prove more fruitful.

The paradigm best suited to explicating structural change in the global economy is an evolutionary one. Joseph Schumpeter was a pioneer of an evolutionary approach to economics. More than any other economist, he helped to advance the view that innovation was central to the process of economic growth and to fluctuations that are a necessary consequence of growth. He opposed what he described as the Marshallian theory of evolution and denied that the structure of the economy evolves in a steady or smooth fashion.

In the *Theory of Economic Development* (1934), Joseph Schumpeter set out to construct a coherent account of economic change by showing how the economic system incessantly transforms itself. The mechanism of transformation consists of entrepreneurs (with access to credit) who exercise economic leadership by pursuing equilibrium-destroying innovations in continuous winner-and-loser producing competition. In *Business Cycles* (Schumpeter, 1939) he introduced English-speaking audiences to the concept of long waves of fifty to sixty years as a bunching of innovations. He named them Kondratieff-waves after Nikolai Kondratieff. Further detail is provided on these K-waves in a later section of this chapter titled "the evolutionary paradigm."

More recently, Richard Nelson and Sidney Winter (1982) have taken up the Schumpeterian themes in *An Evolutionary Theory of Economic Change*. Theirs is a critique of the neoclassical model based on equilibrium and rational choice, and a proposal for an alternative perspective based on the distinction between routine operations and innovative search and selection. In their view, the main theoretical commitments of evolutionary theory have application in relation to transitions from one period to the next. While their focus is on the behavior of individual firms, it is also clear that their emphasis on transitions (and not equilibrium) is a great aid to understanding long-range processes.

Other students of innovation have also been drawn toward an evolutionary perspective. Gerhard Mensch saw these problems as necessary features of industrial evolution. For Christopher Freeman, Carlotta Perez, and Giovanni Dosi, economic evolution is a succession of technological or socio-technical paradigms, with each K-wave embodying one such paradigm (the latest defined by what is called here "the information revolution"). K-wave studies find a good home in an evolutionary framework because innovation and transition are keys to understanding such processes of social structural change. The distinguishing characteristics of evolutionary processes include the following:

1 they embody mechanisms of search and selection;
2 they occur when the necessary and sufficient conditions are present;
3 they are constitutive of generational lineages; and
4 they co-evolve with other evolutionary processes.

Let us look briefly at the first three points, leaving the last for the next section.

Ever since Charles Darwin, search and selection have been the central mechanisms of the evolutionary process. Search is generated by variation (mutation) or, in our context, innovation that advances solutions to social problems.

In favorable conditions, the economic system generates a stream of innovations that are then subject to a process of selection. In Darwinian biology it is the natural environment that exerts selective pressure; in social contexts the process is a competitive one in a market sense. K-waves describe the rise of clusters of innovations that respond to the demands of a competitive marketplace and put in place new industrial or commercial sectors or new forms of economic organization. The rise of new firms and leading sectors is the micro-level mechanism that drives growth in what becomes the lead economy. Economies that create the most favorable conditions for innovation and market selection are also likely to be those that originate K-waves.

The necessary and sufficient conditions for the initial rise of a K-wave in a potential lead economy are innovative entrepreneurs:

1   operating in market economies with access to resources and credit;
2   in the context of an open society;
3   in favorable political circumstances; and
4   in conditions of global competitiveness, including responsiveness to global problems.

But the outcomes of evolutionary events do not exist in a vacuum, rather they are linked at the macro-level in chains of processes that trace distinctive lineages. Darwinian macroevolution traces the origin of all life on earth through lines of common descent. While social change is much faster, structures of behavior, too, are related in lineages and may be seen to build on antecedents and to accumulate. By a process of accumulation, a succession of K-waves have shaped the emergence and the functioning of the global economy.

Co-evolution

Co-evolution is the last characteristic of evolutionary processes that do not unfold in a vacuum, but may be presumed to co-evolve. That is, to relate in a determinate manner to other evolutionary processes. World system evolution engages a cascade of processes of which several components must be distinguished and their mutual relationship traced (Devezas and Modelski, 2003).

The author proposes that co-evolution occurs for two reasons: substantively, because of the necessity of co-action; and as regards form, because of synchronization – that is, the concurrence of events in respect to time.

Co-action

The author's research (Modelski, 1999; Modelski and Thompson, 1996) indicates that long-run economic innovation and global political leadership of nation-states are two structurally similar global evolutionary processes, and that this structural similarity alone makes it more likely that the two processes are interrelated. But these event sequences are not just interrelated – each is the necessary condition of the performance of the other. In other words, co-action is called for and occurs *in time* because it is necessary over the entire length of that process. It occurs *in space* because, in all the cases we have looked at so far, both processes were based on one and the same area – in the four most recent cases, a nation-state.

What, then, might be the reasons for such coordination? In the first place, these are constraints of efficiency that have to do with ease of communications and costs of supplying inputs. Locational studies have shown that innovation is highest at sites at which communication is swift and easy between producers and their markets, and where a variety of input is available. K-waves have not only been dominated by countries such as Britain and the United States, but also by regions within those countries. In Britain, for instance, the first industrial wave was dominated by Lancashire, Shropshire, and the Black Country, with the second wave dominated by newer regions such as South Wales and the North East. In the United States, the west has now become a major center of the information industries, with Silicon Valley in California already becoming a textbook example of that process.

All this suggests that a nation-state, being the common site of these two processes, also serves as a coordinating factor because proximity helps to expedite both of them. Transaction costs are lowered, communication is cheaper, and factors of production common to these processes are more easily mobilized. This national "basing-mode" affords both security and openness of conditions, and provides the arena within which all kinds of innovations thrive. We might add, though, that the specialization of one site, based on one innovative paradigm, also makes it more difficult to replace such a tradition with a new paradigm in the same place – that is why transitions to new waves and new long cycles tend to be associated with shifts of location.

Second, coordination occurs because both processes respond to a common agenda of global problems as transmitted by global politics. If we postulate that structural change responds to priority global problems – authoritatively formulated by global leadership – then such solutions might derive from both political and economic sources. More concretely, we might think of such solutions being expected (or demanded) by world opinion via global media – as represented by markets, the press, and scholarly or scientific (epistemic) communities. Thus we might think of the problem of discoveries in the fifteenth and sixteenth centuries as being articulated by sets of opinion-makers in several parts of western Europe, who viewed it as a search for new routes to India and responded to both through political and economic processes – thus innovating new sources of supply, as well as a new global political structure. Or we might think of contemporary global problems – for example, climate change as discussed in Chapter 7 – centered on integration of the global community as being responded to both through the building of a democratic community and the expansion of information industries without which a global community could not function.

We observe that in the experience of the past half-millennium the co-evolution of global processes occurred in a national basing-mode. We might attribute this both to the high costs of coordinating global activities in any other mode and to the fact that world opinion and world media, such as they were, could be found predominantly among the populations of the world powers. In the nineteenth century, and for William Gladstone, for example, the British public would have constituted the court of world opinion, especially as articulated by Parliament and the British press, and would play a privileged role in formulating global problems and translating them into actions. But we notice, too, that costs of communication and transport at the global level have been falling steadily in the past century or so. The difficulties of coordination are declining in the information age and the base of world opinion has also expanded steadily. These developments suggest that the predominantly national basing-mode for coordination of global processes ought to be broadening at it evolves.

Synchronization

In form, this co-action takes place via synchronization that shows up in the empirically confirmed fact that K-waves of economic innovation tend to be one-half the length of a long cycle of global political leadership by a nation-state (see the section "K-waves and global political leadership" later in this chapter). In principle, synchronization should not be surprising because without it global processes would be chaotic. But for those raised on the idea that world politics is anarchic and global economics is no more than a jungle, some explanation might be in order.

Why the synchronization of K-waves and long cycles, or the effective co-evolution of global economics and politics? In physics, the phenomenon of synchronization is known as the problem of "coupled oscillators"; the classic case is two close-by pendulum clocks spontaneously adopting the same rhythm, which was observed by the Dutch mathematician Christiaan Huygens in 1665. More recent research has extended this problem to biology, including that of biological clocks (Strogatz and Stewart, 1993). J.W.S. Pringle (Modelski, 1990: 19) has pointed out that coupled oscillators possess a type of mechanism capable of "selection of variation over time," leading to an evolutionary increase in the complexity of rhythm, thereby leading to learning.

An oscillator is any system that exhibits periodic variation or fluctuation over time. We have reason to believe that the global economy, and the global political system, might properly be regarded as oscillators because they execute periodic behavior. Our work (Modelski and Thompson 1996: chapters 9 and 10) now argues that the global economy has experienced regularly recurring K-waves over a period of a millennium, with an average period of fifty-eight years; these eighteen completed K-waves have ranged in length from forty to seventy-four years, with ten of them in the range of fifty to sixty years. The global political system may be estimated to have shown, over the same period, long cycles with a period of some 116 years; with sea power concentration over the shorter period of one-half millennium (1494–1993) showing average periodicity (between five peaks) of 108 years (Modelski and Thompson, 1988).

We notice that periodicity is average rather than strict, but we have no reason to require that social periodicity be as precise as physical or mechanical systems. But biological systems also tend to have not only a characteristic period, but also amplitude – for once disturbed they return to their accustomed path and are therefore known as limit-cycle oscillators. On our evidence we have reasons to think that both the global economy and the political system belong to that type.

Coupled oscillators exhibit more complex behavior, hence potentially learning. We have previously shown grounds for thinking that the global economy and global politics are a coupled system exhibiting co-evolution. Just as in the case of two pendulum clocks where the coupling was a function of proximity, so also in our case: the coupling of K-waves and long cycles is a product of collocation – the fact of basing in one political-economic base and one opinion base, that, most recently, has been delimited by the boundaries of a nation-state. We have also shown that the rhythm of global war that was, until recently, the most spectacular event of the long cycle has also marked the coming and going of K-waves. That leads us to believe that this is a case of "pulse coupling," because interactions need not necessarily be continuous, but could be particularly marked when one or the other of the systems "fires" (as in producing a global war) or fails to fire (as in the case of a great depression).

For coupled oscillators, synchrony is the most likely manner of coordination. Physics and biology research has shown that oscillators started at different times will tend to become synchronous. Synchrony is not inevitable, but exhibits the general effect of phase-locking. In communities of oscillators, synchrony depends on the strength of coupling and emerges cooperatively. We suspect that the same principles apply in the case of the two systems we have been studying.

The evolutionary paradigm

We have now cast our analysis in an evolutionary mold. In our opinion, it is one that is appropriate to the study of long-term economic processes and developments. Let us restate the advantages and special insights of that approach.

1 The paradigm explains structural change in the global economy as an evolutionary process of determinate shape in which K-waves are the (agent-level, organizational) pulses of growth in innovative sectors that help to build the global economic structure. It opens up a range of issues, both in respect to understanding past change and in looking to the future outside the lens of rational-equilibrium models. We need not postulate a rational plan or grand design to explain the emergence of a world market or global organization.
2 The idea of co-evolution helps us conceptualize the relationship of the global economy to global politics. The broad concept of social evolution is made more tractable, yet analytically more useful.
3 Even while cultivating the big picture of global evolution, this approach enables us to view individual K-waves (the micro-foundations), via search

Table 2.1 Rational choice and evolutionary approaches compared

Characteristic features	Rational choice	Evolutionary
Perspective (time horizon)	Short-term	Long-term
Focus of explanation	Decisions, equilibrium	Institutions,transitions
Choice process	Rational maximization	Trial and error, search and selection
Ends-means schema	Given constraints and preferences, choice of means	Both constraints and preferences are variable

and selection of a global macro-development. in a new, sharper light and with greater analytical power. This makes it possible to say which economies, and what conditions, are likely to harbor new K-waves.

The features of the evolutionary approach might be seen more clearly when contrasted with the standard "rational choice" paradigm of neoclassical economics. Table 2.1 singles out four such characteristic features and compares them for the two perspectives. It makes it clear that each have their own place and domain of maximum effectiveness, and that in important respects they might indeed be regarded as complementary; but it also makes plain that an evolutionary approach is the one that is best suited for problems of analyzing patterns of long-range change. That is so because such an approach naturally inclines toward a long-term perspective; it focuses on structural transformations rather than on equilibrium states; it does not require the postulate of rationality and it sees collective choice processes as resulting from trial and error search and selection procedures. Best of all, it gets away from a purely instrumental rationality and allows for ends to be seen to be changeable, and for constraints to be altered as the result of evolutionary processes.

World economic history

World history is conventionally regarded as comprising the ancient, classical, and modern eras; the first two, of about two millennia each, and the last, the modern, taking up a single millennium, as shown in Table 2.2. Together, these three categories yield a basic grid against which long-term trends might be appraised in more detail. But they might also be seen as presenting such history as a continuum, as successive phases in the evolution of the social organization of the human species, and it is within that grid that the world economy assumes shape.

That is why economic history, too, might be seen as a process of such continuity, as proposed by John Hicks (1969). Within the overall framework of the ancient, classical, and modern eras unfolds world economic organization, over millennia-long periods marking major institutional innovations. These innovations fall into two broad categories: supply-side, concerning broad productive and construction undertakings; and demand-side, relating to distributive,

Table 2.2 Evolution of the world economy

From about (year)	Era	World economy process
3400 BC	Ancient	Command economy
2300		Bronze
1200	Classical	Fertile Crescent
100		Iron
		Silk Roads
AD 930	Modern	Market economy
1850		Market systems
		World market

commercial, and trading aspects. The result is that millennial (supply-side) periods of production achievements might be seen to alternate with (demand-side) periods of similar length, of trade networking that bring about a diffusion of technology and wealth.

The ancient era is commonly also known as the Bronze Age, because it is that new alloy that is characteristic of the material culture of that time, especially in Mesopotamia. The tools, weapons, and art objects fashioned of that material were keys to the development of irrigation agriculture, public works, water and land transportation, and warfare. But within the ancient era, two periods might then be distinguished: first, the launching of bronze metallurgy, centered on Sumer, and second, the development of the Fertile Crescent into a wider and more dispersed economic and trading zone.

The classical era, after 1200 BC, opens with the age of iron, as the innovation that makes possible yet greater strides in agriculture and weaponry, and produces rapid population growth and urbanization in China and India. In the second period of that era, the Silk Roads create, for the first time, a transcontinental system of trade, where products such as silk, spices, or silver, travel from one end of Eurasia to the other.

These four periods might be said to have instituted and comprised the command economy as the paradigmatic institutional arrangement for the world economic system. The command economy is an economic system in which the great instruments of production are publicly owned, either by the temple or the state, and in which basic economic decisions on investment, production, and exchange are centrally controlled. That is not to say that the pre-modern period saw no individual property or private transactions, but only that the differentiation between economic and political functions was weak, and that the great projects of investment or long-distance trade were strongly dominated by public concerns.

John Hicks (1969) has argued that the central tendency of economic history has been the movement from command to market economy. The larger an economy, the more difficult, if not impossible, it is to coordinate economic and political activities from one central point. That is why in a general sense and over the very long-run, the command economy is unstable, and tends toward "decline";

in comparison, the market economy is more flexible and more resilient and therefore more likely to endure. But that is not to say that in the short-run, central direction might not yield better results for certain limited purposes, particularly at times of major warfare when a large share of economic output is directed to the one goal of achieving military victory. In the twentieth century, the global war periods of World War I and World War II saw the resurgence of such planning on all sides. That is why the rise of the market economy has hardly been a smooth or straight-line process.

In the temporal dimension, this great evolutionary transition over the last millenium – from command to market – is represented by periods shown in Table 2.2 as "market systems", and "world market." "Markets systems" stands for the "invention" of reliable markets serving productive centers on a national or regional basis. According to William McNeill (1982), this first occurred in China, in the Sung period, between 1000 and 1200; it was followed by the trading system of the Italian Renaissance that organized the western end of the Silk Roads; it reached high gear with the rise of a "West Europe with a global reach" after 1500, and culminated in what we call the Industrial Revolution in England after 1700. "World market" is the second phase in this story, whose central feature, after 1850, is the increasing globalization of economic activities and the progressive extension of the reach of world markets to more and more segments of the world economy. There is no reason to believe that this process is about to end anytime soon; more probably, this drastic and unprecedented transformation of the way humanity earns its living is likely to remain the salient feature of the world economy for a long time to come.

In perspective, the transition from command to market has been a gradual one, spanning centuries. The factor mediating this transition was the rise of the Silk Roads, to which reference was made earlier, and is illustrated in Table 2.3. This transcontinental system of transportation and communication formed the backbone of the economy of the "Old World" until about 1500, well into the "market system" period, and the industrial and commercial activities upon which it thrived did in fact help to stimulate the growth of markets in the several areas it did traverse, even though at other times political interventions would, for long periods, block and immobilize entire segments of those routes.

Overall, the Silk Roads reveal the central portions of the world economy to be a living, pulsating thing, even if the volume of transactions, or the speed of interactions, might have been low by today's more exacting standards. Table 2.3 shows how the intensity of activity along that central artery alternated in a fairly regular manner between the northern and the southern routes, and in a way that correlated with surges of activity in China and Europe. Most importantly, the Silk Roads and the key industrial and commercial structures they supported became the scaffolding upon which arose the truly global economic system of the modern era.

This has been so far, in broad strokes, a sketch of the evolution of the world economy as marked by major institutional changes, and above all, viewed as a fundamental transition from command to market economy. It covers the entire

Table 2.3 Evolution of the silk roads 100 BC to AD 1500

Period	Major linkages	Anchor cities	K-waves
Silk Roads			
100–250	Silk via Parthia	Rome, Luoyang	
200–500	Red Sea route to India	Alexandria, Guangdong	
500–650	Byzantium develops the northern route	Constantinople, Changan	
750–1000	Abbasids develop Persian Gulf route	Baghdad, Changan	
Market systems			
930–1125	Northern Song via Central Asia	Constantinople, Kaifeng	K-1–2
1150–1250	Southern Song	Cairo, Hangzhou	K-3–4
1250–1350	Mongols restore northern route	Genoa, Beijing	K-5–6
1350–1500	Mamluks, Venice work Red Sea route	Venice, Cairo, Calicut, Malacca, Hangzhou	K-7–8

historical experience with world economic systems, from the very inception of the possibility of such arrangements, inherent even in the pre-historical trading linkages of maybe 6,000–7,000 years ago, right up to the contemporary experience of an increasingly globalized economy.

The next question is: how did the process work itself out at the global organizational level? That is, what were the organizational structures that mediated and orchestrated these changes such that a movement toward greater economic interdependence might in fact be observed? An answer is suggested in Table 2.4.

Table 2.4 shows the main outlines of the evolution that has moved the world economy toward market solutions, that is, economic globalization, in this case with emphasis on the global level (that is, in respect of long-distance and intercontinental trade, and the activities of leading industrial sectors). This concerns the institutional setting within which innovation occurs, and without which it is

Table 2.4 Evolution of the global economy

From about	Phases	Centered on	
Breakthrough to market systems			
930	Song move to national market	China	Experiments
1190	Nautical–commercial revolution	Italy	Clusters
1430	Oceanic trading	Atlantic Europe	Critical mass
1640	Industrial take-off	Britain	Pay-off
World Market			
1850	Information economy	United States	Experiments
2080			Clusters

unlikely. It includes the creation of markets, new types of enterprises and communication systems, the background of political security, and the launching of new productive facilities.

As noted in Table 2.3, for over a millennium China had been an anchor of the Silk Road system, and as such a major participant in the world trading system as it then existed, exporting silk (an early innovation whose secrets were for a long time very well guarded) and porcelain, and importing jade from Central Asia and spices from Southeast Asia. It is therefore not altogether surprising that about the year 1000, under the Song Dynasty, China laid the foundations for a "first" national market economy, and became "the" market of the world system, attracting traders from far and wide (ultimately even serving as the ultimate destination for Columbus). But in the longer run, this proved to be basically an experiment with wide ramifications and lessons for others; soon the ball was taken up by the Italians, whose commercial and industrial organizations and practices have been more directly foundational for global economic evolution.

Italian commercial and nautical enterprise helped to launch Portugal and Spain on their global ventures creating the first truly global trading (and political) system that in turn served as the foundation for the Industrial Revolution. Britain built the factories that made that revolution, a feat to be imitated worldwide. The United States completes the picture, for the time being, with its leading role in the twentieth and early twenty-first century.

Interestingly, though broadly speaking, these great organizational waves have been reflected quite closely in the long-term movements in English prices of consumables since about 1200. A series first constructed by Sir Henry Phelps-Brown and Sheila Hopkins, and recently interpreted by David Hackett Fischer (Fischer, 1996), reveals four great "price revolutions" (each a period of rapidly rising prices): the medieval one (1200–1350); the sixteenth century one (1475–1650), the eighteenth century one (1729–1812), and the twentieth century one (1896–2000?). They could equally well be called the Italian, Atlantic, British, and American price revolutions – and reorganizations.

Both the organizational sequence and the price data make it plain that global economic development is to be seen as an evolutionary series of path-breaking innovations by a number of organizational centers, rather than a matter of a sudden unprecedented and miraculous "revolution" in the British Isles of the eighteenth and nineteenth centuries.

K-waves and economic evolution

What drives global economic evolution, the process depicted in Table 2.4? It is the thesis explored in George Modelski and William R. Thompson's 1996 work, *Leading sectors and World Powers: The Co-evolution of Global Economics and Politics*, that global economic evolution of the millennium just past has been driven by a succession of K-waves.

What are K-waves? They may be defined as "processes of rise and decline of leading sectors," or as paradigm shifts in the global economy. K-waves are surges of innovation that create new sectors either of industry or commerce. These sectors are initially of local and national significance but ultimately impact the entire global economy. A classical example is the rise of the cotton textile industry in the second half of the eighteenth century. On the basis of innovative techniques in spinning and weaving, and the organization of factory production around steam engines the cotton textile industry became a leading sector of the British economy. Then, through exports of these products, and the technology used to create them, Britain provided a leading industrial sector of worldwide impact, the foundation of which – at the end of the nineteenth century – came to be described as the Industrial Revolution.

The term K-wave is short for Kondratieff wave. That latter term, coined by Joseph Schumpeter in 1939, was intended to honor the fact that the first to draw attention in a sustained manner to this important characteristic of the modern world economy was Nikolai Kondratieff (1892–1938), a leading Russian economist writing in the 1920s. For a recent translation of his work on this topic see Kondratieff (1984); a full commentary in the light of more recent work may be found in Van Duijn (1983). Well received in the 1930s, but neglected in the 1950s and 1960s, Kondratieff's arguments found greater resonance again in the 1980s and 1990s.

Some basic features of K-waves are quite widely agreed. The first is their period, generally seen to last between fifty and sixty years. These are figures derived in the first place from empirical observations, going back to long-range studies of both price and output series. More recently the emphasis has been on sectoral output and growth, and on international perspectives. In a more general context, the period of the K-wave might also be seen to be related to generational turnover. A generation period is usually reckoned as the time required for a generation to replace itself, some twenty-five to thirty years. A K-wave would then be made up of two generation-long phases. Indeed, looking again at the empirical record, two phases can usually be discerned, a take-off phase that launches the innovations but needs to contend with alternative paradigms in a context where earlier leading sectors have lost their edge and are in decline; and a high-growth phase, in which the new paradigm prevails and, for a while at least (again, for a generation), occupies center stage, brings prosperity, and leads the world economy. Most recently, the period from 1972 to 2000 might be regarded as the take-off for the information industries, including the internet, while the period from 2000 to 2020–2030 might be seen as its high-growth phase.

The substantive content of a K-wave is given by the set of innovations that it launches. Table 2.5 lists a dating scheme for K-waves of the modern world economy, starting with developments in Song China just over a millennium ago, and tentatively shows, for each K-wave, the innovations that constitute successive paradigm shifts.

The concept of innovation guiding this listing is Schumpeterian. Schumpeter proposed that economic development is the product of entrepreneurial innovation of the following types: launching new products; pioneering new methods

Table 2.5   K-waves: the sequence of global leading sectors

K-wave	From about	Leading sector	Major innovation
K-1	930	Printing, paper	Learning society, book printing
K-2	990	National market formation	North–south market unification
K-3	1060	Fiscal/administrative framework	Monetization, paper money
K-4	1120	Maritime trade expansion	Compass, large junks
K-5	1190	Champagne fairs	European market organized
K-6	1250	Black Sea trade	Innovations from East Asia
K-7	1310	Venetian galley fleets	New markets in North Europe
K-8	1350	Pepper trade	Alexandria-connection institutionalized
K-9	1430	Guinea gold	"Discovery" of African trade
K-10	1494	Indian spices	Operating oceanic route
K-11	1540	Atlantic, Baltic trades	American silver
K-12	1580	Asian trade	Dutch East Indies Co. (VOC)
K-13	1640	Amerasian trade	Plantations
K-14	1688	Amerasian trade	Tobacco
K-15	1740	Cotton, iron	Factory production
K-16	1792	Steam, rail	New forms of transport
K-17	1850	Electrics, chemicals, steel	Invention of invention
K-18	1914	Electronics, autos, aerospace	New products
K-19	1972	Information industries	Computers
K-20	2026		

of production; opening new markets; creating new sources of raw materials; and introducing new forms of business organization. Table 2.5 shows that K-waves have been produced by all of these.

What is more, the list in Table 2.5 shows the individual K-waves arrayed into groups of four. This grouping reflects the fact that individual paradigm shifts, however powerful they might be in and of themselves, such as that to railroads, do not stand alone but "stand on the shoulders of others," and in their turn serve as launching pads for new endeavors. That is how K-waves 9–12, in Table 2.5, might be seen as adding up to the establishment of an "oceanic trading" system in Table 2.4; in effect, a change in the organization of the global economy.

Table 2.5 is, in effect, a "short history of the global economy." It is also a dating scheme for K-waves. It shows them for the entire time span of the modern era – a greater length than some other studies. Analysts who do not focus on the long-term are often content to notice the last five well-known pulses, including the most recent one focused on information industries. Students of economic history, including Joseph Schumpeter and Fernand Braudel, have proposed pushing the analysis back to the early modern period. Starting analysis with rise of the Song market economy recognizes the role of China, as earlier proposed.

It remains an open question, though, whether "leading sector" innovation waves of this length (some fifty to sixty years) can also be discerned in pre-modern economies. The earlier account of the Silk Roads as having mediated the transition from "command" to "market" economies (Table 2.3) did point to a regular alternation between northern and southern routes even before what we now call the modern era. But our data are at present insufficient for tracing economic fluctuations and the rise and decline of leading sectors in those earlier times.

The agents of innovation driving the K-waves are clusters of entrepreneurs: in individual or family firms, companies, or more recently, multinational corporations. In earlier periods it is hard or impossible to identify such individuals whose deeds have been recorded with less assiduity than those of kings or military heroes. Such families as the Grimaldi or the Spinola led much of Genoese activity; South German merchant houses such as the Fugger or the Welsers cooperated with the King of Portugal (and his *Casa da India*) in organizing and financing the crucial voyages to the East. It was the advent of the Dutch East Indies Company (VOC) in 1600 that not only put the organization of Asian trade on a solid footing, but also served as a potent model of corporate management, superior by an entire order of magnitude to the organization that the King of Portugal put together a century earlier.

By the mid-nineteenth century, the innovations can be clearly linked to individual entrepreneurs and their companies: e.g. the locomotive, and the Liverpool and Manchester Railway (Stevenson), with the railway K-wave (K-16), or the electric dynamo (Siemens) and the electricity K-wave (K-17). More interestingly, no single entrepreneur or even firm can confidently be named as the single carrier of any one K-wave; mostly it is a cluster of related and competing individuals and firms that carry forward these great changes, and the more recent the K-wave, the thicker these clusters become. That is how evolutionary changes of global proportions are carried forward by the concerted action of individual agents, many of whom are difficult to name so long after the event, but whose initiatives continue to impact our lives.

An essential dimension of innovation and waves of innovation is location. This is not merely a matter of geography: innovative activity tends to be localized within particular regions of a country, as textiles were in northwest England, or more recently, the information industries in Silicon Valley. More importantly however, all K-waves have been prominently located in distinct national economies. Such economies would afford a supply of factors of evolutionary potential: markets that generated the initial demand for its products; and capital resources as supply factors, openness to trade and financial institutions ready to support innovation. Beyond that, political support and security are important. This high degree to which innovative activity initially centers on one key economy is a key to understanding the linkage between global economics and politics.

Data brought together by Modelski and Thompson (1996, tables 6.11–6.13) make plain these two crucial characteristics of K-waves: surges of innovation have their origin in one national economy and then diffuse more widely, at first to other major economies, and ultimately worldwide. Second, K-waves are not the automatic property of the largest countries or the wealthiest economies; they occur in certain specific conditions that favor innovation. It is, of course, the case that hosting a K-wave greatly adds to the value of the output of an economy for a period of at least two generations, and therefore greatly adds to its size. But size alone does not place an economy into the vanguard of economic evolution.

The Modelski–Thompson data on national shares for key products of K-waves 15–18 show Britain leading in cotton consumption, a good indicator of textile production until well past the mid-nineteenth century (not to be overtaken by the United States until 1900). Britain also leads in pig iron production, only to lose its lead by 1890. In railroad construction the lead in the indicator used here passes to the United States by 1870, but much of the rail construction in the world continues to be undertaken by British builders, with British expertise and machinery, and on the basis of British capital investment. The picture changes with K-17. Sulfuric acid is one indicator of the output of the chemical industry that was a locus of innovation of that K-wave. Britain starts well in 1870, but is outpaced by the United States in 1900, and is followed closely by Germany, a country that is also strong in other new branches of that industry, particularly dyestuffs. The story is the same in steel production. In electric power, Britain falls behind right from the start. In motor vehicle production (and the closely linked oil industry), the American lead is decisive from the beginning. European production is less substantial, and by the 1980s the important competition comes from Japan and the Asia-Pacific area.

This reiterates the central point that in the experience of the modern economy for the past millennium, K-wave-animated leading sectors have invariably originated in one well-organized national economy linked to a wider network, and then diffused from there. It happened in the early (Song) China economy, with its links via the Silk Roads, and in the Italian city-states that organized the western end of those linkages, and in the successive stages of the Atlantic economy. The source of strength of these economies was not so much population, or size of territory, but evolutionary potential married to innovation that met the needs of the time. That is how, broadly speaking, David Landes also explains economic history in *The Causes of the Wealth and Poverty of Nations* (1998). The alternative view would argue, as does Andre Gunder Frank (1998), that because of their relative size, Asia in general, and China in particular, were the center of the world economy through most of the millennium, and right up to 1800. While it is true that Asia did hold some 50–60 percent of the world population throughout that period, its economies contributed much less than their share to major innovations, and stopped leading global evolution after about 1200.

The association of major innovations and specific location might once again be illustrated in Table 2.6. An independently compiled list of 160 major innovations over the best part of the nineteenth and twentieth centuries shows that in K-16, the plurality of such advances in industrial competitiveness occurred in

Table 2.6 Clustering of major innovations, (K16–K18)

K-wave	(data for)	Total of major innovations	Originating in (percentage shares)	Examples
K16	(1811–1849)	18	Britain 44 U.S.A. 22	Steam locomotive Vulcanized rubber
K17	(1850–1914)	67	U.S.A. 45 Germany 18	Telephone Electric dynamo
K18	(1915–1971)	75	U.S.A. 57 Germany 17	Microprocessor Jet airplane

Source: Derived from list of major innovations in Van Duijn (1983: 176–179).

Britain (44 percent), followed by the United States. In the next two K-waves, the United States holds the lead, followed by Germany. In each case, these lead-ins to key industrial sectors are linked to major innovative firms: e.g. the telephone, with the Bell company, since reorganized into ATT and "Baby Bells" and now one of central players in the information industry; and the microprocessor, the product of Intel, a major participant in Silicon Valley.

K-waves and global political leadership

The localization of K-waves, and their initial close association with a particular national economy, means that national leading sectors translate rather smoothly into global economic leadership. The successful launching of new industries of global impact confers high standing on an entire economic system. It means new high-growth industries, products and services meeting a worldwide demand, and consequently, prosperity and added wealth. But does it also automatically confer political leadership in international affairs, and does it directly lead to global leadership?

Global leadership is here understood as the exercise of a role that has been central to world politics in the last half-millennium. This world power role has evolved from early experiments by Portugal and the Dutch Republic, to a mature form fashioned by Britain that shaped the nucleus of the global system. After about 1850, it became a building block of the emerging global organization. Held most recently by the United States, this has been a role for a nation-state with a commanding presence on the world ocean and a decisive role in the global wars that periodically reorganized the system in a pattern of "long cycles" at intervals of about a century.

In the experience of the modern era, the rise and decline of leading sectors – discussed above – is paralleled quite closely by the rise and decline of world powers exercising global leadership. We have seen that the first is a process driving economic transformation. The latter, too, is an evolutionary process. This "co-evolution of global economics and politics" is shown in Table 2.7. Just as K-waves of economic innovation can be numbered consecutively for the

Table 2.7   The co-evolution of global economics and politics

About	K-waves (global leading sectors)	Long cycles (world powers after 1500)
930	K-1 Printing and paper	LC1 Northern Song
990	K-2 National market	
1060	K-3 Fiscal framework	LC2 Southern Song
1120	K-4 Maritime trade	
1190	K-5 Champagne fair	LC3 Genoa
1250	K-6 Black Sea trade	
1300	K-7 Galley fleets	LC4 Venice
1360	K-8 Pepper	
1430	K-9 Guinea gold	LC5 Portugal
1492	K-10 Indian spices	
1540	K-11 Atlantic, Baltic	LC6 Dutch Republic
1580	K-12 Asian trade (VOC)	
1640	K-13 Amerasian trade	LC8 Britain I
1688	K-14 Amerasian trade	
1740	K-15 Cotton, iron	LC9 Britain II
1792	K-16 Steam, rail	
1850	K-17 Electrics, chemicals, steel	LC10 United States
1914	K-18 Autos, air, electronics	
1972	K-19 Information industries	

entire modern period, so can successive long cycles of global political leadership and the powers associated with them.

Table 2.7 shows that global economic leadership that is earned by innovation has consistently gone hand-in-hand with both global political leadership and political innovation, including new forms of world organization. But the relationship has not been an automatic one, but rather a mutually interdependent one: with the economic line of enterprise being supportive of, and supported by, political initiatives. What precisely has been the pattern of that relationship?

Most prominently, the basic relation has been in the form 2:1. For each pair of K-waves in the global economy we can observe one cycle of global politics, that is, one term of political leadership at the global level. The first of the pair of K-waves lays down the economic base of prosperity and affluence; and upon that base, a political position can be erected. Once the political structure is in place – and in the past this has been the work of a world power acting as an agent of innovation after a prolonged, generation-long period of global wars – the second K-wave is ready to go into high gear.

To give an example: the economic transformation wrought by K-17 (steel, chemistry, electric power) put the United States, by 1914, in the top-rank of industrial powers and created the basis for a powerful "arsenal of democracy" that proved to be of decisive significance in the period of World War I through World War II (1914–1945), not only in iron, steel, and electric power, but also in telephones and wireless communications. The second K-wave (K-18) that took off after 1914 moved into high gear after 1945, when a new political order was firmly put in place; that K-wave achieved a peak in 1973. That is how one such long political cycle might be thought of as two K-waves between which is sandwiched a period of major political disturbance, the evolutionary selection process of macro-decision that in the past half-millennium took the form of a global war.

This means that economic and political evolution at the global level are closely related, at the basic level of agents of innovation, and that the relation is a mutually supportive one. It is also closely synchronized (because oscillators tend to synchronize), as is apparent from the table on co-evolution. The synchronization is facilitated by the fact that the same nation-state is the locus both of surges of economic innovation and of political initiatives that are at the heart of new forms of world order.

The right-hand column of Table 2.7, with its sequence of leading powers, may also be read as a "short history of evolutionary global politics." It shows the results of a process whereby world politics is subject to a regular *selection* process that produces leadership (world powers, etc.) for the solution of global problems. That process is strongly motivated by the relationship of challengers to receding and ascendant global powers in the democratic lineage, together with their allies. Out of that competition that, at its strongest, took the form of global wars, arise innovations (*mutations*) in world political arrangements: both military, in the form of new formations and weapon systems, and political, such as diplomacy, alliances, world organizations, and arms-control regimes (*cooperation*). Such innovations characterize the eras of world order associated with the respective world powers (*reinforcement*). The entire process has governed a steady increase in the scale and complexity of world politics over the entire millennium (see Modelski, 1996).

The K-wave-global leadership relationship is empirically grounded and may be documented both quantitatively and qualitatively for most of the modern era. Table 2.8 summarizes some key empirical evidence for the period since 1500.

In Table 2.8, the interaction of economics and politics may be systematically observed over a long time-span. The first column reports the results of a series of observations on leading sector growth rates in Portugal, the Dutch Republic, Britain, and the United States, and records the years of peak rates (for data and methods see Modelski and Thompson, 1996, Chapter 6). In each case, the

Table 2.8 K-waves and the attainment of global leadership

First K-wave peak (observed)	*World power*	*Occasions for global leadership*	*Sea power threshold attained*	*Second K-wave peak (observed)*
1480s	Portugal	1494, 1499	1510	1500s/1530s
1560s	Dutch Republic	1601, 1608	1610	1620s
1670s	Britain I	1689, 1701	1715	1710s
1780s	Britain II	1793, 1815	1810	1830s
1870s/1900s	U.S.A.	1917, 1941	1945	1960s

Source: Based on Modelski and Thompson (1996), Table 7.3.

observed peak anticipates the "occasions for global leadership," most of which are linked to, or are occasioned by, global wars. The first date for Portugal, 1492, refers to the establishment of the Tordesillas global political regime – dividing the ocean space with Spain – and 1499 confirms the King's strategy of creating an oceanic route to India. For the United States, 1917 stands for entry into World War I, while 1941 stands for the Atlantic Charter – the statement of the war aims of the United Nations coalition that brought World War II to a victorious conclusion. To these might be added 1947, for the Truman Doctrine and the European Recovery Program (Marshall Plan), that put the final stamp of approval on America's peace-time role in international affairs (full documentation in Modelski and Modelski, 1988).

The fourth column of Table 2.8 is a reminder that economic power is not all that matters. A crucial element in fighting and gaining victory in all the five global wars covered here has been sea power. Those attaining, or coming close to, a monopoly share of capital ships (ships of the line earlier, battleships, carriers, and missile submarines more recently) are those having won, or those likely to win, global wars; the year of attainment of the naval threshold (more than 50 percent of the world total of such ships) marks the conclusion of major conflicts (world sea power distributions are documented in Modelski and Thompson, 1988). The final column shows the peak years of the second K-wave, and unsurprisingly it is the 1960s for the United States.

The information economy

At the opening of the new millennium, at this time of writing, the most prominent feature of the economy, and its leading sector, appears to be information, marking this undoubtedly as the information age, with computers and communications as its most essential elements.

Those taking the longer perspective adopted in this chapter will not be surprised, and will recognize the contemporary prominence of information industries as the breakthrough phase of an "information economy" that has been in the making since the mid-nineteenth century (see Table 2.4). First came the telegraph, initially linked to railroads; then two cable lines successfully crossed the Atlantic as early as 1866 and set in motion the era of global communications. Later in the nineteenth century came the telephone, initially centered on the United States, but that over time became an inexpensive international service, more recently relayed by space satellites. In the twentieth century, radio and television made the electronic media a fully global system. At the dawn of a new millennium it is the World Wide Web that is setting the pace, with the number of users to reach the hundreds of millions in the near future. We observe that each of these developments was powered by K-waves: K-17, the electric power wave of the dynamo; and K-18, the wave of electronics. With those two laying the foundations, the current K-19 of computers and digital telecommunications clinches the case for an information economy as the basic requirement of world markets. And K-20 will probably put the finishing touches on it.

Expert observers have been aware since the 1970s that the world economy was ready to spawn new leading sectors. Those who coined the term of "new socio-technical paradigm" correctly anticipated that the focus of these new developments would be the information industries. It is interesting to note that this was the opinion not just of American experts. British students of innovation such as Christopher Freeman, drew their analyses along similar lines. The (then) Soviet experts, too, looked forward to major breakthroughs in computers and microelectronics. Japanese electronics companies, followed by South Korean and Taiwanese concerns, invested heavily in semiconductor (amongst other) manufacturing facilities. In other words, it was hardly a secret that information technologies would be the sources of future growth. Yet the basic shape of the information revolution resembles that of earlier leading sector surges: a nucleus of high growth in one national economy, in this case the American, followed by gradual diffusion worldwide.

The information industries matter not just because they produce valuable equipment, such as computers. Their impact is felt throughout the economy because, via innovative software, these products enter into a wide range of production processes, and an even wider range of services, and it is services in particular that are coming to comprise an increasingly large proportion of the output of modern economies. Table 11.2 in Modelski and Thompson (1996) illustrates how broad and deep that impact has become. A decade later, the internet and the World Wide Web, not listed in that table, have become the other major features of the information landscape, and of the economy as a whole.

Computer technology has now been around for several decades, and some economists have wondered why it was that the important investments represented by such equipment did not appear to show results in the statistics of productivity for the U.S. economy. But in 1990, Paul David, to the contrary, proposed a solution to this "productivity paradox" by drawing on the lessons from the introduction of the electric motor in the 1880s (that is, in K-17, the electric power wave). He showed that it took tens of years for serious gains to be registered, not just because technology diffusion takes time, but also because businesses had to reorganize work around the new industrial assembly line. He argued that a similar delay was at work in the introduction of the computer.

Economists are slowly coming around to this position. In 1999, Federal Reserve Chairman Alan Greenspan himself endorsed the role of information industries in spurring growth when he said that the United States may be experiencing a structural shift similar to those that have visited its economy from time to time in the past due to innovations built around computers that have made businesses operate more efficiently. Spending on information technology is rising, comprising about one-half of the cost of all new business equipment.

As shown for earlier K-waves, a crucial question concerns the location of the K-19 process. We also know that awareness of the importance of information technology has been widespread, among specialists and among business leaders, for the previous two to three decades. Computers certainly have already spread worldwide. Is it still the case that the new technologies are centered in one economy, and why is that so?

On the evidence of the three decades between 1970 and 2000, the central locus of K-19 information industries has substantially been the United States. The early leader in the computer manufacture was the IBM Corporation, with up to 70 percent of market share in mainframes and equipment. The 1980s saw the rise of the personal computer, with IBM losing its lead to a variety of producers, including Apple, Compaq, and Dell. Over time, powerful Japanese electronics companies such as Toshiba, and NEC, as well as South Korean, and Taiwanese firms, assumed important positions in some portions of the industry (such as in memory or flat screen monitors). In the late 1980s it appeared as though Japan might be catching up in high technology.

But the PC itself was rapidly becoming a "mere" commodity and attention soon focused on two key components: microprocessors, seen as the heart of the computer; and software. In the 1990s, American producers controlled over 90 percent of the market in microprocessors (Table 2.9). In software, it was Microsoft that was installing up to 90 percent of the world's operating systems, and half of its applications (and then coming under pressure from government regulators) later in the 1990s. Moreover, the Internet emerged with astonishing rapidity, approaching 2000 with a user-base of the World Wide Web of some 100 million. One half of these users were in the United States. And the principal operators were American too, such as Cisco Systems for Internet servers, and AOL for service providers. That is also where a tremendous expansion was occurring in web commerce. Figure 2.1 shows the "learning curve" growth pattern of the internet, one that is similar to that of earlier K-waves.

All these developments surely do not exhaust the range of the Information Revolution. Wireless telephony (cell phones) is now experiencing rapid growth in Europe and Japan, areas less well covered by traditional telephony, and helped by agreement on a common standard, and the application of 3G techno-logy that may make the wireless phone (rather than the PC) the main access to the Internet.

The reasons for the American focus on information industries are not really

Table 2.9 World microprocessor market shares

Company	HQ location	Marketshare			
		1991	*1993*	*1998 (4Q)*	*2006 (1Q)**
Intel	U.S.A.	53.2	74.1	75.7	81.7
Motorola	U.S.A.	12.3	8		
Advanced Micro Devices	U.S.A.	5.1	5.8	15.6	16.9
Hitachi	Japan	3.6			
NEC	Japan	3.5			

Note
* x86 CPU.

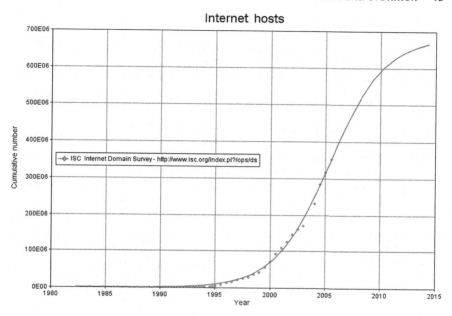

Figure 2.1 Growth in the number of internet hosts (Internet Domain Survey) fitted to a logistic curve (source: Devezas *et al.*, in Modelski *et al.*, 2007).

surprising. Firms in the United States have been the leaders of the world information economy at least since the mid-nineteenth century. Starting with the telegraph and Morse code, through the telephone, radio, and television, with a vibrant press and media sector, this has been an economy that flourished on information. An open society that values freedom of speech and fosters flexibility and entrepreneurship (and rewards it well: the world's richest man in 2000 was a product of the U.S. information industy), and a political system that assures stability with a military that fosters research and demands "smart weapons": all these have joined to create elements of evolutionary potential that forged this new K-wave. The nearest competitor, Japan, by contrast, did build on its manufacturing prowess and the strength of its K-18 industries in automobiles and electronics, but was lagging in other sectors of the economy, as well as in openness and flexibility. Only one of the six Japanese in the world's top-100 derived his wealth from an information industry.

Some implications for world politics

In the light of this analysis (see also Modelski and Thompson, 1999), what are the broader implications of these considerations for the future world politics in particular?

In the first place, if the United States continues as the principal locus of the information industries K-wave, carrying through the high-growth phase into the

2020s, then these developments lay a sound base for the bid for a second term of U.S. global leadership in the next generation.

Second, the fact that the information revolution is now underway and is yet to run its full course bodes well for the continued spread of democracy in the world. The information industries depend upon open societies, but they also strengthen them, and make them work better, because democracies feed upon good information. In 1900, just over 10 percent of the world's population lived in democracies; by 2000, that proportion had risen to 50 percent. At that rate, the world might be expected to be substantially democratic by the end of the twenty-first century. That is good news, and raises the prospects for the success of cooperative arrangements worldwide in the coming century.

Finally, in the experience of the past, a pair of K-waves sandwiched a longish period of major warfare. Are global wars to be expected in the transition from K-19 to K-20, that may be anticipated maybe for the 2030s, and is that also likely to yield the usual economic strains? The information revolution, and the rising salience of a democratic community make it likely that such an outcome is avoidable, even if a period of major tensions and political discomfort is quite likely in two to three decades time. And the role of global leadership will evolve too, to include an increasing role for democratic world governance.

References

David, Paul A. (1990) "The Dynamo and the Computer," *The American Economic Review*, 80 (2): 355–361.

Devezas, T. and G. Modelski (2003) "Power law behavior and world system evolution: A millennial learning process," *Technological Forecasting and Social Change*, 70: 819–859.

Fischer, David Hackett (1996) *The Great Wave: Price Revolution and the Rhythm of History*, New York: Oxford University Press.

Frank, Andre Gunder (1998) *ReOrient: Asia in the Global* Economy, Berkeley: University of California Press.

Hicks, John (1969) *A Theory of Economic History*, New York: Oxford University Press.

Kondratieff, Nikolai (1984) *The Long Wave Cycle*, trans. Guy Daniels, New York: Richardson and Snyder.

Landes, David (1998) *The Wealth and Poverty of Nations*, New York: W.W. Norton.

McNeill, William H. (1982) *The Pursuit of Power: Technology, Armed Force, and Society since A.D. 1000*, Chicago: University of Chicago Press.

Modelski, George (1990) "Is world politics evolutionary learning?" *International Organization*, Winter, 1–24.

—— (1996) "An evolutionary paradigm for global politics," *International Studies Quarterly*, 40, September, 321–342.

Modelski, George and Sylvia Modelski (eds.) (1988) *Documenting Global Leadership*, London: Macmillan.

Modelski, George and William R. Thompson (1988) *Sea Power in Global Politics 1494–1993*, London: Macmillan.

—— (1996) *Leading Sectors and World Powers: The Co-evolution of Global Economics and Politics*, Columbia: University of South Carolina Press.

—— (1999) "The long and the short of global politics in the 21st century: An evolutionary approach," *International Studies Review*, October, 109–140.

Modelski, G., T. Devezas, and W.R. Thompson (eds.) (2007) *Globalization as Evolutionary Process: Modeling Global Change*, London: Routledge.

Nelson, Richard and Sidney Winter (1982) *An Evolutionary Theory of Economic Change*, Cambridge, MA: Harvard University Press.

Schumpter, Joseph (1934) *The Theory of Economic Development*, Cambridge, MA: Harvard University Press.

—— (1939) *Business Cycles*, New York: McGraw Hill.

Strogatz, Steven and Ian Stewart (1993) "Coupled oscillators and biological synchronization," *Scientific American*, 269: 102–109.

Van Duijn, J.J. (1983) *The Long Wave in Economic Life*, London: George Allen and Unwin.

Part II

Globalization and development

Chapter 2 outlined the evolution that moved the world economy toward market systems, with major regional and institutional breakthroughs occurring from approximately AD 930 in China, 1190 in Italy, 1430 in Atlantic Europe, and 1640 or so in Britain, leading to its industrial take-off period. Chapter 2 also discussed the institutional setting within which the modern world economy developed from these regional centers of innovation, especially after the 1850s, including the creation of international markets, new types of enterprises and communication systems, the background of political security, and the launching of new productive facilities.

More recently, especially since the 1980s, innovations in information-processing technology and government deregulation have accelerated the expansion and globalization of financial markets as well as trade in goods and services. "Global" and "globalization" as used here combine the elements of international (activities taking place between nations) and multinational (activities taking place in more than one nation) with a strong degree of integration and ecological interdependence between nations.

This recent economic globalization is the subject of Part II, which covers its effects on economic growth and development, poverty and inequality, etc. Through this economic globalization literature, one can identify whatever common understanding of the global economic system is currently available, including an understanding of what might be needed to sustain the system – the major goals of this book.

With few exceptions, Part II finds that the evidence is not conclusive to support either strong pro- or anti-globalization viewpoints concerning the impacts of globalization on poverty, inequality, and growth and development. Thus, how can the two sides of this debate make such strong claims about the correctness of their positions? And, how are we to proceed toward solutions to these problems?

The human ecology economics framework helps us identify four explanations for the uncertainties surrounding globalization. First, the globalization processes are extremely complex and hard to measure and model. Second, people with different prior beliefs about globalization frequently attach different interpretations to the same evidence. Third, people may have hidden agendas and incentives to disguise their true beliefs about globalization. And fourth, the cognitive styles of how people think, as opposed to what they think, seems to play an important role in perpetuating the controversies.

Donald Snyder's Chapter 3 advances these debates on globalization, and Ravi Bhandari's Chapter 4 extends these debates to a human ecology study of land reform in general, and Nepal in particular, of how strong "politically correct" beliefs can lead to dangerous policy conclusions.

3 Strange priors

Understanding globalization

Donald Snyder

> No one can escape the anti-globalists today. One can simply turn on the TV, read the news reports on the street theater in Seattle last year and in Washington, D.C. this year. ... This motley crew comes almost entirely from the rich countries and is overwhelmingly white, largely middle-class, occasionally misinformed, often wittingly dishonest, and so diverse in its professed concerns that it makes the output from a monkey's romp on the keyboard look more coherent.
>
> (Jagdish Bhagwati)[1]

> Since the questions they raise are real, adequate answers have to be sought, no matter how unpolished, crude and breathless the protesters may look to the world establishment. There is a need for change. The world of Bretton Woods is definitely not the world of today, and there is a strong case for far-reaching re-examination of the institutional structure of the international world.
>
> (Amartya Sen)[2]

Introduction

Globalization has become an increasingly contentious topic in recent years: this chapter explores the reasons why. It utilizes the human ecology analytical framework and emphasizes the role of belief systems as drivers of the globalization debate. A taxonomy of globalization belief systems is developed. Attention is focused on the extremes of opinion which generate most of the controversy: free-market beliefs on the one hand, and leftist/nationalist beliefs on the other. The chapter then turns to the effects of globalization on economic growth, poverty and inequality; pro- and anti-globalization viewpoints are presented and compared with presently available empirical evidence. With few exceptions, the evidence is not strong enough to confirm either viewpoint as "correct." In light of that, how can the two sides continue to make such strong claims about the correctness of their views? The chapter suggests several possible reasons, including one not previously considered in the economics literature: the cognitive styles of the opinion-leaders.

"Globalization" is taken to mean growing interdependence among all nations and peoples. Our primary concern is with economic globalization, defined as the integration of the world's markets for goods and services, financial capital, and labor.[3] During the 1990s a vigorous debate emerged regarding globalization's benefits and costs; the quotation from Bhagwati re-evokes the strong feelings that were characteristic of that time. Forty thousand protesters, representing every conceivable interest group, descended onto Seattle's streets in 1999, shutting down the WTO meetings; large and sometimes violent demonstrations against globalization subsequently occurred in Washington, Québec, and Genoa. In recent years, these protests have become smaller and quieter, and have attracted less media coverage. That doesn't mean the issues have been resolved: what has happened instead is that the debate has spread from the streets to the halls of government and into the consciousness of the general population. Strong feelings about globalization continue to manifest themselves through sudden outpourings of public sentiment over outsourcing, immigration, foreign ownership of domestic firms, and similar issues. International economic affairs are in the thoughts of the average citizen today perhaps more than at any time since the 1930s.

Despite many years of argument, globalization's defenders and attackers seem no closer to a meeting of minds. Paul Krugman, in a foreword to a recent book about globalization, writes: "I don't expect this book to settle the debate over globalization...there are too many people firmly committed to their views to be shaken by any argument or evidence."[4] Opposing positions continue to be pushed beyond what the evidence will support: Conway's review of IMF performance during the financial crises of the 1990s, for example, concludes that on many of the important issues, "both (Stanley) Fischer and the IMF's critics made logically consistent arguments with little empirical support."[5] Similarly, a recent study of trade and globalization by Stiglitz and Charlton notes that:

> The weakness of the evidence in favor of a direct relationship between trade liberalization on economic growth has not prevented some economists from pursuing free trade at full throttle. ... It is difficult to identify the evidentiary source of the bullishness for unqualified trade liberalization. ... The theoretical and empirical evidence ... rules out extreme positions on both sides. It is therefore worth asking why these extreme positions have proved so enduring.[6]

That question is the subject of this chapter. The following section links this chapter to human ecology economics. The third section reviews the major ideologies of globalization, while the fourth section assesses the evidence on some key globalization controversies. The fifth section takes up the question of why globalization is persistently controversial. The chapter is summarized and concluded in the final section.

A human ecology approach to globalization

One of the goals of human ecology, as discussed in Chapter 1, is to understand humankind's present problems and the ways that they can be solved. H.G. Wells used the term "human ecology" to denote a forum for describing "what is happening to mankind." This forum was supposed to "bring all the scattered and ineffective mental wealth of our world into something like a common under- standing." To Wells in the 1930s, this project was urgent because he felt that neither the League of Nations, nor Roosevelt's "brain trust," understood enough about what was needed to sustain the global system.

Through the globalization literature of today, one can identify whatever common understanding of the global human ecology is currently available, including an understanding of what might be needed to sustain the system. By identifying the belief systems surrounding globalization, this chapter also sets out many of the belief systems that are in play in the human ecology. Identifying these competing beliefs, and reconciling and verifying them where possible, constitutes a response to H.G. Wells' challenge and to the challenge of this book.

A human ecology consists of the four elements shown in Figure 3.1: belief systems, social agreements, human populations, and physical environments and resources. In the long-run, no doubt the four components all affect each other (with the possible exception of such things as geography and geology which may be truly exogenous), but for the purposes of this chapter, it is

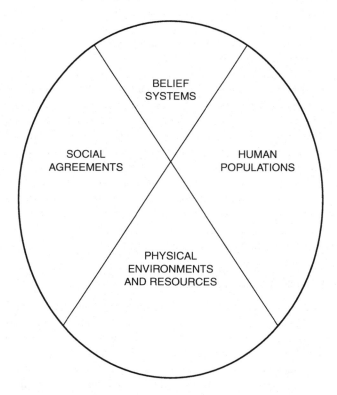

Figure 3.1 The four elements of a human ecology.

assumed that belief systems change much more slowly than social agreements, institutions, and organizations, and are therefore fairly exogenous in the short-run. This chapter takes the term "belief" to refer to any conceptualization of the nature of reality that has an observable effect on behavior; this would include religious beliefs, philosophical constructs, scientific and mathematical methodologies, mythological systems, and political and other ideologies. In addition, superstitions and prejudices, common heuristics, and broad cultural values are also considered to be "beliefs," even when they are learned and applied subconsciously.

The focus here is on the belief systems of those who theorize about globalization, not those who have to live it out. Kevin Watkins cites a short essay by Jean Dreze, written at the end of a field visit to villages in Rajhastan, India, which comments on the clash between the world of academic debate on poverty and the world as experienced by poor people themselves. Dreze writes: "Social scientists are chiefly engaged in arguing with each other about issues and theories that often bear little relation to the real world."[7] It is hoped that the present chapter might help bring the academic debate a little closer to the actual lives of the poor.

In Chapter 9, Allen broadens the notion of human ecology belief systems by asking: What "ways of being" are at play in the global human ecology? "Ways of being" cluster together belief systems (as identified here) with personality traits, social behaviors, and even physical energies of various globally-important actors. The goal is the same: to identify key structural components of the global ecology so that we can respond to global concerns.

A troubling aspect of the conclusions of this chapter, and of Allen's Chapter 9, is that competing belief systems and ways of being can, at present, point to little in the way of hard evidence that might help the non-believer evaluate their relative merits. Given the weakness of the evidence, how can competing camps make such strong claims about the correctness of their views? This chapter suggests several possible reasons, including one not previously considered: the cognitive styles of the opinion leaders. Allen goes further, to provide a longer historical account of how the current belief systems, cognitive styles etc. as per "ways of being," have grown to their current dominance. And, Allen suggests ways of holding at arms length and reconciling these beliefs and ways of being, so that debate and policymaking can be more intelligently informed.

But first, to identify the belief systems of globalization ...

Economic globalization and belief systems

This section describes the major belief systems that drive the globalization debate. The strong proponents of globalization advocate a free-market belief system. The strong opponents of globalization can be broken down into two ideological camps: a rightist group which is nationalistic and protectionist, and a rather diverse leftist group where some members espouse updated versions of Marxism; others advocate local self-sufficiency; and a small but visible minority are identified with anarchist ideas and tactics.

All of these groups are driven by ideology first and foremost. Collectively, they constitute a minority in the globalization movement, albeit an influential one. Most participants in the movement would probably consider themselves pragmatists, who think in terms of practical outcomes, compromise and shades of gray rather than absolute imperatives. The pragmatists generally want to see globalization continue, but under different, more humane rules; their strategies and concerns are well described by Elliott *et al.*[8] They are not the focus of this chapter, because ideology and movement-building is not what drives them. They are globalization's (relatively) silent majority. It is from the strong believers on the extremes that the movement has gotten its public image, much of its energy, and many of its contradictions.

It may be helpful at the outset to give some historical perspective to the ideologies of globalization. Since the eighteenth century at least, economics has been concerned not only with describing how society works, but with redesigning social institutions to make for a better world. This led to the emergence of two grand interpretations of economic history, each with an aura of inevitability and a prescription for a just society. One belief system developed around the ideas of Karl Marx and favored socialism. The other arose to defend market-based capitalism from this socialist challenge. During the first two-thirds of the twentieth century, Marxian-based beliefs were in the ascendancy and economic ideas were often defined by their relationship to that world-view, even when they were adamantly opposed to it. The momentum began to shift towards capitalism in the 1970s as socialist economic performance lagged and Thatcher–Reagan policies gained popularity. By the start of the 1990s, state socialism had collapsed and capitalism stood alone on the stage. The free-market belief system is now playing the same role that the socialist belief system played earlier: all economic positions, even hostile ones, are defined by their relationship to it.

Figure 3.2 categorizes the various participants in the globalization debate according to who they are and what attitudes they hold towards globalization. The categories are suggestive, not definitive. Not all NGOs are pragmatic for example, nor are all finance ministry professionals unabashed free-traders. But the stereotypes are sufficiently accurate to serve as a basis for discussion.

Who participates in the globalization debate? There are those who generate and exchange ideas both inside and outside of academia; there are government agencies involved in activities related to globalization; and there is civil society, which essentially means everybody else who might be involved. These categories take their inspiration from a widely-cited analysis by Kanbur.[9]

Figure 3.2 identifies three general attitudes towards globalization: pro, anti, and a pragmatic middle ground. Those in the first group want to see globalization continue or accelerate. The second group wants it to stop or go into reverse. The third group wants to see it continue, but in a supervised fashion. These categories are adapted from Elliott *et al.*[10] These authors provide a thorough analysis of the middle column in Figure 3.2, but say little about column 1 and devote only a single footnote to column 3.[11] This chapter focuses on columns 1 and 3,

	Pro	Pragmatic	Anti
Academics and intellectuals	Neoclassical economists	Other social scientists	Neo-Marxists, Dependency theorists World system theorists Localists, anarchists
Government	Finance ministries	UN Aid ministries Social ministries	
Civil society	Financial community	Many NGOs Average citizen	Nationalists

Figure 3.2 Attitudes towards globalization.

so as to gain a better understanding of the ideological differences that drive the whole debate.

Two stylized facts stand out for the academics and intellectuals in Figure 3.2. First, mainstream economists are somewhat isolated in their enthusiasm for economic globalization, an enthusiasm largely based on the outcomes their models generate. These outcomes are contingent on certain assumptions built into the models, in particular: disregard for short-term adjustment costs; and a presumption of no significant market power effects.[12] Other social scientists, who are conditioned by different world-views, tend to give globalization more mixed reviews. Second, the political orientation of academics and intellectuals who oppose globalization is predominantly leftist, but not exclusively so.

With respect to government, there is a split between attitudes in the finance ministries, where views are heavily conditioned by neoclassical economics, and attitudes in the agencies responsible for dispensing foreign aid and assistance to the poor. Austerity programs imposed by the IMF according to Washington Consensus ideology are widely believed to have resulted in cutbacks in social expenditures in many developing countries, which may help explain the relative lack of enthusiasm for globalization among aid and social agencies. These agencies have to deal with the real problems of individual human beings rather than impersonal economic models, and rightly or wrongly, they attribute some of the problems their clients face to the forces of globalization.

In civil society, pro-globalization opinion is centered in the financial community, that is, the financial press and Wall Street, which by and large shares the world-view of the finance ministries and often works closely with them. The anti-globalization center-of-gravity is the Nationalists, who see unrestrained globalization as inimical to the interests of the state. Nationalists have little support among academics and intellectuals, but they do enjoy the sympathies of a fairly large number of citizens and business people. They are usually protectionist. They agree with Marxists and Localists that globalization should be reversed, but disagree with them on just about everything else. NGOs have a wide distribution of views ranging from pro-globalization to anti-globalization. Elliott *et al.* attempted to identify "engager" NGOs, who are inclined towards compromise, and "confronters," who are not.[13] However, they were not able to classify the majority of NGOs one way or the other; therefore all NGOs are placed, somewhat subjectively, in the middle column of Figure 3.2. Finally, one might ask where the average citizen stands. For this we must turn to survey research. General questions about people's attitudes towards globalization do not reveal much, and more detailed surveys have so far only been conducted in wealthier countries. Analysis of the latter by Scheve and Slaughter[14] suggests that the average citizen in wealthy countries is aware of the benefits of specialization and comparative advantage, but is also sensitive to the short-run costs of lowering trade barriers; his support for globalization is highly conditional on compensation schemes and support nets for the losers. This suggests that the average citizen belongs in the "pragmatist" column of Figure 3.2. However, it should be borne in mind that most citizens of the poorer countries have yet to express their opinion.

The major globalization belief systems are now described in more detail.

The free market belief system

The cornerstone of the free-market belief system is a view of capitalism in which the interaction of numerous, self-organizing firms, each seeking to maximize its own profit, leads to an optimal social outcome. Although this vision incorporates elements of Smith, von Mises, and Hayek, its promulgation owes much to the Chicago School of economics; it is an American, more than a European, ideology.[15] The glue that holds it together is the neoclassical belief system.

One of the most important concepts in the neoclassical belief system is specialization. When human beings collaborate to produce things, the way they collaborate matters: if the group practices division of labor so that individual members specialize in specific tasks, the result is increased output and/or lower unit costs. The neoclassical term for this is "scale economies." The group can then exchange the extra output for things that it wants but does not produce. Taking the same idea to the national level leads to the theory of comparative advantage: a nation can specialize in producing things for which its relative costs are low, trade with other nations for what it needs, and the world gets to consume more as a result. Other important neoclassical concepts are that economic behavior is presumed to be rational, and that exchange, when it occurs, is presumed to be voluntary.

The neoclassical belief system does not lead inevitably to the free market belief system: that requires auxiliary assumptions. Neoclassical economics cautions that markets can fail for a variety of technical reasons, in which case there is no guarantee that numerous self-organizing firms will generate an optimal social outcome. The free-market belief system deals with this problem by assuming that if a market fails, the government can be called in to correct the problem. Some free-market enthusiasts assert that government failure is more common and serious than market failure, leading to the conclusion that markets should be tolerated even when they fail, the alternative being worse.

Buttressed by the neoclassical belief system, the free-market belief system makes the following claims:

- Market competition is widespread. It is best to let markets operate unimpeded because government interference usually makes society worse off.
- Market failure is less common than government failure, so the government should serve mainly as a social referee; rarely should it provide goods and services, or own assets.
- Globalization is the product of voluntary exchange, free trade, and market liberalization.
- Globalization is beneficial to all countries, rich and poor alike, that participate in it. Based on the lessons of history, it is the only route to long-term prosperity.
- The multinational corporation is an important vehicle for facilitating trade and transmitting technology to the developing countries. It also provides useful competition against local monopoly.
- Poor nations should follow the dictates of the "Washington Consensus": institute sound fiscal and monetary policy; sell off state-owned industries; create secure property rights; and open the economy to foreign trade and investment.
- The IMF, World Bank, and WTO have been very helpful in stabilizing the world economy, helping the poorest countries, and encouraging trade.
- Poor nations that trade more and attract foreign investment will narrow the gap between themselves and the rich nations, thereby reducing inequality, a process known as "convergence."
- Taxation should be avoided where possible, because it is coercive and creates perverse incentives. The poor should be helped through economic growth, not tax/transfer redistribution.
- Global governance is undesirable because it co-opts rights and functions of the territorial state.

The Marxian tradition

A summary of the Marxian point of view on globalization might begin with a second look at specialization. The free-market belief system claims that specialization leads to scale economies and therefore to a higher standard of living. Marx, in contrast, doubted that specialization yields net benefits to society, for two reasons. First, scale economies usually lead to oligopoly or monopoly. Marx's Law of Increasing Concentration predicts that the drive for profit will lead capitalists to substitute capital for labor, which will consolidate many small competing firms into a few large-scale enterprises, as the firms which realize scale economies are able to lower their costs and drive competitors out of business, absorbing their assets. In Marx's world, a purely competitive economy cannot last for long: scale economies ensure that industries become monopolized and economic power becomes increasingly concentrated in the hands of the few.

Second, specialization increases vulnerability. In Marx's words:

> The whole system of capitalist production is based upon the fact that the worker sells his labor power as a commodity. Thanks to the division of labor, this labor power becomes specialized, is reduced to skill in handling a particular tool. As soon as the handling of this tool becomes the work of a machine...the worker becomes unsalable, like paper money which is no longer legal tender.[16]

Extending this line of reasoning, any major disruption in a capitalist economy (new products, new competitors, changing technologies, etc.) carries the potential for making some workers' skills obsolete and creating unemployment. The association between specialization and vulnerability carries over into international trade in the form of layoffs caused by outsourcing. A nation that carries specialization to the limit by, say, becoming a mono-crop exporter will find its standard of living held hostage to world market conditions.

For Marx, the fundamental realities were modes of production (feudal, capitalist, etc.) and social classes. Marx had no theory of imperialism, and no real theory of nationalism either: nations were said to be subject to class relations. From the standpoint of globalization these are awkward gaps: if you are being exploited from abroad, is it being done by capitalists (a class-based concept) or by the United States (a nation-based concept)? Lenin provided the Marxian tradition with a theory of imperialism, which he saw as a force that would transplant capitalism into the less-developed countries, weakening the dominance of the capitalists of the advanced countries.[17] Paul Baran reversed this theory in the 1950s, arguing that capitalists in the advanced countries were forcing the developing world into the role of permanent raw materials supplier and using trade as the means of extracting economic surplus.[18]

In the 1970s, the dependency theorists further modified the notion of imperialism by arguing that the periphery was not just selling primary products: industrialization was occurring in the periphery as well, undertaken by local elites and local states with the assistance of foreign capital. This "triple alliance" was a new form of imperialism.[19] The dependency theorists also tried to bring nationalism more formally into their analysis, but were not wholly successful because nations often believe and do things at odds with Marxian (class-based) thinking. Dependency writers had trouble distinguishing between external dependency (relations between nations of the center and nations of the periphery) and structural dependency (external relations and their impact on classes and modes of production within a nation).[20]

The ambiguity between nation and class was addressed in a different way by another offshoot of Marxism known as world-systems theory.[21] Roughly speaking, world-systems theory is dependency theory without nationalism. It views the whole world as an integrated class system, capitalist in nature, which has been with us since the sixteenth century. National units exist and are categorized as core, periphery, and semi-periphery, but these terms are intellectual tools, useful mainly for gaining an understanding of the world class system with its all-inclusive division of labor and system of trade, and its multiple forms of class conflict. A unifying theme of world-system theory is that the core capitalist economies became developed by exploiting the periphery.

At the middle of the twentieth century, developing countries were busy either separating themselves from their colonial masters (Africa and parts of Asia) or contending with the entrenched power of the descendents of former colonial masters (Latin America). Theories of exploitation, surplus extraction, and unequal exchange had wide appeal at that time. But subsequent decades saw improvement in the fortunes of some former colonies, mainly in Asia. This demonstrated that under-development could be overcome, at least in the right circumstances: victimization was not insurmountable. As living standards began to rise in the developing world, the Marxian-based theories became less popular. Today they have appeal mainly in countries where the legacy of colonialism remains strong, especially in sub-Saharan Africa. Barbara Epstein writes:

> The traditional socialist left in the United States now mostly consists of several magazines and journals, a few annual conferences, a small number of intellectuals. Hope for the revival of the left appears to lie with the anti-globalization movement and the young radical activists at its core.[22]

Because a theory is no longer popular in intellectual circles, however, does not mean that it has nothing of value to say. Marxian-based theories raise fundamental issues about the desirability of globalization. In the Marxian view, globalization is something that has been inflicted on the world by the United States and Western Europe for their own advantage. Present-day globalization is seen as the latest manifestation of a set of processes that began gathering steam in the early nineteenth century: processes characterized by unequal exchange, growing inequalities in the world distribution of wealth and power, and in earlier times by colonialism, slavery, and empire. Marxist-oriented writers see a strong correlation between globalization and imperialism. They would not be surprised by the fact that Cecil Rhodes, the founder of Rhodesia, once said:

> We must find new land from which we can easily obtain raw materials and at the same time exploit the cheap slave labor that is available from the

natives of the colonies. The colonies would also provide a dumping ground for the surplus goods produced in our factories.[23]

Major themes of Marxian-based thinking on globalization are as follows:

- The competitive ideal of numerous similar-sized firms cannot happen under capitalism: scale economies cause market competition to degenerate into oligopoly or monopoly.
- Market failure is more common than government failure.
- Globalization contains strong elements of coercive exchange, managed trade, and restricted markets.
- Globalization disproportionately benefits wealthy capitalistic countries and firms. The wealthy countries achieved prosperity in part by exploiting the developing countries.
- The multinational corporation is an important contemporary vehicle for this exploitation.
- IMF structural adjustment programs based on Washington Consensus policies have not helped LDCs grow or develop. In some cases they have made things worse, forcing cutbacks in social services. Today's wealthy countries did not achieve their wealth by following Washington Consensus-type policies.
- The IMF, World Bank, and WTO are often pressured by wealthy countries to promulgate policies that primarily benefit multinational corporations and large international banks.
- Under capitalism, economic growth disproportionately benefits the wealthier countries and classes; the poorest cannot catch up.
- Growth alone is not sufficient to reduce inequality: Tax/transfer redistribution is also needed.
- Global governance is essential to assert control over the exploitative activities of multinationals, which can evade the rules of any one nation-state.

One does not have to be Marxist to hold some of these beliefs. It is hard, for example, to find a mainstream economist who is willing to speak in defense of current U.S. and European agricultural subsidies: vested interests have prevailed over economic rationality and social justice on that issue. And neoclassical economists are not in agreement amongst themselves. For example, Jeffrey Sachs expresses the following conservative view:

> Since Marx, if not before, the gains of the capitalist economies (and of the rich within those societies), have been viewed as ill-gotten exploitation. ... After all, the rich countries did indeed grossly exploit the rest of the world, via slavery, colonial rule, military pressures, and the like. Yet the causality was mostly the other way around: exploitation was made possible by superior power and wealth, and was not the cause of that superior power and wealth.[24]

This last statement might make Cecil Rhodes smile were he still alive. The mainstream World Bank economist Branko Milanovic expresses a very different opinion about the free-market view of globalization:

> Economists who deal in models of individual rational behavior are not well equipped to treat conquests and plunder. Thus, they prefer to stick to the "nice" face of globalization, to describe how the global working of the "invisible hand" brought late nineteenth century technological marvels. Globalization was not merely accompanied by the worst excesses of colonialism… globalization *was* colonialism because it is through being colonies that most of the non-European countries were brought into the global world.[25]

The localists

> I sympathize, therefore, with those who minimize, rather then with those who would maximize economic entanglements between nations. Ideas, knowledge, art, hospitality, travel – these are the things which should of their nature be international. But let goods be homespun whenever it is reasonably and conveniently possible, and, above all, let finance be primarily national. … Yet, at the same time, those who seek to disembarrass a country of its entanglements should be very slow and wary. It should not be a matter of tearing up roots but of slowly training a plant to grow in a different direction.
>
> (John Maynard Keynes)[26]

Localists are fond of citing the above passage because it conveys the flavor of their belief system and gives the impression that Keynes may have been one of them. Of course, he wrote those words in 1933 when external pressures were causing the world trading system to fall apart and the optimism of free-traders was being sorely tested. In any event, localism has a long history, stretching back to Gandhi and well before. The broad outlines of modern localism are laid out in *Alternatives to Economic Globalization*.[27] The localists want to roll back globalization, devolving international economic activity back down to the regional or local level. Views vary on how much of a rollback is appropriate, with the more extreme proponents calling for elimination of the WTO, the Bretton Woods institutions, and all multinationals.[28] Complete autarky is not advocated however, and moderates only want to declare specific things off-limits to international exchange. Localists claim that they do not oppose trade per se, but rather trade agreements as they are currently undertaken, which are dominated by the interests of the multinationals and strip away social and environmental protections at the local level: governance, more than trade volume, is the issue.[29]

Localism is a collectivist ideology, but it is not socialist in the usual sense of the term. Localists argue that socialism and capitalism are equally misguided, because both ideologies centralized the power of ownership in institutions that could not be held accountable: the state in the case of socialism and the corporation in the case of capitalism. Both worked against the classic liberal economic ideal of self-organizing markets, markets in which communities organize themselves to respond to local needs within a framework of democratically determined rules.[30]

But many localists don't really aspire to that classic liberal economic ideal either. In the developing countries they seek to replace foreign-owned MNCs with locally owned and operated enterprises accountable to local stakeholders. Reliance on market prices is viewed with suspicion: "the goal of society should not be to find cheaper prices for products. ... If people grow their own food, produce their own necessities and control the conditions of their lives, the issue of price becomes irrelevant."[31] Localists believe that firms should pay greatest attention to "democratically determined rules" when making decisions: in other words, to some sort of collectivist political process. They are simultaneously pessimistic that democracy can tame national collectivist governments (state socialism) and optimistic that it can make collectivism work at the local level.

Important elements of the localist belief system are the following:

- The principle of subsidiarity should govern economic affairs – whatever decisions and activities can be undertaken locally, should be. It is interesting to note that this principle is inscribed in the Treaty on European Union.
- Control of the common heritage resources which make up the global commons should not be allowed to fall into the hands of persons or corporations who, in the interest of monetary gain, would limit the public's right to use these resources.
- The limited liability corporation, especially in its multinational form, is opposed to the needs of sustainable societies: it should be reformed or eliminated.
- The World Bank, the IMF, and the WTO are dominated by multinational corporate interests; their policies facilitate the agenda of the multinationals more than they improve the lot of the poor. They should be reformed or eliminated.
- Economic systems should be ecologically sustainable, and protective of the interests of future generations.

Localists have strong opinions about common heritage resources, which they define as resources that belong to a group by birthright and should be shared among the members of that group. Water supplies, the atmosphere, pastures, and forests are often given as examples.[32] Neoclassical economists refer to such goods as common property goods, goods which are rival (the more you consume of it, the less is available for me) and non-excludable (both of us have a right to consume it). Such goods are notoriously difficult to manage: one user's actions impose costs on other users, but there is often no mechanism in place to hold a user accountable for such costs. The result, too often, is Hardin's famous "tragedy of the commons,"[33] where a group of herders overgraze a common pasture and drive it to ruin. Any one herder might say to himself: "I'm best off to graze as much livestock on the commons as I can...if I don't, my neighbor will." Hardin termed this type of situation "a rebuttal of the invisible hand" because self-interested behavior not only fails to make society better off, it actually makes everyone worse off – their collective behavior costs all the herders the future use of their pasture. Many societies have expended considerable effort and ingenuity trying to devise ways to avoid the tragedy of the commons. The potential solutions fall into three categories: regulation through local interaction among the users themselves; regulation by an outside party (such as a government); and privatization of the common resource.[34] The localists oppose the third alternative, especially when the resource is privatized by a multinational corporation. Their concern is that the multinational will not manage it in the interests of local users to whom it belongs by birthright. In extreme cases, the multinational might sell off the resource in the world market for its own gain, leaving local users with nothing.

Localists are suspicious of all limited liability corporations, not just multinationals. They believe separation of ownership from control encourages irresponsible investor behavior. Since owners cannot be punished for harm done by the corporation's managers, they may be prone to overlook such harm if profits are good. Localists seem to reserve special contempt for multinational corporations, accusing them of a long list of misdeeds in the developing countries, and rarely crediting them with doing anything positive.[35]

The anarchist element

Localists are part of a larger group, the globalization activists, which is a major source of energy for the movement and is responsible for much of the publicity the movement has received. The views and behavior of this group sometimes puzzle mainstream economists, evoking comments such as "I don't understand what is getting the protesters into the streets," and "I understand what they're against, but I have no idea what they are for." Milanovic observed earlier in this chapter that economists seem to be temperamentally disinclined towards incorporating coercion and violence into their models.[36] Elliott *et al.* comment that "Economists sometimes find conflict and protest intrinsically baffling, in contrast to negotiation."[37] Not surprisingly then, many economists believe that the globalization protesters have no central theme or coherent ideology, are opposed to all forms of structure and organization, and are engaging in nothing more significant than Bhagwati's "monkey's romp on the keyboard." On the more positive side, in responding to global concerns such as climate change, as concluded by Asbjorn Moseidjord at the end of Chapter 7, "economics offers a peaceful and cost effective way [to accomplish necessary change]."

The globalization activists beg to disagree with their critics. In the words of one of them:

It's distressing that ... I should have to write this, but someone obviously should: ... this is a movement about reinventing democracy. It is not opposed to organization. It is about creating new forms of organization. ... It is about creating and enacting horizontal networks instead of top-down structures like states, parties or corporations; networks based on principles of decentralized, non-hierarchical consensus democracy.[38]

He goes on to say that activists in North America have been using their groups' own internal processes as laboratory experiments, "to create viable models of what functioning direct democracy could actually look like."

But what, precisely, is the ideology guiding the experiment? Much creative energy for radical globalization politics today appears to be coming from anarchism, which competed with Marxism in pre-World War I days, and is enjoying a new lease on life now that state socialism is defunct. Many mainstream economists know little of anarchism. Elliot *et al.* for example, refer to "the anarchists of the Black Bloc, who are against all forms of institutional control."[39] In actual fact, neither the Black Bloc nor anarchists in general oppose all forms of institutional control. The term "anarchism" comes from a Greek word which means "without archons," that is, "without rulers." It is the belief that institutions of centralized authority are antithetical to freedom and equality, and should be abolished. Anarchists reason that centralized government is granted – by society – a monopoly right to use force and violence, and routinely exercises that right in unjust and oppressive ways. The primary targets of anarchism are the institutions of the modern bureaucratic nation-state, be it state socialism or large-scale capitalism.

What would life be like in a stateless society? On this the anarchists differ widely, some favoring a communal, horizontally-organized structure with no private property, others favoring a purely competitive capitalistic structure, and still others advocating something in between. But all seem to agree that the stateless society should be horizontally (not vertically) organized, should consist of small units, and should be governed by a democracy based more on consensus than on majority vote. Proudhon distinguished between ownership coinciding with use (possession) and absentee ownership (property),[40] arguing that the community should only protect the former: a concept which pre-figures contemporary localist ideas about the proper disposition of common heritage resources.

Anarchists and Marxists have a history of mutual antagonism, the Marxists maintaining that the state can be taken over and used for benevolent ends, the anarchists arguing that the state is an instrument of oppression no matter who controls it. The histories of Mao's China and Stalin's Soviet Union suggest that the anarchists got the better of that argument. Anarchism's own history, however, is not of great relevance to what is happening today in the globalization movement:

The anarchist mindset of today's young activists has relatively little to do with the theoretical debates between anarchists and Marxists ... it has more to do with an egalitarian and antiauthoritarian perspective. There are versions of anarchism that are deeply individualistic and incompatible with socialism. But these are not the forms of anarchism that hold sway in radical activist circles, which have more in common with the libertarian socialism advocated by Noam Chomsky and Howard Zinn than with the writings of Bakunin or Kropotkin.[41]

This observation is of particular relevance when it comes to the question of the role of violence in political protest. There have been both pacifistic and violence-advocating anarchists over the course of the movement's history. Regarding today's globalization activists:

> Where once it seemed that the only alternatives ... were either Gandhian nonviolent civil disobedience or outright insurrection ... [the anti-globalization militant groups] have all, in their own ways, been trying to map out a completely new territory in between ... what can only be called non-violent warfare ... non-violent in the sense adopted by, say, Black Bloc anarchists, in that it eschews any direct physical harm to human beings.[42]

It is somewhat of an irony that the anarchist paradigm is able to function well only in a general atmosphere of peace, when the institutions of the centralized nation-state are in a tolerant mood. In the late nineteenth century, when most people believed that war between the European powers was irrational and inconceivable, anarchism was an influential belief system in radical circles. It went into forced eclipse with the onset of World War I, and remained there with the ascendancy of state socialism. But then, when the Cold War ended at the end of the twentieth century, it reappeared as an energizing element in radical politics.

Anarchism by its nature is not good at certain things. Movements need leaders, and it discourages leadership. Movements are more effective when they are large and well-organized, and these traits are antithetical to anarchist thinking. As a consequence, "movements dominated by an anarchist mindset are prone to burning out early."[43] It remains to be seen, therefore, whether anarchism (or localism) will continue to play a catalytic role in the progress of the globalization movement, or whether momentum will shift to the moderates and compromisers who occupy the center column of Figure 3.2. The less prominent role of demonstrations in recent years hints that such a shift may in fact be happening.

Critics maintain that anarchists and localists, if they wish to present a viable alternative to large-scale capitalism, need to deal realistically with the issue of economies of scale. Since the days of Adam Smith, it has been recognized that economic organization on a large scale can lead to significant gains in productivity and efficiency. Opponents of globalization almost never mention this positive aspect of size and centralization, choosing instead to focus on the negative aspects: concentration of power, unjust use of force, vulnerability to change. However, the positive and negative aspects of concentration seem as inseparable as the two faces of Janus. It is laudable to want to improve the democratic process and eliminate undesirable power relationships, but how does one replace large-scale nation-state capitalism with atomistic, horizontally-organized units without unwinding specialization and division of labor, a side effect which would drive up unit costs and lower living standards? A similar argument exists if one advocates eliminating vulnerability to international market fluctuations by curtailing international trade. Some localists might welcome a return to a simpler, leaner life, but most of the world's citizens who are below the $2 per day poverty standard are trying hard to move their living standards in the opposite direction.

An assertion leveled at globalization critics in general is that they have a tendency to blame foreigners for problems that occur in developing economies. More than one mainstream economist has pointed out that local malfeasance is often the most pressing problem. Pranab Bhardan writes:

> At the micro level of firms, farms, neighborhoods, and local communities, there is scope for a great deal of efficiency-enhancing egalitarian measures that can help the poor and are not primarily blocked by the forces of globalization ... like land reform, expansion of education and health facilities for the poor, organizing cooperative and peer-monitored credit and marketing for small firms and farms, facilitating formation of local community organizations to manage the local environmental resources, etc. The main hindrance ... is the considerable opposition from domestic vested interests – landlords, corrupt and/or inept politicians and bureaucrats, and the currently subsidized rich. Closing the economy does not reduce the power of these vested interests.[44]

The localist response to this line of thought is to agree that local governance can sometimes be authoritarian, oppressive, even brutal, but then to assert that globalization is worse because it "actually guarantees absentee rule by giant corporations that are designed to act solely in their own economic interests and have no real concerns about conditions faced in the daily lives of most people."[45] The possibility that competition from abroad might help weaken the control of domestic vested interests is implicitly rejected. Harry Flam probably speaks for many mainstream economists when he offers the following opinion: "The international institutions and globalization serve as scapegoats, when the really important barriers to economic development and well-being lie in the national, not the international, arena."[46] A provisional conclusion: this is an aspect of the globalization controversy where hard evidence is in shorter supply than strong opinions.

Economic nationalism

The opinions of those concerned about globalization vary as to what constitutes the proper relationship between the market and the state. At one extreme are those who favor a global market and wish to match it with a global state of some sort.[47] At the other extreme, the localists advocate fragmenting the global market into local submarkets matched to local jurisdictions. Decamped somewhere in the middle are the nationalists, who want to force markets back within the borders of existing nation-states and erect trade, migration, and investment barriers to keep them there.

Opinion leaders for the economic nationalists include Jean Marie LePen in France, Patrick Buchanan in the United States, and Jörg Haidar in Austria. As Figure 3.2 suggests, economic nationalism has little support in the academic/ intellectual community: mainstream economists question its logic and abhor the protectionism it promotes; left-leaning intellectuals concur with the nationalists that globalization should be reversed, but disagree with them on just about everything else. Nationalism resonates, however, with industrial-country workers who fear outsourcing and plant shutdowns; with xenophobes, especially in Europe;[48] and with businessmen wanting to shield themselves from foreign competition, a category that includes small businesses and older, nation-rooted industries, but excludes the new species of transnational firm which has thrown off its national roots.[49]

The ideology of economic nationalism is based upon the following propositions:

- The nation-state – not the world, not local jurisdictions – is the unit around which economic activity should be organized.
- Protection is more economically efficient then free trade.
- Trade policy should expand the nation's manufacturing base and maintain its social and political stability.
- International repercussions of a country's trade policy are of secondary importance: the international tail shouldn't be allowed to wag the domestic dog.
- Multinational governing bodies such as the WTO, which can overrule the internal prerogatives of the nation-state, should be reduced in power or abolished.

Economic nationalists point out that, globalization rhetoric to the contrary, most of the world's economic activity still takes place within the boundaries of the nation-state. Furthermore, despite globalization's new footloose internationalists, the loyalties of most people and most businesses continue to be firmly rooted in the nation-state. This is good, say the nationalists, because the nation, not the free-market, is the institution most likely to act in their best interests.

The nationalist assertion that protection is economically superior to free trade is more sweeping than arguments for isolated interventions such as infant industry tariffs. The logic runs as follows:

> Free trade is usually justified in terms of the cornucopia of low-priced goods in the shopping mall. This is hedonistic nonsense, particularly if you have no job to earn income to buy those goods. Production, not consumption,

is the basis of economic activity, the source of wealth. The wealth of a nation consists of domestic industries with high-paying jobs. This wealth must be protected from foreign competition.[50]

If the logic of the economic nationalists is accepted, the corollary must be that trade policy should be designed to protect industries and jobs. This usually translates into trade barriers and/or subsidies for most domestically produced products, limitations on outward foreign investment, and barriers to immigration, especially of low-skilled workers.

Economic nationalism is a close cousin to mercantilism, that venerable nemesis of free trade, which advocates increasing the wealth of a nation by maximizing the current account surplus. These two ideologies share a certain indifference to the possible international consequences of a nation's actions. For mercantilism, the blind-spot is the zero-sum nature of current account transactions for the world as a whole.[51] What are the blind-spots for economic nationalism? One issue is the potential for foreign retaliation to protectionist barriers. Brazil's imports are Argentina's exports and vice versa. Many observers have noted that worldwide retaliation spinning out of control can produce an outcome similar to the tragedy of the commons, where the gains from trade get destroyed and all nations (and their workers) wind up worse off than before. The 1930s come to mind in this regard. Another issue is that outsourcing or foreign investment by domestic firms may be a response to foreign protectionism rather than anti-patriotic behavior. A machine tool manufacturer who prefers to produce in the United States but also wishes to sell in India, upon encountering prohibitively high Indian tariffs on machine tool imports, may feel that he has no choice but to invest in an Indian manufacturing plant.

Economic nationalists are prone to the accusation of inconsistent argument. Patrick Buchanan, for example, is said to maintain that free trade is both inefficient and overly efficient. Inefficient, because America had more prosperity during the nineteenth century (when protectionism prevailed) than in the post-1970s era of free trade; overly efficient, because free trade ideology exalts the efficiency gains from trade and downplays the human costs to its losers. But his critics point out that free trade can't be both at the same time.[52]

It is possible to make a reasoned case for a certain degree of economic nationalism without totally abandoning arguments in favor of globalization and trade. The neoclassical economist Dani Rodrik makes such a case by starting with three stylized facts about modern capitalism. First, markets cannot work well unless state-provided institutions are doing their job properly:

> The paradox of markets is that they thrive best not under laissez-faire but under the watchful eye of the state. ... Markets are not self-regulating, self-stabilizing, or self-legitimizing. As Adam Smith complained, businessmen seldom meet together without the conversation ending up in a conspiracy against the public. In the absence of regulations pertaining to antitrust ... and other externalities, markets can hardly do their job correctly. Without a

lender-of-last-resort and a public fisc, markets are prone to wild gyrations.
... And without safety nets and social insurance ... markets cannot retain
their legitimacy for long.[53]

The second fact, not widely appreciated, is that a given institutional function,
such as reassuring investors that the fruits of their efforts will not be confiscated,
can be provided by widely differing institutional forms in different countries: the
Household Responsibility System in China, for example, as compared to private
property in the United States. The third fact is that societies resist changing their
institutional forms, especially if the change is socially disruptive or goes against
deeply-held values (picture Americans being asked to switch to the Household
Responsibility System for example); this reluctance throws up a serious road-
block to extensive globalization, which requires international convergence in
many economic institutions such as contract enforcement and the rules of doing
business.

These stylized facts lead Rodrik to postulate a political trilemma in the global
economy today:

> the nation-state system, democratic politics, and complete globalization are
> mutually incompatible. We can have at most two out of the three. Because
> global policymakers have yet to face up to this trilemma, we are headed in
> an untenable direction: global markets without global governance.[54]

The trilemma plays out as follows. To attain complete globalization and
retain the nation-state, it is necessary to give up a large slice of democracy.
This is because globalization requires standardized economic institutions everywhere (for example, if a country joins the WTO it must give up the right to
trade any way it wishes). Or, to attain complete globalization and retain democracy, it is necessary to create a global federation, a sort of "United States of
the World" in which former nations are the member units. Thus, the nation-
state is lost. Finally, to retain democracy and the nation-state, it is necessary to
stop short of fully standardizing the world's economic institutions, and therefore complete globalization is not achieved. This was the approach taken at
Bretton Woods.

Rodrik favors the third approach, arguing that the first is feasible but not
desirable, and the second is desirable but not feasible. He argues for a
reinvention of the Bretton Woods compromise for a new era. In his model, the
nation-state plays a useful role as a vehicle for democracy and a buffer to impersonal world economic forces, without invoking the isolationist extremism of
Buchanan's world-view.

This historic debate between nationalism/mercantilism and free trade is
revisited in Chapter 5 by Roy Allen and Chapter 6 by Guillaume Daudin.
Examining case studies from France in the eighteenth century as well as the
modern-day U.S., both authors conclude that nationalist/mercantilist policies
have proved to be more beneficial (to the countries that favor them) than is

commonly understood. Governments that have followed an approach Allen calls "money-mercantilism," have benefited from an inflow of foreign monetary wealth, which has been used to expand domestic money, credit, economic growth, and wealth. This process has allowed economic activity to be better coordinated and more efficient on a large scale, and has encouraged more intensive production and consumption activities. The mainstream growth literature has had difficulty modeling such effects because it looks for the source of new economic growth more narrowly in technology, physical resources, and labor productivity. Money, changing institutions, and international political power are assumed to have no independent effects on growth. Allen and Daudin challenge that assumption.

In the human ecology approach, as used by Allen and Daudin in Chapters 5 and 6, as in any natural science ecology approach, interspecies negotiations and transactions are exploratory, adaptive, and often individualized. Thus, all outcomes are not known to all members of the species; there is imperfect information, and transaction costs can be significant. This belief system has different consequences than the belief system of neoclassical economics with its full-information assumptions. In the human ecology approach, because full information on interspecies transactions is not available to all, the evolution of prices is not as straightforward; prices cannot be changed by spontaneous unanimous social agreement. From this it follows, as Allen and Daudin find, that money is not a veil for the influence of real variables: money and financial institutions have actually played a major role, in the eighteenth century as well as nowadays, in determining the comparative and absolute prosperity of nations.

Globalization and development

Overview

Some of the most intense controversies in the globalization debate concern the influence of globalization on the developing countries. Does globalization stimulate or inhibit economic growth? What effect, if any, does it have on poverty and inequality in the world? This section looks at the theoretical arguments and reviews the empirical evidence on these questions. To fix ideas, consider Figure 3.3, which follows Bourguignon.[55] The incomes of all households in the world are portrayed as lognormal distribution A.

The mean of this distribution represents the average level of household income and the dispersion represents the distribution of income. Assume that if a household earns less than $1 per day it is considered poor. Visual inspection of distribution A suggests that about 10 percent of the households are below the poverty line. How can these households be brought out of poverty?

One way that could happen is if a surge of economic growth were to raise average household income without altering the shape of the distribution. The entire distribution would then move rightward from A to B, bringing everybody's

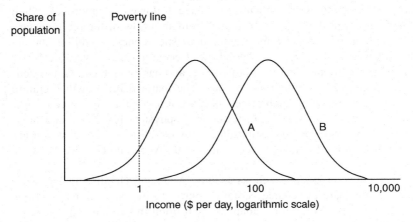

Figure 3.3 Eliminating poverty through growth.

income above the poverty line. Another way to eliminate poverty would be to redistribute income from the rich to the poor, which achieves the desired result in a very different way, as shown in Figure 3.4.

Neither the pure growth approach of Figure 3.3 nor the pure redistribution approach of Figure 3.4 would be easy to achieve in practice, since policy and social changes in the real world are likely to affect growth and distribution simultaneously in ways that are difficult to control. A policy change designed to increase growth, for example, might inadvertently make the distribution of income more unequal, spreading out B as in Figure 3.3. If this redistribution

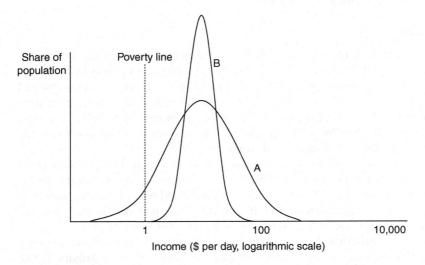

Figure 3.4 Eliminating poverty through redistribution.

effect were sufficiently strong, it could swamp the growth effect, resulting in more people below the poverty line than before. Alternatively, if an income-redistribution campaign created widespread social disruption, then average household income might fall, resulting in more people below the poverty line than before. With such possibilities in mind, let us now turn to the relationship between globalization and growth.

Globalization and growth

As far as the LDCs are concerned, it is probably fair to say that at least a crude sort of "justice" prevails in the economic policy realm. Countries that have run their economies following the policy tenants of the professionals have on the whole reaped good fruit from the effort; those that have flown in the face of these tenants have had to pay the price.

(Arnold Harberger *circa* 1985)

When you get right down to business, there aren't too many policies that we can say with certainty deeply and positively affect growth.

(Arnold Harberger *circa* 2003)[56]

The two main channels through which globalization might affect economic growth are openness to international trade and openness to international financial flows. Let us consider trade openness first. The proponents of globalization claim that no country has ever eliminated poverty by closing itself off to trade or by relying on income redistribution alone. Rising living standards, they maintain, have always been rooted in economic growth. Since globalization encourages trade, which in turn stimulates growth, it is argued that the poorest countries would be better off if they traded more; they are not victims of globalization, they are victims of the lack of it.[57]

Globalization's critics on the left[58] respond that many LDCs, including the most successful, have experienced sustained growth without throwing themselves wide open to trade. They frequently cite China as an example, a country that experienced rapid growth for many years before embarking on a policy of trade liberalization. Moreover, they point out, trade-induced growth may carry undesirable side effects. Leftist theories of surplus extraction and unequal exchange suggest that trade might be used by capitalist multinationals to exploit poorer countries and suppress their development. In general, the critics predict that trade is likely to have either negligible or negative effects on growth in the less-developed countries.

What does the empirical evidence show? Assessment of the trade–growth relationship is complicated by two factors: the practical problems of measuring "openness to trade," and the fact that trade is only one of many factors that influence growth. Consider the first issue. When deciding on a measure of trade openness, it is important to distinguish between variables that measure trade policies (such as tariff changes) and variables that measure trade volume (such as (exports+imports)/GDP). One generally wants to know how the government can control or influence growth, so openness should be measured by trade policy variables. However, trade policy variables can be difficult to quantify, which has forced many studies to use trade volume variables as proxies. This is problematic, because trade volume can be affected by factors other than trade policy. For example, a government might lower its tariffs, yet experience a decrease in trade volume if trade volume were also reacting to, for example, a shrinking domestic economy. Several researchers have pointed out that this has been a source of confusion in the trade–growth literature.[59] The proponents of globalization have tended to use trade volume when evaluating the effects of trade on growth; there is a positive association here, leading them to claim that their hypothesis has been confirmed. But this brings us to the second issue: many factors besides trade influence growth. The models are not well enough specified to rule out the possibility that trade volume is picking up the effect of forces other than trade policy. And even if there is a positive association between trade policy and growth, causation may run in the direction opposite from what is usually supposed: countries that grow faster may find that they trade more as a result. The globalization skeptics have tended to use trade policy variables as their measure of globalization, which makes better theoretical sense. Unfortunately, the relationship between trade policy variables and growth has proven to be statistically weak.[60] It is not certain whether this means trade policy has little effect on growth, or whether the weak relationship just reflects the ambiguities inherent in conceptualizing and constructing trade policy variables. Countries that have liberalized their trade have done so in strikingly different ways and have adopted a range of complementary growth-enhancing policies at the same time, all of which makes it difficult to sort out what is causing what.[61]

Taken as a whole then, the empirical literature on trade and growth does not support the most extreme critics of globalization, since there is no evidence that a country can grow faster by totally forsaking its trade with other nations, or that trade leads to negative growth. But neither does the evidence support globalization's strong enthusiasts; being open to trade, by itself, is no guarantee that a country will grow. Dani Rodrik, referring to the Washington Consensus reforms of the 1980s and early 1990s, writes:

> It would be fair to say that confronted with these radical changes in policies, most economists would have expected an equally radical improvement in economic performance. ... That has not happened. While the interpretations of why vary, the facts are not in doubt. Economic growth rates in those countries that adopted the "stabilize, liberalize, and privatize" agenda have turned out to be low not only in absolute terms, but also relative to other countries that were reluctant reformers and relative to the reforming countries own historical experience. Perhaps the disappointments in Africa are due to special circumstances: the ravages of civil war and crises in public health. But how can one explain the Latin American story, which is one of

poor growth and productivity performance in the 1990s – much worse than in the 1950–1980 period?[62]

What the empirical evidence strongly suggests is that the determinants of growth are complex, and while trade may be one of them, it is not in any obvious way the most important. In a related article, Freeman compares the writings of advocates of the Washington Consensus with those of the moderate globalization protesters and concludes that both groups may have exaggerated (in opposite directions) the effects of trade on economic performance.[63]

We turn next to financial liberalization, the second channel by which openness might affect growth. The fundamental issue here is whether nations should open themselves up to foreign financial flows or not. This is an ancient debate, but one which has taken on fresh urgency in the wake of the financial crises of the 1990s. Access to international financial markets allows pooling of risks; facilitates borrowing to deal with temporary recession or national disaster; allows capital-poor developing countries to finance investment; and disciplines the actions of local policymakers and local financial monopolists. In the long-run at least, such attributes can be expected to contribute to economic growth. Globalization enthusiasts feel that these advantages of financial markets outweigh any disadvantages. The more extreme enthusiasts want to lift all restrictions on the movement of financial capital among nations and even reorganize or abolish the IMF, on the grounds that it interferes with efficiency by shielding large commercial banks when they make bad lending decisions.[64]

However, it is also true that international financial markets contain information asymmetries, require democratic states to give up some sovereign control (especially of macro-economic stabilization policy), provide large foreign lenders with the opportunity to exploit small domestic borrowers, are subject to herding behavior, and involve contracts that can be difficult to enforce. Citing issues such as these, anti-globalization leftists have been consistently against letting in foreign capital.

Marx's theory emphasized production but it also recognized the role of money finance in building up capitalist enterprise. Marx seems to have viewed large banks in much the same way he viewed large industrial firms: as monopolies that obtain their surplus by capturing market share and exploiting labor. Until recently, Marxist thinkers paid little attention to finance: for example, a major 1985 review of recent Marxist thinking on economic development had little to say on the subject, except to point out that foreign aid could be used as a means of implementing imperialism.[65] This situation changed with the spread of financial markets in the closing decades of the twentieth century. Financial issues have been incorporated into recent Marxist interpretations of globalization, which portray financial liberalization as a device for providing funding to transnational corporations and as a source of destabilizing speculation.[66] Localists have a similar point of view, emphasizing that international finance has an absentee-owner character likely to be opposed to the interests of local and regional economies. They advocate keeping finance local, allowing foreigners to finance projects only under close supervision. American credit unions and the Grameen Bank of Bangladesh are cited as models.[67]

Also opposed (in part) to financial liberalization are a group of mainstream economists, Joseph Stiglitz and Jagdish Bhagwati being two of the most well-known. This contingent is generally in favor of increased trade and is not opposed to long-term foreign investment, which they regard as generating net economic benefits to the developing countries. What they object to is short-term finance, particularly bank loans. The instability of short-term flows is seen as one of the major causes of the financial crises of the late twentieth century. Economists have produced a vast pool of literature on this topic.[68] The core of the problem is succinctly described by Soros:

> Markets do show a tendency towards equilibrium when they deal with known quantities, but financial markets are different. They discount the future, but the future they discount is contingent on how the financial markets discount it...there is a two-way interaction between expectations and outcomes that I call "reflexivity"...[therefore] the future is genuinely uncertain and is unlikely to correspond to expectations.[69]

Such uncertainty is believed to be a major factor in the sudden inflows and out-flows of short-term funds that have plagued many developing countries.

Thus, only the most extreme globalization advocates are in favor of totally unrestricted financial flows between countries; almost everyone else is united in believing that short-term financial flows can be a serious problem. Mainstream economists would address the problem through monitoring, regulation, and financial-institution building. Leftist economists would go further, severely circumscribing or banning most short- and long-term financial flows. However, mainstream economists believe long-term financial flows are non-disruptive and generally beneficial to the developing countries. Overall then, mainstream economists would expect a positive relationship between long-term financial flows and growth, and leftist economists would expect financial flows of all types to exert a negative effect on growth, or at best to have no effect.

What does the empirical evidence show? Two surveys, one by the IMF[70] and the second by the World Bank,[71] reach essentially the same conclusion. As the IMF study puts it:

> Theoretical models have identified a number of channels through which international financial integration can promote economic growth in developing countries. However, a systematic examination of the evidence suggests that it is difficult to establish a strong causal relationship...if financial integration has a positive effect on growth, there is as yet no clear and robust empirical proof that the effect is quantitatively significant.[72]

To which might be added, the literature contains no widespread evidence of a negative relationship either, except for short-term financial flows.

At this point we can summarize the empirical evidence on globalization (openness) and economic growth. Globalization enthusiasts predict strong positive relationships running from both trade and financial flows to economic growth, with the possible exception of short-term financial flows. Globalization skeptics expect trade and financial flows to severely inhibit economic growth. The evidence does not provide overwhelming support for either side. However, short term financial flow volatility is widely found to be harmful and there is general agreement that it needs to be better controlled, although disagreement persists as to what measures are most appropriate.

Globalization, poverty, and inequality

According to its supporters, globalization tends to reduce poverty and inequality. Expressed in terms of Figure 3.3, the argument is that economic growth shifts the mean of world income distribution A to the right, while at the same time triggering a convergence of rich and poor incomes which restrains any increase in the dispersion of A. This story is not accepted by the critics of globalization. Their scenario is that globalization-induced rightward shifts in A are either weak or nonexistent, while at the same time globalization enables rich countries and social classes to pull steadily ahead of poor ones, increasing the dispersion of A. The net result is greater poverty and more inequality.

What does the empirical evidence suggest about world poverty? Wade surveys the evidence and concludes that it is quite likely that the proportion of the world's population living in extreme poverty has fallen over the past 20 years.[73] With regard to the poverty headcount however, there is much less certainty because a large margin of error is present in the World Bank figures. Wade feels that the World Bank has underestimated the number of the world's population living in poverty, but nobody knows for certain.

Has world inequality increased or decreased? Both sides in this particular dispute buttress their arguments with supporting statistics, sometimes based on the same underlying raw data. The controversy is surveyed by Wade and by Ravallion.[74] Ravallion's assessment is that each side in the debate is making a different value judgment about what a fair distribution of the gains from globalization would be. This has led the two sides to choose different metrics for measuring inequality, which has resulted in different empirical findings. In other words, it is differences in value judgments that generate many of the conflicting findings that characterize studies of globalization and inequality. According to Ravallion, value judgments are an issue in three areas: whether equal country weights or equal people weights should be used when estimating a world income distribution; whether horizontal or vertical inequality should be given more emphasis; and whether inequality is best measured relatively or absolutely.

The choice between country weights and people weights arises because of the way world income distribution estimates are constructed. The ideal way would be to line up everybody in the world from poorest to richest, but this is impossible in practice. What is actually done is that, first, country income distributions are derived using national income accounts and/or household survey data. These country income distributions are subsequently combined by weighted averages to arrive at a world income distribution. If country populations are used as the weights (so that people count equally) the results usually show falling between-country inequality in recent decades. But if country weights are used (so that each country counts equally) inequality appears to be rising in recent decades. Which weighting scheme is correct? If one is interested in comparing the well-being of individuals, people weights make more sense. But sometimes one wants to evaluate the effects of policy changes, in which case it makes sense to treat each country as a unit of observation. Another reason for preferring country weights is the possibility of serious errors in the income data for China and India, since these two countries account for 38 percent of the world's population and have a decisive effect on any estimated world income distribution.[75] It is a widely-accepted finding that when China and India are not included in the calculations, the people-weighted results become similar to the country-weighted results. Globalization critics prefer to use country weights, while globalization supporters generally use population weights.

The second distinction is between vertical and horizontal inequality. Vertical inequality refers to a situation where incomes at different levels do not rise by the same proportionate amount. Suppose a growth spurt increases everyone's income, rich and poor, by 10 percent. In Figure 3.3, that will shift the world distribution of income from A to B without affecting its shape. Since rich and poor share the gain in equal proportions, the growth spurt is said to generate no vertical inequality. Now imagine two people in distribution A, each with an income of $10. Suppose that when the distribution shifts, the first person's income rises to $13, but the second person's income drops to $9. Combined, their two incomes are now $22, a 10 percent increase, but this outcome is quite different from the case where the income of each goes up by 10 percent to $11. This is what is meant by horizontal inequality; people who were equal before the change are not equal afterwards. Globalization's supporters are fond of citing studies showing that globalization leaves vertical inequality measures undisturbed;[76] their implicit value judgment is that vertical inequality is more important than horizontal inequality. Globalization critics tend to be more concerned with horizontal inequality, often pointing out that there are losers among the poor even when the net gains to the poor are positive, as in the example above.[77] At times these concerns lead them to ignore vertical impacts which are favorable to globalization.

Ravallion's third key distinction is between relative inequality (ratio inequality) and absolute inequality (difference inequality). Suppose household X has an income of $4 and household Y's income is $20. Now suppose X's income increases to $6 and Y's increases to $30. There has been no change in relative inequality because the two incomes rose by the same percentage amount (their ratio remains constant at 1:5). There has, however, been an increase in absolute inequality, because the difference between the two incomes increased from $16 to $24. When non-economists voice concern about distributive justice they generally have some type of absolute inequality in mind. Critics of globalization can be imprecise when they talk about inequality, but when they cite evidence it usually involves absolute inequality. In contrast, defenders of globalization almost always base their arguments on relative inequality evidence.[78] Choice of evidence is crucial, because relative inequality measures usually show constant or decreasing world inequality in recent decades, while absolute inequality measures most often portray world inequality as rising. To cite one example, a common finding in the literature is that plotting percentage changes in the Gini index against corresponding percentage changes in mean household income yields a near-zero correlation; income growth leaves relative inequality unchanged on average. But if one replaces percentage changes in the Gini with absolute changes, the correlation jumps to 0.64, suggesting that the absolute gap between the rich and the poor rises in growing economies and falls in contracting ones.[79] So whether it is necessary to give up some growth in order to reduce inequality depends on which definition of inequality one uses. Another example where the relative–absolute distinction is important is in the widely-cited growth–poverty cross-country regression studies of Dollar and Kraay.[80] Commentators have sometimes interpreted these studies as demonstrating that the poor share fully in the gains from growth. What the studies actually show, however, is that the percentage change in the incomes of the poor is about the same as the percentage change in average income. From the perspective of absolute inequality, equal percentage gains translate into larger dollar gains for the rich; to the order of four times larger for the richest decile in India, 15–20 times larger for the richest decile in Brazil. The issue actually goes deeper. In Ravallion's words:

> There is no economic theory that tells us that inequality is relative, not absolute. It is not that one concept is right and the other wrong. Nor are they two ways of measuring the same thing. Rather, they are two different concepts. The revealed preferences for one concept over another reflect implicit value judgment(s) about what constitutes a fair division of the gains from growth. Those judgments need to be brought into the open and given critical scrutiny before one can take a well-considered position in this debate.[81]

Wade[82] discusses two additional measurement issues which affect conclusions about globalization, poverty and inequality: whether purchasing power parity (PPP) or market exchange rates are used to make incomes comparable across countries, and whether inequality is measured at the average or at the extremes (PPP exchange rates are the arbitrarily chosen ones that would equate average prices, between nations, of their tradeable merchandise and services). In theory, PPP exchange rates should be used to adjust country income estimates since they are designed to take account of differences in purchasing power and thus material well-being. Market exchange rates should not be used because they often do not reflect the real economy, being subject to well-known distortions (short-term capital flows, non-traded goods, overvalued or undervalued official rates, etc.). However, in practice the matter is not that simple. Sometimes we are interested in residents' purchasing power over goods and services produced in other countries, as when repaying dollar-denominated foreign debts or importing capital goods. In that case, use of market exchange rates makes more sense. And even when PPPs are theoretically preferable, it has to be borne in mind that estimated PPPs for certain important countries (China, India, and Russia especially) are highly unreliable.[83] The choice makes a big difference. When PPPs are used, the resulting world income distribution shows declining inequality in recent decades; substituting market exchange rates for PPPs results in rising estimates of inequality. Wade also notes that average-based measures such as the Gini coefficient are less likely to show rising inequality compared to polarization measures, such as the ratio of top decile incomes to bottom decile incomes. Not surprisingly, critics of globalization prefer polarization-based inequality measures while globalization supporters gravitate towards the average-based measures.

Wade summarizes the measurement situation as follows: one is pretty much guaranteed of coming up with declining inequality in recent decades if one: uses population weights, not country weights; uses PPPs, not market exchange rates; measures inequality at the average, not the extremes; and takes China's questionable income growth statistics at face value.[84]

To summarize this section: our understanding of world poverty and inequality is incomplete at this time. The heart of the problem seems to be a lack of agreement on the meaning of these terms in principle. Different researchers are attracted to different theoretical poverty or inequality concepts (for reasons they may not be fully conscious of), choose their metrics accordingly, and therefore produce studies that are essentially not comparable. At present, it appears that value judgments are driving results, rather than results shedding light on the plausibility of alternative value judgments. Until this situation changes, there is likely to be continuing disagreement about the extent of poverty and inequality in the world, and little progress in resolving the question of whether globalization intensifies or reduces poverty and inequality.

Why is globalization so controversial?

> economists should not engage in serious debates with every critic, every social and political movement. ... Just because the "critics" have strange priors, we should not accept claims based on substandard methodological practices. The debate with the critics must be based on sensible theories and on accepted econometric methods.
>
> (Xavier Sala-I-Martin)[85]

> our beliefs ... can easily become self-perpetuating, insulated from disconfirming evidence by a thick protective belt of defensive maneuvers that attribute dissonant evidence to methodological sloppiness or partisan bias.
>
> (Phillip Tetlock)[86]

In the section "Economic globalization and belief systems," we described the major belief systems of the globalization debate. In the previous section, we surveyed some important areas where globalization enthusiasts and critics disagree, and we concluded that the available evidence is not strong enough to declare any one belief system to be the winner. In this section we consider why so many strong claims are made about globalization despite generally inconclusive evidence. There appear to be four reasons for the strong claims. First, globalization is complex and difficult to measure. Second, people with different prior beliefs may attach different interpretations to the same set of evidence. Third, people sometimes have incentives to disguise their true beliefs. Fourth, psychological research suggests that cognitive style (*how* people think, as opposed to *what* they think) plays an important role in amplifying and perpetuating the controversy. In Chapter 9 Roy Allen expands the notion of cognitive style to identify different "ways of being" at play across the global economy, and he reaches similar conclusions.

The complexity of the globalization process

Few who have studied globalization would deny the difficulty of identifying and verifying its many possible effects. Pick any situation where globalization is thought to be influential and it is usually possible to construct theoretical models that assign either a constructive or a harmful role to it. Since theory by itself cannot determine whether globalization is good or bad, economists often attempt to approach the problem statistically through cross-country regression studies or country case studies. Such empirical efforts are useful, but their analytical weaknesses are widely recognized. Regression studies must contend with bias due to country-specific effects and omitted variables. Endogeneity is a further source of bias because reverse causation is common and it is not easy to find suitable instruments for the affected regressors. Since different regression studies rely on different data sets, different samples of countries, and different time periods, comparisons across regression studies are difficult. Country case studies avoid many of these problems but they are subject to problems of their own, especially interpretive controversies and questions about how to generalize the findings.[87]

Another problem is that globalization is not an easy concept to define or measure. As noted previously, failure to distinguish between trade policy and trade volume has been a major source of confusion in the literature on trade and growth. Trade volume is affected by many other factors besides trade policy, and the two are not strongly correlated. Globalization proponents prefer trade volume measures, globalization skeptics prefer trade policy measures, and as a result it can be difficult to compare findings. Many of the variables globalization interacts with are difficult to measure as well; recall, for example, the ambiguities associated with poverty and inequality.

Although such complexity is widely thought to be responsible for the globalization controversy, it cannot be the whole explanation. Complexity issues are essentially technical issues, and in this regard Aisbett observes:

> if technical issues were the only cause, we would expect to see a world populated by people sitting on the globalization fence, who are awaiting further

evidence before coming down on either [side]. This is clearly not the world in which we live.[88]

What other factors then, might help to account for the persistent disagreements about globalization?

Prior beliefs affect the way the facts get interpreted

A company announces that its quarterly earnings are up 6 percent. One group of investors reasons that this is bullish news and buys the company's stock. At the same time another group of investors sells the stock because the financial press was predicting a 9 percent increase, so 6 percent sounds to them like under-performance. As this example suggests, it is not uncommon for people with different views to interpret the same set of facts in different ways. All of us see reality through the haze of our prior beliefs, and when evidence is ambiguous, we may have a tendency to interpret it in line with those "priors." Since globalization proponents and critics have different priors, it wouldn't be surprising if their interpretations of the evidence were somewhat different. Aisbett argues that this is a major reason why there is so much controversy over globalization.[89] The effects of new evidence on prior beliefs will be discussed in more detail in the sub-section "An overlooked factor: cognitive style."

Beliefs may be purposefully misrepresented

So far we have assumed that what everyone says is what they really believe. If some are saying or advocating things they do not really believe, arriving at an understanding of how globalization works becomes more difficult. The literature does provide examples of purposeful misrepresentation: one such situation is described by Wade.[90] Whereas academic researchers place the highest value on the pursuit of truth, the chief imperative of policymakers is getting things accomplished, and they may be willing to say things they do not believe if they think it will help them with that imperative. A situation occurred during the making of the World Development Report 2000, which was put together by a team of social scientists, originally headed by Ravi Kanbur. This group had been assured that they were to be completely independent. The theme of the report, entitled "Attacking Poverty," was bound to be controversial. Sure enough, the first draft, which de-emphasized growth as an engine of poverty reduction in the LDCs, attracted strong criticism from, among others, the U.S. Treasury, which appears to have been concerned about the protectionist upsurge that followed the Seattle riots. Despite previous assurances of independence, pressure was applied to revise the Report so as to put more stress on the need for open markets. Wade describes the situation as follows:

> Kanbur explained to some members of the team what he understood was going on. He put his hand on the desk and said (to paraphrase), "suppose

this is where US officials 'really' believe the truth to lie. The NGOs, trade unionists and the like argue that the truth is over here, far to the left. The US is saying that you – the World Bank, the WDR – have to position yourself over here, far to the right, in order that, in the end, the middle ground coincides with the truth."[91]

The Treasury was saying, in effect: "you don't believe far-right globalization will help the poor, and we don't really believe so either – but say so anyway, because that will help counteract rising protectionist sentiment." The Treasury's stance might be defended on policy grounds, but from the standpoint of trying to fathom how globalization really affects human welfare, it was unhelpful to say the least.

As a second example, consider Stiglitz and Charlton's observations on the extreme positions on trade liberalization taken by some conservative economists.[92] How can these economists continue to insist – despite weak theoretical and empirical evidence of its potential benefits – that developing countries should pursue rapid and unfettered trade liberalization? The answer, according to Stiglitz and Charlton, is that these economists are more concerned about government failure than market failure. They don't believe that unrestricted free trade is the panacea that globalization advocates claim it to be, and they admit that there are many situations where properly-executed trade interventions by governments would boost welfare. The problem, they claim, is that most developing country officials are not capable of managing anything but the simplest, most liberal trade regime. In other words, they advocate free trade for reasons which have little to do with the intrinsic merits claimed for free trade. Here again, the task of isolating the truth about globalization's effects is made more difficult.

An overlooked factor: cognitive style

belief systems are at continual risk of evolving into self-perpetuating world-views, with their own self-serving criteria for judging judgment and keeping score, their own stocks of favorite historical analogies, their own pantheons of heroes and villains ...

(Phillip Tetlock)[93]

Man is a rationalizing, not a rational animal.

(Anonymous)

The fourth factor which may help explain why globalization is so controversial is the cognitive styles of those involved in the debate. Cognitive styles have been extensively studied in psychology. Of particular interest is the work of Phillip Tetlock. In the early 1980s, Tetlock became involved in exploring the psychological and strategic dilemmas of the Cold War. "I was struck," he writes, "by how frequently influential observers offered confident, but flatly contradictory assessments that were impervious to the arguments that were advanced by the other side."[94] The Cold War is long over, but the phenomenon Tetlock described persists; consider, for example, the current debate over Iraq, the controversies over Islam, and of course, the globalization controversy. One response to such intellectual gridlock is to opt for relativism: declare that all world-views are equally valid and that "objectivity" is an illusion. Tetlock decided instead to see how far back relativism could be pushed, by attempting to scientifically evaluate the forecasting accuracy of the "experts." In his own words:

> I have long been annoyed by how rarely partisans admit error even in the face of massive evidence that things did not work out as they once confidently declared. And I have long wondered what we might learn if we approached these disputes in a more scientific spirit ... if, instead of passively watching warring partisans score their own performance and duly pronounce themselves victorious ... [we were to] take on the role of referees: soliciting testable predictions, scoring accuracy ... and checking whether partisans change their minds when they get it wrong.[95]

A long-term study of how experts probe the future

Beginning in 1984, Tetlock embarked on a 20-year study involving 284 people who made their living commenting on, or offering advice on, political and economic trends. He began by asking them to assess the probability that various things would happen or not: would Gorbachev be ousted in a coup? Would free-markets bring prosperity to Eastern Europe? Would Québec secede from Canada? And so on. The study also asked questions designed to determine how each forecast was arrived at; how the experts reacted when their forecasts proved to be wrong; how they evaluated new information that did not support their views; and how they assessed the probability that rival views were correct. The study ended in 2003, by which time the experts had made 82,361 forecasts. The ultimate goal was to develop objective measures of good expert judgment.

Three broad conclusions emerged from the study. The first was that the experts fell in love with their pet theories and hated to change them. They became highly confident that they were right and everybody else wrong. When their forecasts didn't pan out, they were reluctant belief updaters – admitting their mistakes grudgingly and defending their prior positions tenaciously in a variety of ways: "An exogenous shock made me wrong"; "What I predicted almost did happen"; "I got it right, but my timing was off"; "I made a mistake but it was morally the right mistake to make."[96] And so on. They were also subject to hindsight bias, often managing to convince themselves that "they knew what would really happen all along." Finally, they were prone to apply higher standards of proof to new evidence which disagreed with their preferred theories.

The second conclusion was that nobody was very good at forecasting political and economic trends. Everyone who participated in the study – from Yale undergraduates to famous names in respected research institutes – had to struggle to defeat the proverbial dart-throwing chimp. Experts did do better than undergraduates (fortunately for their self-esteem), but all human participants were decisively out-performed by statistical models. And experts did not necessarily make the best predictions: well-informed dilettantes who regularly read such publications as the *New York Times*, the *Wall Street Journal*, or *The Economist* had average forecasting scores about as high as experts in their specific fields.[97]

The third conclusion was that, despite the pessimistic note sounded above, some individuals were indeed able to generate systematically better forecasts. Forecasting ability was not associated with specialty: economists, political scientists, journalists, historians, and other occupations did about equally well (that is, not very). Those with doctorates did no better than those without, so advanced graduate work was not the key. Home subject advantage, forecasting experience, public reputation: none of these made much difference. Ideological orientation didn't matter: liberals and conservatives, realists and institutionalists, optimists and pessimists, all performed at about the same level when it came to making accurate forecasts.[98]

What did make a difference was how the experts thought: their cognitive style. Tetlock categorized the cognitive styles of his experts according to Isaiah Berlin's famous hedgehog–fox metaphors.[99] A fox is a balanced, circumspect thinker who is skeptical of grand schemes; foxes tend to see the world as a shifting mix which heads in one direction for a while, then self-corrects when people realize things have gone too far. A hedgehog is attracted to a single big idea which dictates the probable course of events. Hedgehogs value parsimony, closure, and simplicity: they are often ideologues and tend towards extremism, whether they happen to be liberals or conservatives. A hedgehog tends to see prediction as a deductive exercise, whereas a fox sees it as a process of integrating diverse sources of information. Milton Friedman was probably a hedgehog; Alan Greenspan is surely a fox.

The foxes turned out to be consistently better forecasters than the hedgehogs. Although they made the same types of mistakes the hedgehogs did, their errors tended to be less severe and they were better able to self-correct, largely because foxes tend to question everything and are more willing to adjust prior beliefs in response to new evidence. Being a hedgehog is not necessarily a bad thing however: hedgehogs are like home-run hitters; they strike-out a lot, but when they get it right, they get it really right. Parsimony is seen as a virtue in the scientific community, and many famous scientists are hedgehogs. Foxes can be overly responsive to the latest trends, and when there are numerous conflicting viewpoints, foxes can be indecisive. Hedgehogs, with their singleness of purpose, will usually be able to forge ahead under such conditions. In policymaking, while the fox's breadth of vision may reduce the chances of getting trapped in a cul-de-sac, the hedgehog's decisiveness is useful when tough decisions have to be made and policies must have backbone. Winston Churchill's hedgehog leadership during World War II is a case in point.

In summary then, Tetlock's research suggests that when "experts" try to forecast political and economic events, they become overly partial to their own theories and reluctant to admit they are on the wrong track. These traits lead to large and unnecessary errors in their forecasts. Everyone makes such mistakes to some degree, but hedgehogs are more prone to them. Foxes have less of a problem forecasting because they are inquisitive, quick to adjust, and more willing to alter their prior beliefs in response to new evidence. Hedgehogs have the advantage in some situations, such as when fast, definite decisions are required, but forecasting political and economic events is not one of their strong suits.

How do the experts alter their prior beliefs?

> When the facts change, I change my views. What do you do, sir?
>
> (J.M. Keynes)

The foregoing discussion suggests that the process by which prior beliefs get revised might play a crucial role in the dynamics of the globalization debate. Aisbett's view is that differing prior beliefs lead to different interpretations of the evidence, hence the seemingly interminable arguments about globalization being "good" or "bad."[100] Yet, shouldn't new evidence that does not support one's prior beliefs eventually cause a revision in those beliefs? Does this actually happen?

Someone who wishes to update his prior beliefs in a rational manner would practice Bayesian belief-updating or something very much like it. Bayesian belief-updating is informally explained below; the Appendix to this chapter presents numerical details.

Suppose a rational observer holds two competing viewpoints about the world: (a) global warming is not increasing the frequency of large hurricanes; and (b) global warming is increasing the frequency of large hurricanes. He is not absolutely certain which viewpoint is correct, but his prior beliefs are that he is 90 percent sure (a) is true and 10 percent sure (b) is true. Our observer is willing to change his prior beliefs in response to new evidence. He thinks that if (a) is correct there is only a 20 percent chance that a large hurricane will hit the U.S. in the next year, but if (b) is correct the chance is 60 percent. Basic probability rules can be used to combine these four subjective probabilities to arrive at a projected 24 percent chance of a large hurricane next year (see Appendix).

Now, suppose it is next year and a big hurricane does in fact hit the United States. Our rational observer's intuition is that, since there is only a 24 percent chance of that happening if world-view (a) is correct, his prior beliefs may need to be a revised. But by how much? After all, the new evidence is not conclusive. Here is where the Bayesian approach is helpful: it enables the observer to calculate the exact amount by which, rationally, he should revise his prior beliefs.

The revised priors turn out to be 75 percent that (a) is correct and 25 percent that (b) is correct (see Appendix).

These revised priors become the rational observer's new priors, and are themselves subject to revision with the next round of new evidence. If a large hurricane strikes for a second year in a row, our rational observer is obliged to revise his priors to 50 percent and 50 percent (see Appendix). Extrapolating this process, it turns out that a sufficiently long series of years with large hurricanes would force our rational observer to become a global-warming convert. Likewise, a long series of years with no large storms would increase his global-warming skepticism, and a series of years in which large storms occur randomly would cause his priors to get stuck at 50/50, and turn him into a frustrated fence-sitter awaiting better evidence.

The Bayesian approach appears to be a reasonable, objective way to conduct introspection and update one's belief systems. But is this an accurate description of the behavior of high-visibility participants in the globalization debate? Tetlock came up with some suggestive evidence on this question, based on his sample of world events experts. One finding was that his experts tended to base their forecasts solely on their own theories, ignoring the possibility that other theories could be right; it was as though, in the example above, the rational observer's initial prior beliefs had been 100 percent and 0 percent respectively. The experts seem to be natural egocentrics, not natural Bayesians. Another finding was that the experts were slower to revise their beliefs than a good Bayesian would be. This was true of both foxes and hedgehogs, but the hedgehogs were significantly slower to update than the foxes were (see the Appendix for references and more details).

Implications of cognitive style for the globalization controversy

Tetlock's findings are consistent with several decades of psychological research on cognitive characteristics.[101] He observes that:

> psychologists are familiar with this dimension of human personality. It bears a family resemblance to the generic openness factor in multivariate studies of personality structure as well as to several measures of cognitive style in the psychological literature, especially those of need for closure and integrative complexity...High need-for-closure, integratively simple individuals are like Berlin's hedgehogs: they dislike ambiguity and dissonance in their personal and professional lives, place a premium on parsimony, and prefer speedy resolutions of uncertainty that keep prior opinions intact. Low need-for-closure, integratively complex individuals are like Berlin's foxes: they are tolerant of ambiguity and dissonance, curious about other points of view, and open to the possibility that they are wrong.[102]

This body of research suggests that cognitive style is one reason why the globalization debate has been so overdrawn. Recall Figure 3.2, which portrays the various attitudes towards globalization. Foxes are likely to be found residing in the center column, a region of compromise and balanced thinking. Hedgehogs gravitate towards the edges, neoclassical hedgehogs to the left, collectivist and isolationist hedgehogs to the right. They fulminate at each other across the intervening gulf in what is called the globalization debate, but which at times has more resembled a dialogue of the deaf. One group that must be happy about this state of affairs is the media: as Tetlock wryly notes, the only thing the media like better than a hedgehog is two hedgehogs who disagree.

Summary and conclusions

Evidence concerning the effects of globalization is ambiguous at best. Heedless of that, the globalization debate has been dominated by strong statements about the supposed benevolent or malevolent effects of globalization. This chapter asks why. Globalization is viewed through the human ecology approach, in which belief systems, social agreements, human populations, and physical endowments and resources all develop interactively. A taxonomy of globalization belief systems is developed, with pro-globalization ideologists (mainly neoclassical economists) on one extreme and anti-globalist ideologists (chiefly left-leaning Marxists and right-leaning nationalists) on the other. The belief systems of each of these groups are explored in depth.

The chapter then looks at some of the empirical evidence on globalization; has globalization, on the balance, accelerated or retarded economic development? Its effect on growth is empirically ambiguous, except that excessive short-term capital flows do appear to harm growth. Its effect on world poverty and inequality is also cloudy because of the difficult conceptual and statistical problems involved in measuring these relationships. Thus, we can't yet tell for sure whether globalization has accelerated or retarded economic development.

Finally, the chapter examines reasons why globalization elicits strong positive and negative reactions despite a general lack of conclusive evidence about its effects. Four reasons appear to be important. First, globalization relationships are difficult to measure accurately. Second, the same globalization evidence is sometimes interpreted differently by researchers with different prior beliefs. Third, some people or institutions may, for strategic reasons, be expressing beliefs about globalization that they do not truly hold. The fourth reason, not previously mentioned in the literature, has to do with the cognitive styles of the participants in the controversy, which can be metaphorically described in terms of Isaiah Berlin's hedgehogs and foxes. Those who strongly favor or strongly oppose globalization are usually hedgehogs. Extensive psychological research suggests that the cognitive errors made by this personality type are one reason why the globalization debate has been so persistent, acrimonious, and disconnected from fact.

As the first decade of the twenty-first century draws to a close, the economic state of the world is not what it was in the late 1990s when globalization protests first caught the public eye. Contrary to the expectations of that earlier time, most emerging economies have grown very fast at the start of the twenty-first century, in the region of 5 percent per year. This is even true of the poorest economies, for Africa has been the beneficiary of an export boom stemming from high world commodity-consumption and low interest rates. Nor is it just a matter of external demand: many developing economies have rationalized their macro-economic policies and enacted structural reforms, leading to growth stability and resistance to external shocks. Especially in Asia, domestic saving has been high, allowing countries to repay foreign debt. Unsustainable, fixed exchange-rates are now much less common, and foreign exchange reserves are high.[103]

As a result of these trends, the role of the IMF is (for the moment at least) different from what it was at the time of the Seattle protests. With more countries repaying than borrowing, the IMF's loan portfolio has shrunk to the levels of the 1980s, its influence over global economic policy has declined, and (to the thinly-disguised delight of many of its critics) falling interest income has forced it to adopt a budgetary austerity program. Neoliberalism has lost favor; the Washington Consensus is no longer seriously advocated as development policy.

On the anti-globalization side, Marxist policy prescriptions based on colonialism and imperialism increasingly seem focused on the past, given the rapid economic growth being experienced in the poorest parts of the world. Localist and anarchist ideas do not seem to be gaining adherants either. On the other hand, nationalist anti-globalization sentiments seem stronger than they were at the turn of the millennium, particularly in the wealthy countries among workers who feel threatened by outsourcing. It is possible that nationalism may wind up exerting a significant drag on globalization's progress in the coming years. Whether this is bad or good is, of course, open to debate: recall the terms of Rodrik's trilemma.

Despite some modest moves away from extremism, the globalization debate still rings out at times with strongly-stated positions. This chapter concludes by passing on a bit of tongue-in-cheek advice for globalization's more ardent boosters and detractors. It is the advice Oliver Cromwell directed to his enemies in 1650: "I beseech you, in the bowels of Christ, think it possible you may be mistaken."

Appendix

This appendix provides numerical detail for the example of Bayesian belief-updating. Suppose that an observer holds two competing viewpoints about the world: (a) and (b). Also suppose that $P(X_1)$ is the subjective probability that a particular event X_1 will occur. If the observer is a card-carrying Bayesian he will estimate the probability of X_1 as follows:

$$P(X_1) = P(X_1|\text{world-view a}) \times P(\text{world-view a})$$
$$+ P(X_1|\text{world-view b}) \times P(\text{world-view b}) \tag{1}$$

Suppose world-view (a) is that global warming is increasing the frequency of large hurricanes, worldview (b) is that global warming is not increasing the frequency of large hurricanes, and X_1 is the occurrence of a large hurricane. Our observer thinks there is a 90 percent chance that (a) is correct and a 10 percent chance that (b) is correct: these are his prior beliefs, or "priors." If (a) is correct he thinks there is a 20 percent chance that X_1 will happen and if (b) is correct he thinks there is a 60 percent chance that X_1 will happen. He therefore calculates the probability of a large hurricane hitting the U.S. next year to be

$$P(X_1) = (0.20 \times 0.90) + (0.60 \times 0.10) = 0.24 \tag{2}$$

Now fast-forward to next year and suppose that a large hurricane does, in fact, hit the United States. Should our observer revise his prior beliefs? If so, by how much? Once again Bayes' theorem provides guidance. Consider the following relationships:

Prior odds $= P$(world-view a)$/P$(world-view b)
Posterior odds $= P$(world-view a$|X_1$ occurs)$/$ $\qquad$ (3)
$\qquad\qquad$ P(world-view b$|X_1$ occurs)

The prior odds ratio represents the observer's beliefs before X_1 happened. The posterior odds ratio represents the observer's beliefs revised to reflect the occurrence of X_1. But how does our observer get from prior beliefs to posterior beliefs? He needs a third relationship, also implicit in Bayes's theorem:

Likelihood $= P(X_1|$world-view a)$/P(X_1|$world-view b) $\qquad$ (4)

The likelihood ratio captures the difference under the two world-views in the probability of X_1 occurring.

If the prior odds and the likelihood are known, Bayes' theorem implies that the posterior odds should be calculated as

Posterior odds $=$ prior odds $\times$ likelihood $\qquad$ (5)

For our observer, the calculation would be as follows:

Prior odds $= 0.90/0.10 = 9$ $\quad$ likelihood $= 0.20/0.60 = 0.33$ $\qquad$ (6)
Posterior odds $= 9 \times 0.33 = 3$

The calculated posterior odds ratio of 3 implies that the observer's revised beliefs should be 75 percent and 25 percent. This is based on the definition of the posterior odds ratio:

$3 = P$(world-view a$|X_1$ occurs)$/P$(world-view b$|X_1$ occurs) $= 0.75/0.25$ $\quad$ (7)

Because X_1 occurred, the observer should reduce his belief that world-view (a) is correct from 90 percent to 75 percent. Similarly, his belief that his world-view (b) is correct should be revised upward from 10 percent to 25 percent.

These revised probabilities become the observer's new prior beliefs and are themselves subject to revision as additional evidence comes in. Suppose that another large hurricane hits the U.S. for a second year in a row. The posterior odds then become $3 \times 0.33 = 1$, and our observer is obliged to assign a 50/50 chance that his world-view is wrong and his rival's is correct. And so on, year after year.

Equation 1 can be used as a test of whether our observer's prediction is based on internally consistent logic, and equation 5 as a test of whether our observer is updating his prior beliefs sufficiently in response to new information. How did Tetlock's experts fare on these tests? The logical coherence of their forecasts was suspect: they formulated their forecasts without taking account of the possibility that other theories could be right.[104] The experts were also much slower to update their beliefs then a Bayesian would be. Reluctance was greatest among the hedgehogs, especially when the revision went against their world-view. In that situation, foxes updated their beliefs by 59 percent of the prescribed amount, hedgehogs by only 19 percent of the prescribed amount.[105]

Tetlock's findings regarding belief updating can be easily summarized. Nobody is a good Bayesian. Nobody takes sufficient account of rival theories when they formulate their predictions. Everyone resists updating their priors in response to new evidence. Hedgehogs are more disposed towards these transgressions, especially when the new evidence contradicts their world-views.

Notes

1 Bhagwati 2000: p. 19, footnote 2; Elliott *et al.* 2004.
2 Sen 2002: p. 15.
3 Scholars identify many other important dimensions of globalization: cultural, technological, military, political, etc.
4 Dehasa 2006: p. vii.
5 Conway 2006: p. 115.
6 Stiglitz and Charlton 2005: pp. 33–36.
7 Watkins 2003: p. 47.
8 Elliot *et al.* 2004: p. 19, footnote 2.
9 Kanbur 2001.
10 Elliott *et al.* 2004.
11 Elliott *et al.* 2004: p. 19, footnote 2.
12 Kanbur 2001: p. 1085.
13 Elliott *et al.* 2004, Appendix.
14 Scheve and Slaughter 2001; Scheve and Slaughter 2006.
15 John Kay refers to the free-market belief system as the "American business model," (Kay 2004, ch. 27). However, this belief system is concerned with more than just the conduct of business.
16 Ekelund and Hebert 1997: p. 243.
17 Ruttan 2003: p. 80.
18 Baran 1957.
19 Packenham 1992: p. 19.
20 Packenham 1992: pp. 111–112.
21 Amin 1976; Emmanuel 1972; Wallerstein 1979.
22 Epstein 2001, section 5. Communism may be a more viable force than Epstein's view would suggest (Anonymous 2006).

23 Broad 2002a: p. 66.
24 Sachs 1999: p. 100.
25 Milanovic 2003: p. 669.
26 Broad 2002b: p. 255.
27 Cavanagh and Mander 2004.
28 See, for example, Bello 2002.
29 Cavanagh and Mander 2004: p. 20.
30 Cavanagh and Mander 2004: p. 26.
31 Wolf 2004: chapter 10, footnote 1.
32 Localists would also like to count culture and knowledge, as well as general public services (health, education, Social Security, etc.) as common heritage resources.
33 Hardin 1968.
34 Bowles 2004: p. 140.
35 A balanced overview of multinationals in developing countries is given in Stiglitz 2006: chapter 7.
36 And that isn't a question of not having the tools to do the job: neoclassical economic theory is perfectly capable of analyzing conflict, threat, violence, and other destructive and coercive behaviors (see Hirschleifer 2001).
37 Elliott *et al.* 2004: p. 40.
38 Graeber 2002: p. 70.
39 Elliott *et al.* 2004: p. 24.
40 Proudhon 1840.
41 Epstein 2001: Introduction.
42 Graeber 2002: p. 66.
43 Epstein 2001: section 3.
44 Bardhan 2003: p. 55.
45 Cavanagh and Mander 2004: p. 160.
46 Flam 2004: p. 62.
47 Not all global market advocates favor a world government. As noted previously, extreme free traders advocate a combination of free global markets and minimal world government. Where one stands on this issue depends on whether one thinks global market externalities are a serious problem or not.
48 Where there is fear of losing cultural homogeneity (acquired through a long process of obliterating their own local cultures, such as the French Bretons) to an influx of Muslim immigrants.
49 As exemplified in the following statement by Gilbert Williamson, the president of NCR:

> I was asked the other day about [the problem of U.S. workers being unable to compete in the global economy]... I replied that I don't think about it at all. We at NCR think of ourselves as a globally competitive company that happens to be headquartered in the United States.
>
> (Buchanan 1998: p. 99)

50 Liberal economic thought since the days of Adam Smith has responded to this line of reasoning in the following way: hedonism is not the reason economics emphasizes the welfare of the consumer. Rather, it is that consumer sovereignty acts as a market discipline on producers, keeping them from wasting resources by producing things people don't want. Trade generates more competition, forcing producers to cut waste and serve consumers better. The ultimate result is more efficiency, more value-added, and more economic growth. This is the process that creates the high-paying jobs the protectionists are concerned about. Protectionism impedes the creation of new, high-paying jobs.
51 Since all countries cannot simultaneously export more than they import and since no

mercantilist country wants a current-account deficit, mercantilism works best in a world of hegemonic imperialism where strong mercantilist economies can impose unequal exchange on smaller and weaker economies.

52 Lindsey 1998.
53 Rodrik 2005: pp. 198–199.
54 Rodrik 2005: p. 196.
55 Bourguignon 2004.
56 Both Harberger quotes are taken from Rodrik 2003a: p. 1.
57 Globalization proponents base their arguments on neoclassical trade theory. However, with appropriate assumptions, neoclassical theory can also generate a negative relationship between trade and growth (Brecher and Diaz-Alejandro 1977: p. 7; Sen 2005: p. 36; Shaikh 2003) and is consistent with a minimal relationship as well (Freeman 2004: p. 27).
58 Globalization's rightist critics, the nationalists, do not take a position regarding globalization and growth in the developing countries, but they believe trade inhibits growth in the advanced countries.
59 Baldwin 2004; Rodriguez and Rodrik 2001; Sumner 2004; Winters 2004.
60 See Sumner 2004: p. 1020. However, there is some new evidence that trade liberalization episodes produce surges in growth (Wacziarg and Welch 2003).
61 Commander 2004; World Bank 2005b.
62 Rodrik 2004: pp. 1–2.
63 Freeman 2004.
64 Meltzer 2002.
65 Griffin and Gurley 1985.
66 Amin 2006; Surin 1998.
67 Barnet and Cavanagh 2001.
68 For reviews of this large literature see Aizenman 2004; Allen 2004; Calomiris 2005; Eichengreen 2003; Obstfeld and Taylor 2004, and more recently, Eichengreen 2006.
69 Soros 2002: pp. 109–110.
70 Prasad *et al.* 2003.
71 World Bank 2005a.
72 Prasad *et al.* 2003: p. 5.
73 Wade 2004: p. 574.
74 Ravallion 2003; Ravallion 2004; Wade 2004.
75 Wade 2004: p. 578.
76 For example, Dollar and Kraay 2002; Dollar and Kraay 2004.
77 This example illustrates the problem of "churning" in the poverty dynamics of developing countries (Baulch and Hoddinott 2000; Thorbecke 2004). In sharp contrast to the advanced countries where poverty tends to be a long-term structural problem, it is common in developing countries for people to cycle in and out of poverty depending on short-term macro-economic conditions and other external shocks. Diminishing marginal utility suggests that losses to losers will exceed gains to gainers in such situations, leading to social discontent. Other factors besides churning can contribute to horizontal inequality. Chua (2003: ch.4) describes a situation in Africa where various tribal groups gained differentially under market reform: the fact that the gains were not distributed equally fueled ethnic hostility. Churning and other types of horizontal inequality often escape detection in distribution measures based on averages.
78 For an exception see Sala-i-Martin 2006.
79 Ravallion 2004: p. 20.
80 Dollar and Kraay 2002; Dollar and Kraay 2004.
81 Ravallion 2004: p. 21.
82 Wade 2004.
83 Wade 2004: p. 575.

84 Wade 2004: p. 579.
85 Sala-i-Martin 2004.
86 Tetlock 2005: p. 161.
87 For examples of country case studies see Rodrik 2003b. In chapter 1 of that book Rodrik describes the role that country case studies can play in analyzing economic growth.
88 Aisbett 2004: p. 22.
89 Aisbett 2004: p. 22.
90 Wade 2001.
91 Wade 2001: p. 1437.
92 Stiglitz and Charlton 2005: p. 36.
93 Tetlock 2005: p. 4.
94 Tetlock 2005: p. xiii.
95 Tetlock 2005: p. xi.
96 Stanley Fischer, for example, in defending IMF loans to Russia in the 1990s, conceded that much of the money may have been misdirected into Swiss bank accounts, but given the risks of allowing a nuclear power to implode financially, nevertheless claimed that issuing the loans was the "prudent thing to do," (Tetlock 2005: p. 135).
97 Tetlock 2005: p. 51, fig 2.5.
98 Tetlock used factor analysis to identify a liberal–conservative (left–right) component in the belief systems of the experts. This component is strongly correlated with attitudes towards globalization. In Tetlock's words:

> the left wanted to redress inequalities within and across borders, expressed reservations about rapid transitions from socialist to market economies and about the impact of trade liberalization and unrestricted capital flows on countries with weak regulatory institutions, and worried about nasty side effects on the poor and the natural environment. The right were enthusiastic about market solutions but had grave reservations about "governmental meddling" that shifted attention from wealth creation to wealth distribution. To quote one: "government failure is far more common than market failure."
>
> (Tetlock 2005: p. 71)

99 Berlin 1997. These metaphors are of ancient origin; Berlin traces them back 2600 years to the Greek soldier-poet, Archilochus.
100 Aisbett 2004: p. 22.
101 See John 1990; Kruglanski and Webster 1996; Suedfeld and Tetlock 2001 for reviews of this literature.
102 Tetlock 2005: p. 75, footnote 6.
103 Of course, this favorable scenario may not last (Eichengreen 2006: pp. 21–22, 28–29).
104 To test the logical coherence of their forecasts, Tetlock asked his experts questions designed to reveal their estimates of each term in equation 1. Almost everyone based $P(X_1)$ on the first two right-side terms in the equation and ignored the terms beyond the plus sign, implying they were 100 percent confident that they were right and everyone else was wrong. Had they taken account of other peoples' theories by using all four terms in equation 1, their forecasts would have been better calibrated, with increases in accuracy of up to 18 percent for foxes and up to 32 percent for hedgehogs (Tetlock 2005: pp. 122–123).
105 To test whether the experts were updating their prior beliefs sufficiently in response to new information, Tetlock asked them questions designed to reveal their estimates of each term in the likelihood and prior odds ratios. Later, after X_1 either occurred or didn't, equation 5 was used to compute the posterior odds ratio and, from that, the "correctly" revised prior beliefs. Finally, the experts were re-contacted, and without divulging the results from equation 5, were asked how much they wished to change

their prior beliefs in light of the X_1 outcome. Their answers were then compared with the results from equation 5 to see if they updated their prior beliefs enough to satisfy Bayesian canons of rationality (Tetlock 2005: p. 128).

References

Aisbett, Emma (2004) "Why are the critics so convinced that globalization is bad for the poor?" to be published in *Globalization and Poverty*, Ann Harrison (ed.) National Bureau of Economic Research (Forthcoming).

Aizenman, Joshua (2004) "Financial opening: evidence and policy options," in *Challenges to Globalization*, Robert E. Baldwin and L. Alan Winters (eds.) Chicago: National Bureau of Economic Research: 473–494.

Allen, Roy E. (ed.) (2004) *The Political Economy of Financial Crises* (2 volumes), Cheltenham, U.K.: Edward Elgar.

Amin, Samir (1976) *Unequal Development*, New York: Monthly Review Press.

—— (2006) "The future of global polarization," in *Critical Perspectives on Globalization*, Maria Della Giusta, Uma S. Kambhampati, and Robert Hunter Wade (eds.) Cheltenham, U.K.: Edward Elgar: 5–15.

Anonymous (2006) "Comrades, come rally" *The Economist*, 69–70, October 28:69–70.

Baldwin, Robert E. (2004) "Openness and growth: what's the empirical relationship?" in *Challenges to Globalization*, Robert E. Baldwin and L. Alan Winters (eds.) Chicago: National Bureau of Economic Research: 499–521.

Baran, Paul (1957) *The Political Economy of Growth*, New York: Monthly Review Press.

Bardhan, Pranab (2003) "International economic integration and the poor," in *Global Governance: An Architecture for the World Economy*, Horst Siebert (ed.) Berlin: Springer-Verlag: 49–60.

Barnet, Richard and John Cavanagh (2001) "Electronic money and the casino economy," in *Critical Perspectives on Globalization*, Maria Della Giusta, Uma S. Kambhampati, and Robert Hunter Wade (eds.) Cheltenham, U.K.: Edward Elgar: 521–533. Originally published as chapter 4 in Edward Goldsmith and Jerry Mander (eds) (2001) *The Case Against the Global Economy: and for a Turn Towards Localization*, London: Earthscan Publications, Ltd.

Baulch, Bob and John Hoddinott (2000) "Economic mobility and poverty dynamics in developing countries," *Journal of Development Studies* 36 (6):1–24.

Bello, Walden (2002) "Toward a deglobalized world," in *Global Backlash*, Robin Broad (ed.) Lanham: Rowman & Littlefield: 292–295.

Berlin, Isaiah (ed.) (1997) *The Proper Study of Mankind*, New York: Farrar, Straus, and Giroux.

Bhagwati, Jagdish (2000) "Globalization in your face," *Foreign Affairs* 79 (4):134–139.

Bourguignon, Francois (2004) *The Poverty–Growth–Inequality Triangle.* Online, available at: www.worldbank.org

Bowles, Samuel (2004) *Microeconomics: Behavior, Institutions, and Evolution*, Princeton: Princeton University Press.

Brecher, Richard A. and Carlos F. Diaz-Alejandro (1977) "Tariffs, foreign capital, and immiserising growth," *Journal of International Economics* 7:317–322.

Broad, Robin (2002a) "Part II: The Historical Context. Introduction," in *Global Backlash*, Robin Broad (ed.) Lanham: Rowman & Littlefield: 65–76.

—— (2002b) "Part V: Rolling Back Globalization. Introduction," in *Global Backlash*, Robin Broad (ed.) Lanham: Rowman & Littlefield: 243–257.

Buchanan, Patrick (1998) *The Great Betrayal*, Boston: Little, Brown & Company.

Calomiris, Charles W (2005) "Capital flows, financial crises, and public policy," in *Globalization: What's New*, Michael Weinstein (ed.) New York: Columbia University Press: 36–76.

Cavanagh, John and Jerry Mander (2004) *Alternatives to Economic Globalization*, San Francisco: Berrett-Koehler.

Chua, Amy (2003) *World on Fire*. New York: Anchor Books.

Commander, Simon (2004) "Comment," in *Challenges to Globalization*, Robert E. Baldwin and L. Alan Winters (eds.) Chicago: National Bureau of Economic Research: 521–525.

Conway, Patrick (2006) "The International Monetary Fund in a time of crisis: a review of Stanley Fischer's IMF," *Journal Of Economic Literature* XLIV (1):115–144.

Dehasa, Guillermo de la (2006) *Winners and Losers in Globalization*, Oxford: Blackwell Publishing.

Dollar, David and Aart Kraay (2002) "Growth is good for the poor," *Journal of Economic Growth* 7:195–225.

—— (2004) "Trade, growth, and poverty," *The Economic Journal* 114, February: F22–F49.

Eichengreen, Barry (2003) "Predicting and preventing financial crises: where do we stand? What have we learned?" in *Global Governance: an Architecture for the World Economy*, Horst Siebert (ed.) Berlin: Springer-Verlag: 153–188.

—— (2006) *The Future of Global Financial Markets*. Online, available at: www.econ.berkeley.edu/~eichengr

Ekelund, Robert B. and Robert F. Hebert (1997) *A History of Economic Theory and Method*, New York: McGraw-Hill.

Elliott, Kimberly Ann, Debanyi Kar, and J. David Richardson (2004) "Assessing globalization's critics: 'talkers are no good doers?'" in *Challenges to Globalization*, Robert E. Baldwin and L. Alan Winters (eds.) Chicago: National Bureau of Economic Research: 17–60.

Emmanuel, Arghiri (1972) *Unequal Exchange: A Study of the Imperialism of Trade*, New York: Monthly Review Press.

Epstein, Barbara (2001) "Anarchism and the anti-globalization movement," *Monthly Review* 53 (4)

Flam, Harry (2004) "Comment," in *Challenges to Globalization*, Robert E. Baldwin and L. Alan Winters (eds.) Chicago: National Bureau of Economic Research: 61–62.

Freeman, Richard B. (2004) "Trade wars: the exaggerated impact of trade in economic debate," *The World Economy* 27 (1):1–23.

Graeber, David (2002) "The new anarchists," *New Left Review* 13:61–73.

Griffin, Keith and John Gurley (1985) "Radical analyses of imperialism, the Third World, and the transition to socialism: a survey article," *Journal Of Economic Literature* XXIII, September: 1089–1143.

Hardin, Garritt (1968) "The tragedy of the commons," *Science* 162:1243–1248.

Hirschleifer, Jack (2001) *The Dark Side of the Force*, Cambridge: Cambridge University Press.

John, Oliver P. (1990) "The 'Big Five' factor taxonomy," in *Handbook of Personality: Theory and Research*, Pervin, Lawrence A. (ed.) New York: Guilford Press: 66–100.

Kanbur, Ravi (2001) "Economic policy, distribution and poverty: the nature of disagreements," *World Development* 29 (6):1083–1094.

Kay, John (2004) *Culture and Prosperity*, New York: HarperCollins.

Kruglanski, A.W. and D.M. Webster, (1996) "Motivated Closing of the Mind: 'Seizing' and 'Freezing,'" *Psychological Review* 103 (2):263–283.

Lindsey, Brink (1998) The great contradiction. Online, available at www.freetrade. org/pubs/reviews/buchreview.html

May, E.R. (1973) *Lessons of the Past*, New York: Oxford University Press. Cited in Tetlock 2005: p. 143.

Meltzer, Allan H. (2002) "Report of the International Financial Institution Advisory Commission," in *Global Backlash*, Robin Broad (ed.) Lanham: Rowman & Littlefield: 29–33.

Milanovic, Branko (2003) "The two faces of globalization: against globalization as we know it," *World Development* 31 (4):667–683.

Obstfeld, Maurice and Alan M. Taylor (2004) *Global Capital Markets: Integration, Crisis, and Growth*, Cambridge: Cambridge University Press.

Packenham, Robert (1992) *The Dependency Movement.* Cambridge: Harvard University Press.

Prasad, Eswar, Kenneth Rogoff, Shang-Jin Wei, and M. Ayhan Kose (2003) Effects of financial globalization on developing countries: some empirical evidence. IMF occasional paper 220.

Proudhon, Pierre-Joseph (1840) What is property? Online, available at www.gutenberg.org/ etext/360

Ravallion, Martin (2003) The debate on globalization, poverty, and inequality: why measurement matters. World Bank policy research working paper 3038.

—— (2004) "Competing Concepts of Inequality in the Globalization Debate," in *Brookings Trade Forum 2004*, Susan M. Collins and Carol Graham (eds.) Washington, D.C.: The Brookings Institution: 1–23.

Rodriguez, Francisco and Dani Rodrik (2001) "Trade policy and economic growth: a skeptic's guide to the cross-national evidence," in *NBER Macroeconomics Annual 2000*, Ben Bernanke and Kenneth Rogoff (eds.) Cambridge: MIT Press: 261–325.

Rodrik, Dani (2003a) Growth strategies. Department of Economics, Johannes Kepler University of Linz, Working Paper 0317.

—— (2003b) *In Search of Prosperity*, Princeton: Princeton University Press.

—— (2004) *Rethinking Growth Policies in the Developing World.* Online, available at: www.ksghome.harvard.edu/~drodrik

—— (2005) "Feasable globalizations," in *Globalization: What's New*, Michael Weinstein (ed.) New York: Columbia University Press: 196–213.

Ruttan, Vernon (2003) *Social Science Knowledge and Economic Development.* Ann Arbor: University of Michigan Press.

Sachs, Jeffrey (1999) "Twentieth century political economy: a brief history of global capitalism," *Oxford Review of Economic Policy* 15 (4):90–101.

Sala-i-Martin, Xavier (2004) "Why are the critics so convinced that globalization is bad for the poor? a comment," To be published in *Globalization and Poverty*, Ann Harrison (ed.) National Bureau of Economic Research (forthcoming).

—— (2006) "The world distribution of income: falling poverty and convergence, period," *Quarterly Journal of Economics* CCXI (2):351–397.

Scheve, Kenneth and Matthew J. Slaughter (2001) *Globalization and the Perceptions of American Workers*, Washington, D.C.: Institute for International Economics.

—— (2006) "Public opinion, international economic integration, and the welfare state," in *Globalization and Egalitarian Redistribution*, Pranab Bardhan, Samuel Bowles, and Michael Wallerstein (eds.) New York:Russell Sage Foundation: 217–260.

Sen, Amartya (2002) "Globalization, inequality and global protest," *Development* 45 (2):11–16.

Sen, Sunanda (2005) "International trade theory and policy: what is left of the free trade paradigm?" *Development and Change* 36 (6):1011–1029.

Shaikh, Anwar (2003) Globalization and the myth of free trade. Paper for the "Conference on Globalization and the Myths of Free Trade: New School University, New York." Online, available at: www.homepage.newschool.edu/~AShaikh

Soros, George (2002) *George Soros on Globalization*, New York: Public Affairs.

Stiglitz, Joseph (2006) *Making Globalization Work*, New York: W.W. Norton.

Stiglitz, Joseph and Andrew Charlton (2005) *Fair Trade for All*, Oxford: Oxford University Press.

Suedfeld, P. and Phillip E. Tetlock (2001) "Individual differences in information processing," in *Blackwell International Handbook of Social Psychology: Intraindividual Processes*, Abraham Tesser and Norbert Schwartz (eds.) London: Blackwell: 284–304.

Sumner, Andrew (2004) "Why are we still arguing about globalization?" *Journal of International Development* 16:1015–1022.

Surin, Kenneth (1998) "Dependency theory's reanimation in the era of financial capital," *Cultural Logic* 1 (2): n.p., online.

Tetlock, Phillip E. (2005) *Expert Political Judgment: How Good is It? How Can We Know?* Princeton: Princeton University Press.

Thorbecke, Eric (2004) "Comment," in *Brookings Trade Forum 2004*, Susan M. Collins and Carol Graham (eds.) Washington, D.C.: The Brookings Institution: 24–26.

Wacziarg, Romain and Karen Horn Welch (2003) Trade Liberalization and Growth: New Evidence. Online, available at: www.nber.org/papers/W10152

Wade, Robert Hunter (2001) "Making the World Development Report 2000: attacking poverty," *World Development* 29 (8):1435–1441.

—— (2004) "Is globalization reducing poverty and inequality?" *World Development* 32 (4):567–589.

Wallerstein, Emmanuel (1979) *The Capitalist World-Economy*, Cambridge: Cambridge University Press.

Watkins, Kevin, "Comment", in *Global Governance: an Architecture for the World Economy*, Horst Siebert (ed.) Berlin: Springer-Verlag: 42–48.

Winters, L. Alan (2004) "Trade liberalization and economic performance: an overview," *Economic Journal* 114, February: F4–F21.

Wolf, Martin (2004) *Why Globalization Works*, New Haven: Yale University Press.

World Bank (2005a) "Financial liberalization: what went right, what went wrong?" in *Economic Growth in the 1990s: Learning From a Decade of Reform*, Washington, D.C.: The International Bank for Reconstruction and Development/World Bank: 203–237.

—— (2005b) "Trade liberalization: why so much controversy?" in *Economic Growth in the 1990s: Learning From a Decade of Reform*, Washington, D.C.: The International Bank for Reconstruction and Development/World Bank: 131–153.

4   The peasant betrayed

A human ecology approach to land reform in Nepal

Ravi Bhandari*

> Human ecology can be defined as both the interrelated world conditions and human systems, and an interdisciplinary field or perspective which studies world conditions and human systems. As a body of studies, it seeks to coordinate previously disconnected knowledge, and make that knowledge available for a wide variety of practical purposes.
>
> (Allen, Chapter 1, this volume)

Introduction

In *World Brain* (1938), H.G. Wells noted an interesting dilemma facing the social sciences. Namely, that as knowledge becomes more fragmented and specialized within disciplines, it also becomes increasingly detached from real development problems facing humanity. This knowledge has become increasingly less useful to policymakers who are forced to confront reality, a reality that trespasses on the boundaries of any single discipline and exists by virtue of its dynamic interconnections between differing fields of knowledge. Using a human ecology framework by integrating the knowledge of sociology, history, and economics, this chapter responds to H.G. Well's challenge in the context of the current global debates on land reform and tenure security.

After decades of silence, calls for various types of land reform have resurfaced to combat poverty, inequality, and agricultural stagnation. Through a human ecology framework, this chapter describes various belief systems associated with visions of land reform, as well as the "strange priors" within each belief system. I introduce another belief system – a human ecology one with a dose of institutional pragmatism – that goes beyond "getting the prices and/or institutions right," by identifying key structural constraints for land reform and attempting to locate these constraints within the wider political economy of developing countries. A human ecology framework reveals that these features (or structural variables) are commonly overlooked in the current global debates on land reform, which include:

1   an adverse macroeconomic environment;
2   how rural markets actually work with respect to existing social arrangements;

3   economic deprivation and related grievances of the poor; and
4   the pressure of modern forms of property rights on the natural and physical
    environment.

These structural limitations not only seriously complicate the role of land reform
as a panacea for rural economic development and larger global sustainability,
but also suggest that the strong and prevailing beliefs in support for land
reforms, which are advocated by both the academic left and right, are largely
ideologically driven. This chapter highlights the importance of a human ecology
approach to understanding not only the limitations of land reform in Nepal, but
also sheds light on Nepal's uncertain future. In fact, Nepal is the sole remaining
place on Earth with an active, aggressive, and growing Maoist insurgency, a
political-economic-social model that has been supposedly discredited by history
by almost all accounts.

The theme of land policy in general, and land reform in particular is a key
issue not only for the agendas of (inter)national (non-)governmental development institutions and states, but for academics as well. Globally, poverty still
has primarily a rural face. Effective control over productive resources, especially
land, by the rural poor is important to their autonomy and capacity to construct
an ecologically sustainable rural livelihood and overcome poverty. This is
because in many agrarian societies, a significant portion of the income of the
rural poor still comes from farming, and hence access to land is strongly correlated to poverty processes.

Moreover, for many rural people land (and landed property rights) has a multidimensional character: in addition to being an economic resource, it also has
significant political, cultural, and social dimensions. As a consequence, lack of
access to and/or loss of land can foster social exclusion, a diminution of human
capabilities, and cultivate violence and conflict. The agrarian question and the
question of global sustainability seem inextricably intertwined.

Historically, land reform has been conceptualized to address the problem of
lack of access to, and control over, land resources by the landless and near-
landless rural poor. The past century had witnessed the widespread, albeit highly
uneven, implementation of land reform in most developing countries. Most of
the land reforms carried out during this period were state-led; today, many are
market-led under the auspices of the World Bank working in partnership with
states and NGOs. A few of these were highly successful in restructuring land-
based production and distribution relations; however, many others were not.
Thus, to a large extent, landlessness, poverty, and inequality have persisted.

This chapter looks at the idea of land reform in Nepal and argues that World
Bank proposals to prime tenure reform by GPS mapping and development of the
titling system will do little to address the underlying issues of low productivity and
inequality. This chapter presents ideas about land reform as reflections of varied
underlying belief systems, some nearly religious in character. To present the
dynamics of the situation in Nepal, I use Allen's four-quadrant human ecology
framework of interrelated sub-systems: demographics, belief systems, social

agreements, and macro-economic and ecological conditions and constraints. This framework is useful for understanding what is happening in Nepal. Human striving is seen as a motor that sets off engagement and negotiation among people within Allen's human ecology system. The striving among the players generates internal opportunity-sets for survival and betterment on the part of individuals and families. These opportunity-sets are malleable. They evolve over a lifetime – although the ability to change one's behavior in response to expanding or shrinking opportunity sets varies from person to person and family to family. In the second expansion, Nepal's trading opportunity-set in the world economy is taken into account. Weakness there, that is, the lack of something profitable to sell to the world, combined with an internal policy regime unfavorable to agriculture, undermines the ability of most rural players to improve their lot. At present, the internal and external opportunities cannot provide support to an ever-rising number of rural people who need a way out of their constrained situations, a way out that does not involve the desperate measure of taking to arms.

This chapter also points out that while on the one hand land reform may seem like a logical solution to Nepal's many rural problems, history has shown it to be no panacea. Previous attempts at land reform in Nepal have, in fact, had the unintended and unforeseen consequence of limiting and undermining opportunity-sets for the rural poor rather than expanding them. I argue that while redistributive land reform could go far to help provide a more stable place in the world for many people in Nepal, it will not solve the underlying problem of providing farmers with something they can grow and sell and better themselves with. Moreover, calls for land reform will do nothing to address the wider dynamics that lead to landlessness and marginality in the first place, making land reform a bad option for achieving its stated objectives.

Underlying belief systems behind land reform

Much of the thinking about land reform can be attributed to a few belief systems. The first, a traditional neoclassical one – exemplified perhaps by Klaus Deininger of the World Bank – believes that land reform must be done so that land does what the World Bank wants it to do, namely: become a mere factor of production that is freely bought and sold until it trades into its most efficient use and hence into the hands of the most neoclassically efficient owner. Enforceable laws and effective armies, police forces, and judiciaries are usually needed to impose or make stick any land reform, which is basically a social agreement. When these three conditions for a full-fledged reform are absent, as they are most of the time in Nepal, adepts of this belief system propose interim measures such as GPS-mapping projects and computerized titling systems. These second-best policies are not just whistling the wind. Developers put them out there in the hopes of gaining some modest efficiency improvements to weak land markets, and at the same time build up local support for more full-blown reforms.

In the human ecology terms of this book, holders of this belief system are worshippers of the god of Efficiency, a God who is a bit like Allen's description of "Zeus" in Chapter 9. Zeus is, after all, somewhat arbitrary and he likes to punish everyone who doesn't do what he wants (in this case, be efficient). The strange priors of this belief system are several: efficiency should be worshipped by all; market-led outcomes represent the best of all possible worlds, and (in a strange contradiction) socialist planning systems such as those generated outside a country by an agency (such as the World Bank) can actually accomplish something so precise, bloody, and local as a land reform, market-assisted or other.

Another strange prior of this view is that the presumed benefits of market-led reform are assumed to be real, although they are but derived from mathematical theories without much in the way of empirical validation. With worshippers of the god of Efficiency, if a mathematical model says one type of land-tenure system is efficient, then it must be true. It will be no surprise that the author imagines the cognitive style of holders of this view as that of "hedgehogs," as used in Chapter 3. The strength and spread of Nepal's Maoists has posed a substantial puzzle for this belief system, not least for the staffs of the World Bank and the IMF who had hoped to modernize and de-feudalize Nepal, and oversee the growth of a society of prosperous peasant farmers on the high slopes of the Himalayas.

A related belief system about land reform is one that tries to temper the violence and assertiveness of the god of Efficiency with a concern for the small producer and the democratic virtues to a larger society of a small-holding class of farmers. These people may be called worshippers of a rural Middle Class, generated by a partnership between Zeus and one of his more human-loving and people-tolerant daughters, such as Athena. Land in this belief system is not just a productive asset, it is an asset that, if evenly distributed, will create a self-protecting middle-class and promote food self-sufficiency and lead to a nirvana of democratic stability. This group often proposes land ceilings, protectionism, and other policies deliberately designed to protect the middle-class farmer rather than the big guys or the completely marginal and landless populations. They often make a natural ally for worshippers of Efficiency.

A third belief system is one shared by the worshippers of Gaia (see Chapter 9). In this system, land is not just a productive asset to be rendered efficient or a source of democratic stability, it is also a physical manifestation of a delicate ecosystem and thus requires care and tending, "husbanding" in the old sense of the term. It is also a home for people, where lives are created and ended, where culture is made. It is, in short, a place in the world. Holders of this belief system are a hodgepodge collection of unlikely and rarely encountered and not-very-loyal allies: localists, defenders of the commons, or in Nepal, Maoists promoting a serious redistribution of land. In this belief system, even if the poor and landless don't end up producing a lot of food for sale, land has a role as a place in the world where people can return when selling newspapers amid the traffic jams of the cities fails as a survival strategy. Pessimists might say it is where they can have a place in the world to await the arrival of the messiah of development economists: foreign investors filled with the intention and means to build factories and hire workers and export something. This belief system generates land reform policies intended to protect the poor, to distribute assets, to safeguard the remaining commons, and promote sustainable husbandry.

A fourth belief system also floats about this discussion, that of institutional pragmatism. In this belief system, land reform is not an exercise determined by a mathematical model about the value of land. It is about changing the rules of the game of survival and betterment that is institutional change. Doing something that radical for the pragmatist or "institutional view" is all about relative power and the enforceability of current and proposed rules. Enforceability is, in turn, about economic power and the physical power of those who can use the police and army to get what they want. Here there is worship of the way of being or god Allen refers to as Buro (see Chapter 9) – modern, hierarchial organized, communitarian, disciplined tendencies. It has nothing to do with ideas about efficiency, husbandry, or a place in the world. Pragmatists ask, who has the means to get what they want? The means in question can be guns, an army, a judge, or just the power of inertia to stay in place regardless of what someone wants. This belief system says: do what policymaking you want, but be clear about who your policies are intended to favor and make sure that their new situation, opportunity-sets, and claims on society can be enforced locally in the legal system and by whatever powers of coercion exist in the society. In the pragmatist school, predatory behavior and the abuse of rules and situations by the powerful is hardly a surprise, it is to be expected. Moreover, pragmatism suggests that rural institutions and contracts do not exist in isolation, but rather embedded in a host of social arrangements that can also influence economic outcomes. For example, the nature of the social relationships between the landlords and tenants can significantly influence economic outcomes. However, although the pragmatists and institutionalists are right to point out that power, institutions, and social arrangements matter, they (just like the other three belief systems) tend to fail to locate the failure of institutions in the wider political-economic context of any given country by almost exclusively worshipping the god of good institutions.

The first two belief systems hopelessly neglect the problem that land reform is a social agreement to do something different: to change, create, and redistribute opportunities. Holders of the third belief system tend to be more pragmatic. For the first two systems, the neglect is a serious problem. Land reform is just not a technocratic exercise of two like-minded bureaucracies agreeing to do what an economics model suggests. The fourth belief system goes even further to understand how economic outcomes are shaped by power rather than political participation, and focuses on a micro-economic approach to getting the institutions right. However, to the extent that the failure of land reform is the outcome of these varying belief systems, they all fail to account for the structural processes of development that generated this failure.

Therefore, a fifth belief system is introduced, a human ecology one. This system builds from the fourth belief system of institutional pragmatism by adding a useful insight: land reform is a *social agreement*. It is explicitly political. One of the first issues then, is how to impose reform: by bureaucratic fiat; by violence;

or by a process that arises out of a widespread social agreement to do reform. A prerequisite for the latter, is to generate some agreement.

In Nepal, however, the Maoists are the main group who frequently bring the issue to national attention. And now that they have a seat at the table of power, the question is, what will they do? Is land reform for them merely a recruitment tool? Is it all rhetoric? And who exactly do they propose to help with reform: middle farmers, marginal farmers, or the landless? After all, there most likely is not enough land to help everyone.

Nepal has a constellation of problems that seem daunting for anyone thinking about reform. A human ecology approach can explicitly take into consideration:

1   Agriculture is not a great business to be in, regardless of how much land you have. There aren't a lot of ways for small or middle farmers (the terms are all relative to Nepal's reality) to improve their lot. Export markets for what they produce are weak and don't really create an avenue for upward mobility, if even an avenue for survival.
2   The land frontier was reached a long time ago. Population pressure and abuse have made soil erosion and deforestation a major problem; the underlying resource has been weakened.
3   Building roads and providing credit might have worked decades ago, but now there are just too many people and not enough business opportunities for an enterprising farmer.
4   Uneven development and political instability coupled with rising inequality and poverty have been the rule rather than the exception, providing a solid economic grievance from the rural population who are demanding new social arrangements with the stakeholders of their country.

In Nepal, the first four belief systems are useful for understanding how different foreign aid players and their policy ideas are animated by particular belief systems, consciously or not. Since the four are generated by strange religious priors and the worship of specific "gods," none of them pay enough attention to either rural reality or the processes that generate such realities. Like the fourth belief system, a human ecology system openly adopts the analytical tools of the pragmatists, without which policy prescriptions and the implementation of any of their reforms is bound to fail. This chapter suggests that a human ecology perspective combined with a simple pragmatism might lead to better informed policymaking in Nepal among the foreign-aid community and the various stakeholders who continue to dominate the decision-making of the country.

Underlying situation of land markets and land reform in Nepal

Abysmal levels of poverty and inequality; over 10,000 lives lost in a Maoist uprising[1]; a king who assumed power and dismissed the parliament after the crown prince's slaughtering of the royal family – these are among the dismal realities that make up Nepal's recent past. This small nation's ability to develop in the future, amid the disparate political and economic forces of nearby China, India, and Pakistan, promises to have significant global consequences.

Nepal, a country widely portrayed as a "mythical kingdom" characterized by stunning landscapes and "exotic, peace-loving people," stands in stark contrast to this Western mythology, a mythology that has firmly taken root to even Nepal's neighbors. Since embracing the concept of Western style "development" as a national priority over five decades ago, local agents have been willing to receive – and outside donors have been willing to extend – unprecedented financial resources. Relative to other recipient nations, Nepal has accepted striking levels of aid from international donors in the name of addressing short-term national wellbeing and to fund longer-term traditional development programs. In spite of these immense efforts to solve the problems of poverty and dismal growth, Nepal remains gripped by economic hardship. The country exists in perpetual political instability (despite recent heroic efforts to include the Maoists into the current government), poor governance and corruption, and continues to be economically divided into urban elites and marginalized lower castes (especially with respect to indigenous groups such as the Magar, Khambu, Limbu, Newa Khala, Tara, and Tharu). Further corroding any budding agenda of economic, political, and social progress is the bloody civil war of brutal and indiscriminant violence between the State and the Maoist forces.

In Nepal, the system of ownership and tenure of land has been used by successive governments to consolidate and widen their power base, and to extract revenues from the state, supporting an inegalitarian economic system and significantly disrupting the relationship between rural populations and their environment. Needless to say, this relationship has been heavily biased and uneven to some groups in society. The poor and landless have considerably increased (in both relative and absolute terms), whilst agricultural innovation and neoliberal policies have stultified land fragmentation, environmental deterioration, desertification (essentially in the form of soil erosion), poverty, hunger, and widespread unemployment throughout the agricultural sector in which the vast majority of Nepalese struggle to survive.

Only a few countries have undertaken genuine agrarian reform: Mexico in the early days of the twentieth century; Japan, Taiwan, and South Korea after World War II; China and Cuba after their revolutions. Almost everywhere else, including Nepal, the laws that were passed all over the world in the 1950s and 1960s have never been faithfully applied, and more often than not led to counterproductive results, especially for the intended beneficiaries. In South Asia, only West Bengal and Kerala states, where 10 percent of the region's population lives and both self-proclaimed communist states, have completed land distribution.

Societies throughout South Asia have experienced a rapid growth in demand for land as a principal means of subsistence and household economic improvement. Land is a critical source of subsistence for many developing countries, including Nepal, since the vast majority live in rural areas. Importantly, land is not simply a physical asset, but also a symbol of prestige, a means to power, a form of social security, and a *social agreement,* as well as a source of inevitable conflict between those who own it and those who do not. It is not surprising that land ownership and the closely associated levels of poverty and inequality remain an explosive issue globally. Nepal is no exception.

In Nepal, with the closing of the land frontier, the resulting increase in the demand for land is often expressed in violence of all types: increased land disputes between neighbors, villagers, and powerful political representatives; killings and extortion of farmers by hired individuals and groups, etc. The strange prior that unites many belief systems as described above is that through institutional interventions in property relations and modernization of agriculture, a basis would be created for a more egalitarian society that would ensure minimum social welfare and justice in rural areas. In particular, land reform has the capacity to target those most vulnerable – the landless, women, indigenous groups, children. However, bringing about these changes must inevitably involve confronting (and coordinating) power relations and associated *social agreements* among various groups, including landlords and tenants, the landless, bureaucrats, NGOs, international institutions, and the entrenched Nepali political and industrial elite.

Land reform, therefore, involves the question of complex structural change through the formulation of policy, activating appropriate government and civil society organizations, and mobilizing the poor. The change that land reforms intend to bring about depends largely on the changing social agreements and relational issues construed and controlled by multiple factors of class, caste, culture, politics, religions, and history. These involve the network of relations and social agreements between institutions and people and their environment, who either draw their livelihood from lands or have an abiding interest in it (Thorner, 1956).

Land reform invariably means significant changes in agrarian structures and relationships for securing access to new land (redistribution), and favorable tenure for those who actually work on the land, including a secured title to land, legally fixed rents, and better working conditions for tenants and agricultural laborers (Carter *et al.,* 2004). It also encompasses the access to agricultural input, markets, services, and other needed assistance such as the introduction of high-yielding varieties of seeds, chemical fertilizers, and irrigation services.

The sheer presence of deep and extensive poverty across the region has generated a demand for land reform that also has strong ideological overtones. For the independent kingdom of Nepal, the impulse for land reform came from South Asian radical demands during the period of undivided colonial India. The nationalist leaders used agrarian unrest as a component for the anti-colonial movement and an independent government, which also brought together a wide range of classes, social groupings, and interests. The South Asian Marxist movement, which was in its crescendo between the 1950s and the late 1970s, had also created significant pressure on the states for structural agrarian change, which resonates among the Maoists in Nepal today.

Unlike most land reforms in the past (which were state-led) or reforms advocated today (which are market-led),[2] which are both piecemeal with respect to intervention and approach, the currently Nepalese Maoists are calling for a radical land distribution targeted not to some idealized "small farmer" (Bernstein, 2006), but rather to the landless, in addition to other structural changes in the economy and society. Interestingly, a human ecology perspective towards land reform is equally critical of both redistributive and tenurial reforms. Alternative theories almost always strongly critique redistributive measures on the grounds that they only delay the process of proletarianization,[3] while neoclassical economists generally critique tenurial reforms. The Maoists of today have transformed the issue of land reforms into a nationalist theme that relies upon an old formula of landlord–tenant relations accompanied by an expanding rural proletariat, and argues for a redistribution of key assets via land reform supported by state-managed credit and services.

In Nepal, since land is in such short supply, or in many cases virtually non-existent, any redistributive measures would provide only limited relief for the poor (the general rule of 3:1 of supply to demand is hard to imagine with the closing of the land frontier). Efforts should therefore be concentrated on raising productivity supported by modern agricultural inputs. Technological innovation and the necessary land improvements which increase agricultural productivity are presumed to be greatly influenced by the ownership and control over land. It is in this context that land titling and tenurial reforms in general are meant to pave the way for redistributive reforms later, by priming the demand side of land markets (as opposed to state-led or radical reforms as suggested by the Maoists, which develop the supply side), leading to a better and more competitive functioning of land sales, land rental, and credit markets.[4]

The underlying dynamic of the reformative strategies of the states was also based on the increased commercialization and development of the agrarian economy, which would generate more income and employment opportunities. In this way, those who did not hold land could also make a decent living. But it became quite clear that regional agrarian economies were subject to an extensive process of polarization between those with increasing ownership of land and those who became landless, with nothing but their labor power to sell. The technological and market inputs have hardly created favorable conditions for improvement for the vast majority of the rural poor and the landless in the region. Instead, in most circumstances, the market economy approach has further deteriorated the existing ecological balance in much of South Asia, including Nepal, while increasing poverty and landlessness (Shrestha, 1991). In fact, the new push for market-assisted land reform has recently been the subject of critical examination by a number of authors over a wide range of case studies.[5]

What dominates the debate taking place in policy circles regarding land reform today are the first two belief systems, as described in the previous section, which both carry the strange prior that the English system of capitalist farming is the ideal model. This strange prior is accompanied by another strange prior, namely that Nepal's history is similar to that of feudal Europe, where individual property rights emerged after a considerable evolution.[6] The ultimate goal of these belief systems is to develop a property rights system, good governance, marketable commodities, voluntary exchanges, and importantly, produce ever more commodities. Western forms of ownership of land, regardless of size, are merely assumed to be more efficient than other all other forms of tenure (be they communal, state, common, religious, or open-access), independent of the country's human ecology – its natural and physical constraints, its particular history, its institutions and social arrangements, and its culture.[7]

Moreover, the fact that the negation of capitalist forms of employment occurs in a region such as the Nepalese Tarai makes the discourse particularly compelling. Agriculturally relatively backward and stagnant, socially mired in class exploitation and caste oppression, the Nepalese Tarai often evokes revulsion both to the north, in the hills of Nepal, and to its south, in neighboring states of India. It is looked upon as a region where feudal domination continues unabated, in violent conflict with Nepal's struggling political democracy which represents modernity and progress. Even in colonial times, the Nepalese Tarai was too far from the imperial centers of Delhi, Calcutta, and Kathmandu. Because of this history of marginality, the region appears to be a place overlooked by the forces of modernization, lending credibility to the mythology that the current state of crisis is linked to its backward legacy of the Tarai's "pre-modern" past.

In the absence of resolving the above theoretical issues, modern proponents have retreated to empirical justifications of small-farmer productivity theory (i.e. small farms are more efficient than large farms), and even though the empirical evidence is anything but clear (even the English system was certainly not a place of triumphant small owners), strong arguments are still made assuming the well-known inverse relation (Bhandari, 2006). The doubt over productivity effects removes the economic façade from land reform arguments which, taken at face value, promote smaller owner-occupied farms (which dominate rural Nepal today as a result of past reforms) as the favored post-reform system.

Despite the lack of empirical evidence, the still strongly held belief and positive presumptions of land reform based on small efficient and egalitarian farms (family-based and self-employed) has been exposed as having a strong Eurocentric and class bias.[8] The fundamental fallacies involved in such an assumption, and the logical implications of an idealized Jeffersonian vision of homogenous and undifferentiated small farms, seem to have little empirical support for such a strong belief on which reforms are based. It seems wholly inappropriate to impose a belief system using an individual behavioral calculus based on leisure preference in a radically different human ecology, i.e. on farmers in the context of extreme poverty. If farmers have higher intensity labor use on small farms, it seems more reasonable to conclude it is the effect of extremely low wages, a lack of alternative income-generating activities, and overall agricultural stagnation, rather than the standard neoclassical labor–leisure tradeoff.

Given no alternative sources of income and employment, a "small farmer" would try to produce the maximum output and hire labor as much as possible to meet his minimum consumption needs and minimum cash needs. The structural imperatives of living in impoverished conditions itself suggests that the factors that drive some "small farmers," at least, to intensify labor input are radically different than those that the dominant belief systems permits them to do so (i.e. there exists a striking gap between the theoretical potential of family-based small farming and the dismal reality of small farming.

In other words, the inverse relationship can be one of distress and "SOS calls" rather than a sign of relative efficiency and small-farm efficiency. In fact, land sales in Nepalese agriculture more often go in the reverse direction from what standard land reform theory would predict: small farms are selling their plots, despite their comparative advantages, to large farms. Small farms are simply not viable alternatives where the majority of small farms in the countryside are on average only one-fourth to one-half of one hectare in size. What is even more revealing is that at the micro-level, so-called "distress sales" are not only common, but are also on the rise since adoption of liberalization and privatization policies implanted by the World Bank and IMF during the 1980s and 1990s (Shrestha, 2001). A deeper examination of the small farm implies that viability itself cannot be assumed (and is misleading) where it is enforced by the acute risks of starvation, poverty, and instability that necessitate severe stress on all family labor (Patnaik, 1979; Kautsky, 1988; Sender and Smith, 1990; Bhandari, 2006).[9]

Distress sales have been accompanied by the changing notion of security itself to accommodate the policies of economic liberalization and privatization. In one study by the World Bank twenty years ago (Feder and Noronha, 1987), it was clearly stated that "in most sub-Saharan African societies, land under cultivation by an allottee cannot be taken away." The definition of security was explicitly changed even then, so as to include the "ability of an occupant to undertake land transactions that would best suit his interests" (p. 159), including the ability of that individual to sell and mortgage the land.

Where small farms appear to be more efficient than large farms, speculation could more than likely be the cause. If this is the case, then a standard redistributive reform might rectify under-utilization in the short-run, but *would not* change the overall attractiveness of land as an asset. Since there would exist a high incentive for re-purchase by investors, re-aggregation, consolidation, and higher land inequality would likely result. As discussed in the next section, this is consistent with what happened after the Land Reforms of 1964. A redistribution of existing rights then would not go towards solving the problem. The error is to assume the inverse relation simply because of the immediate evidence of such as a truism, thereby concealing the *underlying* reasons causing the observed inverse relation in the first place.[10]

The increased integration to the global economy and the increased aid dependency of Nepal bears significant influence in determining the nature and magnitude of land reforms. They are also heavily influenced by the models developed by dominant funding institutions. In particular, in recent years, land reform has been significantly influenced by the policy of the World Bank in its vision of the small, efficient, egalitarian, and privately-owned farm with title and assumed enforcement (Deininger and Binswanger, 1999: 247).[11]

However, the broader context of power structures (IFAD, 2004) is entirely ignored by these belief systems that propose land reform, both international agencies and academic scholarship alike. Although Nepal has in the past adopted a certain number of agrarian reforms affecting the socio-economic status of the agrarian elite to some extent, the basic structure of wealth and power in the society has remained the same. The interests of both rural and urban elites are well entrenched in Nepal's current human ecology. The strong alliance between the business, bureaucracy, and landed classes with support from international capital continues. The state reproduces laws and regulations which tend to be highly in favor of the landed classes. For example, average land ownership among the members of the National Parliament (MPs) representing rural constituencies is significantly higher in their national land–person ratios. In Nepal, 50 percent of farming households have barely 0.15 hectare on average, while MPs possess land over 16.8 hectares in hill areas, and nearly ten hectares in the plains (Ghimire, 2001: 4). The accumulation of land in the hands of a few has curtailed the interests of small farmers, who are unable to constitute a powerful lobby that could effectively pressure the governments.

Little, if any, poverty alleviation has been achieved since 1951, the year donor agencies became actively interested in the country's economic and social "development," and the same year that the multi-party democracy began.[12] Since 1951, Nepal has also become increasingly dependent on foreign aid and external influences. Over 80 percent of the country's budget for development programs comes in the form of grants and loans from donor agencies, the two largest being the World Bank and the Asian Development Bank. In spite of all of the efforts of major donors and policymakers, there are no indications whatsoever of sustainability. Simply, like many developing countries too numerous to mention, Nepal has become an international beggar vulnerable to the whims and desires of the donor community (DeVries, 2003).

Nepal's development is characterized by low incomes; increasing food deficits; increasing unemployment; widening gaps between both rich and poor and urban and rural; growing dependency on foreign aid; persistent political instability and corruption. Traditional elites have maintained their dominance in society, re-legitimizing their influence through the institutions of democracy. Whilst democracy offers political power to the professional middle-classes, left-wing parties and representatives of marginalized social and economic groups remained sidelined from the elite-dominated political processes. Importantly, a minority of the population has benefited from international initiatives – 15 percent of the Nepalese are beneficiaries of foreign aid, and these have been largely the urban and political elite comprising businessmen and powerful bureaucrats.

Along with the formal reinstatement of democracy in 1991 came a significant shift in economic policy, from inward-looking to an extensive structural adjustment program with the standard policies including stabilization; getting the prices right for increased private sector activity; a reduced role for government and fiscal deficits; and increased openness in all areas. With deregulation during the country's experiment with democracy in the 1990s, the NGO sector exploded from seventy in 1994 to over 16,000 NGOs (excluding international NGOs) in 2000. Donors define the development agendas rather than the other way around (Panday, 1999). Moreover, the impact of structural adjustment in the 1990s alongside Nepal's experiment with democracy was anything but benign; Washington Consensus-type policies resulted in rapidly eroding economic security for the middle-peasantry, which provided much fuel for the current insurgency (Deraniyagala, 2005). It should come as no surprise that these factors greatly contributed to the ongoing Maoist revolution, more commonly known as the "People's War."

Financial liberalization in Nepal has led to the spread of financial institutions and financial deepening (reflected in the increase of credit as a share of GDP to about 46 percent in 2001), yet there has been no increase of credit to the rural areas where poverty is concentrated. The government has, in fact, withdrawn from rural development banks and phased-out priority-sector credit programs that benefited rural development. As a consequence, indebtedness and landlessness is on the rise in rural areas.

Micro-finance has been growing in Nepal, but is largely donor-driven and has a small capital base. While it is a valuable tool for stimulating self-employment, micro-finance cannot substitute a viable domestic rural banking system which could provide adequate credit to farmers and employment-generating small and medium non-farm enterprises. Part of the explanation for the unequal distribution of the benefits of trade is the lack of a supply response from poorer farmers and small enterprises when increased trade has broadened economic opportunities. This is a particular problem in rural areas where there is a lack of infrastructure, credit, marketing channels and public services.

Another part of the problem is the unequal distribution of benefits across regions in Nepal. Nepal remains wary of completely opening up their economies because of the potentially devastating effects on their industrial and agricultural sectors, especially if industrial-country markets for exports of agricultural commodities and labor-intensive manufactures from developing countries remain protected.

While Nepal has banked heavily on garment and textile exports, international competition remains intense in these sectors, and foreign direct investment is footloose. Nepal warns us that too many developing countries are specializing in the same low-value-added products such as garments, and have not diversified their manufactured exports. Instead, they should ideally be concentrating on relatively income-elastic and price-inelastic export products.

Also, it should be noted that trade liberalization has only been partial in Nepal. For example, in 2000, the weighted mean tariff on all products was 17 percent in Nepal. Trade liberalization in Nepal has benefited only a small formal sector and an entrenched political, industrial, and urban elite. Exports are narrowly concentrated in garments, carpets, and pashmina, and have not increased as fast as the flood of imports. As a result, the trade deficit has risen to 20 percent of GDP. Whatever income has been generated is becoming more concentrated in the urban industrial and commercial sectors.

Nepal's annual per capita income is around US$210, with most of its income accounted for by consumption and a savings rate at a dismal 14 percent. But by IMF standards, Nepal is a stable economy! Exports grew at an average annual rate of 22.3 percent in the last three years, whereas imports registered a negative growth rate of 2.9 percent. Foreign loans grew at a low average annual rate of 1.3 percent. Furthermore, debt servicing, at less than 5 percent of current deposits, is not a burden, and inflation is not of great concern at a mere 4 percent.

The Nepali elite's subservience to the international financial institutions played a crucial role in the official inclusion of the Maoists in the political arena in 1996 in order to induce investor confidence and the promised panacea of global finance capital for economic development (Patnaik, 2003). Criticism in Nepal concerning privatization, foreign licensing, and the foreign ownership that has begun to dominate their economy continues go grow from all corners. Fiscal expenditures were focused exclusively on enhancing the role of the private sector and free-market forces. Restrictive monetary policy effectively increased the real interest rate in agriculture, making it much more difficult for the vast majority of farmers to obtain loans. Furthermore, as in most developing countries, the planning process of Nepal became inextricably linked to the logic of Bretton Woods institutions, which are premised on the inherent benefits of stabilization and structural adjustment policies. These reforms ignored the structural realities and imbalances of both the agricultural sector and macro-economy, which has reinforced Nepal's continuing uneven development, landlessness, poverty and inequality (Bhandari, 2006).

Today, more than twelve million inhabitants (over half the country's population) live below the poverty line and nearly half of the country subsists on incomes of less than US$1 per day. Differences in living conditions between the rural areas and urban centers are increasing. Prejudice against women, dalits, and other native minorities is also on the rise. Nepal's land ownership figures reveal further internal inequality. Just 6 percent of arable land is owned by 50 percent of the population, compared to the wealthiest 10 percent that holds over 75 percent of the arable land. This situation leaves many farmers unable to support themselves. With so many persistently poor, poverty has become an epidemic (Seddon et al., 2002) and the poor often see their misery increase along with their necessary household debt to government loan offices and local moneylenders. More than half the population faces malnutrition, with 60 percent of children under five years old considered malnourished (UN, 2004). Life expectancy averages below fifty years of age. Combining these factors with the abysmal condition of health care and elementary education, the poor have little reason to believe change is on the horizon. In reaction to these factors and a popular feeling of crisis, a militant left-wing movement has accepted the opportunity to take action. What is remarkable about Nepal, as compared to other developing countries with similarly depressing statistics, is that Nepal has received emphatic financial attention from the so-called donor community. Regrettably, the results of this attention belie the resources injected.[13]

Lessons from other uprisings in the twentieth century show that underdevelopment plays a large role in provoking popular uprising. One common theme in these upheavals is a rural population suffering from landlessness around 40 percent: in the case of Mexico (1911), 62 percent of the farmers were considered landless; Russia (1917), between 32 and 47 percent; Spain (1936), 40 percent; China (1949), between 35 and 45 percent; Bolivia (1952), 60 percent; Cuba (1959), 39 percent; Vietnam (1961), 42 to 58 percent; Ethiopia (1975), 38 percent; Nicaragua (1979), 40 percent; and now Nepal (1996–), 42 percent (Taras, 2005).[14]

Today, Nepal's broad political environment is subject to the volatile combination of systemic economic and social inequalities, marginalization of the rural population by Kathmandu's political order, and extensive underdevelopment. While the cause for Nepal's decline is often attributed to historical, geographical, or cultural factors, the disruption of the political class by the Maoist insurgency is irrefutably in response to the absence of economic and human development.

To complicate things further, the impacts of the current conflict, both on the environment and the natural resource base, have been noted to be a significant barrier for Nepal to move forward. The loss of infrastructure from the protected-area system in Nepal has continued to rise, which, coupled with the loss of political will for environmental conservation, may have created conditions conducive for the opportunistic resource exploitation that seems to be making Nepal a classic case of the tragedy of the commons. High population density, largely due to the high "natural" growth rates, forces the landless class to harvest environmental resources on which they depend, which further causes ecological devastation.

Importantly, the human ecology framework considers key structural variables (and their various feedback effects) such as an adverse macro-economic environment, the root causes of landlessness, as well as the relationship between property rights and the environment. In addition, a human ecology framework does not neglect the role of horizontal and group inequality (chiefly rural/urban) in perpetuating Nepal's internal political conflict, which all other belief systems take for granted or simply ignore; in fact, the notion of a causal relationship between inequality and armed conflict (Collier *et al.*, 2003; 2005; Collier and Cramer, 2003), in what is now known as the "greed versus grievance" debate, can seriously undermine land reform efforts.[15] In these theories, civil war is argued to be the result of "greed," where predatory behaviors of disgruntled civil groups, such as the Maoists, seek control over lootable resources. Of course, this view clearly begs the key question as to what are the causes of widespread predatory behavior in society itself. For that, one cannot ignore the role of persistent and growing horizontal economic-inequality, and the potential role of neoliberal policies in perpetuating and even exacerbating such inequality (Deraniyagala, 2005).[16]

Nepal is a striking example of how group inequality can be a source of violent conflict (Stewart, 2000). Group inequality provides powerful grievances which leaders can use to mobilize people to political protest by calling on cultural markers (a common history such as the landless movement commonly known as "Sukumbasi" movement) and pointing to group exploitation. This type of mobilization seems especially likely to occur where there is political as well as economic inequality, so that the leaders are excluded from political power.

Economic factors, such as "inequality, landlessness, and a general lack of opportunity reinforced by complex systems of caste and related discriminatory patterns, have provided sufficient motivation and support for the Maoist cause" (DFID, 2005).[17] Disproportionately limited opportunities may arise not only as a result of formal discrimination in education or employment towards tribal castes, but also from generations of relative impoverishment in the agricultural sector.[18] While one cannot fully trace Nepal's growing poverty and inequality to IMF and World Bank prescriptions, their homogeneous, one-size-fits-all approach to macro-policy has significantly negatively impacted Nepal by all accounts (Patnaik, 2003).

The interconnections between neoliberal policies, insurgency, economic inequality (both horizontal and vertical), and political instability are emphasized in a human ecology economics approach, and are not assumed to be mere irritants or simply coincide by chance as in other belief systems.[19] A human ecology approach suggests at the outset that any effective policy package for Nepal must directly address the connections between macro-economic reforms, structural imbalances, economic inequality, political stability, landlessness, and insurgency.

Unfortunately, current calls for market-assisted land reform in Nepal ignore these macro-economic structural variables and their critical connections, let alone the impacts on the environment and the ability of the landless to purchase arable land. By exclusively focusing on inequality within the agricultural sector, without an understanding of what are the macro-economic foundations of agricultural stagnation and why so many have become marginalized and landless in the first place, may lead to misguided policy formulation with respect to land reform and tenure security.

The next section more closely looks at the current belief systems that dominate Nepal today, one from the international community as epitomized in World Bank efforts for market-assisted land reform, and the other from various public voices as reflected in proposals from the Maoists.

What is to be done? Current proposals from Maoists and the World Bank

From the initiation of the People's War in 1996 up to the present period, around 80 percent of Nepal has come under the control of the Communist Party of Nepal and United Marxist–Leninist Party (UML–Maoist), while the old state's presence is now limited to the capital, district headquarters, and highways. The most potent mechanism aligning Maoists and their supporters is the common awareness of underdevelopment.

Today, the dominant aspect of the current state of development is the civil conflict which shows no signs of abating. As discussed in the earlier section, the Maoist insurgency erupted in response to the perceived failure of the Nepalese government to address key issues as poverty, landlessness, inequality, corruption, discrimination, and human rights abuses. The Maoists have proclaimed their intention to put an end to social injustice, extreme inequality, corruption, and foreign domination. In particular, they have pledged to empower women, lower-castes, and indigenous groups. They have also taken a strong stand against alcohol, prostitution, child polygamy, gambling, and domestic violence, and called for the establishment of People's Courts, where women are more likely to win justice. Included in their demands is the establishment of a secular state (non-religious), ethnic autonomy, and equal status for all of the country's many diverse languages. However, their reign of terror has done little to support their stated goals, resulting in school closures, extortion, kidnappings, forced conscription of children, bombings, and other acts of extreme violence, all of which have made it harder to move the country's poor state of development forward (Taras, 2006).

At the other extreme, Nepal has been governed by a "development industry" ever since it opened up its borders to both foreigners and foreign aid in 1951 (Khadka, 1997). The United States, following the initial lead of India, eventually became Nepal's largest donor. Until this time, Nepal's main political objectives were independence and sovereignty, and although British colonial rulers ruled Nepal indirectly through India and had considerable influence over the monarchy, Nepal maintained an official position of self-imposed isolation. It is not surprising that the perception of Nepal's development is intrinsically linked to dependence on both foreign aid and the foreign visitors (Kernot, 2006).

Since 1955, beginning with King Mahendra, Nepal has actively pursued a policy of attaining as much foreign aid as possible; today there are over 100 countries represented by diplomatic missions in Kathmandu, and over 200 international NGOs, in addition to foreign government agencies, U.N. departments and development banks. In addition to the considerable levels of foreign aid, foreign organizations bring conspicuous influence, both materially and socially. This influence extends to the formation of their own ways of being – new social, economic, and political echelons within the country that create national policies of the highest consequence. International donors are now seen as the de facto arbiter of nationwide policies, rather than the government itself.

As Daudin argues in Chapter 6, it is rather bizarre, if not inappropriate, to impose a belief system on a country that is completely inorganic and unsuitable to the real conditions of the people, economy, and society of that country. For example, imposing a perfectly competitive model on eighteenth-century France would be absurd (as Daudin indicates is sometimes done in the literature). Moreover, the domination of the foreign development industry from agencies to NGOs to diplomatic missions, etc. has established a firmly rooted *way of being* in Kathmandu that the Maoists (among others) see as part of the problem rather than part of the solution and, hence, want to end.[20]

For instance, unlike in some other recipient countries, aid-givers and other foreign do-gooders are treated with great respect, hospitality and generosity, and are easily allowed to persuade themselves of their usefulness and importance.

It is little wonder that very few people leave this paradise, even under requests from the majority of the population! It is this feature which has spawned what may well be the secret response of many outsiders who are at present living in Nepal, which of course would almost never be admitted to. The country is a haven for the international do-gooder. And the past decade and more of international manipulation and interference in Nepal's polity and economy, while it may have contributed little to the living conditions of the average Nepalese, has enriched and even captivated the lives of the many expatriates who have flocked there over the years. The personnel of these outfits range from experienced and perceptive old Nepali hands to young people who have barely graduated from college, eager to impose their expertise, however inappropriate, on the hapless residents. And young Nepali's with education see the most rapid route to mobility and success as being achieved through working with such organizations, or even through forming NGOs of their own which will receive aid funds. The entrenched ways of being among donors, expatriates, and development consultants not only support a colonial human ecology, but also, and equally important, maintain an exclusionary discourse. These continued ways of being are intensifying rather than ameliorating current ecological, social, and economic conflicts between the rural population and those in Kathmandu.

While the Maoists may pose a genuine security risk, the vast majority of the public in Nepal perceive there to be a lack of commitment on the part of international development workers to make the sacrifices necessary to ensure that funds are actually going where they are supposed to. The relationship between the NGO world and the government is also precarious. Much of Nepal's aid is channeled through NGOs, which has the two-fold effect of removing state control over directing aid money, and making it compete as a recipient of funds at the same time. And although the government recognizes the vital role of NGOs in implementing local programs, each has shown an unwillingness to work with each other, and each has accused the other of both corruption and inefficiency (Shah, 2002). As such, the two sectors continue to operate independently. How any successful land reform can be initiated by the government or NGOs is anybody's guess.[21]

Ironically, the civil war has not reduced the impact of donor–state relations, but rather strengthened their resolve. The Asian Development Bank, among many others, has found a renewed purpose to facilitate the peace process and human rights initiatives, the construction of communication and health facilities, and "capacity-building." USAID's development strategy in Nepal even focuses on the conflict, claiming that good governance and increased income will promote peace (USAID, 2005). How these promises might come to pass is not addressed. However, one thing is clear: Nepal seems all too willing to accept foreign aid and high indebtedness, despite the observed costs of its dependency.

The Maoist movement raises serious questions about the role of foreign development domination of their country as they have witnessed minimal improvements in the past fifty years, and in many cases the poor have been even further marginalized. The lack of progress also raises questions about the validity of international input into Nepal's development. They ask: should current dominant belief systems be maintained, or should the donor community redirect some or all of their aid to other countries which can make more effective use of it? And would Nepal really be worse off if international funding were withdrawn?

Additional discussion may be helpful in understanding the effects of NGO public promotion within the context of the Maoist campaign. Some NGOs publicly express the message that they work to empower community residents with the tools to "solve" their own economic problems. In this way, these agencies may accidentally be priming village communities for Maoist dogma by placing a high value on the language of empowerment and self government. In fact, both the Maoists and the development agencies claim inherent political power because of their self-help mantras, and their ability to foster a sense of solidarity within communities.[22]

The historic and comprehensive state-led reforms in 1964 are now assessed in order to gain further insight about the prospects of policy-changes emanating from these two opposing and antithetical belief systems – market-assisted land reform proposed by the World Bank and the international community, and radical land redistribution advocated by the near majority of the rural sector.

Earlier land reforms in Nepal

The farming class has a long history of providing the bulk of the surplus on which the success of the government's military designs and the pomp and pageantry of the ruling aristocracy crucially depended. The success of the Rana regime also hinged upon the regular supply of income from land. The peasants were left with a bare minimum for subsistence and no efforts were made to ameliorate their conditions until the end of Ranacracy in 1951. Early attempts at land reform measures culminated in the historic Land Reforms of 1964, the first set of countrywide and comprehensive land reforms.

However, the central objective of a more equitable distribution of agricultural land in society has not been fulfilled for several reasons: first, land acquired for redistribution was not substantial; second, the land which was acquired was not fully redistributed; and third, even the land which was distributed did not fall into proper hands. The reforms could hardly speak of the process of progressive "proletarianization" of the peasantry, mainly due to the lack of a dynamically-growing industrial sector, as hoped for by well-known "dual economy" models. In fact, the reforms drove tenancy underground as landlords became acutely fearful of tenants gaining security on the land they rent. For all practical purposes, the tenants have receded into their own oblivion where they are left to sink or swim.

The reforms have also been shown to aggravate employment possibilities. Historically, the Tarai was a frontier and has been peopled by immigrants from the hills and from bordering Indian states. Immigrants from the hills attracted by greater economic opportunities, education, and health facilities came with the capital which gave them access to land. Immigrants from India were also encouraged by the 1964 reforms as this major sociopolitical event created economic reasons for the local landowning class to invite Indians to immigrate. The instant land access for immigrants and evasion of tenancy regulations by the landowners benefited both parties. However, this practice, although mutually beneficial, has unintentionally exacerbated land conflicts by creating multiple claims to land and undermined existing institutions for conflict resolution as occurred in Honduras (Jansen and Roquas, 1998).

Past reforms, both tenurial and redistributive, had the unintended negative consequence of creating a deep insecurity among landlords that continues today, and which leads them to resume self-cultivation, and to evict and rotate tenants, hiring Indian labor who cannot legally claim tenancy rights. This has created a paradox in Nepal: laborers from Nepal's hills seasonally migrate to bordering Indian states to look for employment, and Indians have settled in Nepal permanently and illegally gained access to a considerable amount of land. This, together with the fact that large amounts of land have been subdivided among heirs as a response to past ceilings, has actually led to increasing landlessness, with the landless population concentrated in the Tarai. The emergence and growth of a class of agricultural laborers in the Tarai far exceeds employment demand, hence real wage rates in agriculture have continued to fall (ARTEP, 1994).

Thus, in the liberalized atmosphere since the early 1990s, a key question has emerged among policymakers in Nepal: should the ceilings be reduced or lifted altogether?[23] And should the tenancy law prohibiting leasing out of land (under the "land to the tiller" philosophy) be changed to permit free leasing in and out of agricultural land? The motivation and logic behind such demands are clear: if industry has to invest large sums in cash-crop production of oilseeds and many other biological inputs, they would like to have a sufficient degree of control of their raw materials, which is not possible unless they own the land they cultivate with well-defined property rights. On the other hand, market forces in land markets suggest that widespread and illegal leasing of land is common.[24]

The institution of land reforms has also failed to stimulate agricultural production as expected. In fact, the reforms have most likely weakened peasants' income-earning capacity as wages have decreased, not increased, as land reform theory predicts (Shrestha, 1991; Bhandari, 2001, 2006). The historical conditions for land reforms have changed considerably: severe capital market imperfections, combined with the macro-economic stabilization policies beginning in the 1990s, have generated a process (including higher rural interest rates) that will, in any event, more than likely reverse any potential gains of currently proposed market-assisted land reforms.[25]

This is not to say that tenants are less efficient than owners of land in terms of productivity. However, with the significant injection of modern agricultural technology (mainly irrigation and seeds), the productivity of tenant farmers will be mitigated as the productivity gap should narrow in favor of large farmers with increasing returns to scale (Verma and Bromley, 1987; Bhandari, 2006). Productivity declines have been experienced in many developing countries, with the diffusion of new technology for short periods during periods of transition.

The human ecology framework offers a plausible explanation for such counter-intuitive results. As the Green Revolution spread in rural Nepal from the 1960s to the early 1980s, richer farmers were in a position to reap the benefits, leading to a "coercive treadmill cycle" for poorer farmers (Owen, 1814; Olson, 1964). When the new technology is transferred from agricultural research stations to farm production, owners of larger farms benefited disproportionately. Institutions and services such as extension, credit, and marketing channels, coupled with political power, reflect a strong and well-known bias in favor of big farmers who can adapt early and gain a windfall through high output prices and heavily subsidized input prices.

Clearly, richer farmers have better access to new technology (HYV seeds, chemical fertilizers), credit markets, and new institutions that supply and distribute various inputs. While these biochemical inputs may be scale neutral, adoption leads to greater demand for mechanization, resulting in economies of scale. In addition, as discussed earlier, the average farm size is already so pathetically small (although idealized in small-farmer efficiency theory), that it falls well below any minimum size necessary to reap the gains of new technology, notwithstanding the severe credit constraints the majority of farmers face. In fact, even in the highly cited Griffin *et al.* piece in favor of a more radical redistribution-oriented land reform, they argue, "small farms generate higher land productivity and total social factor productivity except in the very smallest farms in some countries" (2004: 128; Bhandari, 2006).

Poor productivity may have more to do with lack of accessible and affordable credit for most farmers than with land inequality and farm size per se. On strictly economic grounds, redistribution of land that increases landholding size has little theoretical justification. However, this analysis does not necessarily argue against the need of a radical agrarian reform to target the landless or indigenous groups directly on either efficiency or equity criteria as proposed by the Maoists. But it does clearly point out that attempts to achieve tenure security will only create even more tenure insecurity by underestimating landlords' post-reform responses, both legal and extra-legal, as evidenced in the past land reform. And attempts to redistribute land without simultaneously tackling the declining terms of trade against agriculture and rapidly deteriorating natural resource base will also likely be met with failure.

Current and proposed legislation

Recent World Bank land policy centers on the push for market-assisted land reform, which calls for deregulation of land rental markets (Deininger, 2003). It is true that land rental markets are under-used relative to their potential, although this argument is largely based on experience of Latin America where land markets are extremely thin, unlike South Asia where rental markets are highly active and involve at least one-third of the rural population.

According to the cautious proponents of market-assisted land reform however, this is not a result of over-regulation of land rental markets, but rather:

1 the weakness of property rights for landlords who fear that tenants will claim possession rights and not return rented lands when contracts expire;[26]

2   lack of conflict resolution mechanisms in social agreements, particularly between landlords and tenants who belong to opposite ends of the social spectrum and have high levels of "social distance" (Bhandari, forthcoming); and

3   a view that past reforms failed largely due to their redistributive nature, not the rental regulations.

These laws create a loss–loss situation for tenants: they do not provide them with access to land now that classical land reform programs are exhausted; and they block access to rental land as they create insecurity for landlords over land ownership.

Nor do land rental markets provide an adequate solution. Tenancy arrangements do allow the surplus land of the rich to be combined with the surplus labor of the poor, bypassing the drawbacks of hired labor discussed earlier. But at the same time, tenancy creates a new set of incentive problems that again depress labor use and land productivity. The most widespread form of tenancy in many parts of the world is sharecropping, in which the landlord takes a share of the harvest (often half) as rent and the sharecropper gets the rest. As far back as the time of Adam Smith, economists have pointed out that this reduces the tenant's incentive to put labor into the land, since the tenant bears the full cost of each unit of labor but receives only a fraction of the resulting output (Smith, 1904 [1776], 366–367).[27]

Fixed rents avoid this problem, but leave the tenant to bear all the risks of output and price fluctuations. Moreover, tenants have no incentive to make investments that enhance the long-term productivity of the land, unless they have "occupancy rights" that protect them from eviction. Granting such rights to tenants is itself a land reform, since it redistributes one important stick in the property-rights bundle. The landowners' fear of losing property rights is one reason that long-term land rentals are uncommon.[28]

Therefore, proponents often incorrectly argue for regulation of land rental contracts, but regulated to the Western notion of formal contracts based on individual private-property rights, thereby making land rentals more attractive (in theory) to both landlords and tenants. These belief systems take the nature of social agreements between landlords and their respective tenant for granted. One of the major current hurdles to rentals and source of conflicts between landlords and tenants is over tenants' investments in land improvements and the termination of contracts (dual tenancy). Improvements made without the authorization of the landlord become sources of claim over the land by tenants; they are being discouraged from investing in land improvements because rules for compensation of the residual value of these investments when contracts are terminated are not explicit.

As a result, landlords only give land under tenancy, especially formal tenancy, to members with low "social distance" (Bhandari, forthcoming) or within their narrow "circles of confidence" (de Janvry, 2002), such as family and immediate neighbors. In fact, throughout the micro-economic oriented explanations for sharecropping efficiency, only a human ecology perspective can take into consideration the strange prior that permeates throughout land reform debates concerning neoclassical assumption of fully alienated relationships between landlord and tenant. In the world of both cost and output sharing, the widely discussed problem of enforcement over the labor effort of the tenant hinges on the "social distance" between tenant and landlord. In Nepal, the closer the tenant is to his landlord socially, the more likely the tenant will apply the efficient level of inputs. Simply, the less social distance a tenant has toward his landlord, the less *need* for supervision itself, which can therefore reduce excessive supervision costs. By the nature of the specific social arrangement between landlord and tenant, individual non-cooperative behavior can then potentially become identical to the cooperative choice.

Standard explanations rely on transactions costs (e.g. supervision costs), imperfect markets, and risk. As Allen points out:

> intraspecies negotiations and transactions are exploratory, adaptive, often individualized, and the outcomes are not known to all members of the species. This [human ecology] belief system has different consequences than the belief system of neoclassical economics in which transactions costs (a catch-all category for a variety of intraspecies activities) are assumed to be either trivial or not worth exploring except as a general constraint on the otherwise superior "efficiency" of markets.
>
> (Allen, Chapter 1)

In spite of the plethora of empirical studies on sharecropping efficiency, the results are mixed. However, because all other belief systems conceive sharecropping as an undifferentiated category,[29] they cannot shed light as to why some sharecroppers are relatively more efficient than others in overcoming well-known Marshallian disincentives.

Beyond poverty itself being a powerful enough structural incentive to induce high levels of work effort without supervision and monitoring, another feature that induces efficient behavior lies in the tenants own preferences through internalizing the social optimum. The extent to which a tenant internalizes the social optimum is based on the degree of social distance in the particular social arrangement he has toward his landlord (Bhandari, 2007). As Arrow puts it, the most effective way to prevent the occurrence of moral hazards (the incentive to shirk or otherwise cheat by someone whose actions cannot be monitored) is to: "develop the relations of trust and confidence between principal and agent ... so that the agent will not cheat even though it may be 'rational economic behavior' to do so" (Arrow, 1968, p. 537).

Since parties with low social distance embedded in their social agreement are more efficient, agents can seek to build their "reputation capital" (Daudin, Chapter 6) by showing their commitment through increased work effort. This is similar to a "bond" approach to social capital and reputation. Most importantly, in rural Nepal contracts are part of larger social arrangements that are flexible and continue to evolve and adapt to changing ecological environments over time.

Nepal has recently announced the abolishment of "dual tenancy" in its current tenth five-year plan of the National Planning Commission (2002–2007).

Dual tenancy applies only to legal and formal tenants, who comprise a negligible percentage of the total tenants, and refers to the apparent confusion arising from competing claims on the individualized private-property right of the land by tenant and landlord. Formal tenants then have no useful function to perform on the land they own and are likely unable to shift their investments elsewhere. Tenants, who are natural buyers of such land, simply do not have enough resources, while others have no interest to buy land rented out to formal yellow-certificate holding tenants. In reality, landowners become stuck with the land they own.

The Lands Act of 1964 authorized a registered tenant to lay claim to one-fourth of the area or equivalent market value of land from the owner. Since this resulting "dual ownership" is believed to discourage both the owner and the tenant from making land improvements and from adopting productivity-enhancing technology, the government recently abolished dual ownership in favor of a single owner, thereby forcing the tenant and landlord to "strike" an amicable settlement. Of course, this is based on the assumption that landlords are "willing sellers," and tenants are "willing buyers," and both will behave in rational ways given proper institutional incentives, i.e. more productive land will go to more productive farmers. Poor farmers clearly do not have any influence on pushing the price down, while landlords will simply "set" prices, more than likely overpricing their land transactions regardless of the true value of land. Besides, the required 3:1 ratio of land supply–demand certainly does not apply to Nepal.[30]

Moreover, it is assumed in the dominant belief system, that single ownership based on the Western experience will lead to increased productivity-led investments in land. The brief historical sketch of past land reforms shows the unforeseen responses of landlords to circumvent legislation, with a significant bargaining advantage in all rural markets, be they land, labor, or credit (Gine, 2005). The asymmetry of political and economic power can hardly result in an efficient and harmonious outcome when there is significant conflict to begin with and inherent in any redistribution measure (Borras, 2003); on the contrary, conflicts between tenants and landlords will most likely increase in a post-market-assisted land reform environment.

The World Bank now acknowledges that the conventional view that titling promotes market-driven development by increasing security and the incentives to invest has been replaced by an "evolutionary theory" (Fortin, 2005) consistent with our human ecology approach, where individual land rights actually emerge over time from customary systems. There is ample evidence that titling has had a seriously negative impact on socially embedded rights, which are recognized by titling programs if customary tenure systems are as efficient (narrowly defined in the static sense and not including long-run ecological considerations) as owner-operated ones (Griffin et al., 2002; Toulmin and Quan, 2000; Whitehead and Tsikata, 2003; Yngstrom, 2002; Place and Hazell, 1993). Although the World Bank has recently updated its land policy to respect customary rights (2004), it still sees individual ownership rights of land as the best end-state as it represents the most modern form of landholding. Communal systems are mainly judged on narrowly defined efficiency criteria that do not take into account its role, albeit limited, in reducing inequality and poverty and providing a safety-net for the extremely poor.

Given the historical record of past land reforms in Nepal and contrary to conventional land reform belief systems, land rights and land titling in Nepal is endogenous rather than exogenous as assumed in the property-rights school of thought. In reality, many tenants have good reason to believe that they will retain their plots over several years due to an ongoing informal relationship with their landlord. In other words, farmers invest in land over which they have insecure title in order to solidify their claim (Brasselle *et al.*, 2002). It should be pointed out that there is no demonstrable link to date that a person who has a right of occupation through possession and not genuine ownership, implies a reduced incentive for investment (Feder and Feeny, 1991; Place and Hazell, 1993). What Jean-Philippe Platteau (2000) points out for Africa rings true in Nepal: "in customary land areas, basic use rights seem to be sufficient to induce landlords to invest, so that the adding of transfer rights ... does not appear to improve investment significantly" and further, "investment [itself actually] enhances security" (p. 57).

Most farmers would find it extremely difficult to make such investments given their lack of income, weakening their claim to a title. Moreover, as pointed out by Manji (2003), a fact which is invariably forgotten when discussing policies related to land reform: any credit that is likely to be granted will be used for more important expenditures such as food or medical care rather than investing it in land. Even if titling programs may reduce some credit constraints, the effect at best would be highly *selective*. Farmers who are on the margin of access to credit within the existing structure of capital-market imperfections may be helped by gaining title to their land, but the majority of tenants who are severely credit-constrained are entirely neglected, making economic mobility that much more difficult. Thus de jure differences in tenure status may have little, if any, de facto significance.

Even the 2003 World Bank–Deininger report admits, mechanization and the "scope to collateral ... to overcome imperfections inherent in the credit market ... will favor farmers who own larger amounts of land," (Deininger *et al.*, 2003a: pp. 30–31). The report even acknowledges a less than productive ruling elite, and the historical fact that change from collective to individual forms of tenure is anything but automatic, typically involving major historical transitions replete with conflicts, upheavals, and power struggles.

Also, the assumption in market-assisted land reform that decentralization guarantees both transparency and accountability (Borras, 2004), and has the potential for administrative efficiency and speedy policy implementation, is questionable. Contrary to conventional wisdom, power at the local level is often even more concentrated, more urban-biased, and more ruthlessly against the interests of the poor than even in Kathmandu, giving rise to a *more* unequal land distribution. This view negates the differentiation that is taking place within agriculture by treating all farmers as homogenous groups.

The World Bank's policy of promoting the removal of restrictions on land sales markets contradicts the idea that land sales markets are likely to be much less active than land rental markets. This notion is based on higher transactions costs and difficulties obtaining long-term loans. That general economic insecurity affects land prices is acknowledged by the World Bank. All the reasons that make it nearly impossible for the poor to purchase land through such markets also drive the speculative purchases by landlords (making the price out of reach) and cause the "distress sales" of the poor.

While a policy of promoting tenure security sounds good in theory, in a context of immense economic and political instability and insecurity over future economic development that would significantly affect land prices, coupled with very high and rising levels of poverty and inequality, and policy-bias favoring large landlords over the idealized small farmer, legally registering titles and rights will hardly be sufficient for viable small farmer production or as a means to reduce poverty. Greater transferability of land rights cannot lead to greater security in any meaningful way as the World Bank belief system and various other belief systems would have us believe. In fact, in the present context, it can only reaffirm the deep structural imbalances in Nepalese agriculture and reinforce the power of large landowners and those connected with, and thereby supported by, alliances that go up the ladder to the Nepali elite and their partnerships with global capital.

In summary then, 1964 saw attempts at several reforms: the creation of ceilings on ownership; redistribution; the issue of a small number of tenancy certifications; and regulation of tenancy arrangements such as rules about the percentage of a harvest that is sharecropped and the creation of the right of a certificate-holding tenant to a quarter claim on the underlying land. Evaluations of these reforms years later, found not just widespread lack of application of the reforms, but corruption, evasion, and in those areas that did experience some reform, multiple unintended consequences, such as the substitution of wage labor for tenancy contracts. The outcome was increased landlessness, inequality, and the marginality of farming.

Most importantly, tenancy was once an institution with some built-in flexibility. Depending on who you were, it could be either a means to simply survive or a stepping stone to better oneself, if only incrementally. These possibilities (survival or manipulation of tenancy for marginal improvement in opportunity-sets) for tenancy have been undermined by reforms that served in the end to reduce the opportunity set of marginal farmers. Worse, marginal farmers have not been faced with hoped-for-but-never-realized expanding urban or industrial opportunities. The outcome is that people starve, barely survive, or join the Maoists. Current proposals from the foreign-aid community to tinker with the tenure system will do little to change the opportunity-sets of any of the players. The proposal of the Maoists on the other hand, will do so, although how such a radical redistribution is to be accomplished is not at all clear, especially given the structural constraints of the political structure, limited farm size, poverty, landlessness, and ecological devastation.

Landowners found it easy to evade ceilings and redistribution. Given how long it took for your turn to come up, you could simply transfer ownership to close friends and relatives, so when any officials arrived in your area, you were off the hook. Even if your land was not up for redistribution (and very little was), you could evict your tenants and simply start hiring seasonal wage workers from India, or as far as Bhutan and Burma as they have done in the past.

Moreover, economic models that take the laws, culture, and characteristics of the *physical and natural environment* as unimportant or unrelated, and characteristics of particular *social arrangements* as undifferentiated and exogenous, inevitably conceal important dynamic feedback mechanisms that shape the economic outcomes under investigation. For example, even though share tenancy in Nepal may be formally abolished in the hopes of being replaced by fixed-rental contracts and private ownership, the majority of tenants in the rural population are still informal, and as efficient as owners in the second-best sense. Legalizing tenancy has had the adverse effect of pushing it underground while creating deep insecurity among landlords who already hold private claims to land. This insecurity has led landlords to resume self-cultivation, evict or rotate existing tenants, and increasingly hire non-Nepali labor who are not able to seek tenancy rights, resulting in increasing ethnic tensions between Indians and Nepalese in the Tarai, and if it were to happen again, could only provide further fuel for the insurgency and prolong the crisis.

Conclusions

As this chapter has argued, one entirely neglected yet powerful side effect of the "structural adjustment" programs pursued by the World Bank and the IMF in Nepal throughout the 1990s has been to greatly destabilize the ownership of property in rural Nepal. Rather than expanding markets giving options to poor farmers, it has set them traps – or perhaps, it has given them options that they are later extremely angry they have taken. Hence they take up arms. A human ecology framework provides much needed insight into how this seemingly anachronistic movement emerged to pose a threat – not just to Nepal but potentially to the whole of South Asia (in fact, over 25 percent of farmers in India are Maoist, especially in the northeast regions neighboring Nepal).

Past land reforms and further land reforms in Nepal have broken down communal social-insurance relationships more than they have improved efficiency by aligning incentives – especially since there is no evidence in Nepal that previous land-tenure arrangements were incentive-incompatible, and some evidence that previous arrangements captured at least some economies of scale. Previous land reform efforts suffered from not having an appreciation of the human ecology of Nepal, including the problem of large-scale social engineering: it is very difficult to get your interventions right from Kathmandu, let alone from Delhi or Washington. In the presence of a politically-powerful landlord class there on the ground, land reform can easily wind up not transferring property to the landless poor, but rather relieving the landed rich of local tax-and-governance burdens and increasing their bargaining power vis-à-vis their tenants. Moreover, although landlords may have been and continue to be a parasitic class, they are also interested in agricultural improvement, and also play an important intermediary role in Nepal's pre-modern safety net.

The old institutions in Nepal had grown up over a long time and have their wisdom, with which World Bank and IMF technocrats meddle, not at their peril, but at the peril of the Nepalese. The coming of neoliberal reform programs to destabilize property relations in the countryside has reduced the institutions of the social agreements that supported social solidarity that used to provide implicit insurance, and so has increased both risk and the perception of risk in Nepal. Instead of always destroying traditional tenure regimes, sometimes it is best to define them, if only because their true functionality is not understood until they are gone, or because the alternatives are no better and even much worse due to the multiple and complicated unintended consequences of tinkering with rural markets from policy set in Kathmandu.

With the onslaught of neoliberalism and globalization on an external level, and rising domestic economic crisis and conflict on an internal level, like many developing countries, Nepal provides a salient example of how pressure from extreme horizontal inequality, poverty, and macro-economic dysfunctionality can prove to be simply too powerful for the advocated legal mechanisms of suppression in land reform measures.[31] Moreover, such approaches reek of colonialism as it is the job for "development experts" to impose a full Western-style set of property-rights in all things, complete with land administration systems, titles, and deed registries. In the desperate drive to "Westernize" or "proletarianize" agricultural labor, market-assisted land reforms falsely assume liberalization, inequality, political instability, and insurgency are mere irritants, market distortions, or negative externalities.[32] Unlike all other belief systems, the human ecology system takes all these structural variables to be explicitly related rather than co-existing by chance.

With rising input prices (especially land), falling output prices, little if any infrastructure for the majority of poor farmers, full-blown incorporation into the world economy on increasingly unequal terms since the late 1980s, and a recently failed experiment with democracy, it is no wonder the World Bank's new land reforms rely on decentralization and markets. From a human ecology perspective, the current push for market-assisted land reform in Nepal is based more on political arguments to pacify the current Maoist insurgency than the alleged economic benefits of efficiency and equity in both the land sales and land rental markets. Also, with market-led land reforms come the real danger of *increasing* inequality and landlessness as people will still need to harvest natural resources for their very survival. On the other hand, Maoist calls for radical land reforms will also be met with similar results unless broader structural variables are explicitly taken into account in the overall human ecology of Nepal. Moreover, the uncertainty of the impact of a radical redistribution of land on deforestation, soil erosion, and sustainable land-use only serve to make land-market interventions in general, and land-reform measures in particular, even less attractive as a policy lever.

While land reform can make a tremendous difference in the lives of the rural poor, as it has in East Asian land reforms, it is clearly not a panacea for rural poverty. For Nepal, and possibly many other developing countries, in the absence of broader macro-economic policies that support agriculture in general, and small-scale producers in particular, land reform alone will not bring substantial income gains to the poor, nor a reduction in poverty or inequality. Indeed, if the macro-economic context is quite adverse to agriculture as is the case of Nepal – for example, if exchange rate overvaluation and trade policies make agricultural imports so cheap that local growers cannot compete – then to encourage the poor to seek to earn a living in farming is to lure them into debt and penury. For this reason, Acevedo (1996: 209) observed that in El Salvador in the 1990s, "a small farm (particularly one encumbered by debt for its acquisition) and access to agricultural credit is an economic curse to be wished only on one's worst enemy."

Good policy analysis and formulation of proposals about what is to be done then need to be thoroughly anchored in an understanding of the opportunity sets in front of various classes of people and how they use them to survive or better themselves and not in theoretical fantasies. In setting policy, some kind of fair internal process needs to happen. The often non-economic values of Gaia and Athena worshippers need to take on as much weight as those of the worshippers of the god of Efficiency. The relative weighting of these economic and non-economic values should not be done by the foreign-aid world and its one-size-fits-all belief system, but by the society itself and its various constituencies.

Tenancy and associated legislation, landlessness, inequality, agricultural stagnation, tourism, and the overall political economy of the country have each experienced rapid change in their structure, extent, and interactions over the past fifty-five years in response to a variety of structural factors – economic, cultural, political, institutional, and demographic processes. This chapter suggests that policy-design based on a broader human ecology approach will be far more effective in achieving the stated objectives of poverty alleviation, growth, and reduced inequality in agriculture.

Finally, this chapter should be viewed as having provided the basis for a methodological approach, rather than a methodology per se. Such an approach towards land reform implies that people, their environment and society are not separable by rigid and separable boundaries. The boundaries between them are porous and flexible allowing interchange and influence: the unity here is not the uniformity of the fragmented individualism, rather it rests on the continuity of life in its interconnectedness; there are subtle and (unintended) complex connections between Nepal's process of uneven development and its internal microeconomic conditions, including land use, the decay of the ecosystem, breakdown of civil society, agricultural intensification, and private-property rights, just as there are connections in the search for a more sustainable human ecology at all these levels.

Notes

* Ravi Bhandari is an Associate Professor of Economics at St. Mary's College. This chapter has benefited from seminar participants at the annual AEA meetings: Chicago January 7, 2007 "Sustainability of the Global System: New Insights from Human Ecology Economics," sponsored by the Association of Social Economics; the Indira Gandhi Institute of Development Research in Mumbai, India, January 2007; and the International Conference on Social Values and Economic Life, Twelfth World Congress of Social Economics University of Amsterdam June 8–10, 2007. This chapter also benefited from excellent comments received from James K. Boyce, Carmen Dianna-Deere, R. Radhakrishna, George Akerlof, Bradford de Long, M.H. Suryanarayana, Peter Reeves, Saturnino Borras, David Moore, James Putzel, Terence Byres, Mohan Rao, Aaron Bobrow-Strain, Frances Stewart, Ambreena Manji, Terence Byres, Elizabeth Fortin, Roy Allen, Donald Snyder, Guillaume Daudin, Antonio Casella, Edward Chilcote. Thanks to my wife for her encouragement and editing as well as Marco D'Constanza for his research assistance in this project. Financial support is acknowledged from the St. Mary's Faculty Development Fund.

1 Some estimates put the death toll over 12,000, while more than 200,000 have been internally displaced. Hundreds of thousands more have fled to neighboring India (Global IDP Database, 2004). Tens of thousands of school children have been abducted and taken to indoctrination camps (Human Rights Watch, 2003). School teachers, government officials, field staff of development organizations, as well as ordinary citizens have been targeted for extortion (Gersony, 2003; Global IDP Database, 2004; Human Rights Watch, 2003; Rajdhani, 2004). Dwindling government control in rural regions has interrupted or halted effective development efforts for many NGOs, international organizations, and donors.

2 Second-generation land reforms are referred to in the literature as market-assisted (de Janvry and Sadoulet, 2002), market-led (Borras, 2003), market-friendly (Carter 2004), market-mediated (Ghimire, 2001), negotiated or community-based (Deininger and Biswanger, 1999), and neo-populist neoclassical (Byres, 2004).

3 See the special issue in the (2004) *Journal of Agrarian Change* (4) for an alternative critique of redistributive land reform measures. An intriguing response by Keith Griffin to these critiques is also included (Griffin *et al.*, 2004).

4 Bucking the publishing trend, this article is equally critical of both redistributive and tenurial reforms. Alternative theories critique redistributive measures (see the special issue in the *Journal of Agrarian Change*, Vol. 4, 2004) while neoclassical economists generally critique tenurial reforms.

5 In many countries such as Vietnam (Adelman, 1995), Jamaica (Atkins, 1988), Mexico (Bobrow-Strain, 2004), Brazil, Pakistan, India (Dyer, 2004), South Africa (Sender and Johnston, 2004), Zimbabwe (Bernstein, 2004), Honduras and Nicaragua (Carter, 2004), Columbia (Borras, 2003), Nepal, including an econometric critique of the alleged inverse relationship between farm size and productivity (Bhandari, 2006), Philippines (Ramachandran and Swaminathan, 2002); Africa in general (see Place and Hazell, 1993); sub-Saharan Africa (Fortin, 2005), Honduras (Jansen and Roquas, 1998), Nicaragua (Broegaard, 2005), and Laos (Ducourtieux *et al.*, 2005), land reforms have not only failed but also reveal a contradiction that looms large in new land policy. If land reform is based on the capitalizing small farm in the context of a withdrawing state, its implementation requires strong and repressive state intervention as in the cases of East Asia where land reform was successful and paved the way for industrialization. Titles are generally found not to decrease insecurity of the marginal farmer, but merely formalize and modernize the sources which can be used to contest rights in land. Needless to say, the precise mechanisms for growth and equity are mis-specified.

6 Interestingly, the assumed historical inevitability of Western style capitalism permeates

the entire history of economic thought from Adam Smith to Karl Marx (including updated versions of theories of "peasants") fall victim to a form of teleological imperialism in which some implicit end-state becomes the norm against which region-specific problems are diagnosed – which diagnosis then provides the basis for a policy prescription. The multitude and diverse range of agrarian relations and institutions are only conceived in relation to Western capitalism, if only in opposition to it. It is not surprising, then, that these relations themselves are poorly understood. A country's "economic takeoff" (Rostow, 1960) is understood as a successful transformation of "feudal" relations into capitalist ones. However, for Nepal and many poor countries, there is no sight of even reaching take-off speed, let alone making the runway. The implication is that poor countries like Nepal suffer from remnants of a "feudal" past and are therefore described as being in "prolonged transition." Agrarian relations are generally understood as a barrier to the process of economic development, rooted in the non-economic world of culture and tradition, reminiscent of colonial development ideology.

7 Bromley (2004) eloquently points out the Eurocentric fallacies in much of our current theorizing on land policy:

> We show little inclination to ponder the so-called mysteries of Swiss livestock management under common property between June and September when cattle graze in the high Alps, but somehow feel compelled to lament the commons dilemma when we encounter it in Nepal or Botswana. Coherent policy about rangelands and forests awaits the day when we stop seeing many of them as somehow in need of explanation and instead seeing them as coherent *human* responses to a set of *ecological* circumstances that reward mobility, flexibility, and adaptability.

8 Sender and Johnston (2004) point out how the Jeffersonian vision of the family farm masks the prevailing conditions of poverty by excluding the landless and semi-landless, who must depend on wages to survive daily. They are also assumed to suffer less poverty and always find more opportunities for on- and off-farm wage employment than the small farmer. An important contradiction arises entirely unresolved by even successful land reforms that benefit small farmers – since if small farms are supposed to rely on their comparatively cheaper family labor input to be successful, then how will they simultaneously become the engine for growth and employment?

9 Two main reasons exist why land sales go in reverse in Nepal. The first is the familiar chicken-and-egg problem: the poor need credit to buy land, but without land they lack the collateral to secure loans. The second is that in practice the distribution of land in Nepal is determined by political power rather than changes in relative prices, as the standard economic theory predicts. Historically, inequitable land ownership patterns did not originate in the free play of market forces; rather they emerged through processes involving conquest, fraud, and outright force. Today political power and land rights remain fused in rural societies, each reinforcing the other. For landed elites, the value of land lies therefore not only in its agricultural productivity, but also in the power, status, and economic advantages that land ownership confers. These economic advantages include access to subsidized credit, favorable tax treatment of agricultural incomes, and landholding as a hedge against inflation. For discussion, see Binswanger *et al.* (1995: 2710–2711). Hence, speculation on land is expected and prices are far out of reach for the average farmer, undermining the redistributive impact of land reform, i.e. only those who can afford to buy land will buy land as epitomized in the World Bank's "willing seller–willing buyer" market approach to land reform. Efforts to promote "market-assisted land reform" by earmarking credit for land purchases for small farmers often founder on this fundamental and structural stumbling block.

10 Kevane (1996) shows a positive relationship between wealth or size of farm and output even when the supervision constraint is controlled, which should favor small

farms. Wealthier or bigger farms have less need to engage in off-farm labor, so the amount of labor available for production is higher. However, because of rental-market imperfections, they are unable to match this labor with additional land, so that labor input per unit of land rises with farm size. This mechanism seems to be at work not only in Sudan, but also Nepal where a positive relationship between size and productivity seem to exist (see Bhandari, 2006).

11 From its position advocating the abandonment of customary communal systems and the subdivision of the commons into plots over which freehold title would be granted (Deininger and Binswanger, 1999), today there is an official recognition, and sometimes support, that customary or communal systems often provide secure and long-term land rights. At the same time though, the World Bank's recent formulation still sees individual property rights as preferable; group rights can only be acceptable under several conditions, at low levels of development. The new policy emphasizes the land-rental market, whereas the older policy the land-sales market, but the strange priors remain unchanged (World Bank, 2004).

12 Donor narratives have largely created the mythology that pre-1951 Nepal was an isolated medieval kingdom without the most rudimentary infrastructure; this dominant discourse serves to de-emphasize the complexity and sophistication of Nepal's human ecology processes.

13 In fact, according to recent statistics, around 43 percent of the government's budget is financed by aid (CBS, 2004). In addition, there are aid inflows to NGOs, many of whom then fund other NGOs within the economy. These flows may be relatively small in the total portfolio of donors, but they are huge in relation to Nepal's tiny economy, and dwarf the effects of other sources of foreign exchange, which are mainly through tourism and garment exports. Such aid is what explains how the capital Kathmandu is literally swarming with donors and experts of all varieties and many nationalities. As Easterly argues in "White Man's Burden" (2006), aid advocates measure success by how much money rich countries spend. Praising the G-8 industrialized nations for their increased aid to Nepal (to help King Gyanendra squash the People's War) is like reviewing Hollywood films based on their budgets.

14 In several countries, disputes over land rights are at the core of what later appears as ethnic violence. In Kenya, the Kikuyu benefited from colonial policies increasing land rights and were also the main beneficiaries of educational improvements and business credit programs after independence. Kimenyi and Njuguna (2002) explain that this caused a negative reaction against the Kikuyu, leading to their expulsion from Masai-land after independence. In Senegal, land-rights disputes were also a key factor in the Casamance civil war; the conflict started with large-scale expropriation of indigenous land in 1979 (Humphreys and Mohamed, 2002). Similarly, it is hard to find any account of the civil war in El Salvador that does not emphasize the highly unequal distribution of wealth and land (see, for example, Johnstone *et al.*, 1997).

15 Stewart (2005) convincingly argues that horizontal inequalities, in addition to the well-known vertical inequality measures captures in the Gini that compares individual to individual, matter both from the perspective of the well-being of individuals within groups, who are concerned about how their group is faring relative to others, and instrumentally, through the impact of group inequalities in reducing growth potential and provoking violence. In the economic sphere, inequalities in ownership of land in Nepal are significant, as well as in employment and income. Where there is considerable intra-group inequality as well as inter-group, vertical inequality will be high. The fact that group inequalities can have a direct impact on members' well-being is one of the most important aspects. People's well-being may be affected not only by their individual circumstances, but also by how well their group is doing relative to others. This is partly because membership of the group is part of a person's own identity, and partly because relative impoverishment of the group increases the perceptions of members that they are likely to be trapped permanently in a poor position, or, if they

have managed to do better than many in the group, that they are likely to fall back into poverty. In a recent innovative piece, Akerlof and Kranton (2000) enter the relative position of the group into a person's welfare function.

16 Besides Nepal, group inequalities have been found to be a factor in provoking conflict in: Côte d'Ivoire, Rwanda, Northern Ireland, Chiapas, and the Sudan to mention just a few (Gurr, 1993; Stewart, 2000; Gurr and Moore, 1997; Langer, 2005; Murshed and Gates, 2005).

17 Murshed and Gates (2005) also find a significant correlation between landlessness and the number of fatalities in the conflict. However, other accounts such as Thapa (2004) attribute the conflict mostly to poverty and under-development of the country. Gersony (2003) and Wagle (2006) both find that caste and ethnic divisions are not a major contributor to the conflict. There is also the possibility that government repression might have generated further grievances which led to greater support for the Maoist rebels. Nepal has a history of human rights abuses by the police forces, such as the crackdown against CPN political activists as part of a highly contentious police operation (Operation Romeo) in the districts of Rolpa and Rukum in 1994. As would be expected, where poverty is especially pervasive, as in Western Nepal, the Maoist insurgency is strongest. Unlike so many rebel movements elsewhere in the world (including in Iraq), however, the Maoists do not identify themselves as defenders of a particular ethnic or communal group. Therefore, one generalization that has been advanced is that the Maoist uprising in Nepal points to the dangers of focusing too narrowly on the ethnicity, important and neglected as it has been, to the exclusion of class interests (Fisher, 1999).

18 This is largely because: (i) family background including nutrition and educational levels influence a child's chances in life; (ii) social networks and social agreements operate disproportionately within a group and less between groups – indeed economists and sociologists regard having more in-group than out-group interactions as a defining characteristic of a group.

19 Given the fact that social and economic stability are still very distant for Nepal, interference by outside powers such as the U.S. and India is expected to only contribute to prolonging the agony of the country.

20 The development industry has greatly contributed to new luxury services that cater to the rich. It is no wonder that the lifestyles and working conditions of foreign expatriates are well removed from those of the people they have supposedly come to assist. The influx of international development workers has resulted in a market for expensive commodities, and the shops which crowd these neighborhoods in Kathmandu take pride in catering to the very rich. For example, the World Bank has its offices in Kathmandu's premier five star luxury hotel, the Yak and Yeti, whose famous casino, like all five star hotels, permits access to only non-Nepali citizens. In addition, although the primary beneficiaries of aid are allegedly the rural poor, it should be pointed out that there is a virtual absence of any international presence outside of Kathmandu.

21 What is even more telling is that even though donors have expressed concern over the dismal performance rate in Nepal, they are all very reluctant to pull out. Nepal's experience has been that donors are willing to support it as long at they show a willingness to comply with their demands (which has always been the case) – the continuing flow of aid substantiates this perspective. The World Bank, for example, which has over three decades of experience in Nepal, evaluated its overall performance in Nepal as unsatisfactory – yet it later *upgraded* its lending program (World Bank, 2003b).

22 A further irony is that there is ample evidence that although the Maoists and the Monarchy are ideologically poles apart, in present day Nepal they both seem to share a common stand, at least in the short-term: they hate the entire multi-electoral democratic system (Adhikary, 2005). Indeed, senior Maoist leader Baburam Bhattarai has publicly claimed at a recent press conference in Delhi (January 12, 2007) that he had

forged a working unity with King Birendra a few months before he was slain in a mysterious palace carnage, in June 2001.

23 In 1995, the government formed the High Level Land Reform Commission to suggest corrective measures. Although the report is not available to the public, one can assume that it calls for a further reduction in land ceilings which has raised the question of "optimal holding size" or "economically viable minimum size of holding." The issue is moot because in the Nepalese Tarai, intense demographic pressure functionally puts automatic ceilings on land. Freeing the land market is not likely to lead to large scale selling of land by large farmers to small farmers or the private sector because of the high premium on land due to its collateral value. Reducing ceilings in the interest of redistribution would face a similar problem in a population-induced competitively determined land market.

24 See Goeschl and Igliori (2006), who convincingly argue that that the limitations of a static property rights structure narrowly focuses on the management of the natural resource base of the community is quite evident, particularly when communities operating a severely constrained production function is expected to somehow (with more defined rights) to develop economically in brutal market competition with unconstrained monopolistic and powerful firms.

25 See Jonakin (1997) who argues that the impact of structural adjustment and stabilization polices in Nicaragua in the 1980s increased credit market imperfections, undermining any potential gains from previous land reforms. Deteriorating terms of trade against agriculture have also been shown to wipe out any potential gains in land reform for Tanzania and Egypt in the 1970s (Powelson and Stock, 1987). Still others go even further showing how in the context of domestic and international instability, market-based approaches in agriculture will most likely *increase* poverty and inequality by reinforcing colonial legacies of dual economies and regulatory systems (Fortin, 2005) while others explicitly show how these policies are simply tailored to larger privatization, deregulation, and liberalization policies (Patnaik, 2003).

26 de Janvry and Sadoulet (2003) found an inverse relation between the weakness of property rights and land rental markets for Latin American countries, suggesting the importance of the informal economy, often strengthened by the same policies of neoliberalism that were designed to remove it.

27 For discussion of the efficiency impacts of sharecropping and the critical role of culture and social agreements in shaping economic outcomes that is ignored in the vast literature on sharecropping see Bhandari, 2007.

28 It should be pointed out that neither hired labor nor tenancy arrangements completely resolve the inefficiencies that result from a dichotomy between the ownership of land and labor on it in a first-best sense. The strange prior of land reforms lies in the assumption that reform can mythically end this dichotomy by fiat and bring forth higher agricultural output as well as a more egalitarian distribution of that output. As IFAD (one of the leading proponents of land reforms in developing countries) argues, if the poor get a bigger share of asset control or benefits, efficiency and economic growth also improves. By creating a bigger pie as well as a wider slice for the poor, land reform offers a potent strategy for reducing rural poverty. If land reform has positive spillover effects on the urban economy, too, as the East Asian experience suggests, then its contribution to poverty reduction can be even greater (IFAD, 2004: 71).

29 One notable exception is de Janvry (1997) who explains sharecropping efficiency by the important role of kinship relations between landlords and tenants.

30 Even if redistribution leads to a higher average farm size, whether the farm is sustainable is taken for granted in almost all calculations. It has been estimated that the minimum feasible holding in Nepal, below which its output is too small to maintain the family at what is considered to be a reasonable standard, is between three and four hectares in the Tarai. Floors might also be established with regards to full employment, including full employment of farm draught animals. The inverse relation

though, suggests an optimal farm size of less than two hectares. Therefore, the concept of viability itself imposes severe limits to redistributive land reform if not making the case altogether moot to begin with.

31 Nepal is an excellent example of a society with a relatively unchanging value of vertical inequality but an increasing level of horizontal inequality. A human ecology approach implies that policies aimed at reducing poverty or vertical inequality may not be effective unless a group approach is adopted where there are severe horizontal inequalities or where social exclusion of various groups are significant.

32 The political instability of Gyanendra's coup demonstrated that democracy was not inevitable as the market fundamentalist belief system suggests and as reflected in end-of-history (Fukuyama, 1993) and third-wave-of-democratization (Huntington, 1991).

Bibliography

Acevedo, Carlos. 1996. "Structural Adjustment, the Agricultural Sector, and the Peace Process." In James K. Boyce (ed.) *Economic Policy for Building Peace: The Lessons of El Salvador*. Boulder: Lynne Rienner, pp. 209–231.

Adelman, Irma. 1995. *The Selected Essays of Irma Adelman*. Volume I: Institutions and Development Strategies. Volume II: Dynamics and Income Distribution. Aldershot: Elgar Edward Press. See Preface by Paul Streeten.

Adhikary, D. 2005. "Monarchy Stands Firm." *Asia Times*. 23 July.

Akerlof, George and Rachael Kranton. "Economics and Identity." *The Quarterly Journal of Economics*. Vol. 115 (3): 715–753.

Alavi, Hamza. 1973. "The State in Post-Colonial Societies: Pakistan and Bangladesh." In K. Gough and Hari Sharma (eds.) *Imperialism and Revolution in South Asia*. London and New York: Monthly Review Press.

Alesina, Alberto, Reza Baqir, and William Easterly. 1999. "Public Goods and Ethnic Divisions." *Quarterly Journal of Economics*. Vol. 114 (4): 1243–1284.

Amin, Samir. 1990. *Delinking: Towards a Polycentric World*. London: Zed Books.

Arrow, K.J. 1968. "The Economics of Moral Hazard: Further Comment." *American Economic Review*. Vol. 58: 537–539.

Asian Development Bank. 1982. *Kathmandu*. Volume I and II. Nepal: Nepal Agriculture Sector Strategy Study, His Majesty's Government of Nepal.

Asian Regional Team for Employment Promotion (ARTEP). 1994. *The Challenge for Nepal*. Bangkok: ILO.

Atkins, Fiona. 1988. "Land Reform: A Failure of Neoclassical Theorization?" *World Development*. Vol. 16 (8): 935–1946.

Bahadur, K.C., Ram. 1996. "Land Reform: Progress and Prospects in Nepal." *Research Report Series, no. 2*. Kathmandu: Winrock International Institute for Agricultural Development.

Banaji, J. 2002. "The Metamorphoses of Agrarian Capitalism." *Journal of Agrarian Change*. Vol. 2 (1): 96–119.

Banerjee, Abhijit and Maitreesh Ghatak. 2002. "Empowerment and Efficiency: Tenancy Reform in West Bengal." *Journal of Political Economy*. Vol. 110 (2): 239–280.

Baral, Lok Raj. 2000. "Clash of Values: Governance, Political Elite and Democracy in Nepal." In D. Kumar (ed.) *Domestic Conflict and Crisis of Governability in Nepal*. Kathmandu: Center for Nepal and Asian Studies.

Bardhan, Pranab K. 1979. "Wages and Unemployment in Poor Agrarian Economies: A Theoretical and Empirical Analysis." *Journal of Political Economy*. Vol. 87 (3): 479–500.

——. 1984. *Land, Labor, and Rural Poverty*. Oxford: Oxford University Press.

Barham, Bradford, Stephen Borcher, and Michael Carter. 2004. "The Impact of Market-Friendly Reforms on Credit and Land Markets in Honduras and Nicaragua." *World Development*. Vol. 33 (1):87–105.

Barker, Randolph and Violeta Cordova. 1978. "Labor Utilization in Rice Production." In: *Economic Consequences of the New Rice Technology*. Los Banos, Philippines: International Rice Research Institute.

Battachan, Krishna B. 2001. "Sociological Perspectives on Gender Issues in Changing Nepalese Society." In L.K. Manadhar and K.B. Battachan (eds.) *Gender and Democracy in Nepal*. Kathmandu: Tribhuvan University.

Bernstein, Henry. 2004. "Changing Before Our Very Eyes: Agrarian Questions and the Politics of Land in Capitalism Today." *Journal of Agrarian Change*. Vol. 4 (1–2): 190–225.

——. 2006. "Once Were/Still Peasants? Farming in the Globalizing South." *New Political Economy*. Vol. 11 (3): 399–406.

Bhandari, Ravi. 1994. "*Dynamic Efficiency in 'Semi-Feudal' Contracts through Interlocked Markets.*" *USAID Report #145823566757*. USAID: Nepal.

——. 2001. "Is the Land Tenure System a Constraint on Economic Growth? A Comprehensive Theoretical and Empirical Analysis of Nepalese Agriculture." *World Bank Report*. Kathmandu: World Bank.

——. 2006. "Searching for a Weapon of Mass Production in Nepal: Can Market-Assisted Land Reform Live Up to its Promise?" *Journal of Developing Societies*. Vol. 22 (2): 111–143.

——. 2007 (forthcoming). "The Role of Social Distance in Sharecropping Efficiency: The Case of Two Rice Growing Villages in the Nepalese Tarai." *Journal of Economic Studies*. Vol. 34 (3–4).

Binswanger, A., Klaus Deininger, and Gershon Feder. 1995. "Power, Distortions, Revolt, and Reform in Agricultural Relations." In: J.R. Behrman and T.N. Srinivasan (eds.) *Handbook of Development Economics*. Amsterdam: Elsevier.

Blaikie, Piers, John Cameron, and David Seddon. 1980. *Nepal in Crisis: Growth and Stagnation in the Periphery*. Oxford: Clarendon Press.

——. 2002. *Peasants and Workers in Nepal*. New Delhi: Adroit Publishers.

Bobrow-Strain, Aaron. 2004. "(Dis) Accords: The Politics of Market-Assisted Land Reforms in Chiapas, Mexico." *World Development*. Vol. 32 (6): 897–903.

Borras, Saturnino. 2003. "Questioning Market-Led Agrarian Reform: Experiences from Brazil, Colombia and South Africa." *Journal of Agrarian Change*. Vol. 3 (3): 367–394.

——. 2004. "Redistributive Land Reform in Public (Forest) Land? Rethinking Theory and Practice with Evidence from the Philippines." *Progress in Development Studies*. Vol. 14 (1): 143–175.

Boyce, James K., Peter Rosset, and Elizabeth A. Stanton. 2005. Land Reform and Sustainable Development. Political Economy Research Institute. Working Paper Series 98.

Brasselle, A.S., F. Gaspart, and J.P. Platteau. 2002. "Land Tenure Security and Investment Incentives: Puzzling Evidence from Burkina Faso." *Journal of Development Economics*. Vol. 67 (2): 373–418.

Bray, John, Leiv Lunde, and S. Mansoob Murshed. 2003. "Nepal: Economic Drivers of the Maoist Insurgency." In Karen Ballentine and Jake Sherman (eds.) *The Political Economy of Armed Conflict: Beyond Greed and Grievance*. Boulder, Colorado: Lynne Rienner Publishers.

Broegaard, Rikke J. 2005. "Land Tenure Insecurity and Inequality in Nicaragua." *Development and Change.* Vol. 36 (5): 845–864.

Bromley, Daniel. 2000. "The Prejudices of Property Rights: On Individualism, Specificity and Security in Property Regimes." *Development Policy Review.* Vol. 18 (4): 365–389.

——. 2004. "Property Rights: Locke, Kant, and Peirce and the Logic of Volitional Pragmatism." In Henry Jacobs (ed.) *Private Property in the 21st Century.* Cheltenham: Elgar Edward Press.

——. 2005. The Diminishing Assets of the Poor: Immerization in Sub-Saharan Africa. Working Paper. Department of Agriculture and Resource Economics. University of Madison.

Byres, Terence J. 2004. "Introduction: Contextualizing and Interrogating the GKI Case for Redistributive Land Reform." *Journal of Agrarian Change.* Vol. 4 (1–2): 1–16.

Carter, Michael, Stephen Boucher, and Bradford Barham. 2004. "The Impact of Market Friendly Reforms on the Operation of Credit and Land Markets in Honduras and Nicaragua." *World Development.* Vol. 33: 107–128.

Chandak, Naresh. 2003. "Quiet Governance Revolution: World Bank." *Nepali Times.* 31: 6.

Collier, P. and Hoeffler, A. 2002. Greed and Grievance in Civil War. World Bank Working Paper.

——. 2005. *Understanding Civil War: Evidence and Analysis.* Volume 1. World Bank Publications.

Collier, Paul, V.L. Elliott, Havard Hegre, Anke Hoeffler, Marta Reynal-Querol, and Nicholas Sambanis. 2003. *Breaking the Conflict Trap: Civil War and Development Policy.* Washington, DC: World Bank.

Cramer, C. 2003. "Does Inequality Cause Conflict?" *Journal of International Development.* Vol. 15: 397–415.

Deininger, Klaus. 2004. *Causes and Consequences of Civil Strife: Micro-Level Evidence from Uganda.* Mimeo. World Bank.

Deininger, Klaus and Hans Binswanger. 1999. "The Evolution of the World Bank's Land Policy: Principles, Experiences, and Future Challenges." *World Bank Research Observer.* Vol. 14 (2): 247–276.

Deininger, Klaus and S. Jin. 2003. Land Sales and Rental Markets in Transition: Evidence from Rural Vietnam. World Bank Policy Research Paper 3013.

De Janvry, Alain and E. Sadoulet, 2002. Land Reforms in Latin America: Ten Lessons toward a Contemporary Agenda. Prepared for the World Bank's Latin American Land Policy Workshop, Pachuca, Mexico.

——. 2003. "Rural Poverty in Latin America: Determinants and Exit Paths." In: S. Mathur and D. Pachico (eds.) *Agricultural Research and Poverty Reduction: Some Issues and Evidence. Economics and Impact Series 2.* Centro Internacional de Agricultura Tropical (CIAT), Cali: Colombia.

De Janvry, Alain, E. Sadoulet and Marcel Fafchamps. 1991. "Peasant Household Behavior with Missing Markets: Some Paradoxes Explained." *Economic Journal.* Vol. 101: 1400–1417.

De Janvry, Alain, A.G. Gordillo, J.P. Platteau, and E. Sadoulet. 2002. *Access to Land, Rural Poverty and Public Action.* Oxford: Oxford University Press.

Deraniyagala, Sonali. 2005. "The Political Economy of Civil Conflict in Nepal." *Oxford Development Studies.* Vol. 33 (1): 47–62.

De Soto, Hernando. 2000. *The Mystery of Capital: Why Capitalism Triumphs in the West and Fails Everywhere Else.* London: Bantam.

DeVries, Lucia. 2003. "The Real Struggle Has Just Begun." *Kathmandu Post.* February 19, 10th anniversary special supplement.

Duclos, J.-Y., J. Esteban, and D. Ray. 2004. "Polarization: Concepts, Measurement, Estimation." *Econometrica.* Vol. 72 (6): 1737–1772.

Ducourtieux, Olivier, J. Laffort, and S. Sacklokham. 2005. "Land Policy and Farming Practices in Laos." *Development and Change.* Vol. 36 (3): 499–526.

Durand-Lasserve, Alain and Lauren Royston. 2002. *Secure Land Tenure for the Urban Poor in Developing Countries.* London: Earth Scan.

Dutta, B., D. Ray, and K. Sengupta. 1989. "Contracts with Eviction in Infinitely Repeated Principal Agent Relationships." In Pranab Bardhan (ed.) *The Economic Theory of Agrarian Institutions.* Oxford: Clarendon Press.

Dyer, Graham. 2004. "Redistributive Land Reform: No April Rose. The Poverty of Berry and Cline and GKI on the Inverse Relationship." *Journal of Agrarian Change.* Vol. 4 (1–2): 45–72.

Escobar, Arturo. 1995. *Encountering Development. The Making and Unmaking of the Third World.* Princeton: Princeton University Press.

Economist, The. 2004. A Failing State. December 4. p. 10.

Ellingsen, T. 2000. "Colourful Community or Ethnic Witches' Brew: Multiethnicity and Domestic Conflict During and After the Cold War." *The Journal of Conflict Resolution.* Vol. 44 (2): 228–249.

Ellsworth, Lynn. 2004. A Place in the World: A Review of the Global Debate on Tenure Security. Ford Foundation Report.

Fafchamps, Marcel. 1992. "Solidarity Networks in Preindustrial Societies: Rational Peasants With a Moral Economy." *Economic Development and Cultural Change.* Vol. 41 (1): 147–176.

Fanon, Frantz. 1965. The Wretched of the Earth. New York: Grove Weidenfeld. See Preface by Jean-Paul Sartre. Tr. Constance Farrington.

Faruqee, Rashid and Kevin Carey. 1997. Land Markets in South Asia: What Have We Learned? World Bank Policy Research Paper. Washington, DC: World Bank.

Fearon, James and David Laitin. 2003. "Ethnicity, Insurgency, and Civil War." *American Political Science Review.* Vol. 97: 75–90.

Feder, Gershon and David Feeny. 1991. "Land Tenure and Property Rights: Theory and Implications for Development Policy." *The World Bank Economic Review.* Vol 5 (1): 135–153.

Feder, Gershon and Raymond Noronha. 1987. "Land Rights Systems and Agricultural Development in Sub-Saharan Africa." *World Bank Research Observer.* Vol. 2 (2): 143–169.

Fisher, J.F. 1999. "Review of Gellner, D., J. Whelpton, and J. Paff-Czarnecka, Nationalism and Ethnicity in a Hindu Kingdom." *Journal of Asian Studies.* Vol. 58 (3): 863–865.

Fortin, Elizabeth. 2005. "Reforming Land Reform: The World Bank and the Globalization of Agriculture." *Social and Legal Studies.* Vol. 14 (2): 147–177.

Frank, Andre Gunder. 1998. *ReOrient: Global Economy in the Asian Age.* Berkeley, CA: University of California Press.

Fukuyama, F. 1993. *The End of History and the Last Man.* New York: Harper Collins.

Gersony, R. 2003. *Western Nepal Conflict Assessment.* Portland: Mercy Corps.

Ghimire, Krishna. 2001. *Land Reform and Peasant Livelihoods: The Social Dynamics of Rural Poverty and Agrarian Reforms in Developing Countries.* Colchester: UNRISD.

Gine, Xavier. 2005. Cultivate or Rent out? Land Security in Rural Thailand. World Bank Working Paper.

Global IDP Project and Database. 2004. *Internal Displacement: A Global Overview of Trends and Displacements.* Geneva. (Feb).

Goeschl, Timo and Danilo Camargo Igliori. 2006. "Property Rights for Biodiversity Conservation and Development: Extractive Reserves in the Brazilian Amazon." *Development and Change.* Vol. 37 (2): 427–451.

Griffin, K., A.Z. Rahman Khan, and Amy Ickowitz. 2002. "Poverty and the Distribution in Land." *Journal of Agrarian Change.* Vol. 2 (3): 279–330.

Griffin, K., A.Z. Rahman Khan, and Amy Ickowitz. 2004. "In Defence of Neo-Classical Neo-Populism." *Journal of Agrarian Change.* Vol. 4 (3): 361–386.

Grossman, Herschel I. 1994. "Production, Appropriation, and Land Reform." *The American Economic Review.* Vol. 84 (3): 705–712.

Gurr, Ted Robert. 1993. "Why Minorities Rebel: A Global Analysis of Communal Mobilization and Conflict since 1945." *International Political Science Review.* Vol. 14 (2): 161–201.

Gurr, Ted and Will H. Moore. 1997. "Ethnopolitical Rebellion: A Cross-Sectional Analysis of the 1980s with Risk Assessments for the 1990s." *American Journal of Political Science.* Vol. 41 (4): 1079–1103.

Hachhethu, K. 2004. "The Nepali State and the Maoist Insurgency, 1996–2001." In M. Hutt (ed.) *Himalayan People's War: Nepal's Maoist Rebellion.* Bloomington, IN: Indiana University Press. Pp. 58–78.

Hemming, Richard, Michael Kell, and Selma Mahfouz. 2002. The Effectiveness of Fiscal Policy in Stimulating Economic Activity: A Review of the Literature. IMF Working Paper. WP/02/208. International Monetary Fund.

Himalayan Times. 2005. Nepal Does Not Need U.N. Mediation: Brahimi. July 15.

HMG, Nepal. 1983. *Agricultural Statistics of Nepal.* Kathmandu: Department of Food and Agricultural Marketing, Ministry of Agriculture.

———. 1995. *National Sample Census of Agriculture, 1991/1992.* Kathmandu: Central Bureau of Statistics, National Planning Commission.

Human Development Report. 2005. United Nations Development Project. Oxford University Press.

Human Rights Watch. 2003. Nepal/*Bhutan: Bilateral Talks Fail to Solve Refugee Crisis.* New York.

Humphreys, Macartan and Habaye ag Mohamed. 2002. Senegal and Mali. Working Paper prepared for Case Study Project on Civil Wars.

Huntington, Samuel P. 1968. *Political Order in Changing Societies.* New Haven, CT: Yale University Press.

———. 1991. *The Third Wave: Democratisation in the Late Twentieth Century.* Norman, OK: University of Oklahoma Press.

IFAD. 2004. *Rural Poverty Report 2004.* New York: Oxford University Press.

Iyer, Lakshmi and Quy-Toan Do. 2006. Poverty, Social Divisions, and Conflict in Nepal. Harvard Business School, Working paper.

Jansen, K. and E. Roquas. 1998. "Modernizing Insecurity: The Land Titling Project in Honduras." *Development and Change.* Vol. 29 (1): 81–106.

Johnstone, Ian, Michael W. Doyle, and Robert C. Orr. 1997. *Keeping the Peace: Multidimensional U.N. Operations in Cambodia and El Salvador.* Cambridge: Cambridge University Press.

Jonakin, Jon. 1997. "The Interaction of Market Failure and Structural Adjustment in Producer Credit and Land Markets: The Case of Nicaragua." *The Journal of Economic Issues.* Vol. 31 (2): 349–357.

Kautsky, K. 1988. *The Agrarian Question*. London: Zwann.

Kernot, Sarah. 2006. "Nepal: A Development Challenge." *Journal of South Asian Studies*. Vol. 29 (2): 279–292.

Kevane, Michael. 1996. "Agrarian Structure and Agricultural Practice: Typology and Application to Western Sudan." *American Journal of Agricultural Economics*. Vol. 78: 236–245.

Khadka, Narayan. 1997. *Foreign Aid and Foreign Policy: Major Powers and Nepal*. New Delhi: Vikas.

Kimenyi, Mwangi S. and Njuguna S. Ndung'u. 2002. Sporadic Ethnic Violence: Why Has Kenya Not Experienced a Full Blown Civil War? Paper prepared for Case Study Project on Civil Wars.

Langer, A. 2005. "Horizontal Inequalities and Violent Group Mobilisation in Cote d'Ivoire." *Oxford Development Studies*. Vol. 27 (7): 25–45.

Lecomte-Tilouine, M. and P. Dollfus (eds.) 2003. *Ethnic Revival and Religious Turmoil: Identities and Representations in the Himalayas*. New Delhi: Oxford University Press.

Manji, Ambreena. 2003. "Capital, Labor, and Land Relations in Africa: A Gender Analysis of the World Bank's Policy Research Report on Land Institutions and Land Policy." *Third World Quarterly*. Vol. 24 (1): 97–114.

Marshall, Alfred. 1961. *Principles of Economics*. London: Macmillan.

Maskey, Vishakha, G. Gebremedhin Tesfa and Timothy J. Dalton. 2006. "Social and Cultural Determinants of Collective Management of Community Forest in Nepal." *Journal of Forest Economics*. Vol. 11 (4): 261–274.

Miguel, Edward, Shanker Satyanath, and Ernest Sergenti. 2004. "Economic Shocks and Civil Conflict: An Instrumental Variables Approach." *Journal of Political Economy*. Vol. 112 (4): 725–753.

Ministry of Land Reforms. 1998. Proposal for Land Reform System in Nepal (in Nepali). Kathmandu: His Majesty's Government of Nepal.

Montalvo, Jose G. and Marta Reynal-Querol. 2005. "Ethnic Polarization, Potential Conflict and Civil wars." *American Economic Review*. Vol. 95 (3): 796–816.

Moore, David. 2004. "The Second Age of the Third World: From Primitive Accumulation to Global Public Goods." *Third World Quarterly*. Vol. 25 (1): 87–109.

Murshed, Mansoob S. and Scott Gates. 2005. "Spatial–Horizontal Inequality and the Maoist Insurgency in Nepal." *Review of Development Economics*. Vol. 9 (1): 121–134.

North, Douglass and Robert Thomas. 1982. "The First Economic Revolution." *Economic History Review*. Vol. 30: 229–241.

Olson, Mancur. 1964. *The Logic of Collective Action: Public Goods and the Theory of Groups*. Cambridge, MA: Harvard University Press.

Otsuka, Keijiro and Frank Place. 2005. *Land Tenure and Natural Resource Management: A Comparative Study of Agrarian Communities in Asia and Africa*. Baltimore: Johns Hopkins University Press.

Otsuka, Keijiro and Agnes Quisumbing. 2001. "Land Rights and Natural Resource Management in the Transition to Individual Ownership: Case Studies from Ghana and Indonesia." In Alain de Janvry, Gustavo Gordillo, Jean-Philippe Platteau, and Elizabeth Sadoulet (eds.). *Access to Land, Rural Poverty, and Public Action*. Oxford: Oxford University Press. Pps. 97–128.

Owen, Robert. 1814. *A New View of Society*. London: R&A Taylor.

Panday, Devendra. 1999. *Nepal's Failed Development: Reflections on the Mission and the Maladies*. Kathmandu: Nepal South Asia Center.

Patnaik, Prabhat. 2003. *The Humbug of Finance. In The Retreat to Unfreedom.* New Delhi: Tulika Press.

——. 2005. *The Value of Money, a Critique of Economic Theory.* Oxford: Oxford University Press.

Patnaik, Utsa. 1979. "Neo-Populism and Marxism: The Chayanovian View of the Agarian Question and its Fundamental Fallacy." *Journal of Peasant Studies.* Vol. 6 (4): 375–420.

——. 1987. *Peasant Class Differentiation. A Study in Method with Reference to Haryana.* Delhi: Oxford University Press.

——. 2003. "Global Capitalism, Deflation, and Agrarian Crisis in Developing Countries." *Journal of Agrarian Change.* Vol. 3 (1–2): 33–66.

Perelman, Michael. 2000. *The Invention of Capitalism: Classic Political Economy and the Secret History of Primitive Accumulation.* Durham, SC: Duke University Press.

Persson, T. and G. Tabellini. 1994. "Is inequality harmful for growth?" *American Economic Review.* Vol. 84: 600–621.

Place, Frank and Peter Hazell. 1993. "Productivity Effects of Indigenous Land Tenure Systems in Sub-Saharan Africa." *American Journal of Agricultural Economics.* Vol. 75 (1): 10–19.

Platteau, Jean-Philippe. 2000. "Does Africa Need Land Reform?" In C. Toulmin and J. Quan (eds.) *Evolving Land Rights, Policy and Tenure in Africa.* London: DFID/IIED/NRI. Pps. 51–74

Polanyi, Karl. 1944. *The Great Transformation.* New York: Beacon Press.

Powelson, John P. and Richard Stock. 1987. *The Peasant Betrayed: Agriculture and Land Reform in the Third World.* Lincoln Series of Land Policy Book: Cambridge, MA: Cato Institute

Prasad, Eswar, Kenneth Rogoff, Shang-Jin Wei, and M. Ayhan Kose. 2003. *Effects of Financial Globalization on Developing Countries: Some Empirical Evidence.* International Monetary Fund.

Prasad, Krishna, Mark L. Murphy, and Steve Gorzula. 2005. *Conservation in Conflict: The Impact of the Maoist–Government Conflict on Conservation and Biodiversity in Nepal.* Canada: International Institute for Sustainable Development (IISD).

Raj, Prakash A. 2004. *Maoists in the land of Buddha: an Analytical Study of the Maoist Insurgency in Nepal.* Delhi: Nirala Publications.

Rajdhani. 2004. *Tax for Insurgency.* Washington, DC: Institute for Conflict Management.

Ramachandran, V.K. and Madhura Swaminathan (eds.). 2002. *Agrarian Studies: Essays on Agricultural Relations in Less-Developed Countries.* New Delhi: Tulika Pubs.

Rankin, Katherine Neilson. 2004. *The Cultural Politics of Markets: Economic Liberalization and Social Change in Nepal.* London: Pluto Press.

Regmi, Mahesh. 1963. *Land Tenure and Taxation,* Volume 1. Berkeley, CA: Institute of International Studies, University of California.

——. 1976. *Landownership in Nepal.* Berkeley, CA: University of California Press.

——. 1978. *Thatched Huts and Stucco Palaces: Peasants and Landlords in Nineteenth Century Nepal.* New Delhi: Vikas.

——. 1988. *An Economic History of Nepal, 1846–1901.* Varanasi: Nath.

Rostow, W.W. 1960. *The Stages of Economic Growth: A Non-Communist Manifesto.* Cambridge, U.K: Cambridge University Press.

Schock, Kurt. 2005. *Unarmed Insurrections: People Power Movements in Nondemocracies.* Minneapolis: University of Minnesota Press.

Scott, James. 1974. *The Moral Economy of the Peasant. Rebellion and Subsistence in Southeast Asia.* New Haven, CT: Yale University Press.

Seddon, D. and A. Karki. 2003. *The People's War in Nepal: A Left Perspective.* New Delhi: Adroit Publishers.

Seddon, David, Piers Blaikie and John Cameron. 2002. "Understanding 20 Years of Change in West-Central Nepal: Continuity and Change in Lives and Ideas." *World Development.* Vol. 30 (7): 1255–1270.

Sen, A.K. 1966. "Peasants and Dualism With or Without Surplus Labor." *Journal of Political Economy.* Vol. 74 (5): 425–450.

———. 1997. *On Economic Inequality,* Oxford: Clarendon Press.

Sender, John and Deborah Johnston. 2004. "Searching for a Weapon of Mass Production in Rural Africa: Unconvincing Arguments for Land Reform." *Journal of Agrarian Change.* Vol. 4 (1–2): 142–164.

Sender, John and S. Smith. 1990. *Poverty, Class, and Gender in Rural Africa: A Tanzanian Case Study.* London: Routledge Press.

Sengupta, Somini. 2005. Where Maoists Still Matter. *The New York Times.* October 30.

Shaban, R.A. 1987. "Testing Between Competing Models of Sharecropping." *Journal of Political Economy.* Vol. 95: 893–920.

Shah, Saubhagya. 2002. "From Evil State to Civil Society." In Kanak Mani Dixit and Shastri Ramachandaran (eds.) *State of Nepal.* Lalitpur: Himal Books.

———. 2004. "A Himalayan Red Herring? Maoist Revolution in the Shadow of the Legacy Raj." In M. Hutt (ed.), *Himalayan People's War: Nepal's Maoist Rebellion.* Bloomington, IN: Indiana University Press. Pps. 192–224.

Sharma, S. 2004. "The Maoist Movement: An Evolutionary Perspective." In M. Hutt (ed.), *Himalayan People's War: Nepal's Maoist Rebellion.* Bloomington, IN: Indiana University Press. Pps. 38–57.

Sharma, Shiva Prasad. 1983. *Landowner's Output Shares and Factor Payment to Land: A Case of Nepalese Sharecroppers.* Kathmandu: Nepal Institute Development Studies (NIDS).

———. 1985. *Tenancy Issues in Nepal.* Mimeo. APROSC, HMG.

———. 1987. *Agrarian Change and Agricultural Labor Relations: Nepalese Case Studies. Research Report Series.* Kathmandu: Winrock International Institute for Agricultural Development.

Shiva, Vandana. 1988. *Staying Alive: Women, Ecology, and Survival in India.* New Delhi and London: Zed Press.

Shrestha, Nanda R. 1991. *Landlessness and Migration in Nepal.* Boulder, CO: Westview Press.

Singh, Nirvikar. 1983. "Tenurial Insecurity and Land Improvements." In Pranab Bardhan (ed.) *Land, Labor, and Rural Poverty.* Oxford: Oxford University Press.

Smith, Adam. 1904 [1776]. *An Inquiry into the Nature and Causes of the Wealth of Nations.* 5th edn. Republished from: Edwin Cannon's annotated edition, 1904. Methuen & Co., Ltd.

Stewart, France. 2000. "Crisis Prevention: Tackling Horizontal Inequalities." *Oxford Development Studies.* Vol. 28 (3): 245–262.

———. 2005. Horizontal Inequalities: A Neglected Dimension of Development. Working Paper. Center for Research on Inequality, Human Security, and Ethnicity, (CRISE). Queen Elizabeth House, University of Oxford.

Taras, Raymond C. 2006. "Rising Insurgency, Faltering Democratization in Nepal." *Journal of South Asian Development.* Vol. 1 (1): 59–90.

Thapa, D. 2004. "Radicalism and the Emergence of the Maoists." In M. Hutt (ed.),

Himalayan People's War: Nepal's Maoist Rebellion. Bloomington, IN: Indiana University Press.

Thapa, Ganesh. 1989. The Impact of New Agricultural Technology on Income Distribution in the Nepalese Tarai. PhD dissertation. Ithaca: Cornell University.

Thorner, Daniel. 1956. *Agrarian Prospect in India.* Delhi: Delhi University Press.

Toulmin, Camilla and Julian Quan. 2000. *Evolving Land Rights, Policy and Tenure in Africa.* London: DFID/IIED/NRI.

Ukiwo, Ukoha O. 2005. "A Study of Ethnicity in Nigeria." *Oxford Development Studies.* Vol. 33 (1): 7–23.

United Nations. 2001. *Nepal Human Development Report: United Nations Development Project.* Oxford: Oxford University Press.

——. 2004. *United Nation's Human Development Indicators 2004.* United Nations Development Program. New York: United Nations.

——. 2005. *Human Development Report: United Nations Development Project.* Oxford: Oxford University Press.

USAID. 2005. *The USAID Program in Nepal and the Development Challenge.* Online, available at: www.usaid.gov/policy/budget/cbj2005/ane/np.html.

U.S. State Department. 2003. *Patterns of Global Terrorism.* Washington, DC: U.S. State Department.

Verma, B. and Bromley D. 1987. "The Political Economy of Farm Size in India: the Elusive Quest." *Economic Development and Cultural Change.* Vol. 35 (4): 791–808.

Wagle, Udaya R. 2006. "Economic Inequality in Kathmandu: A Multi-Indicator Perspective." *Himalayan Journal of Development and Democracy.* Vol. 1 (1): 1–29.

Walker, T.S. and J.G. Ryon. 1990. *Village and Household Economies in India's Semi-Arid Tropics.* Baltimore: Johns Hopkins Press.

Wallerstein, Immanuel. 1996. *Open the Social Sciences: Report of the Gulbenkian Commission.* Stanford: Stanford University Press.

Wells, H.G. 1938. *World Brain.* Garden City, NY: Doubleday, Doran & Co.

Whitehead, Ann and Dzodzi Tsikata. 2003. "Policy Discourses on Women's Land Rights in Sub-Saharan Africa: The Implications of the Return to Customary." *Journal of Agrarian Change.* Vol. 3 (1–2): 67–112.

World Bank. 1993. *Agriculture Sector Review.* World Bank Agriculture and Natural Resources Department.

——. 1998. Thailand: Land Reform Areas Project (Loan 2198-TH) – Second Land Titling Project (Loan 3254-TH). Performance Audit Report. Report No. 17974, Washington, DC.

——. 2001. *A World Bank Country Study. Nepal: Poverty and Incomes.* Washington, DC: World Bank.

——. 2003a. Nepal: Country Assistance Strategy Progress Report.

——. 2003b. Country Brief: South Asia Region (SAR)-Nepal.

——. 2003c. *Land Policies for Growth and Poverty Reduction. A World Bank Policy Research Report.* Washington, DC: World Bank.

——. World Bank. 2004. *Key Issues in the Update of World Bank Policy.* Washington, DC: World Bank.

Yngstrom, Ingrid. 2002. "Women, Wives, and Land Rights in Africa: Situating Gender Beyond the Household in the Debate over Land Policy and Changing Tenure Systems." *Oxford Development Studies.* Vol. 30 (1): 21–40.

Zaman, M.A. 1973. "Evaluation of Land Reform in Nepal." *Ministry of Land Reform Sharecropping and Economic Efficiency in Bangladesh. Economic Review.* Vol. 1 (2): n.p.

Part III

Money, capital, and wealth in the human ecology

Part III, comprising Chapters 5 and 6, discusses the increasingly important role that money, capital and wealth play in the global human ecology. The expansion and globalization of financial markets in recent decades has created a new "infrastructure of the infrastructure." High-tech, symbolic, and even transcendental financial markets are increasingly "where the action is." Invisible expectations, preferences, and social consensus, as incorporated into the ideologies and institutions of finance, increasingly determine social and economic power across the world system.

The financial processes identified in Chapter 5 to explain recent prosperity in the U.S. dollar core of the global economy are similar to those identified in Chapter 6 to explain early European history – especially the detailed case study of France's success in the 1700s that is presented from a human ecology economics framework. Then as now, the ability of the human population to work with the physical environment and resources to produce wealth can be significantly affected by social agreements regarding the use of money and by financial institutions. In particular, both the *ancien régime* of the eighteenth century and the U.S. in recent decades benefited from the inflow of foreign monetary wealth, which was used to expand domestic money, credit, economic growth, and wealth. This process allowed economic activity to be better coordinated and more efficient on a large scale, and it encouraged more intensive production and consumption activities. With regard to one historic debate in economics, these findings lend support for the belief systems associated with mercantilism as compared to the belief systems associated with neoclassical economics and free trade – support in the sense that mercantilism can benefit the mercantilist country (France in the 1700s, and the U.S. in recent decades being "money mercantilist" countries).

In the human ecology approach used to arrive at these conclusions, as in any natural science ecology approach, intra-species negotiations and transactions are exploratory, adaptive, often individualized, and the outcomes are not known to all members of the species. This belief system has different consequences than the belief system of neoclassical economics in which transaction costs (a catch-all category for a variety of intra-species activities) are assumed to be either trivial or not worth exploring except as a general constraint on the otherwise superior "efficiency" of markets. For example, if full information, to all, on intra-species transactions is not available, as per the human ecology approach, the evolution of prices is not as straightforward, because prices cannot be changed by spontaneous unanimous social agreement. Thus, money is not simply a veil on the real economies, but can actually play a major role, in the eighteenth century as well as nowadays, in determining the comparative and absolute prosperity of nations. Money, as a "social agreement," as well as related notions of "capital" and "wealth," within a complicated process of intra-species negotiation and transaction, are shown to be system drivers.

5 Money and wealth in the human ecology

Recent U.S. "money mercantilism"

Roy E. Allen

Introduction

Recent financial history shows that "invisible" structural conditions, such as the law of compound interest, widespread acceptance of new forms of electronic money, preferences for offshore finance, faith in the U.S. dollar, etc., all have important consequences for wealth formation, destruction, and transfer. In the human ecology framework of Chapter 1, these intangible "belief systems" and "social agreements," through the institutions of finance, mutually impact the tangible "human populations" and their "physical environments and resources" through new channels.

As argued in this chapter, an innovative conclusion arising from this human ecology approach, compared to other economics literature, is that invisible belief systems and social agreements – as emphasized in the human ecology approach – can engender or destroy wealth independently of physical processes. And, this kind of wealth can be first represented and distributed through the institutions of finance. Economic wealth, which includes purchasing power, production power, and a wide variety of social powers, is thus recognized to have transcendental (unobservable, subjective) content as well as the usual empirical (observed, objective) content. Invisible expectations, preferences, and social consensus, as incorporated into the ideologies and institutions of finance, can thus be "where the action is," and where differential economic power is determined across the world system. I would like to make clear that I am not advocating, as a matter of ethics or social policy, transcendental notions of value over empirical notions, but rather find that, for the best explanation of recent economic history, one should allow that transcendental, belief-system processes (e.g. financial activity) have driven changes in empirically-observed phenomenon (e.g. tangible merchandise and services activity), as well as vice-versa.

There are several links between this chapter and Daudin's Chapter 6. Both chapters use a human ecology approach to investigate money, capital, and wealth processes. And, Daudin's case study of eighteenth-century France proves similar to the case study of this chapter: present-day U.S. Like the mercantilist ancien régime of the eighteenth century, the U.S. in recent decades has benefited from the inflow of foreign money and capital, which has been used to expand domestic money, credit, economic growth, and wealth. In both cases, this capital inflow process allows economic activity to be better coordinated and more efficient on a large scale, and it encourages more intensive production and consumption activities, especially with regard to labor force participation. According to the human ecology analysis, typical literature has been puzzled by both the successful *ancien régime* and the 1980s-onward U.S. prosperity, because it looks for the source of new economic growth more narrowly – in technology, physical resources, and inherent labor productivity, i.e. the tangible resources – while assuming incorrectly that the impact of intangible belief systems and social agreements are fairly neutral – i.e. the impact of money, changing institutions, the role of financial intermediaries, and the international political power of the nation-state.

More generally, it is argued in this chapter that the U.S. and the "hard-currency-core" of the new globalized financial system have benefited from what the author calls "money-mercantilism" at the expense of the "soft-currency-periphery." Because of the way that the international monetary system works, with the U.S. dollar as the dominant reserve currency, over time various monetary-wealth transfers from the periphery to the core have occurred without any other inherent instabilities in the real economy.

Supporting these results is the author's econometric work (Allen, 1989, 1994, 1999), which confirms that financial markets can both "absorb" existing money and create and "store" new money in ways such that the money is not contemporaneously used to support and induce the "real economy." This process shows up as a decline in the GDP-velocity of money – a process which the author's econometric research has isolated relative to other monetary processes. This absorbed or newly-created money-power might be used at a later date to command production or consumption, or it might be destroyed in an economic crisis before its title-holders can use it. Therefore, monetary-wealth is also not a neutral driver of the real economy over time. And, the wealth and social power that such monetary power represents has been allocated to the benefit of the U.S. and other "dollar core interests" of the global system – although somewhat haphazardly during recent decades and not necessarily in a sustainable way.

Depending on the magnitudes of the transfers and re-valuations of monetary wealth over (how much) time and space in the global system, serious real effects can be produced over time and space. These processes, generally not accepted by either mainstream or Marxist economics, can nevertheless account for what the mainstream has understood as "business cycles" and "debt-deflation crises," including depressions (Fisher, 1933), etc., and what Marxists have understood as crises of "underconsumption," "overproduction," and "disproportionality" (Clarke, 1994).

The ideologies and institutions of finance, are not only "where the action is" and where differential economic power is determined across the world system, but are also increasingly key to the sustainability of the current global economic system – a necessary "infrastructure of the infrastructure" as argued in this chapter, that requires an appropriate "international financial architecture."

Recent developments and instabilities in financial markets

In terms of system dynamics, the last few decades has been an "evolutionary" period for financial markets as defined by Modelski in Chapter 2 – across the world system, processes of human "search and selection," in an unfolding process of market globalization, have co-evolved with new political and social agreements and structures. For example, many government restrictions between national financial markets have been removed, and with the help of new information-processing technologies, financial players now move more money, more quickly and more profitably, across the world economy than ever before. Various "one-world financial markets" now exist in which interest rates, and the prices of similar financial assets, are arbitraged closer together. Processes of borrowing low and lending high, and buying financial assets low and selling high (arbitrage), result in "the law of one price" across the international system as middlemen inexpensively exploit more globalized financial markets.

By the 1990s, global financial markets were generating a net international flow of funds of more than $3 trillion each month, that is the flow of funds between countries which reconciles end of the month balance-of-payments data. The gross monthly flow is several orders of magnitude higher than this net flow, and it is increasingly impossible to measure given the often unregulated use of electronic funds transfers. Of the $3 trillion net monthly flow, $2 trillion is so-called "stateless money," which is virtually exempt from the control of any government or official institution, but available for use by all countries, as from "offshore markets," which are discussed later.

In globalizing financial markets, arbitrage has been an extremely profitable win–win business; therefore a rapid expansion of effective money and credit has been justified. Electronic money and other "quasi-moneys" are now being created and swapped with more traditional "real money" as electronic payment systems expand. Networks that have handled staggering amounts of money include the Clearing House Interbank Payments System (CHIPS) run by private banks out of New York. CHIPS mostly handles foreign exchange and other large-value, wholesale-level international transactions, and the net settlement of its transactions is in dollar reserves through the Federal Reserve Bank of New York. Transfers through CHIPS increased from $16 trillion in 1977 to more than $310 trillion in the late 1990s. The Federal Reserve's Fedwire is its electronic facility, and transfers reserve balances among private banks through dedicated wire and is the favored system for large domestic transfers. Transfers through Fedwire increased from $2.6 trillion in 1977 to more than $225 trillion in the late 1990s. On a daily basis, CHIPS and Fedwire now move more than $2 trillion. Retail systems such as credit and debit cards transfer an additional several hundred billion dollars per day. These daily recorded flows amount to half the entire broad money (M3) stock of the U.S., and more than one-third of the U.S. GDP for the whole year (Solomon, 1997, p. 7). Compared to the U.S., Europe uses even more electronic transfers: for example, its GIRO credit transfer system sends money directly from the buyer's account to the seller's, and accounts for

19 percent of transactions, whereas indirect and debit-based cheques account for only 2 percent.

Countless other new technologies which enhance the opportunities in boundary-less electronic finance include automatic transfer machines (ATMs), electronic points of sale, telephone banking, interactive screen communications between financial intermediaries and their wholesale and retail customers, ever more innovative debit and credit and smart cards, and even electronic wallets. Computer, telecommunications, and other "non-bank" firms have begun to enter these markets. Globalization of plastic payment cards is now being realized. Worldwide spending at merchant locations on general-purpose bank cards totaled $1.47 trillion in 1995, $3.26 trillion in 2000, and $6.43 trillion in 2005. The U.S. has generally had close to a 50 percent share, Europe 25 percent, and Asia–Pacific close to 20 percent.[1]

Globalization of payment systems is now moving from plastic to the Internet, with alliances between banks and companies like Microsoft. Electronic funds transfer systems have allowed "fast money" or "hot money" flows, and now "virtual money." Virtual money is a catchphrase for a host of innovative payment forms such as electronic (e-) cash and digital money. As with Internet communications, virtual money deliveries can be non-centralized and "non-physical" beyond the 0/1 on/off digital switching of computer systems.

In this new global financial infrastructure, the measured value of financial transactions is now mostly in the form of electronic debits and credits. Electronic money credits can be converted to traditional currency, but most of these credits are never converted – they remain in the system to accommodate never-ending financial transactions and reconciliations between financial institutions.

> Today's money: the synthesis. [Bank] reserves perch atop the money pyramid. Conventional money (the measured M's) is next [as the pyramid widens]. The e-transfers, or EFT as earlier known, follow. One level below is the newest kind of e-money: the smart card and computer cybermoney forms slowly taking shape. Free money, by definition without specific formal backing, and e-barter collect at the base of the pyramid. ... As you get further away from the reserve base and the money that passes through banks, it becomes harder to track "money." This is especially true with bundling a lot of different corporate information or settlement in some kind of commodity account (e.g. oil or futures). The value of an aggregate-flows gross becomes supported by a dwindling reserve and money base relative to the expanded electronic blob as a whole.
>
> (Solomon, 1997, pp. 91, 95)

Given these developments, it is becoming difficult to separate the money stock (M) from its rate of use or "velocity" (V) as it recycles quickly through the system. "The expanded electronic blob" of money transactions, or ($M \times V$), remains measurable as an aggregate, but on electronic networks the two components coalesce.

Thus, increasingly we do not really know what the underlying money stock is, and therefore how much money is being created.

Global money and monetary-processes are further complicated by the role of the dollar (and to lesser extent the yen, euro, etc.) as the world reserve currency or "high-powered money." Just as quasi-money supplies can be created and destroyed based upon real money supplies within a national economy, "soft-currency" supplies can be created and destroyed based upon their convertibility into the U.S. dollar and other "hard-currencies" in the world economy.

For example, the Mexican peso and the Thai baht functioned as quasi-moneys or soft-currencies during the recent financial crises in those two countries (1994 and 1997, respectively). Initially, increased dollar supplies in those two countries, often borrowed from abroad, or earned through trade, were used as the reserve currency upon which new peso and baht loans were issued. But many new loans and money accounts were not used profitably. For example, too much commercial real estate was built with borrowed money, and it could not be rented or sold profitably.

People could not pay back their loans to the banks, and the banks had to write-off various accounts. The money supply held by the banks therefore declined, and they had less ability and incentive to continue creating money through lending procedures. The situation deteriorated until banks could not honor their own financial commitments. The Mexican and Thai governments themselves were "banks" that had borrowed dollars and other hard currencies, and both governments lost the ability to honor their hard-currency debt. There was a general loss of confidence in the financial system. Many who could, transferred their local soft-currency into dollars and moved the dollars into safe-havens outside the country. But, just as gold notes may not fully convert into gold during a crisis, or bank deposit accounts may not fully convert into bank reserves, excessively-created quasi-money supplies of pesos and bahts did not fully convert into dollars.

In both Mexico and Thailand there was a sudden devaluation of the domestic currency (failure to fully convert) relative to the dollar, and a sudden drop in the money supply and the monetary-wealth which was available to purchase domestic goods. International holders of pesos and bahts "ran" on those currencies just as deposit holders typically run on a bank during a national financial crisis. National holders also ran on these currencies, demanding dollars, because the dollar was available domestically. And, the most attractive thing to do with the limited supplies of dollars that could be obtained with the devaluing domestic currency was often to put the dollars in safe-haven accounts outside the crisis-ridden domestic economy.

Similarly, at the end of August 1998, a run on rubles occurred in Russia as domestic and international holders of rubles rushed to convert them to dollars and then move the dollars out of the country. Perhaps $40 billion were then held domestically by Russians. Before the run, approximately $20 billion worth of rubles was held; at the end of the run in September the ruble had lost most of its exchange value and what rubles remained were worth less than $5 billion, measured at international exchange rates.

Rubles are the less-secured, less-accepted quasi-money and dollars are the real money in Russia, despite long-standing attempts by authorities to implement just the reverse. This distinction is based upon intangible belief systems and social agreements as well as upon the observable material conditions of the economy – there is superior confidence in the institutions and organizations which support the dollar across the global economy. When the run occurred, the dollar value of the quasi-money (rubles) held by Russians dropped by more than 75 percent. The decline in ruble-wealth was much larger than the wealth that could be converted into dollars. Russians experienced (and agreed to) a sudden decline in wealth – a decline in the ability to exploit productive resources and a decline in the ability to purchase things, including their own products. Having temporarily lost their effective monetary system of institutions and agreements, more wages went unpaid, less work was done, money and goods were hoarded, incentives and means to coordinate economic activity deteriorated, and recessionary conditions worsened.

Mexico, Thailand, Russia, Argentina, and others have suffered not only from a severe contraction of their quasi-money economy, but the rush to convert local-money wealth into dollars also involved a capital-flight of wealth out of the country in order to best establish interest-earning dollar accounts. The U.S. and other hard-currency countries thus gained monetary wealth at the expense of less-developed countries and other quasi-money users. Safe-havens are also wealth havens.

Common patterns have emerged in these recent financial crises. Typically, a country or region initially experiences a financial liberalization phase. The financial sector expands as it captures profit from new efficiencies and opportunities allowed by globalization. The country or region, for a time, may be favored by international investors; thus the banking system, including government, is well-capitalized and able to expand money-liquidity. Assets increase in monetary value and interest rates are low. Consumption, borrowing, business investment, and government spending are encouraged. Productive resources are more fully utilized and economic growth is well supported. There is a boom, as measured by increased (a) monetary wealth held by private and public sectors of an economy, such as the value of stocks, real estate, currency reserves, etc.; and/or (b) the current production of merchandise and services (GDP). In this financial liberalization phase, excessive, risky speculation and investment is sometimes encouraged by the notion that "if I fail, a lender of last resort or government institution will bail me out," i.e. the "moral hazard problem."

Then, typically, the stock of secure currency (M) times its rate of circulation or velocity for GDP purposes (V) contracts, and therefore so does the equivalent nominal GDP. The decline in nominal GDP is usually split between its two components, real GDP which is the volume of current production measured in constant prices (Q), and the GDP price level (P). By definition, the "equation of exchange" requires ($M \times V = P \times Q$). If Q declines for a sustained period (typically at least six months) we call it a recession, and if P declines we call it deflation. After this process starts, monetary policymakers may react by rapidly expanding M, but this action may be too little too late – individuals and institutions may have unpayable debts, banks may even be failing, and international confidence in the country or region may be damaged. An excessive expansion of M may cause the domestic currency to lose much of its value in undesirable episodes of depreciation and inflation (increases in P might then occur even though Q continues to fall).

The initial contraction in effective money ($M \times V$) may be caused by national and international investors draining money from the country or region, or there may be a decline in V if the financial system is unable to direct money toward productive activities. A contraction in effective money or withdrawal of international investment may undermine equity markets, debt markets, bank capital, or government reserves, and monetary wealth is revalued downwards. General economic or political uncertainty worsens the situation – the resulting austerity-mentality causes a contraction of spending and credit, and an increased risk premium attached to business activity scares away investment. Interest rates rise, the demand for quasi-money and credit – i.e. the desire to hold and use the insecure "monetary float" – declines and people try to convert the monetary float into more secure form of money such as cash. No reserve-currency banking system is able to cover all of its monetary float with secure bank reserves if customers try to redeem all of the float at once, and thus "runs" on banks can destroy the banks. A deteriorated banking sector may be unable to honor its deposits, bad loan problems surface and a "lender of last resort" such as the International Monetary Fund may need to be found.

A decline in monetary wealth and effective money in a *peripheral* country or region may be initiated by the financial *centers* or dominant reserve-currency countries. The secure money used in the periphery, which backs its less secure quasi-moneys and credit expansion, may even be the centralized global reserve currency – typically the U.S. dollar. For example, the 1982 debt crisis hit Latin America when the U.S. dollar became scarce. Dollars had been loaned to Latin America in the 1970s at low interest rates, which provided the hard-currency monetary base for the dramatic expansion of local soft currency and credit – Latin America's financial liberalization and economic growth phase. Then, because of U.S. monetary and fiscal policies in the early 1980s, dollar interest rates soared and dollars were both pushed and pulled out of Latin America into U.S. deposits. Latin America lost the dollar reserves which were necessary to pay dollar-denominated debts; thus Latin America lost its internationally recognized source of value which could maintain the redemption value of local currencies. Policymakers desperately increased domestic currency supplies trying to reverse this process. Confidence in pesos, cruzados, and other local currencies was lost as they depreciated rapidly, i.e. inflation (P) surged even faster than the growth in money; therefore the real money supply (M/P) declined, and a decline in real GDP (Q) followed. In the equation of exchange, V declined – in many cases due to bank problems and private hoarding of money – therefore Q had to decline. The 1980s became known as "the lost decade" for Latin America.

In crisis episodes, the monetary contraction in the periphery is usually more severe than in the center, because the periphery uses the large monetary float which is sustained by the smaller monetary base in the center. Furthermore, if savings and monetary wealth in the periphery country are transferred to the financial center to take advantage of its higher interest rates, or for safe-haven purposes (typically when the crisis hits), then the periphery experiences an even greater contraction.

In the nineteenth and early twentieth centuries, London was the secure financial center, and the U.S. was more of a periphery that depended on the British pound to back dollar-expansion. As documented by Mishkin (1991), most of the financial crises in the U.S. during this period began with a monetary-contraction and a rise in interest rates in the London markets, which then caused a contraction in U.S. money-liquidity and a sharp rise in U.S. interest rates, U.S. bank problems, and so on. Since World War II, the dollar has been the dominant world reserve currency – the secure monetary core of the global economy. Thus, recent crises in the global economy are typically initiated by dollar monetary-contraction and increases in dollar interest rates. The effects can be especially severe in the periphery if the contraction occurs suddenly and follows a more liberal dollarization period in the periphery.

A human ecology understanding of "wealth"

As demonstrated by the earlier case studies, financial market participants – including central banks – can be the "driving agents" whose actions might either increase or reduce the economic product and wealth of various nations. Former U.S. Federal Reserve Board Chairman Alan Greenspan wrote:

> The fiat money systems that emerged [after the gold-standard system was abandoned in the early 1970s] have given considerable power and responsibility to central banks to manage the sovereign credit of nations. Under a gold standard, money creation was at the limit tied to changes in gold reserves. The discretionary range of monetary policy was relatively narrow. *Today's central banks have the capability of creating or destroying unlimited supplies of money and credit.* ... The changing dynamics of modern global financial systems also require that central banks address the inevitable increase of systemic risk. It is probably fair to say that the very efficiency of global financial markets, engendered by the rapid proliferation of financial products, also has the capability of transmitting mistakes at a far faster pace throughout the financial system in ways that were unknown a generation ago, and not even remotely imagined in the nineteenth century. Today's technology enables single individuals to initiate massive transactions with very rapid execution. Clearly, not only has the *productivity* of global finance increased markedly, but so, obviously, has the ability to generate losses at a previously inconceivable rate.
>
> (Greenspan, 1998, pp. 247, 249 [my emphasis])

The author would emphasize that "the capability of creating or destroying unlimited supplies of money and credit" in Greenspan's quote is equivalent to "the capability of creating or destroying monetary wealth." Money and credit are "stores of value," as determined by social consensus within nations and between nations.

Regarding financial operators, innovations, and productivity, the author would use Joseph Schumpeter's classic definition (1934, p. 66) of "innovation" to include the opening of new markets and the pioneering of new forms of business or commercial organization, as well as the development of new products and methods of production. Clearly, financial operators have been innovative in each sense, perhaps especially with regard to new global forms of commercial organization. Schumpeter argued that clusters of innovations destroy many of the old ways of doing things, while simultaneously creating new ways to produce value – a process of "creative destruction." Economic development thus proceeds as an evolutionary process, with difficult "transition crises." Innovations are adopted in "search and selection" processes as we proceed through transition periods.

These processes are elaborated by Modelski in Chapter 2. Elsewhere he has written:

> the period since 1973, and lasting in our analysis until about 2000, is one of transition. The industries that have been the bearers of post-World War II prosperity – the "auto-industrial" complex (including oil) and electronics (even including mainframe computers) – have become mature industries. They are no longer sources of rapid growth and major innovation ... competition [worldwide in these industries] has brought unemployment, restructurings, and shocks to world trade balances. ... In the meantime, the [1973–] information industries have been slow in making their impact felt. The large investment in the new technologies has not yet had noticeable effects on *productivity* [my emphasis]. This is a "lag" that is characteristic of paradigmatic shifts in industrial organization. Early in this century, a similar delay, on the order of two decades, was seen in the impact of strong commitment to electric power equipment.
>
> (Modelski and Thompson, 1996, p. 223)

The word "productivity" as it is used in the above two quotes, and as it is typically used in economics literature, means the rate of current production of merchandise and services (GDP) per unit of input (land, labor, tangible capital, financial capital, etc.). I would call this statistic "GDP-productivity." An alternative statistic would be the rate of current production of wealth per unit of input – "wealth-productivity." "Wealth" includes GDP, but it also includes the monetary value of financial assets, real estate, and other property. The *socially-agreed* value of the latter group, as discussed previously, is affected by the flow of effective money ($M \times V$), expectations of the future as well as assessments of the present, the influence of noise traders versus information traders, and other invisible conditions. To the businessperson, wealth-productivity is pursued through maximization of shareholder value, whereas GDP-productivity is pursued through maximization of net income. Economic models typically focus on net-income processes rather than shareholder value processes, although the latter is usually more important to the owners and operators of corporations.

The (1973–) information industries have as yet been slow to significantly increase GDP-productivity, as noted by Modelski in Chapter 2. However, these industries have noticeably supported an increase in wealth-productivity. Financial operators, using these new information-technologies, and taking advantage of new opportunities in deregulated financial markets, have increased the monetary value of financial assets, real estate, and other property. Innovation has reduced the transactions costs of creating and transferring money, as well as the transactions costs of owning and handling property. These reduced owning and managing costs of property give newfound value to property, which is reflected in higher prices. People have been more able to enjoy a net benefit from property ownership; thus, increased demand for existing property has increased property prices and recognized values. This process has occurred mostly independently of what can be observed in GDP markets; instead we observe high stock and real estate prices, higher prices for bonds, and therefore lower interest rates, etc.

Thus, the (1973–) information industries have already had the following economic impact: non-inflationary growth of GDP has been possible consistent with historical trends, while socially-recognized wealth and purchasing power accumulates faster than ever before in financial markets. This effect has been possible even though the (1973–) information industries have yet to significantly increase the growth rate of the "good old" physical productivity of people to bring forward tangible goods within the household, office, or factory.

To date, the entrepreneurs and innovators of the new information-age capitalism can be primarily observed realizing the fruits of their labors in financial markets, with stock options, arbitrage trading profits, global money and credit operations, etc. Those analysts who look only at the "good old" household, office or factory and claim that "the new technology is overrated," might be unaware of this important arena within which capitalism reinvents itself, and within which capitalists maintain their ability to accumulate wealth.

This wealth-creation as captured in financial markets is now, in turn, supporting GDP-productivity. Because the cost of obtaining financing has dropped, whether from loans or participating owners, and because the price of land and other real property has increased, there is an increased incentive to develop property for the market. Some of the wealth that has recently accumulated in financial markets is spent for these purposes, and an "industrious revolution" occurs as resources are more fully exploited and more intensely used for further innovation – business investment and labor participation increases. Also, accumulated wealth allows consumption spending to expand. For example, massive wealth-productivity from information industries realized itself in the mid-to-late 1990s in the U.S.; the U.S. stock markets boomed, household savings out of current income dropped close to zero as the extra wealth supported consumption; unemployment dropped to record lows and economic growth continued beyond all consensus forecasts. Government tax revenues collected from economic activity exceeded expectations, and in 1998 the U.S. Federal Budget moved into surplus. Inflation in GDP markets did not increase.

The author would like to be clear that regarding the U.S. as a "winner" due to international transfers of monetary wealth, and Japan and some other countries as "losers," is a somewhat unconventional position. The new global monetary system, with the dollar as the secure store of value and currency of accumulation, and with the rise of offshore finance and other innovations, has transferred wealth to dollar havens. The devaluation of soft currencies and capital flight in the "periphery" of the global economy has pushed those regions into relative poverty and pushed the dollar-haven core of the global economy into relative wealth. The Japanese yen has also given way to the dollar, not in terms of the unit-to-unit currency exchange rate, but in terms of the share of the world's wealth which is denominated in yen – probably it has been reduced by 50 percent since 1989. Ronen Palan – among other international political economists familiar with offshore finance – began grappling with this issue in the mid 1990s:

> Indeed [after World War II] a hierarchy was produced as the new global currency [mainly the dollar] became the core currency of "hard" to which all other currencies, "soft" currencies were attached. The "off-shore" financial markets may be understood as a reproduction of one of the central features of the post-war international financial system, namely, this hierarchy among currencies. ... The whole off-shore market then operates, whether intentionally or not, as a huge transmission mechanism, transferring the accumulated capital of the old periphery to the financial centers of the "core."
>
> ... about 30 percent of third world debt has found its way into tax havens. The figures rise sharply concerning Latin America. By 1981 five of the havens considered by the Caribbean Task Force report (Bahamas, Bermuda, Liberia, the Dutch Antilles and Panama) had approximately 14.3 percent of the total estimated investment stock which had flowed from OECD to all developing countries, although the economies of these five accounted for less than 0.3 percent of the total GNP of all developing countries. ... With current third world debt outstanding at US $1.6 trillion, these figures imply a net [accumulated] inflow of US $500 billion into the tax havens. Such figures quite simply dwarf anything traditional theories of third world's exploitation and unequal exchange have managed to come up with. This is arguably the saddest of all aspects of third world plight.
>
> (Palen, 1994)

Where do tax havens invest and transfer this wealth? Swiss banks, the earliest modern tax havens "rarely squander it [money accumulated from the periphery] or speculate with it. They invest it prudently and cautiously in the rich Atlantic world" – the big three Swiss banks actually made a policy decision in 1957 to invest only in the "first world" (Fehrenbach, 1966, p. 126). More recently, as shown by Brown (1996), flows into tax havens and other offshore markets have, as their major counterpart, inter-bank lending into the U.S.

Thus, in the author's framework, economic wealth can be initially *created* in financial markets – not only, as commonly believed, through the production of merchandise and non-financial services. Independently of the efforts of labor in non-financial markets, financial market participants might reduce owning and handling costs of property, create new financial assets in the process, revalue existing financial assets upward, and translate this newfound, socially-accepted wealth into sustainable purchasing power over time, without inflation. Likewise, financial market participants also have the power to reverse these processes, and reduce wealth and real purchasing power over time. There need not be any other initial drivers of these changes in wealth other than the labors and social agreements of financial market participants.

Regarding the role of "social agreement," and using the human ecology framework, the author's position is that invisible "belief systems" can engender wealth, independent of physical processes, and this kind of wealth can be first represented and distributed through the institutions of finance. Economic wealth, which includes purchasing power, production power, and a wide variety of social powers, is thus recognized to have transcendental (unobservable, subjective) content as well as the usual empirical content.

Transcendental notions of value need not reflect, or even be compatible with, the observed empirical world. For example, the purely transcendental "law of compound interest" is a social agreement, which may not correlate with the way that the physical economy grows. Growth in the physical economy is subject to thermodynamics, biological growth processes and carrying capacity, endowments of resources, sunlight and rain, etc. Perhaps debtors as a group, who are required to pay *exponentially* increasing interest under this transcendental law, can generate goods and services and therefore economic revenues only in *arithmetically* increasing increments over time. Therefore, perhaps some debtors have to fail, and yield their economic resources to the others, so that the others can meet their obligations.

Whether or not this type of debt-repudiation crisis is systemically required in modern capitalism has been debated. Mainstream economic thinking is generally confident that "hard-to-qualify" lending restrictions, wherein all parties are conscious of systemic risk, can avoid over-lending and debt-failure. In contrast, Marxists and others, such as Frederick Soddy, are convinced that these crises are endemic to capitalism. As discussed in the previous section, massive debt-repudiation crises continue to happen in the world system. Therefore, we have not yet been able to avoid over-lending and periodic disjuncture-crises between, on the one hand, the belief system which includes mathematical compound interest, and on the other hand, the ability to generate money from tangible "real world" processes. The author's position is that some borrowers and lenders are fully conscious risk-takers who know that periodic failures are required in "casino capitalism" (John Maynard Keynes' phrase), whereas other borrowers and lenders underestimate systemic risk and allow over-lending based upon a mistaken ideology regarding the stability of capitalism. Thus, on both accounts, debt crises are likely to remain with us.

Invisible belief systems, including those of money-gamblers and optimistic market capitalists, have supported a money economy based on exponential interest payments, and an easing of lending restrictions. The acceptance and growth of offshore finance, as discussed earlier, without reserve requirements or other significant regulations, is an example of how belief systems – in this case market capitalist ideology – drive institutional change. Offshore market institutions, such as the Bangkok International Banking Facility, encouraged unsustainable overlending, excessive unprofitable construction of real estate etc., and ultimately contributed to the risk of crisis, recession and misery in the Asian financial crisis of 1997. Transcendental belief systems and their supporting institutions can thus drive empirical changes in human populations and their physical environments. Much of the economic wealth that was initially created through deposit-lending, as it exercised itself in production power, consumption power, and power to change institutions, was destroyed in the recent Asian crisis; but it nevertheless did exist as a broad social agreement. And, less of it would have been destroyed if financial capitalists had been more patient in accepting lower, less risky rates of return which were more compatible with the ability of human populations working with the physical environment to yield economic growth.

U.S. money mercantilism

The author's long-time econometric work (Allen, 1989, 1999) confirms that financial markets can "absorb" money so that the money is not contemporaneously available to support and induce the "real economy," which shows up as a decline in the GDP-velocity of money. This absorbed money-power might be used at a later date to command production or consumption, or it might be destroyed in an economic crisis before its title-holders can use it. Therefore, monetary wealth is not a neutral driver of the real economy over time.

The policy implications of these results are profound:

As long as new, profitable opportunities arise in financial markets due to advancing technology, deregulation, and internationalization, and as long as a reasonable degree of confidence in the markets is maintained, then money supplies can be increased faster than historical rates without over-stimulating the markets for merchandise and services. Financial markets absorb the above-normal liquidity and add extra value to household, business, and government assets. Assuming that this extra wealth is used to buy foreign assets, merchandise and services or that it is used sparingly to buy domestic merchandise and services, then the financial side of the economy experiences a sustainable, profit-justified inflation without the necessity of GDP inflation. The author would call this phenomenon the "golden egg." Similarly, failure of financial institutions to support the circulation of effective money (M times V) can, unnecessarily, destroy monetary wealth and cause recessions – the golden egg can be "dropped."

(Allen, 1999, pp. 90–1)

Reversing the causality of Karl Marx's materialism philosophy, it is increasingly true that autonomous, invisible financial processes drive change in the physical relations of production, rather than vice-versa. As part of this process, central banks and other financial market participants such as offshore banks can in some cases (haphazardly) increase or reduce wealth independently of any initial changes in the production of GDP or other "real" economic prospects. *And, this wealth – literally created or destroyed out of thin air (or cyberspace) in some cases – is generally allocated through the arbitrary customs and interest rates concessions of particular social networks. Wealth itself in the global human ecology, in these cases, can thus be derived entirely from "pure social agreement" depending on how well one can participate in the financial system.*

A review of the author's controversial position as italicized here, especially critiquing it from the Marxist and other philosophical materialist frameworks, appeared in *Review of International Political Economy* (1996). To the reviewer, the author's approach incorrectly "... privileges financial changes vis-à-vis changes in the real economy [production of value]" (p. 532). Furthermore, to the reviewer, any perceived initial creation and distribution of wealth or "value" that happens in "the thin air" of financial markets could not be sustained over time without corresponding supportive GDP activity.

In contrast, to the author, "money is wealth" in the sense that it gives the holder a claim on the entire social product. The "social product" includes not only consumption power and production power, but also the power to direct and control large social processes – such as those which are dependent on (gaining access to) the institutions of government, courts, communications, and so on. The accumulation of monetary assets, or what Marxists would call the accumulation of finance capital, represents a social-power-claim that becomes a key driver in the evolution of the world system. Once monetary wealth is understood as power-claims over the social product, then monetary wealth is "real," and it is limited only by the degree to which power can be exerted over others. Presumably this limit would only be found in the unlikely event that an all-encompassing global monopoly has maximized its differential power.

Recent research in the field of international political economy also treats monetary wealth, or finance capital (as opposed to physical capital or capital goods such as machines and factories) as an accumulation of broad social powers:

Drawing on the institutional frameworks of Veblen and Mumford, our principal contribution is to *integrate power into the definition of capital.* Briefly, the value of capital represents discounted expected earnings. Some of these earnings could be associated with the productivity (or exploitation) of the owned industrial apparatus, but this is only part of the story. As capitalism grows in complexity, the earnings of any given business concern come to depend less on its own industrial undertakings and more on the *community's overall productivity.* In this sense, the value of capital represents a *distributional* claim. This claim is manifested partly through ownership, but more broadly through the *whole spectrum of social power.* Moreover, power is not only a means of accumulation, but also its most fundamental end. For the absentee owner, the purpose is not to "maximize" profits but to "beat the average." The ultimate goal of business is not hedonic pleasure, but *differential* gain. In our view, this differential aspect of accumulation offers a promising avenue for putting power into the definition of capital. ... In the eyes of a modern investor, capital means a *capitalized earning capacity*. It consists not of the owned factories, mines, aeroplanes or retail establishments, but of the present value of profits expected to be earned by force of such ownership.

(Nitzan, 1998, pp. 173, 182)

Building upon this quote, Nitzan argues that wealth accumulation processes allowed by monetary capital have favored pecuniary business activities and owners over tangible industrial productivity and working consumers. He argues that, increasingly, "the causal link runs not from the creation of earnings to the right of ownership, but from the right of ownership to the appropriation of earnings" (p. 180). This causality is consistent with the writings of Thorstein Veblen, who insisted that the "natural right of ownership" conferred by society to various people (initially to own slaves, then animals, land, and now capital), can be used coercively or even as a form of sabotage to obtain further social powers at the expense of others:

For the transient time being, therefore, any person who has the legal right to withhold any part of the necessary industrial apparatus or materials from current use will be in a position to impose terms and exact obedience, on pain of rendering the community's joint stock of technology inoperative for that extent. Ownership of industrial equipment and natural resources confers such a right legally to enforce unemployment, and so to make the community's workmanship useless to that extent. This is the Natural Right of Investment. ... Plainly, ownership would be nothing better than an idle gesture without this legal right of sabotage. Without the power of discretionary idleness, without the right to keep the work out of the hands of the workmen, and the product out of the market, investment and business enterprise [as distinguished from other economic activity or forms of organization] would cease. This is the larger meaning of the Security of Property.

(Veblen, 1923, pp. 65–7)

Based on these processes, the author's research confirms that the U.S. and the "hard-currency core" of the new global economy has benefited from what he calls "money-mercantilism" at the expense of the "soft-currency periphery."

Historically, as discussed by Daudin in Chapter 6, "mercantilism" is the use of restrictive trade policies and colonial empires, especially by the European *ancien régime* of the seventeenth and eighteenth centuries, in order to centrally accumulate precious metals. Various nineteenth-century German historians, especially Georg Friedrich List, gave coherence to mercantilist notions of how wealth is accumulated, and they critiqued the laissez-faire economics of Smith, Ricardo, and Say. The institutional advantage used by powerful and hegemonic European states to appropriate unequal win–win or even win–lose gains from international commerce was recognized by the German Historical School as an important determinant of "the wealth of nations." More recent defenders of the mercantilist perspective include the Caribbean School and the World-System School (Wallerstein, 1980).

What I would add to the historical mercantilist perspective, in order to make it "money-mercantilism," is the notion that extraction of monetary wealth from the periphery, through institutional advantage, does not require GDP trade flows – instead, it only requires dominance in financial affairs. In the *ancien régime* period, there was an international financial system, but it was associated more with national debts rather than with commercial finance. Hence, it was easier for France and England, among others, to extract money-species from the colonies through favorable trade and export of goods and services rather than more directly through commercial finance. However, in the current period, well-developed international commercial financial markets allow various trade channels to be bypassed.

The current mercantilists, who are typically financial intermediaries, are less government-affiliated, and thus mercantilism is not so intentionally associated with nationalism. However, the wealth-enhancing effects obtained for the home country or its currency bloc might be the same as with old mercantilism. The official government players in this process might act as direct or indirect agents or partners for the private financial intermediaries, and thus maintain much of the nationalism or core-regionalism that is historically associated with mercantilism.

Also, because of the way that the international monetary system works with the U.S. dollar as the dominant reserve currency, over time various monetary-wealth transfers from the periphery to the core have occurred without any other inherent instabilities in the real economy. As argued by President de Gaulle of France and others, the Bretton Woods system gave the U.S. an unfair advantage by allowing the U.S. to freely finance itself around the world and then settle its obligations in dollars without limit. Unilateral devaluations of the dollar, as long as the dollar remains the international currency of choice, unilaterally devalues U.S. foreign debt – a privilege enjoyed by the U.S. as the only major country whose foreign debt is mostly denominated in its own currency. Currently, over 50 percent of all international notes and bonds are denominated in dollars, 45 percent of all cross-border bank loans are in dollars, and 60 percent of the world's money supply is denominated in the U.S. dollar. Thus, currently more dollars circulate outside the U.S. than inside.

This dominance in debt markets gives dollar-issuers such as the U.S. government a "liquidity discount" or reduced transaction costs of perhaps 25 to 50 basis points (hundredths of a percentage point). Non-U.S. holdings of U.S. government debt amount to $2 trillion, which means the U.S. government saves between five and ten billion dollars per year in interest expense on its debt due to the liquidity discount. Also, an additional five to ten billion dollars per year may be "earned" from other countries by the U.S. due to "seigniorage," which is the profit earned by the monopoly issue of coins and notes. That is, other countries give up real goods and services to holders (and therefore issuers) of dollars in order to obtain dollars for their reserve accounts.

Monetary-wealth transfers to the U.S. dollar core of the international monetary system need not translate into undesirable inflation. Whether inflation is affected depends on the production capacity that is available in the core, the capacity that can be added, the "thickening" and "commodification" of markets as new activity or non-market activity becomes part of the income-expenditure flow, the degree to which U.S. dollars are added to non-circulating reserve accounts versus use in income-expenditure flows, etc.

These remarkably successful labors in the core by the Federal Reserve Bank, the "Wall Street–U.S. Treasury complex" (Bhagwati, 1998), and the millions of international financial market participants, as allowed by the dollar-based international monetary system, need not be conscious or conspiratorial, but they have favored U.S. dollar havens. Because the dollar is a "store of value" and not neutral, dollar havens are wealth havens. And, wealth havens are power havens where production power, consumption power, and social-process-power are gained relative to non-havens. The author's research indicates that global monetary capitalism currently supports institutional arrangements whereby dollar havens gain mercantilist benefits from "dollar colonies" (Allen, 1999).

Consistent with Daudin's findings for France in the 1700s (see Chapter 6), economic growth might thus be largely driven by a thickening and commodification of domestic markets as social agreements and institutions allow foreign monetary wealth to be used domestically. Furthermore, new wealth derived from the labors of financial operators and from the innovations of the post-1973 information industries can accumulate first in financial markets, which then encourages investment in fixed capital and consumerism. And, "money mercantilism" has supported all of these developments in favor of the U.S. and other dollar-core regions of the global economy.

In recent decades, the U.S. economy thus boomed ahead with an unexpectedly high labor-force participation rate (from 60 percent of the population aged 16 and over in 1970 to 66 percent currently, alongside a lengthening work-week) despite a much less significant increase in the inherent physical GDP-productivity of the average worker (which has fluctuated around a 3 percent growth rate per year for several decades).

Thus, reflecting these financial processes, recent research, including from the World Institute for Development Economics Research of the United Nations University indicates that a "widening gap between the global haves and the have-nots in large measure reflects the failure of less-developed countries to develop, while rich countries – particularly the United States – have experienced fast economic growth and a spectacular buildup of assets" (*New York Times*, 2006). And, while beyond the scope of this chapter to explain further, current "social power" across the global human ecology does indicate continued global political-economic success for the U.S. as per Modelski's K-wave analysis in Chapter 2:

> In 2000 the United States accounted for 4.7 percent of the world's population but 32.6 percent of the world's wealth. Nearly four out of every ten people in the wealthiest 1 percent of the global population were American. The average American had a net worth of nearly $144,000, losing only to the average Japanese, who had $180,000, at market exchange rates; the average person in Luxembourg, who had $183,000; and the average Swiss, who had $171,000.
>
> By contrast, in 2000 the average Chinese had a net worth of roughly $2,600, at the official exchange rate. China, home to more than a fifth of the world's population, had only 2.6 percent of the world's wealth. And India, with 16.8 percent of the world's people, accounted for only 0.9 percent of the world's wealth.
>
> (Ibid.)

Conclusions

Although beyond the scope of this chapter to elaborate further, the author's research thus allows the following conclusions:

- Advances in information processing technologies and related innovations since the early 1970s – K-wave 19 identified by George Modelski in Chapter 2 in the continuous history of the global economy – much of which originated in the U.S. and then spread globally, has increased the profitability of financial market participation and arbitrage across the global system.
- Government deregulation of national financial markets to allow international competition and participation has also encouraged seamless "one-world" financial markets. This government deregulation, based upon "the free market belief system" described by Donald Snyder in Chapter 3, was pushed by President Ronald Reagan in the U.S. in the early 1980s, while others pushed it in other countries, such as Margaret Thatcher in Britain.
- As "money-mercantilist" countries, the U.S. and others in the "dollar-core" of the global human ecology have increased their wealth at the expense of other countries in the soft-currency periphery – the U.S. population now holds approximately one third of the world's wealth, i.e. social power, and thus continues to lead world economic evolution through its influence in international financial institutions and markets.
- The new global financial markets have allowed a remarkable expansion of no-reserve banking and money and wealth creation through offshore markets, new financial products, and other ways to securitize and market the ownership of tangible property – increasingly "everything is for sale across the global system."
- The author's econometric research indicates that significant portions of new money created through reserve banking and other processes, as well as use

of the expanded "float" of the purchasing power that is based upon core monies, can be allocated to people over time and space arbitrarily based upon social agreements within the new financial infrastructure. Wealth can be created and reallocated, without necessarily affecting the "good old" political economy of merchandise, non-financial services, GDP productivity of labor, etc.

- These innovations and processes have helped coordinate and direct the global economy, and they have produced efficiencies and sustainable new wealth. They have also increased instabilities, such as the financial crises and recessions in Latin America (1982–), Asia (1997), and Russia (1998).

In the spirit of this book, what responses to these developments might improve the "global sustainability" of the economic system? Elsewhere I have argued for three policy responses (Allen, 1999, pp. 161–9). International financial institutions and policymakers should, in concert:

1   Reduce the number of currencies worldwide, while at the same time supporting regional currency blocs such as the euro model in Europe, so that destabilizing financial flows between currencies are reduced, and so that the dominant U.S. dollar core of the global system gains less money-mercantilist benefits at the expense of other less organized currency areas – thus reducing the rising inequality of wealth across the global system that feeds into the undesirable "Seige of Troy" scenario described by Antonio Cassella in Chapter 8.
2   Develop more forward-looking financial markets, so that financial market participants of all types can better manage their levels of future risk against destabilizing changes in interest rates, exchange rates, financial crises and recession, etc.
3   Maintain better money-liquidity throughout the global system with continued research and monetary policy. As discussed, the econometric research of the author (Allen, 1999, pp. 57–98) indicates that greater money supplies have been necessary to accommodate the growth of money-absorbing financial activity as well as non-financial activity, and based upon the quantity equation $(M) \times (V) = (P) \times (Q)$, changes in the velocity of money (V) need further study so that appropriate supplies of money (M) can be directed to productive uses in the rest of the economy to create non-inflationary economic growth – appropriate levels of (P) and (Q).

Note

1 Data from Nilson (1996).

References

Allen, Roy E. (1989) "Globalisation of the US Financial Markets: The New Structure for Monetary Policy," in *International Economics and Financial Markets*, Oxford University Press: Oxford. Chapter 16.

Allen, Roy E. (1994) *Financial Crises and Recession in the Global Economy*, Edward Elgar Publishing: Cheltenham, UK, and Northampton, MA.

Allen, Roy E. (1999) *Financial Crises and Recession in the Global Economy*, 2nd edition, Edward Elgar Publishing: Cheltenham, UK, and Northampton, MA.

Bhagwati, J.N. (1998) "The Capital Myth: The Difference Between Trade in Widgets and Dollars," *Foreign Affairs*, 77 (3): 7–12.

Brown, Brendan (1996) *Economists and the Financial Markets*, Routledge: London and New York.

Clarke, Simon (1994) *Marx's Theory of Crisis*, St Martin's Press: New York.

Fehrenbach, R.R. (1966) *The Gnomes of Zurich*, Leslie Frewin: London.

Fisher, Irving (1933) "The Debt-Deflation Theory of Great Depressions," *Econometrica*, 1: 337–57.

Greenspan, Alan (1998) "The Globalization of Finance," *The Cato Journal*, 17 (3): n.p.

Mishkin, F.S. (1991) "Asymmetric Information and Financial Crises: A Historical Perspective," in R.G. Hubbard (ed.) *Financial Markets and Financial Crises*, University of Chicago Press: Chicago. Pp. 69–108.

Modelski, George and William R. Thompson (1996) *Leading Sectors and World Powers: The Coevolution of Global Politics and Economics*, University of South Carolina Press: Columbia.

New York Times (2006) December 6, Section C, Page 3, Column 1.

Nilson, Spencer (1996) *The Nilson Report*, Oxford, CA.

Nitzan, Jonathan (1998) "Differential Accumulation: Towards a New Political Economy of Capital," *Review of International Political Economy*, 5: (2): 169–216.

Palan, Ronen (1994) "Tax Havens and the Market for Sovereignty," paper presented at the International Studies Association Convention, Washington, DC.

Review of International Political Economy (1996) 3 (3): 528–37.

Schumpeter, Joseph (1934) *Theory of Economic Development*, Harvard University Press: Cambridge, MA.

Solomon, Elinor Harris (1997) *Virtual Money*, Oxford University Press: New York and Oxford.

Veblen, Thorstein (1923 [1967]) *Absentee Ownership and Business Enterprise in Recent Times: The Case of America*, Beacon Press: Boston, MA.

Wallerstein, Immanuel. (1980). *The Modern World system II: Mercantilism and the Consolidation of the European World Economy 1600–1750*. Academic Press: New York.

6 Money and capital in the human ecology

Rethinking mercantilism and eighteenth-century France

Guillaume Daudin

Introduction

Mercantilism

In the language of human ecology as per Chapter 1, academic fields, as well as schools of thought within a field, are "belief systems," i.e. "ways of organizing alleged truths and convictions." Within economics, two of the most significant belief systems, historically, have been "mercantilism" and "neoclassical" framework. The "neoclassical" framework is now dominant in the economic profession, but the recent failure of the Doha round of trade talks shows that governments and economic leaders may actually believe in the "mercantilist" framework. Both are placeholders for heterogeneous school of thoughts that share some common ideas.

Following Adam Smith, early quantitative historians (called cliometricians after Clio, the Muse of history, and their taste for quantitative methods) challenged in the 1960s and 1970s the idea that empires and worldwide trade were important ingredients of European economic prosperity. They argued that trade with the empires and the rest of the world had profits too small to be of any significance for early modern European economies. They argued also that revenue from external settlements was less than would have been gained if the same capital stock (including administrative and military costs) had been invested in mainland Europe; and even that restrictions on trade and the exclusion of foreigners from colonial trade caused an increase in colonial goods prices which made the colonies a net liability for the domestic economies.

To these arguments it was replied that, considering the organization of the international economy, the real alternative to restrictive trade practices was not free trade, but predatory behavior from the foreign partners: there is no reason to think that prices would have been lower. Furthermore, seemingly non-profitable investments in the colonies were justified by diminishing returns, or the lack of investment opportunities, in the domestic economies. Some quarrels about numbers also took place, showing that, compared with the rather small amount of industrial and colonial investment during the eighteenth century, returns from the empires were not that small. Keynesians affirmed that the empires increased the effective demand in the economy. And, finally, the most ironic arguments in favor of the colonial systems evolve around the fact that slavery and empires allowed different regions of the globe to be open to trade: this, according to basic trade economics, could only lead to a general increase in welfare. It also implies that the suppression of slave trade was a net loss for Africa, as its abolition actually reduced international movement of production factors (Engerman, 1972; O'Brien, 1982; Thomas, 1968; Coelho, 1973; Solow, 1985; Caves, 1971; Findlay, 1990; Darity, 1982).

Did mercantilism have a fair trial?

None of these discussions, even those arguing for the importance of European empires, uses a mercantilist belief system. Thus, their general conclusion is either that Europeans at least were not doing it the right way – it was a good idea to open transoceanic markets, but free trade would have done the trick better – nor for the right reasons. Yet, there is something wrong in this whole debate. It is that it uses classic and neo-classic models that may be valid for modern economies – and were devised to be such – but miss many important features of the *ancien régime* economy.

Crucially, the study of mercantilist external policies should not be separated from the study of the way domestic economies worked. Hence, this chapter justifies and defends a mercantilist view of the relations between world trade and domestic prosperity. It does not try, though, to defend every mercantilist theory and practice. First, because they were often in contradiction with each other, and second, because many were economically unsound. More specifically, this chapter is not directly interested in trade tariffs (a simple price adjustment to the neoclassical economist), but rather in Navigation Acts-type trade policies, which gave domestic traders uncompetitive advantage over foreigners (a complicated intraspecies negotiation and individualized transaction to the human ecology economist). The aim is to devise a model that attains its aims through mechanisms that would have been recognized by mercantilists.

Belief systems have effects on social agreements and the way human populations deal with their physical environment to increase their wealth and welfare. As such, it is preposterous to analyze economic phenomena exclusively with the tools of one belief system when another belief system is dominant among the society being analyzed. This chapter provides an example of this in the case of one of the major disputes within economics: to what degree has free trade, as advocated by neoclassical thinking, been more desirable for the nation-state, as opposed to the aggressive export promotion, trade, and financial protectionism advocated by mercantilism? The answer depends on the belief system that is dominant. The specific example investigated here concerns the *ancien régime* of France before the industrial revolution. This chapter asks: "What are the mechanisms (i.e. elements of the human ecology) that would have been recognized by the mercantilists and were sustained in part by the mercantilist belief system, but which would not be recognized by neoclassical economists?"

Part of the answer is that eighteenth century early modern mercantilists were very much aware of the difficulties inherent in economic exchange – a sub-variety of intraspecies negotiations and transactions. This corresponds to an important aspect of the human ecology approach which recognizes, as any natural science ecology approach, that intraspecies negotiations and transactions are exploratory, adaptive, often individualized, and the outcomes are not known to all members of the species. This belief system has different consequences to the belief system of neoclassical economics in which transaction costs (a catch-all category for a variety of intraspecies activities) are assumed to be either trivial or not worth exploring except as a general constraint on the otherwise superior "efficiency" of markets.

For example, if full information, to all, on intraspecies transactions is not available, as per the human ecology approach, the evolution of prices is not as straightforward, because prices cannot be changed by spontaneous unanimous social agreement. Thus, as I find in this chapter, money is not simply a veil on the real economies, but could actually have played a major role in the eighteenth century in determining the comparative and absolute prosperity of nations. Money, as an invisible element of the human ecology, or "social agreement," as well as related notions of "capital," within a complicated process of intraspecies negotiation and transaction, are shown to be system drivers; this recognition allows support for mercantilism over neoclassical economics in the specific context of the eighteenth century.

The links between this chapter and Roy Allen's Chapter 5 are obvious. It is probably the case that, despite the apparent dominance of the neoclassical belief system, money nowadays has the same importance in the global economy and can be an important determinant in the relative wealth and prosperity of nations. Three conclusions arrived at for the *ancien régime* are consistent with Allen's conclusions in Chapter 5 regarding current U.S. hegemony: (a) the ability of *the human population* working with *the physical environment and resources* to produce wealth can be significantly affected by *social agreements* regarding the use of money and by financial *institutions;* (b) the *ancien régime* of the eight-eenth century – and the U.S. in recent decades according to Chapter 4 – benefited from the inflow of foreign monetary wealth, which was used to expand domestic money, credit, economic growth, and wealth. This process allowed economic activity to be better coordinated and more efficient on a large scale, and it encour-aged more intensive production and consumption activities, especially with regard to labor force participation; (c) compared to typical literature, the human ecology approach to economics might allow for better modeling of both the suc-cessful *ancien régime* and recent U.S. prosperity. Typical literature has been puzzled by these two epochs, because it looks for the source of new economic growth narrowly – in technology, physical resources, and inherent labor produc-tivity – while assuming incorrectly that the impact of money, changing institu-tions, and international political power is fairly neutral. The root of this error is in the fact that it does not properly take into account belief systems and social agree-ments, in opposition to what is advocated by the human ecology approach.

England, like France, supported its economic growth before the industrial revolution period with massive amounts of imports and appropriation of wealth from its empire. The "Malthusian Trap" of overpopulation and poverty was avoided, and human populations grew fast, as aided by new political-economic institutions and organizations, and by belief systems regarding work and exploitation of the physical environment and resources. Enhanced money transactions systems brought under-utilized rural labor into the formal economy in Britain as well as France. Thus, invisible, subjectively allocated money – itself a social agreement – was a "driver" of human populations. And, exploitation of coal, and thus railroads, steam engines, and other changes in the physical environment and resources all co-evolved with these other structural conditions in the human ecology.

Outline

The first step is to devise an appropriate "human ecology model" of the domestic economy: this chapter argues that domestic prosperity depended crucially on the supply of circulating financial capital, because the main limit to economic activity was not *production* but *transaction*. The nature and role of transaction, so basic to inter-species negotiation, coordination, and behavior in ecological models, is often ignored in neoclassical models; the latter may even assume the absence of transactions costs.

The second step is to show that, considering the state of financial markets, this supply of capital ultimately depended on the sign of the balance of "invisibles," as the net export flow of goods and services was compensated mainly by inflows of precious metals that formed the monetary base. Using endogenous growth theories, it is possible to show that the external sector could allow a way out of diminishing returns into unbounded domestic economic growth. Unlike neoclassical models, the human ecology framework thus gives "invisible" money and capital transfers an important role as ecological "drivers" of transactions, coordination, and productive activity. As per the framework of Chapter 1, the invisible can thus drive the visible conditions in a useful predictive sense.

The chapter discusses all these points in the context of France in the eighteenth century. This context is crucial in a human ecology approach, as the structural conditions of the economy are often unique to specific places and times. It adds a new set of evidence to the point developed by other chapters in this volume: money is not simply a veil on the real economies, but actually plays a major role, in the eighteenth century as well as nowadays, in determining the comparative and absolute prosperity of nations.

On the importance of the invisible for the development of the visible French economy

Despite the usual clichés about pre-modern economies, the visible French economy was growing during the eighteenth century. This depended crucially on the payment of transaction costs by traders that allowed other economic actors to integrate further into the domestic economy. "Thick/thin-markets" models were developed in the 1980s to explain the persistence of long-run under-utilization of production factors. Economic growth in France during the eighteenth century can be viewed as a thickening of markets.

Population and resources

Economic growth

Economic growth in France during the eighteenth century was probably as fast as it was in England (for the first presentation of this see Crouzet, 1966). According to *Institut de Science Economique Appliquée* (ISEA) research, based on contemporaneous estimations, annual growth of the nominal gross physical product (GPP) between 1701–1710 and 1791–1794 was 1.2 percent, from 1,470 million livres to 4,059 million livres (Marczewski, 1961 – this work owes a lot to Molinier, 1957). These macro results are compatible with what we know of the product at the beginning of the nineteenth century (compare Bourguignon and Levy-Leboyer, 1985). Their weakness lies in the quality of the data for the beginning of the period. As the population grew 0.24 percent a year (Dupâquier and Lepetit, 1988), this yields a per capita nominal growth of nearly 1 percent a year.

Starting from sectoral evidence would yield the same result. Agricultural growth was faster than population growth, but not by very much (Toutain, 1995). The rise in the production of wool products – the least dynamic of large French industries – was 1.15 percent (Markovitch, 1976). The growth of linen production can be estimated between 1.5 percent and 2 percent a year, while that of silk was 2 percent (Léon, 1970a). Future "modern" industries were of course growing much faster, but they did not form an important part of the product and are less

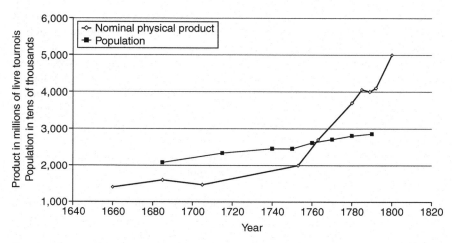

Figure 6.1 French nominal physical product and population.

interesting. Apart from textiles, the other two large industries were farm products (including wine) and construction: no rate of growth of their production can be estimated. Yet, there is enough data to affirm that our global evaluation of GPP growth is plausible.

There is no reliable price index that could be used to deflate this number. However, Labrousse's estimation of the evolution of agricultural prices from 1701–1710 to 1771–1789 can be used, and yields a per capita growth of 0.6 percent. The general evolution of prices is over-evaluated by the evolution of agricultural prices. Yet this is probably compensated for by the abnormally high prices caused by the War of Spanish Succession and the 1709 winter.

The existence of labor reserves

Technical progress only took off with the industrial revolution which happened at the beginning of the nineteenth century in France. In the absence of any exogenous productivity revolution, this growth was possible because more production factors were integrated into the domestic economy. There are three main visible production factors: land, capital, and labor. The stock of land did not change. In so far as fixed capital played a small part in industrial production (compare Grenier, 1996, pp. 84–91; Chapman, 1973; Hudson, 1986, pp. 48–52; Cailly, 1993, pp. 203 *passim;* Caspard, 1979, p. 117; Dornic, 1955, pp. 206–208; Vardi, 1993, p. 131), any increase in the stock of capital was probably too small to explain the speed of growth. A large part of this speed must have come from a more extensive use of human labor.

This was only possible because, in direct opposition to what is usually said about "Malthusian" pre-modern economies, a large part of the labor of the French populations was under-utilized. Demographics tell us that the potential size of the active population was 66 percent of the total population. Grantham has plausibly argued that only between 26 percent and 47 percent of it were needed to produce grain – including part-time workers required during harvest (Grantham, 1994). The proportion of agricultural workers in the actual active population at the end of the eighteenth century was 65 percent of an actual active population estimated at 43.5 percent of the total population (Marchand and Thélot, 1991). This can be interpreted in two ways. If the active population is well measured, 23 percent of the total population could have taken part in the work force and did not. If the active population has been underestimated but if its distribution among sectors is right, between 18 percent and 39 percent of the active population were part of the agricultural population and were not needed – even part-time – to produce grains. Many of them were probably occupied with the production of market agricultural goods, but it seems implausible that it was the case even for most of them.

Of course, considering the measurement difficulties, these numbers should be interpreted with caution. They show however – contrary to common wisdom about "blocked" early modern economies – that the basic subsistence activities required only a small part of the labor force. Hence, there were large reserves of labor in the countryside. Accordingly, an important potential source of growth was the extension of rural market activities, both industrial and agricultural.

Cost of market participation and growth

A Smithian growth potential

Something had to make worthwhile the integration of under-utilized rural labor in the economy. The claim of this chapter is that it was the development of exchanges between different existing economic cells. This increased the number of potential patrons for rural industries. The markets, to use Alfred Marshall's words (Hall, 1991), gained in thickness. This allowed social returns to scale in the number of participants needed to increase labor effective productivity (for a review of different thick/thin markets-type of models, and a reflection on their utility for the study of pre-industrial growth, see Grantham (1997)). Because of this movement from thin markets to thick markets, this growth phenomenon can be seen as "Smithian," as Adam Smith insisted on the importance of market integration for economic development. This chapter suggests one mechanism for such growth.

A non-integrated market can be compared to an archipelago economy. Social relations at the level of the canton (a 5–10 kilometer radius circle dominated by a market center) were probably strong enough to make the economy look like a perfectly competitive market. Hence, we consider them as the basic cell of economic life, as our "islands": their number was nearly 5,000 in eighteenth century France. Peasant households on these islands have the choice between producing autarkic goods which they can directly consume, or participating in the market domestic economy by producing specialized commercial goods, selling them and buying with the proceeds a basket of commercial goods coming from other economic cells.

Let us first consider a case where trading has no cost. Following the same kind of intuition as the "Big Push" models (Rosenstein-Rodan, 1943; Murphy *et al.*, 1989), one can imagine two different kinds equilibria. When no canton produces market goods, a single canton which would like to start producing market goods would not do it, as it is not interested in the consumption of a single, highly specialized, market good. Hence, no canton participates in the domestic market economy. However, if all cantons participate and produce market goods, the offer of market goods for consumption is enticing enough that each canton has an interest in continuing its production of specific market goods to be able to buy a basket of market goods. There is an optimal level of production of market goods that can be reached if all the cantons can be convinced to produce enough. This level is probably larger than is achievable by spontaneous market mechanisms. As each canton has monopoly power on its specialized market good production, it wants to reduce its own production to increase the price of its variety and increase the amount of its consumption. As everyone is playing this game, the actual production level is smaller than the optimum.

Moving from the "no market good production" situation to the "some market good production" situation is a form of one-time growth, as the economy moves between two equilibria. However, this transition is instantaneous and depends on a change in expectations. This could fit in the human ecology approach: the movement from one equilbrium to the other could be caused by a change in belief systems, as everyone simultaneously decides that market participation is a good thing, and in so doing makes it sustainable. Yet, it does not describe French growth experience: one needs an explanation of the fact that growth was gradual. The suggestion of this chapter is that the costs of participating in the domestic economy were declining through time, thanks to financial capital accumulation by traders. But to understand that explanation, one needs to recognize the role of traders in the domestic economy.

The role of traders in the domestic economy

Representing the domestic market economy as the result of transactions between isolated economic cells neglects the fact that the French market economy was organized around the traders. Except on the canton level, there were always middle-men between the producer and the consumer. Most areas were dealing with a huge part of the national market. Data about goods movement in France at the end of the period show that even the most backward rural areas were drawing goods from many different and distant places (Le Roux, 1996, pp. 135, 144).

There are no comprehensive data or studies on the intensity of domestic trade. Nevertheless, the circulation of goods was probably growing faster than the nominal growth of industry: as each individual industry grew, it had to find consumers further and further away. The circulation of information, on which we have more data, was certainly growing fast: the nominal revenue of the *Poste*, for example, grew 3.4 percent a year – with declining prices – between 1738 and 1791. The revenue of fairs and tolls was also growing faster than global product (Léon, 1970b).

Someone had to deal with these goods movements. Accordingly, most districts had dynamic traders dealing potentially with the whole national market. A perfect example of this has been extensively studied in England (Willian, 1970). In France, the Colombo House in Nice can be said to be representative of these activities. It was quite a small firm of retailers that was drawing supply from as far away as Normandy, using credit and commercial paper extensively. During the French Revolution, its traders showed they were dynamic entrepreneurs by regularly adapting their commercial networks to changing circumstances and trying to mount new speculations (Carlin, 1965). Traders were also responsible for the organization of the production in numerous cases – as the abundant literature on proto-industrialization has shown (for French examples: compare Engrand, 1979, pp. 68–70; Guignet, 1979, p. 29; Vardi, 1993, p. 194). Hence, traders were effectively allowing inter-canton transactions.

That this operation was vital to the way the *ancien régime* economies worked can be shown by the social agreements embedded in the domestic industrial policies, notably the regulation system. It set down, in a very precise way, how each good should be produced. From the production point of view, the whole system seems to be inefficient. However, information was very valuable in the *ancien régime* economy, and particularly difficult to obtain. In an era when traders would trade whatever would come their way, identifying the quality of each product was impossible. The customers were even more liable to be cheated on what they were buying. No private trademark existed and thus no one could commit himself to the quality of a product – even if through privilege, a form of personal identification could be put on cloth (for an example, see Gayot, 1979, pp. 136–137). Products could become anonymous very quickly, because of multiple middle-men (this was all the more complex as quality did not only refer to the value usage of each good, but also to its integration in an a priori social hierarchy: Grenier, 1996, pp. 63–70; Reddy, 1984). Hence, transaction costs were very high: you had either to trust your partner or to implement a complete inspection of the good each time. Regulations were a good way of partially solving the problem. First, they established a control. Also, because the whole reputation of a town or production centre was at stake in a case of fraud, some auto-monitoring took place. The real obligation was not for a trader to give fair information on the product – even if he should, no large or effective administration was going to control him. The main burden rested on the producer, who could only produce certain qualities and could neither introduce product or production innovations. Quality control helps trade and impedes production.

As such, it is a social control that reveals something important about the interplay of the structural conditions in eighteenth-century France human economic ecology. The idea that trade was more crucial than production was an important part of its belief system (this is confirmed by Bossenga, 1988). Studying the examples of Lille, Lyon, Paris, and Orléans, he shows the way "by which merchants manipulated the corporate regulations in order to secure a monopoly over the sale of reputable goods produced by both urban artisans and rural weavers" (Bossenga, 1988, pp. 694–695).

The role of monetary capital in allowing transactions

The activity of traders can be divided into three parts. First, they were insuring the actual movement of goods along space and time (the cost of keeping inventories), along with their packaging and their bundling. They had to take precautions in order to insure that each member of the trading network behaved well. They had also to adapt to a lack of information – even in the absence of misbehavior – and changing states of the market.

Some of the forms of capital needed by traders for their activity are familiar. On one hand, the exchange activities – especially their transformation side – require what we are used to calling capital in production economies: carts, buildings, etc. (fixed capital). This capital is of the same nature as in most economic models; it needs to be produced the usual way, through work and other capital. This is also the case of circulating capital: the wool that is to be threaded, the threads that are to be woven, etc.

They needed also what is usually called "merchant capital": circulating financial capital to buy intermediary consumption, used to package and present goods, and the circulating capital embedded in each good as they kept inventories between its purchase and its sale.

They were tackling the problems of misbehavior with work entailed by the inspections and the capital needed to access the legal system that was supposed to enforce propriety rights. However, they could save dramatically on these operations if they had developed enough social and legal links with their partners. This stock could be inherited by offspring of a trading family; be produced out of social capital, by sending members of their family abroad; be produced in its own right out of their work – during travels or apprenticeship; be produced out of financial capital, by buying lands and offices which were tools of integration in a stable community and hence commitment to good behavior. This stock was also very fragile, and it was commonplace to affirm that nothing was at the same time more precious nor more fragile than a reputation – the other term for a large stock of social capital (compare, among numerous examples: how the Pellet brothers started their carrier by sending one of them to the West Indies (Cavignac, 1967); the frequent travels of Pourtalès – knowledge capital was also accumulated in this case (Bergeron, 1970); and the catastrophic effect for Lacoube's trade and credit of the misbehavior of his nephews (Cornette, 1986). However, there is no machinery that can be used to build up reputation capital. One way to do it is to expend part of one's wealth to show the commitment – this wealth only has to be symbolic. This is similar to a "bond" approach to social capital and reputation.

Tackling the problems of market uncertainties and changeability required traders to spend time in getting information from all their correspondents and interpreting it. Yet, they could also save on this by using their own knowledge of the market. We can represent this by a stock of market cultural capital: a mix of tricks, best practice, and knowledge. Most of this knowledge could only be transmitted with difficulty. Experience of a particular type of network or market could only be the fruit of day-to-day operations once traders had created the first link. To create this link they had to stake a lot of money, suffer many rebuffs and learn from them (the cost of this was less important if it was done during apprenticeship – see for example Thomson, 1982, p. 302). Hence, traders were sacrificing the money they could get from operations that they were acquainted with in order to get a larger stock of knowledge capital.

Hence, even though the development of transactions required specific production factors, they were highly personal and bound to depreciate very quickly. However, both social and knowledge capital could be increased through a costly transformation of monetary capital. This capital was not the ideal transaction factor, but it was the easiest to exchange and socially accumulate. Hence, in the absence of institutional transformations, what was crucial for the long-run development of transactions was the accumulation of circulating monetary capital.

This was the case in France. Arnould estimated that the circulating stock of metallic money grew 0.8 percent a year between 1715 and 1788 (Arnould,

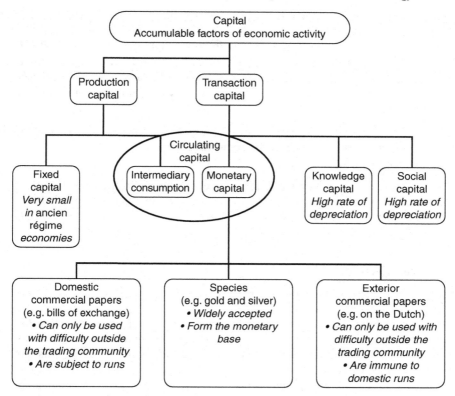

Figure 6.2 Different types of capital.

1791, p. 153). This number is compatible with the growth rate of 0.785 percent a year between 1700 and 1788 computed by modern researchers (Riley and McCusker, 1983, p. 280). The total stock was approximately two billion livres at the end of the period – half the value of the physical product. This specie stock was not the whole money stock, which was also composed of commercial papers like the bills of exchange. Yet according to the sketchy evidence we have, an increase of the real money stock and hence of the circulating monetary capital stock seems a very plausible description of the eighteenth-century situation.

Traders accumulated capital and increased the amount of means of transaction they controlled. The best way to employ this capital in order to increase their profits was to increase the integration of rural producers into the domestic market economy. This is an explanation for French economic growth in the eighteenth century that is compatible with the belief systems and social agreements that can be observed (this model is formalized in Daudin (2002) and Daudin (2005)). France was not at the forefront of the development of the market economy. This explains why there was still benefits to be reaped from the development of national markets, even if, as discussed in Chapter 2 by George Modelski, this is seen as a very early innovation associated with Sung China. Certainly, the Low Countries, for example, already benefited from a nearly full commitment of their producers in the domestic market economy by the eighteenth century. That was not yet the case in France. However, France did participate in Amerasian trade, associated with the K-wave of the late seventeenth to early eighteenth century. The next section shows how the external sector encouraged increased integration of the domestic market.

On the role of external trade in accumulating circulating financial capital

This section discusses chryshedonism – the attachment to the increase of the stock of precious metals in the economy – and the important role of predatory external trade in allowing more economic growth. Both of these were important tenets of the mercantilist belief system.

The real effects of species

The non-neutrality of the real stock of money

Promissory bills, exchange bills, commercial credit: the preceding section has proffered the idea that money *largo sensu* was the capital that mattered for growth in eighteenth-century France. To think of money as capital is not common in economics. It cannot be avoided though, if one accepts the fact that making transactions is a proper economic activity that should be studied for itself. This can even be extracted from such a money-veil theorist as J.S. Mill:

> There cannot, in short, be intrinsically a more insignificant thing, in the economy of society, than money; except in the character of a contrivance for sparing time and labour. It is a machine for doing quickly and commodiously, what would be done, though less quickly and commodiously, without it. ... The introduction of money does not interfere with the operation of any of the Laws of Value laid down in the preceding chapters. ... Things which by barter would exchange for one another, will, if sold for money, sell for an equal amount of it, and so will exchange for one another still.
>
> (Mill, 1909, book III, chpt. VII, §3, p. 488)

The last part of this quote is quite typical; here, the first part is more interesting. The use of the term machine is telling. What Mill is saying about money could be said as well of any machinery or other fixed capital. What is a tool, a device, a machine, if not "a machine for doing quickly and commodiously, what would be done, though less quickly and commodiously, without it"? Capital is a device that helps to save on other production factors. If money helps to save on production factors, can it be considered as capital, in the mercantilist way? (compare Locke in Heckscher, 1935, t. II pp. 203–204). Obviously, in a pure production world, where transactions do not require the use of resources, as money could not help production, money could not be capital. However, that is not the case in actual economies. Transactions are important: and somehow the society must pay their cost. If money can help, it is right to consider it as capital.

Is it possible to increase a real stock of money? Augmenting a stock of capital is conceptually an easy task, as one has just to add more machines and tools. Increasing the stock of money is trickier. Money is only important as a symbol of real wealth: real money. However, the nominal stock of money is not neutral on prices, and an increase in the nominal stock of money will not lead to an increase in the real stock of money if prices adjust. This can be studied in a variant of Hume's famous thought experiment. If the nominal money stock is divided by two overnight, and if everyone knows it, prices should decrease as well and the real money stock should stay the same. According to what everyone thinks money is, if everyone knows about this division of the nominal stock, everyone would expect to see the price of money multiplied by two, whatever the situation. As a consequence, prices would be divided by two. Yet this implies rational expectations, knowledge of the neoclassical models of money, and more important, perfect information on the evolution of private stocks of money of everybody.

The contrast between neoclassical models and the human ecology approach to economics is obvious here: in the human ecology approach, as per any ecological approach, intraspecies negotiations and transactions are exploratory, adaptive, often individualized, and the outcomes are not known to all members of the species. If full information, to all, on intraspecies transactions is not available, as per the human ecology approach, the evolution of prices is not as straightforward, because prices cannot be changed by spontaneous unanimous social agreement. There are two main effects that may change the output in the long term. The first effect of the discrete shock – cutting the money supply in half – is to disorganize exchanges, as agents have to renegotiate new contracts to take the modification into account. The demand and supply curves for each good are modified. Sellers face buyers who ask for lower prices. This can only engage distrust: are they giving their practice to someone else? Why do they want the prices to decrease? Sellers are themselves more eager to get money to compensate their mysterious loss. The terms of transactions have to be changed, and new relationships must be implemented. Relation-specific human and social capital become obsolete as relations are changed and the very process of renegotiation requires the use of new transaction goods to get back to the status quo ante. Hence, even if this is possible, the stock of transaction goods is reduced in the economy: the costs in nominal price changes are in themselves important (the whole point of new Keynesian literature is to show that small menu costs may have large effects on the aggregate. The point here is that the cost of changing nominal price is not small – because it entails transaction costs and the destruction of social and human capital. For a textbook presentation of new Keynesian views on this, see Romer (1996, pp. 276–302). For a collection of articles see Mankiw and Romer (1991, vol. 1, pp. 29–211).

The second effect takes place if prices do not adjust fully to the modification of the stock of money. How prices react depends on the way bargaining takes place among the population. If a Walrasian (*tâtonnement*, or an efficient broker) process takes place, no transaction is implemented before the prices take into account the information of the decrease of the nominal stock of money: prices should adjust fully – they are divided by two and the stock of real monetary wealth in the economy does not change. However, this is probably not the case. If for any reason prices adjust only slowly, for example with a one-period lag, or partly because of the menu costs studied before, the stock of real monetary wealth in the economy is reduced. In consequence, the means to create social and human capital in subsequent periods are divided by the evolution of the real stock of money. Furthermore, symbolic relations which allow the building of trust may be subject to nominal illusion and may not adapt at all. As in many monetarist and new classical models, an unexpected modification of the money supply has an effect on output. Contrary to them, though, this short-term nominal shock has a long-term effect because the modification of prices directly changes the assets stock of the economy (an example of these models is the Lucas–Phelps one of limited information, in which agents do not know if evolution in prices are due to changes in relative or absolute prices (Lucas, 1972; Phelps, 1970). For a presentation and a discussion see Romer (1996, pp. 242–251). This model is interesting in our case because its imperfect information hypothesis looks like ours. For a study of new classical economics see Hoover (1988).

Hence, the Humian result has very few reasons to be expected. P is not the only variable reacting to the decrease of M in $M \times V = P \times Q$ (Cambridge equation or quantity equation as discussed in Chapter 5). Q is decreasing too, as may be V. The level of transaction actually decreases in the long term following a large discrete nominal shock. Even though the value of money is symbolic, the way its pricing is organized and the importance of transaction costs makes it possible for a discrete nominal shock to have a long term real effect.

Furthermore, no actual modification in the stock of money looks like Hume's situation. People are affected in different manners by the evolution of the money stock in the economy. Increasing the money stock in the hands of traders who put it into circulation certainly has not the same effect as increasing the peasants' hoarding stock.

The role of specie in the ancien régime monetary system

Chapter 5 defends the idea that the control of the monetary base by the United States, in the form of the U.S. dollar, gave the United States decisive advantages in the twentieth century. In the same way, the control of the monetary base was a decisive question for the increase in the stock of money in France, and hence for the growing integration of producers into the national market economy. Because of different belief systems and social agreements, the monetary base was obviously not the stock of some national currency in the eighteenth century – it was the stock of precious metals.

Money is in essence a problem of convention. That is why in all monetary systems a continuous process of money creation is always possible. In eighteenth-century France, there was no real banking system. Hence, most money creation was undergone by commercial agents. By issuing bills of exchange, which they would remit only some time after, perhaps with other commercial papers, or by extending commercial credit, agents were simply creating means of exchange – that is, money (an approach to these conceptual problems can be seen in Bernanke and Blinder (1988). For an empirical study see Carrière *et al.* (1976, pp. 49–71)). All the more as the flexibility of the use of commercial papers was very high in the eighteenth century (compare Roover, 1953; Carrière *et al.*, 1976). However, this system was completely decentralized, the result of which was the uncoordinated behavior of agents. If a trader had a good reputation, it would be easy for him to place his promissory bonds. On the contrary, if he was not trusted he would probably find it impossible to do any commercial operation except with the support of high-powered money, i.e. precious metals. At a macroeconomic level, the amount of accepted money in the economy would be in close relation with the size of the monetary base, i.e. the amount of precious metal. This result is intuitive. Imagine an economy where commercial paper circulates without any means of personal insurance on its backing in precious metal. Creditors ask randomly to be repaid in precious metal. This has a domino effect on their debtors who, in order to face their obligation, demand the same of their own debtors. The smaller the stock of precious metal in the economy, the more difficult it will be to satisfy these commands. If this is not possible, exceptional shocks would result in failures and more generally in a brutal contraction of the money supply in the economy (this problem was important in the 1930s (Bernanke, 1995); mercantilists were aware of it (Heckscher, 1935 (1994), t. II pp. 221–224, 231–237)). Hence, the smaller the monetary base compared to the monetary mass, the less stable the whole system is.

Furthermore, each extremity of the trade chain – producers and consumers – were not integrated in the commercial financial system: the only form of money they accepted was species. Hence, the real monetary supply was closely related to the stock of precious metal in the economy. Its increase was the aim of chryshedonist mercantilist policies.

A role for mercantilist policies toward trade

French mercantilist policies and their achievement

The aim of external mercantilist trade policies was not as much to "protect" domestic production as to maximize the current account surplus – and hence inward specie flow. They planned on doing that not only through a positive trade balance in goods, but also by encouraging the sale of trading services by French actors to the rest of the world.

This is clear in the following text by Colbert in which he analyzes Franco-Dutch trade at the beginning of the reign of Louis XIV. At the time, Dutch traders controlled a large part of French maritime trade, external and domestic. His argument is that although French exports were 12 to 18 million livres a year, only between four and six million livres entered as specie each year since the Dutch were paying the French using the following goods and services:

Maritime freight between French ports:	3 million
Colonial goods coming from the French islands:	2 million
Fine clothes, Indian goods, spices, silk, etc.:	3 million
Goods coming from Northern Europe and naval stores	1.5 million

Their ingenuity and our weak-mindedness has been so high that, through the agents they were able to install in every ports of the kingdom, having become the masters of all trade and navigation, they were able to dictate the price of all the goods they sell or buy.

(Clément, 1861–1882, t. II, p. CCLXIX, quoted in Deyon, 1969, p. 100)

There is more than the usual balance of trade theory in this text. Colbert realizes that the main Dutch imports in France were not Dutch-produced goods, but shipping services or re-exports. What is more, the second paragraph stresses that the real problem is the trade position of the Dutch that allows them to make huge commercial profits. What Colbert was complaining about was not Franco-Dutch trade as such, but rather the numerous imports in freight and commercial services caused by the weakness of French traders.

The idea was that trade was to a certain extent a zero-sum game and that each country should help its own traders to get as much as possible from it. The usage of state resources taken from the whole economy in order to secure monopoly profit was but a way of giving back to traders some of the externalities to which the multiplication of exchanges stimulated by their private activity gave rise.

A century later, France had, in effect, taken control of many of these activities, notably by re-exporting colonial products to the whole of continental Europe – effectively controlling a large part of trade between continental Europe and the West Indies. On a smaller scale, the taking over of some parts of inter-Asian trade had the same effect and also yielded important revenues (Haudrère, 1989; Manning, 1996). The distribution of these gains had been decided by the incessant commercial wars and commercial diplomatic agitation of the eighteenth century, notably between France and England. By losing Canada and keeping its West Indies possessions after the worst part of this struggle in 1763, France kept the most profitable part of its Empire and removed a cause for solidarity between England and the Thirteen Colonies. Only during the Wars of the Revolution would England eventually win the Second Hundred Years' War (1689–1815).

French dynamism can be seen in the evolution of French external trade, which is quite well-known (on the production of French trade statistics, see Beaud, 1964). The main aggregate data (from Bruyard (former head of the Bureau de commerce), cited in Romano, 1957) gives a growth rate of 2.25 percent per annum between 1716–1720 and 1776–1780. The other important set of data is Arnould's – Arnould was second-in-command of the Bureau de

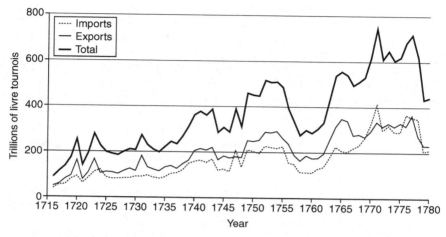

Figure 6.3 Evolution of French trade.

commerce. It implies a growth of 2.34 percent per annum between 1716–1720 and 1784–1788: the results are not so different, especially if we remember that 1778–1783 was a time of maritime war with England, and hence that Bruyard's figures for the end of the period are abnormally low (his numbers are higher than English ones – for a synthesis on these see Thomas and McCloskey, 1981). According to Arnould's figure, the openness of the French economy (the ratio between the mean of imports and exports and the GPP) at the end of the period was more than 14 percent. If we consider services were 17 percent of GDP (data from Bourguignon and Levy-Leboyer (1985) for 1820), this yields a usual measure of openness of a little less than 12 percent. The structure of this trade corresponds to what we have pointed out. From 1716 to 1787, the growth rate of exports in manufactured product to the rest of Europe was only 1.5 percent per annum, whereas the growth rate in re-exports of colonial products was 2.7 percent per annum. This last sector represented as much as 40 percent of French exports to Europe.

Effect of mercantilist policies

As mercantilists knew, external trade was the only means for a country to get a steady inward flow of precious metals and restrictive trade practices were the best way to make this flow as high as possible. There are two sides to this argument.

As domestic production of precious metals was negligible, the external world was their only possible source. During the eighteenth century, European production of precious metals was very small (even the famous Maria-Theresa Thalers were minted out of American silver rather than German (Dermigny, 1954)). It is commonplace to say that Europe was the relay between the production in the Western hemisphere and the hoarding of precious metals in Asia. The problem for Europe was to keep them as long as possible (on why the pure Ricardian specie flow mechanism could not apply to relations between America, Europe, and Asia see Blitz, 1967), and the aim of each country was to get as large as possible a share of this scarce commodity.

For numerous reasons, it is very difficult to compute the current account balance. Even if the global export and import values are trustworthy, the difference between them is probably not. Furthermore, that would give us only information on the trade balance, not the balance of invisibles. I have tried to compute the balance of invisibles for a specific year (Daudin, 2006). Yet, beside the balance of invisibles, there were other leaks in the system – hoarding, political expenses abroad, etc. – that prevented the evolution of the stock of specie to be equal to the trade balance.

Another effect of external trade was to encourage capital accumulation by domestic traders. For that, external trade had to yield higher rates of return than domestic uses of capital. This can be checked.

It has been argued that capital was in fact in excess in the economy, and was often invested in productive ventures with difficulty – this is in apparent contradiction with the presentation we have made of circulating financial capital being the limiting factor in production. This paradox can be explained by the non-substitutability of a large number of forms of capital – most notably hoarding by all classes of society – with the actual circulating financial capital in the hands of traders. Capital was not a homogenous good. Its characteristic depended on who was using it, or rather on the specific and personal forms of social capital and knowledge it was completed by. Hence, any activity that could transmit it from the other classes of society to dynamic traders was growth enhancing.

Two different families of arguments can be used to show that profits were higher in external than internal trade. The first one is empirical, and based on micro-economic study of actual profits. It was made based on a large database of profit rates (Daudin, 2004). Profits in external trade were only around 6 percent – far from the very high numbers that were advertised in the literature. Yet, this was 40 percent higher – taking into account risk, duration, and liquidity – than what was available in the rest of the economy.

Another family of arguments – macroeconomic and theoretical – also exist. External trade was also the realm of politics, conflict and power. This implies that there was a lot of rent seeking for the profit of traders looked upon favorably by the state. Accordingly, many cliometricians would agree that the only reason the Empire was kept is that it yielded high premium profits to traders and planters (Coelho, 1973). Yet, as in a simple economic framework it is difficult to explain why rates of returns on capital should be constantly higher in one sector, most of them would at the same time defend the idea that the organization of colonial trade, notably slave trade, was competitive and should not have given higher returns than domestic trade (Thomas and Bean, 1974). These two sides of the argument are unmistakably contradictory. To use Smith's words, why would a government influenced by shopkeepers go into important sacrifices to preserve a system that was not even profitable to shopkeepers? The second hypothesis can be more readily dropped than the first one.

Indeed, external speculation yielded much more scope for profits than domestic transactions. The quality of capital needed for a relationship between two continents, or even two different countries, was different from what was needed for domestic trade. Knowledge and social capital were often relations-specific, and they were in even shorter supply in this case – hence the higher apparent rate of return on money capital. Even money capital was specific, as the usage of commercial papers was more difficult in these relationships. Capital immobilization and risks were much higher: considering the probable risk-aversion and preference for the liquidity of agents, it would be only fair that profit rates should be higher.

Moreover, the suggestion that external trade was competitive can certainly be contested. The small number of towns controlling colonial trade, their special-ization, and the existence of strong social structures that facilitated co-ordination encouraged oligopoly. The important activity of the Chambres de Commerce and Députés de Commerce, institutions created at the beginning of the century to legalize and facilitate lobbying, are proof that the caste of *négociants* had a real sense of solidarity. The way local institutions worked is another one. The group also ensured its coherence by constant social interactions (see Carrière, 1973, pp. 211–236 for the example of Marseille).

What is more, if profits had not been higher in the external sector, how could we explain the higher rapid growth of external trade compared to the domestic economy and the constant attraction by port cities of trader migrants? This fact alone would indicate that premium profits were indeed being secured. A last point, of course, is that the "small country" hypothesis is at least partly valid here. Compared to the rest of the world, the activities of France (in Europe and the world), or even core Europe for that matter, were small. Hence, an increase in the activity of French traders could not have a large depressing impact on worldwide trade profits.

To sum up, it is plausible that external trade offered a potential for higher profits than any domestic use of capital – even if this potential may have been overstated by the old conventional wisdom. Hence, the encouragement of trading activity abroad by mercantilist policies had an effect on specie accumulation via a mechanism linked to "endogenous growth" theory. The "productive" specie supply was the one in the hands of traders. Their incentive to accumulate specie was linked both to their ascetic behavior (or small preference for the present) and to the returns yielded by circulating financial capital in the domestic economy. As these returns were decreasing, the capital stock accumulation was bound to be smaller than what would be needed to reap the maximum social profits from divi-sion of labor. However, according to the predictions of "heart of growth" models (Rebelo, 1991; Glachant, 1995; Lucas, 1988), if traders could have access to a sector with a lower boundary on the return of capital, and insubstantial needs in primary factors (i.e. factors which cannot be freely accumulated, like land and labor), they will tend to accumulate capital without limits as long as it can help goods production. In so far as we are looking for a sector with no links to labor and land, the profits we are interested in are not so much those associated with a positive balance of trade *stricto sensu* as those associated with the positive balance of invisibles, including commercial and shipping profits. These activities, often overlooked, played an important role in the accumulation of capital in France during the eighteenth century, as they do nowadays in the accumulation of capital in offshore markets – which is a source of the "money mercantilist" profits currently accumulating in the U.S., as argued by Allen in Chapter 5.

Because of these two effects, it was socially optimal to allow traders to make supra-normal profits in the external sector in order to encourage capital accumulation. That was one of the effects of mercantilist policies.

Conclusion

We have shown that a main potential source of growth in *ancien régime* economies was Smithian. Transactions, traders, and money played a central role in allowing this growth to occur. In the absence of a proper banking system, the stock of money depended crucially on the stock of precious metals in the economy. Hence, chryshedonist mercantilist policies aiming at increasing the share of specie of each country through a positive balance of invisibles were growth enhancing.

As in the contemporaneous financial world system, core countries were able to attract specie for the benefit of their domestic economies. There was, actually, already an international finance system. However, it was mainly concerned with national debts and its movement only very rarely had any effect on the commercial financial system, and even less on the monetary base. Hence, this extraction of specie was only possible through trade and the export of both goods and services.

Bibliography

Arnould, Ambroise Marie. (1791). *De la balance du commerce et des relations commerciales extérieures de la France dans toutes les parties du globe particulièrement à la fin du règne de Louis XIV et au moment de la révolution.* Paris.

Barro, Robert J. and Sala-i-Martin, Xavier. (1995). *Economic Growth.* McGraw-Hill: New York.

Beaud, M. (1964). "Le Bureau de la Balance du Commerce, 1781–1791." *Revue d'histoire économique et sociale*, 357–377.

Bergeron, Louis. (1970). "Pourtalès et Cie, 1753–1801, Apogée et déclin d'un capitalisme." *Annales*, 2: 498–517.

Bernanke, Ben S. (1995). "The macroeconomics of the Great Depression: a comparative approach." *Journal of Money, Credit and Banking*, 27 (1): 1–28.

Bernanke, Ben. S. and Blinder, A.S. (1988). "Is it money or credit, or both, or neither? Credit, money and aggregate demand." *American Economic Review*, 78: 435–439.

Blitz, Rudolph C. (1967). "Mercantilist policies and the pattern of world trade, 1500–1750." *Journal of Economic History*, XXVII (1): 39–55.

Bossenga, Gail. (1988). "Protecting merchants: Guilds and commercial capitalism in eighteenth-century France." *French Historical Studies*, 15: 693–703.

Bourguignon, François and Levy-Leboyer, Maurice. (1985). *L'Economie Française au XIXe siècle*. Economica: Paris.

Brown, Michael Barrat. (1974). *The Economics of Imperialism*. Penguin: Harmondsworth and Baltimore.

Butel, Paul. (1974). *Les Négociants Bordelais, l'Europe et les îles au XVIIIe siècle*. Aubier: Paris.

Cailly, C. (1993). "Mutations d'un espace proto-industriel: Le perche au XVIIIe-XIXe." *Fédération des amis du Perche*, 2: 742.

Carlin, Marie-Louise. (1965). *Un commerce de détail à Nice, sous la révolution: la maison Colombo*. La Pensée Universitaire: Aix-en-Provence.

Carrière, Charles. (1973). *Négociants marseillais au XVIIIe siècle*. Institut historique de Provence: Marseille.

Carrière, Charles, Courdurié, Marcel, Gutsatz, Michel, and Squarzoni, René. (1976). *Banque et capitalisme commercial. La lettre de change au XVIIIème siècle*. Institut Historique de Provence: Economies Modernes et Contemporaine: Marseille.

Caspard, P. (1979). "L'accumulation du capital dans l'indiennage au XVIIIe siècle." *Revue du Nord*, LXI (240): 115–124.

Caves, Richard E. (1971). "Export-led Growth ant the New Economic History." In. Bhagwati, J., Mundell, R., Jones, R., and Vanek, J. (eds) *Trade, Balance of Payments and Growth*. North-Holland: Amsterdam.

Cavignac, J. (1967). *Jean Pellet, commerçant en gros (1694–1772). Contribution à l'étude du négoce bordelais au XVIIIe siècle*. SEVPEN: Paris.

Chapman, S.D. (1973). "Industrial capital before the Industrial Revolution: an analysis of the assets of a thousand textile entrepreneurs c.1730–1750." In Hart, N.B. and Ponying, K.G. (eds) *Textile History and Economic History*. Manchester University Press: Manchester.

Clark, John G. (1981). *La Rochelle and the Atlantic Economy During the Eighteenth Century*. Johns Hopkins University Press: Baltimore.

Clément, P. (1861–1882). *Lettres, instructions et mémoires de Colbert*. Paris.

Coelho, Philip R.P. (1973). "The profitability of imperialism: the British experience in the West Indies, 1768–1772." *Exploration in Economic History*, X (2): 253–280.

Cornette, Joëlle. (1986). *Un Révolutionnaire Ordinaire: B. Lacoube, Négociant 1750–1819*. Champ Vallon: Seyselle.

Crouzet, François L. (1966). "Angleterre et France au XVIIIe siècle: analyse comparée de deux croissances économiques." *Annales E.S.C.*, XXI (2): 254–291.

Crouzet, François L. (1990 [1985]). *British Ascendent: Comparative Studies in Franco-British Economic History*. Cambridge University Press: Cambridge.

Darity, William, Jr. (1982). "A general equilibrium model of the eighteenth century atlantic slave trade: a least-likely test for the Caribbean school." *Research in Economic History*, 7: 287–326.

Daudin, Guillaume. (2002). "Coûts de transaction et croissance: un modèle à partir de la situation de la France du XVIIIe siècle." *Revue Française d'Economie*, XVII: 3–36.

Daudin, Guillaume. (2004). "Profitability of slave and long distance trading in context: the case of eighteenth century France." *Journal of Economic History*, 64 (1): 144–171.

Daudin, Guillaume. (2005). *Commerce et Prospérité: La France au XVIIIe siècle*. PUPS: Paris.

Daudin, Guillaume. (2006). "Do frontiers give or do frontiers take? The case of inter-continental trade in France at the end of the ancien régime." In Pétré-Grenouilleau, O.,

Emmer, P., and Roitman, J. (eds) *A Deus Ex Machina Revisited: Atlantic Colonial Activities and European Economic Development*. Brill: Leiden.

de Vries, Jan. (1994). "The industrial revolution and the industrious revolution." *Journal of Economic History*, 54 (2): 249–270.

Dermigny, Louis. (1954). "Circuits de l'argent et milieux d'affaires au XVIIIe siècle." *Revue Historique*, CCXII (1): 239–278.

Dermigny, Louis. (1960). *Cargaisons indiennes: Solier and Cie*. SEVPEN: Paris.

Dermigny, Louis. (1964). *La Chine et L'occident: Le commerce de Canton au XVIIIe siècle: 1719–1833*. SEVPEN: Paris.

Deyon, Pierre. (1969). *Le mercantilisme*. Flammarion: Paris.

Dornic, François. (1955). *L'industrie Textile Dans Le Maine Et Ses Débouchés Internationaux (1650–1815)*. Edition Pierre-Belon: Le Mans.

Dupâquier, Jacques and Lepetit, Bernard. (1988 [1995]). "Le peuplement." In Dupâquier, J. (ed.) *Histoire de la Population Française*, volume 2. Puf: Paris.

Engerman, Stanley L. (1972). "The slave trade and British capital formation in the eighteenth century: a comment on the William thesis." *Buisness History Review*, 46 (Winter): 430–443.

Engrand, Charles. (1979). "Concurrences et complémentarité des villes et des campagnes: les manufactures picardes de 1780 à 1815." *Revue du Nord*, LXI (240): 61–81.

Findlay, Ronald. (1990). "The trianguar trade and the Atlantic economy of the eighteenth century: a simple general-equilibrium model." *Essay in International Finance*.

Gayot, Gérard. (1979). "Dispersion et concentration de la draperie sedanaise au XVIIIe siècle: l'entreprise des Poupart de Neuflize." *Revue du Nord*, LXI (240): 127–148.

Glachant, Jérôme. (1995). "Croissance et structure du système productif dans une économie log-linéaire." *Annales d'économie et statistiques*, 39 (Juillet–septembre): 33–66.

Goubert, Pierre. (1959). *Familles marchandes sous l'Ancien Régime: Les Danse et les Motte, de Beauvais*. SEVPEN: Paris.

Grantham, George W. (1994). "Division of labour: agricultural productivity and occupation specialization in pre-industrial France." *Economic History Review*, 46 (3): 478–502.

Grantham, George W. (1997). *On the macroeconomics of pre-industrial economies*. Paper presented at the Cliometric Conference, Munich, 15 August.

Grenier, Jean-Yves. (1996). *L'économie d'Ancien Régime, Un monde de l'échange et de l'incertitude*. Albin Michel: Paris.

Guignet, Philippe. (1979). "Adaptations, mutations et survivances proto-industrielles dans le textile du Cambrésis et du Valencinnois du XVIIIe au début du XXe siècle." *Revue du Nord*, LXI (240): 27–59.

Hall, R. (1991). *Booms and Recessions in a Noisy Economy*. Yale: New Haven.

Haudrère, Philippe. (1989). "Fortunes orientales et commerce d'Inde en Inde au XVIIIe siècle." In Crouzet, F. (ed.) *Le Négoce International*. Economica: Paris.

Heckscher, Eli F. (1935 [1994]). *Mercantilism*. Routledge: London.

Hoover, Kevin D. (1988). *The New Classical Macroeconomics: A Sceptical Inquiry*. Basil Blackwell: Oxford.

Hudson, Pat. (1986). *The Genesis of Industrial Capital: A Study of the West Riding, c.1750–1850*. Cambridge University Press: Cambridge.

James, C.L.R. (1938 [1963]). *The Black Jacobins: Toussaint l'Ouverture and the San Domingo Revolution*. Vintage: New York.

Le Roux, Thomas. (1996). *Le commerce intérieur de la Frane à la fin du XVIIIe siècle: les Contrastes Économiques Régionaux de L'espace Français à Travers les Archives du Maximum*. Nathan: Paris.

Léon, Pierre. (1970a). "L'élan industriel et commercial." In Braudel, F. and Labrousse, E. (eds) *Histoire Économique et Sociale de la France.* Puf: Paris.

Léon, Pierre and Carrière, Charles. (1970b). "L'appel des marchés." In Braudel, F. and Labrousse, E. (eds) *Histoire Économique et Sociale de la France.* Puf: Paris.

Lespagnol, André. (1997). *Messieurs de Saint-Malo: Une Élite Négociante au Temps de Louis XIV.* Presses Universitaires de Rennes: Rennes.

Lucas, R. (1988). "On the mechanics of economic development." *Journal of Monetary Economics,* 22 (1): 3–42.

Lucas, R. (1972). "Expectations and the neutrality of money." *Journal of Economic Theory,* 4 (2): 103–124.

Mankiw, N. Gregory and Romer, David. (1991). *New Keynesian Economics.* MIT Press: Cambridge.

Manning, Catherine. (1996). *Fortunes à Faire: The French in Asian Trade, 1719–1748.* Variorum: Aldershot.

Marchand, Olivier and Thélot, Claude. (1991). *Deux siècles de travail en France.* INSEE: Paris.

Marczewski, Jean. (1961). "Some aspects of the economic growth of France, 1660–1958." *Economic Development and Cultural Change,* 9 (3): 369–386.

Markovitch, Tihomir J. (1976). *Histoire des Industries françaises (t. 1): Les Industries Lainières de Colbert à la Révolution.* Librairie Droz: Genève-Paris.

Meyer, Jean. (1969). *L'armement nantais dans la deuxième moitié du XVIIIe siècle.* SEVPEN: Paris.

Mill, John Stuart. (1909 [1848]). *Principles of Political Economy with Some of Their Applications to Social Philosophy.* Longmans, Green, and Co.: London.

Molinier, J. (1957). "Les calculs d'agrégats en France antérieurement à 1850." *Revue d'Economie Politique,* 857–897.

Murphy, Kevin M., Shleifer, Andrei, and Vishny, Robert. (1989). "Industrialisation and the Big Push." *The Quarterly Journal of Economics,* 97 (5): 1003–1026.

O'Brien, Patrick. (1982). "European economic development: the contribution of the periphery." *Economic History Review,* 35 (1): 1–18.

Phelps, Edmund S. (1970). "Introduction." In Phelps, E.S. (ed.) *Microeconomic Foundations of Employment and Inflation Theory.* W.W. Norton: New York.

Planhol, Xavier de. (1988). *Géographie Historique de la France,* 2nd edn. Fayard: Paris.

Rebelo, R. (1991). "Long-run policy analysis and long-run growth." *Journal of Political Economy,* 99 (3): 500–521.

Reddy, W. (1984). *The Rise of the Market Culture: the Textile Trade and French Society.* Cambridge University Press: Cambridge.

Richardson, David. (1975). "Profitability in the Bristol–Liverpool slave trade." *Revue Française d'Histoire d'Outre-Mer,* 62 (226–227): 301–308.

Riley, James C. and McCusker, J.J. (1983). "Money supply, economic growth and the quantity theory of money: France 1650–1788." *Explorations in Economic History,* 20 (3): 274–293.

Romano, Ruggiero. (1957). "Documenti e prime considerazioni interno alla balance du commerce della Francia dal 1716 al 1780." In *Studi in onore di Armando Sapori,* Volume 2. Instuto editoriale cisaopino: Milan.

Romer, David. (1996). *Advanced Macroeconomics.* McGraw-Hill: New York.

Roover, R. de. (1953). *L'évolution de la lettre de change, XIVe–XVIIIe siècles.* Armand Colin: Paris.

Rosenstein-Rodan, Paul N. (1943). "Problems of industrialisation in eastern and south-eastern Europe." *Economic Journal*, 53 (June–September): 202–211.

Solow, Barbara. (1985). "Caribbean slavery and British growth: the Eric Williams hypothesis." *Journal of Development Economics*, 17 (1): 99–115.

Tarrade, Jean. (1972). *Le Commerce Colonial de la France à la fin de l'Ancien Régime: L'évolution du Régime de L'exclusif de 1763 à 1782.* Presses Universitaires de France: Paris.

Thomas, R. and Bean, R. (1974). "The fishers of men: the profits of the slave trade". *Journal of Economic History*, 34 (4): 885–914.

Thomas, Robert Paul. (1968). "The sugar colonies of the old empire: profit or loss for Great Britain?" *Economic History Review*, 21 (1): 30–45.

Thomas, R.P. and McCloskey, D.N. (1981). "Overseas trade and empire 1700–1860." In Floud, R. and McCloskey, D. (eds) *The Economic History of Britain since 1700.* Cambridge University Press: Cambridge.

Thomson, J.K.J. (1982). *Clermont-de-Lodève, 1633–1789: Fluctuations in the Prosperity of a Languedocian Cloth-making Town.* Cambridge University Press: Cambridge.

Tilly, C. (1964). *The Vendée.* Edward Arnold: London.

Toutain, Jean-Claude. (1995). "La croissance inégale des régions françaises: l'agriculture de 1810 à 1990." *Revue historique*, CCXCI (2): 315–359.

Vardi, Liana. (1993). *The Land and the Loom: Peasants and Profit in Northern France, 1680–1800.* Duke University Press: Durham and London.

Wallerstein, Immanuel. (1974). *The Modern World System I: Capitalist Agriculture and the Origins of the European World-Economy in the Sixteenth Century.* Academic Press: New York.

Wallerstein, Immanuel. (1980). *The Modern World System II: Mercantilism and the Consolidation of the European World Economy 1600–1750.* Academic Press: New York.

Wallerstein, Immanuel. (1989). *The Modern World System III: The Second Era of Great Expansion of the Capitalist World-Economy, 1730s–1840s.* Academic Press: San Diego.

Williams, Eric Wilson. (1944 [1966]). *Capitalism and Slavery.* Capricorn: New York.

Willian, T.S. (1970). *Abraham Dent of Kirkby Stephen.* Manchester University Press: Manchester.

Part IV

Global concerns, ways of being, and the future

Part IV, comprising Chapters 7, 8, and 9, extends the human ecology framework to "coming challenges to humankind." Most of these ecologically-interrelated challenges within the global system threaten the sustainability of what we know and value, and they include climate change, a rise in poverty and inequality, scarcity of energy, food, and other resources, decline in biological diversity, pandemics, use of weapons of mass destruction, loss of the support of communication and other infrastructures, social strife and violence, large scale economic instability and crisis, failure of global institutions, etc.

Parts I, II, and III have already shed some light on these problems. For example, Part I has discussed periodic "clashes of civilizations" that occur with the rise and fall of political and economic leaders over long cycles of innovation, creative destruction, and evolution within the world system. Part II has discussed causes of poverty, inequality, and other challenges of economic growth and development in the current age of globalization. Part III has discussed causes of large scale financial instabilities and other destabilizing wealth transfers. In most of these investigations, much debate and controversy remains among the experts. And, in most cases, the traditional belief systems and human institutions brought to bear upon the particular problem seem inadequate. Hopefully the human ecology economics framework has been helpful in identifying these inadequacies, and reframing these problems in more comprehensive ways so that better ways of responding to them can be found.

The climate change challenge, as discussed in Chapter 7, may be the ultimate example of an existing institutional framework and its supporting beliefs that have been inadequate, and where reframing institutions is necessary. The fundamental challenge is to transform our energy system and the social organization around it, which stems from an earlier era, and align a new system with the long term needs of humans and other species populating the earth. As discussed in Chapter 7, human ecology economics offers a peaceful and cost-effective way to help.

Yet, however insightful and comprehensive we become in our understanding of climate change and other global concerns, and however cleverly we design new technologies and institutions, it is increasingly clear that the "ways of being" of people may still need to change if what we know and value is to be sustained. Ways of being are defined here to include not only belief systems, but also associated personality traits, social behaviors, and physical energies of the people involved in the ecology in question. Chapters 8 and 9 elaborate these points.

Two scenarios of civilization's future, up to the year 2060, presented in Chapter 8, both prove to be untenable unless, in addition to reaching various state-of-the-art energy efficiencies and other scientific and economic innovations, we also (re)discover ways to co-create the world with other species and nurture new institutions based less on self-importance, hatred, fear, greed, ambition, aggression, and more on altruism, cooperation, humility, responsibility, etc. Sustainability requires reconciliation between increasingly connected people and cultures rather than destructive competition between them. Chapter 8 discusses various methods of cognitive intelligence available to us, which can help with this reconciliation.

It is also concluded, in Chapter 9, that a mentally healthy person, as well as a healthy human ecology, needs to find better balance, tolerance, and appropriate hierarchy between various interrelated ways of being that are currently at play across the global system. Various ways of being are identified in Chapter 9, which can then be better understood and reconciled along the path to a better future.

7 The role of economics in climate policy

Asbjorn Moseidjord

> This approach [the human ecology approach to economics] is proposed to give economists maximum conceptual freedom to rethink the boundaries and methods of their discipline ... it seeks to coordinate previously disconnected knowledge, and make that knowledge available for a variety of practical purposes.
>
> (Allen, Chapter 1)

Introduction

Economics is part of the web of human knowledge that spans the totality of human experience. This web of knowledge is the greatest resource humans have when it comes to facing the challenges of the future. When adopting this broad, human ecology view, the economist aims to contribute to the growth of knowledge generally. It includes being willing to assess the strengths and weaknesses of one's professional area by, in particular, paying attention to the nature and quality of that which passes through the boundaries of the field, i.e. imports from and exports to other disciplines. It also includes being open to insights from other fields that may contradict or supplement the economist's own beliefs and practices.[1]

This paper uses global climate policy as a case study to focus on the role of economics and economists. The climate issue brings into focus a series of issues: purely scientific issues; inter- and intra-generational equity issues; the responsibility of humans towards other species and the natural world generally; as well as the ultimate question of the place of humans in creation. Human societies have always grappled with these issues and come up with solutions reflecting their time and place, sometimes appropriately and sometimes not.[2] Climate policy, by contrast, requires humans to mobilize all of the traditional disciplines (the sciences, including the social sciences, and the humanities) to fully understand the challenge and to act in concert to avert a likely catastrophe, all subject to a time constraint and great uncertainties. Recognizing the emerging danger to the world as a whole, the United Nations Environment Programme and the World Meteorological Organization jointly established the Intergovernmental Panel on Climate Change (IPCC) in 1988 as an interdisciplinary body to become the standard resource and reference when it comes to analyses and information about global warming issues. Subsequently, and partly in response to the IPCC's findings, the U.N. entered into the United Nations Framework Convention on Climate Change in 1992, with the essential objective being "... stabilization of greenhouse gas concentrations in the atmosphere at a level that would prevent dangerous anthropogenic interference with the climate system."[3] The Convention laid out principles and procedures to further develop climate policy, which in turn led to the 1997 Kyoto Protocol.[4] Accordingly, a subset of the parties to this Protocol, not including the U.S., has committed itself to bringing its annual emission of global warming gases down to a little less than the 1990 level during the time period 2008–2012. In addition, other countries and jurisdictions (e.g. individual states and cities in the U.S., and even private corporations) have adopted climate policies independently of the Kyoto Protocol.[5] In effect, humans have started on the extremely ambitious and challenging path of climate change mitigation, an undertaking which, in terms of complexity, resource needs, coordination requirements, and time perspective, is likely to exceed anything human societies have jointly committed to so far.

What should be the role of economics in climate policy? What are the strengths and weaknesses of the field that determine the limits of its usefulness? This chapter addresses these questions by first characterizing climate policy in terms of a physical process and, subsequently, linking this to a social choice process. It then explains the way economists understand the social choice process and the two major traditions – natural resource economics and environmental economics – that are closest to the climate change process. The general claim is made that global warming is the result of a specific institutional failure and that it requires appropriate institutional change. The new institutions proposed by economists are based on beliefs and assumptions and they come with their own set of vulnerabilities. Attention is then directed at the role of economics in addressing the two basic questions in climate policy: what policies and institutional changes should be made to reduce emissions? How significant should the emission cutbacks be in each year? The position taken is that economics is and should be the monopoly source of cost-effective policy approaches. On the other hand, the economist's favored decision criterion for deciding on the annual sequence of emission reductions (present value maximization based on cost–benefit analysis) is insufficient and needs to be supplemented by other criteria. This chapter ends with some observations on the relative roles that economic and sustainability criteria should play in policy decisions.[6]

The climate challenge

Over the past three to four decades, global warming has evolved from an interesting scientific hypothesis to being virtually unanimously accepted as fact by those paying attention to the issue. Moreover, the explanation of the causes of global warming and the degree of human responsibility has become fairly standardized.[7] The earth's climate history can be constructed from a variety of sources, most recently from direct measurements. Other sources include glaciers, the changing ocean level, trees, and coral reefs. It is obvious from this record that the global climate has varied significantly over time. In turns out, for example, that the emergence of civilization over the last 5000 years or so corresponds to a particularly warm period in the Earth's history, sometimes called the long summer. Of concern, however, is that there has been a sudden, significant warming of the Earth over the last 100 years, against a background of a general cooling since about 1000 AD. Why?

Global climate models aim to explain variations in global temperatures over short or long periods of time by accounting for variations in the set of circumstances believed to be responsible: the position of the earth relative to the sun, solar activity, naturally occurring phenomena (such as volcanic eruptions), atmospheric concentrations of global warming gases, and others. These models convincingly attribute the recent spike in temperatures to rapidly growing emissions of greenhouse gases leading to higher concentrations of these gases in the atmosphere (Figure 7.1). The Kyoto Protocol of 1997 identifies six such gases, the most important being CO_2, which results primarily from burning fossil fuels. Since the industrial revolution, these fuels have powered our transportation systems and manufacturing processes, as well as much of our electricity generation. As a result, the atmospheric concentration of CO_2 has increased from 270 parts per million (ppm) pre-industrial revolution to 377 ppm in 2004 (Figure 7.1).[8]

The acceleration in global climate related change is indicated by temperature and sea-level data. The estimated increase in average global temperatures over the last century was 0.4–0.8°C (IPCC, 2001a, p. 5) and the level of the world oceans rose by 10–20 cm. The IPCC expects global temperatures to increase 1.4–5.8°C by the year 2100 and the sea level to increase between 9 and 88 cm (IPCC, 2001a, p. 69). Of course, absent emission cutbacks, the process of global warming will not stop at these levels, but stretch into the indefinite future with

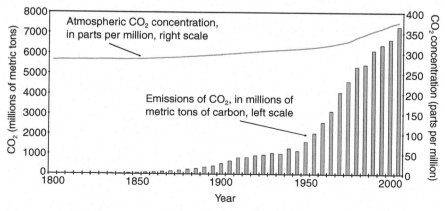

Figure 7.1 Global CO_2 emissions and atmospheric concentrations, 1800–2001 (source: Marland *et al.*, 2006).

likely irreversible changes for the worse in living conditions. There are good reasons to worry. The abundance of oil, gas, and coal resources (particularly coal) in the Earth's crust may continue to fuel our energy needs and the global warming process for some 700 years at present consumption rates. Add in even greater resources of methane frozen on deep ocean floors ("clathrates") and current consumption of carbon fuels can go on for more than a millennium. Combine these enormous resources with an ever increasing demand for energy as population and incomes increase. Lastly, add to the mix the human ingenuity leading to ever more sophisticated technology that puts more and more resources within technical and economic limits. Unless the world is put on a different track, the inescapable conclusion is that humans are overwhelmingly likely to experience "dangerous interference with the climate system" – the concern expressed in the United Nations Framework Convention on Climate Change.

It is useful to see the climate change process in a simplified way for the purpose of identifying key issues and parameters (Figure 7.2). It starts with emissions arising from global economic activity. Let's focus on changes taking place over time. Following the Kaya (1990) identity, desirable emission reductions can come from three sources. First, overall economic activity can slow down temporarily ("a recession") or the economy's growth trend can decline. Second, the production and use of energy may become more efficient or the composition of GDP may change to favor less energy intensive products. Finally, carbon emissions may be reduced by switching over to nuclear or renewable energy sources, by carbon capture and storage, or by substituting low-carbon energy sources for high-carbon sources, e.g. natural gas for coal. All of these options continue to be extensively discussed in the literature.[9,10]

Now, consider the timescale of the climate change process. Economists are most comfortable with a time perspective measured in years and, at most, decades. Expressing this tendency towards a short time perspective, John M. Keynes once famously remarked that "in the long run, we are all dead." With that in mind, consider a scenario in which CO_2 emissions are stabilized within a hundred years and then decline to pre-industrial levels relatively rapidly.

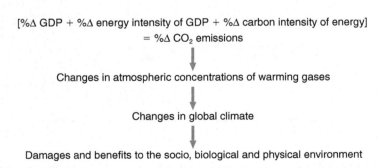

[%Δ GDP + %Δ energy intensity of GDP + %Δ carbon intensity of energy]
= %Δ CO_2 emissions

Changes in atmospheric concentrations of warming gases

Changes in global climate

Damages and benefits to the socio, biological and physical environment

Figure 7.2 Global warming process: a simplified description.

The consequent adjustment periods are simply enormous by the economist's standards: stabilization of CO_2 concentrations in the atmosphere will take 100–300 years; global temperature stabilization will take a few centuries; and the sea level thermal expansion due to ice melting will take between centuries and several millennia (IPCC, 2001a, p. 17). Nevertheless, the usual time perspective adopted in economic analyses is one century, which follows the practice in the IPCC scenarios.

In Figure 7.2, a given sequence of events that plays itself out over a century or more constitutes "a scenario" originating from economic decisions regarding fossil fuel use. The Business As Usual (BAU) benchmark scenario is simply the century or longer sequence that results if no policies are adopted to influence economic activities, either through market incentives or direct activity restrictions. Obviously the formulation of the BAU scenario is subject to great uncertainty from numerous sources, including economic parameters such as the future path of energy prices; population growth; economic growth; and technological innovations that affect energy sources and uses. But there is also major uncertainty about physical parameters. The most serious is probably the relationship between greenhouse gas concentrations in the atmosphere and global temperature ("climate sensitivity"). There are various ways to express the size of this parameter, but the common benchmark is to consider a doubling of atmospheric concentrations of CO_2 from the pre-industrial level (from 270 ppm past our present 377 ppm to 540 ppm). The expected increase in the average global temperature is between 1.5°C and 4.5°C. Future physical damages and the risk of catastrophes are, however, likely to differ significantly whether the true value of the climate sensitivity parameter is at the low or high end of this range. It is noteworthy here that such a doubling of CO_2 concentration is often mentioned as a desirable stabilization level.

Not surprisingly, the identification of the true BAU scenario is the "holy grail" of climate research. Recognizing the wide range of uncertainty about key parameters, the common approach – used by the IPCC, for example – is to produce a range of assumed BAU scenarios based on best available information. The well accepted view is that the range of BAU scenarios implies serious danger to the human ecology. The climate policy debate has therefore largely shifted from being a debate about the science involved to being a debate about the level, the type, and the timing of mitigation efforts.

The challenge to the human ecology

Considering the human ecology framework, climate change is a threat to the survival of the system as a whole, including the social and economic components. The threat comes from the prospect of moving carbon that is now sequestered in the Earth's crust or plant population, first, into the Earth's atmosphere and then, slowly over centuries and millennia, into the deep oceans. Referring to resource use generally, the 30 year update to *Limits to Growth* asks: "Are current policies leading to a sustainable future or to collapse?" (Meadows *et al.*, 2004, p. ix).

The same essential question underlies the IPCC assessment reports and, increasingly, the public debate about global resource use. Within Meadows *et al.* and other system approaches, the BAU scenario is that economic growth overshoots natural resource and ecological limits. This overshoot is reinforced by positive feedback loops, and eventually the global ecological system reaches a tipping point and collapses. The system is kept on this disaster track "by the efforts of those pursuing narrow national, corporate, or individual self-interests" and, one would assume, some degree of ignorance of consequences (Meadows *et al.*, 2004, p. xiii).

The opposite path, guided by appropriate policy and corresponding commitments, is captured by the term "sustainable development." The standard definition is the one provided by The World Commission on Environment and Development (1987): "Development that meets the needs of the present without compromising the ability of future generations to meet their own needs." The specific challenge arising from climate change is to set in motion a socially coordinated and powerful negative feedback loop targeting behaviors that generate carbon emissions. To accomplish this, it is necessary to have a notion of what is meant by a "sustainable energy system" and being able to create this system through appropriate policy.

The common definition of "sustainability" given above emphasizes the ability to satisfy human needs over time. And here is where the controversy starts. To an economist there are usually numerous ways to satisfy the same need because practically all goods have substitutes. As a result, the economist's notion of a sustainable energy system tends to be relatively flexible. A reasonable *economic* definition of a sustainable energy system is one where the level of energy use can be continued indefinitely while being benign to the environment. For example, a system based on fossil fuels with carbon capture and storage slowly transitioning over decades or centuries to a system based on renewables, nuclear, and efficiency gains could satisfy this definition (for example, see Jaccard, 2005).

Regarding new institutions, the remainder of this chapter deals with how economics can be of help in steering the global path away from collapse and towards sustainability. Building new institutions takes time, however. The analogy of a supertanker changing course may come to mind – the captain orders a change of course, the wheel is turned, and several miles later the supertanker is on its new course towards its proper destination. However, this analogy to climate policy captures only a portion of the challenge. For starters, remove the simple decision-making structure of the supertanker as well as all maps (electronic and otherwise). Now think about steering it away from disaster to a safe harbor.

It is reasonably clear to economists how to diagnose the problem. Building on this diagnosis, it is similarly quite straightforward to outline the new set of cost-effective institutions that should be created to transform the energy system. To the extent that there is controversy among economists, it is about the degree and timing of mitigation. In the view of this author, the major obstacles to an effective climate policy come from the politics of the problem and therefore from the political arena. From this arena arises another danger from climate change: that controversies having their roots in the energy system may not be resolved through the market or through negotiation, but by military force. In the event that political obstacles prevent meaningful economic policies and the human ecology proceeds on the path towards collapse, it is hard to believe that this path will be a peaceful one.

In the sections that follow, the economic approach will be explained and justified based on the economist's own criteria. But there is another reason to pay attention, not often brought up by economists, to the effect that good economic policy is a good substitute for the use of force, whether military or some other form of pressure. The economist's proposals for creating new institutions to address climate change are not only aimed at cost effectiveness, but also provide a peaceful bridge from the collapse scenario to the sustainable scenario.

The economic traditions and beliefs

Economists have been relatively slow to pay careful attention to the linkages between economic actions and the physical environment. They have been even slower to recognize that the world, as a natural system, is vulnerable to human interference and may change dramatically and irreversibly for the worse. The two relatively young sub-fields of economics most closely linked to the climate issue, natural resource economics and environmental economics, have their theoretical roots in the 1920s and 1930s, but didn't really start blossoming until the 1960s and 1970s, the period of emerging social concerns over economy versus nature issues.[11]

Economics is relevant to both ends of the climate change process. At the front end, consumption decisions regarding the use of fossil fuels by final buyers in decentralized fuel markets cause emissions of warming gases. The fuel market is therefore the market where climate policies need to be targeted and implemented and where the *costs* of climate policy will originate to finally end up as reductions in GDP. These policies should aim to minimize the GDP impact of reducing emissions to a socially desirable level, i.e. they should be "cost effective." The analysis of fuel markets is the focus of energy economics, a sub-discipline of natural resource economics.

At the back end of the physical process, global warming inflicts damage which can, to some extent, be quantified and compared in dollar terms under various emission scenarios. The *benefits* of climate policy will show up at this end as the difference between damages incurred without climate policy (the "business as usual" or "do nothing" scenario) minus the damages incurred with a policy-induced emission scenario. This difference equals the value of avoided damages that can be attributed to policy. The business of environmental economics is to value this difference – including both market and non-market values – and develop policy recommendations. Ideally, these would include identifying the socially preferred emission scenario that balances costs and benefits in the best possible way.

The basic approaches of these two sub-disciplines of economics and the dominant, current beliefs of their practitioners are summarized next.

Natural resource economics

This sub-field is concerned with how a market economy uses its endowment of natural resources over time and whether the actual use should be altered as seen from a broader social perspective. In the context of climate change, the most relevant resources are, of course, fossil fuels in particular and energy resources in general. The classic statement of optimal use of an exhaustible resource over time is by Hotelling (1931), who inspired a considerable amount of literature on exhaustible natural resource management. The basic idea behind this literature is that the resource owner/manager should think of himself as having two assets: a resource in the ground and a bank account balance earning interest. The manager's problem is to maximize the combined value of these two assets over time. In any year, the solution to the choice problem is that the portion of the resource in the ground that is growing in value faster than the interest rate should be kept in the ground while the portion not growing that fast (if any) should be produced, sold, and the profits put in the bank account to grow at the interest rate. This decision takes into account the expected path of production costs, the price of the product in the market, and the interest rate.

Suppose Hotelling gave a fair sketch of the typical resource owner, what are the expected features of, say, the fossil fuel market as a whole? It turns out that under a set of conditions which include: competitive markets; well defined property rights; equality between the private and social discount rates; and the producer taking into account all economic costs – including pollution costs – the privately chosen production path happens to also be the socially optimal path. In the climate context, the catch here is, of course, that the producer cannot be expected to take into account pollution costs unless that is a requirement imposed from the outside, perhaps in the form of a corresponding per-unit tax.

On the basis of Hotelling's model, one can make a series of interesting predictions. For example, if the expected future price of fossil fuels increases due to an expected increase in scarcity, the incentive to producers is to cut back on current production and save the resource for future buyers. Needless to say, under those circumstances, there is also an incentive to explore for and develop more resources. Future market conditions and the urgency of the needs of future buyers, as expressed by their expected willingness to pay, are thereby taken into account in present exploration and production decisions. This price-driven conservation can turn a resource which is exhaustible from a geologist's point of view into one that is inexhaustible from a practical, economic point of view. As price escalates, buyers switch to substitutes covering the same basic needs. Since buyers do not care about whether the price they pay goes to the producer or is a tax, this substitution process can be induced by government policy. This is, of course, the desired outcome from government policy aimed at switching the economy away from fossil fuels by adding the cost of the externality to the price of the fossil fuel.

Despite the reassuring findings in the theoretical literature, the 1970s became a decade of turmoil in the natural resource markets generally and the fuel markets in particular. The question of the decade became whether or not society is running out of natural resources, as highlighted by Meadows *et al.* (1972). The world market for oil, for example, saw a four-fold price increase in 1974–1975, associated with an event that became known as "The Arab Oil Embargo." Then again, in 1979, the same price shot up another three-fold, this time associated with the Iranian revolution of that year. In the U.S., physical shortages were experienced in both the natural gas and gasoline markets, leading to media drama that served to underscore the public worries over resource scarcity. Politicians responded to the concerns by enacting various laws serving to increase government control of energy prices and to escalate its involvement in the energy industries. However, by the early 1980s, the price of oil in the world markets had nearly collapsed and there was a substantial natural gas production capacity surplus in the U.S. The sense of urgency was over and the doomsayers had been proven wrong. Fossil fuel scarcity was replaced by abundance and, except for the most recent period, fuel prices have stayed low. In retrospect, the crises of the 1970s seem like an aberration. A later survey of empirical studies of natural resource scarcity observes that "the finite availability of nonrenewable resources at a particular point in time has not yet led to increasing economic scarcity of nonrenewable resources for production and consumption activities" (Krautkraemer, 1998, p. 2103). Krautkraemer cites the development of substitutes, improvement in extraction and processing technology, and greater efficiency of use as mitigating factors. In general, natural resource economists are resource optimists, many following in the tradition of Simon (1996) and, later, Lomborg (1998). Some have earned the nickname "flat Earth economists" from a prominent geologist, Campbell (1997), who is one of many geologists whose beliefs are opposed to those of most economists.[12]

Estimates of the world's energy reserves (those known and producible at present prices) and resources (reserves plus other deposits) are shown in Table 7.1. The second to last column shows that current fossil fuel consumption can go on for centuries. Crude oil seems to be in the shortest supply, yet critical to the world transportation system. This seems irrelevant, however, since both natural gas and coal can be used to produce substitutes for crude oil refinery products, e.g. gasoline, at costs that are substantially below the prices of crude oil that have prevailed in 2005 and 2006. Thus the numbers in Table 7.1 are consistent with the economist's view that resources are abundant, the real problem is with environmental impacts of the world energy system. If the carbon contained in the resources in Table 7.1 are transferred from the Earth's crust into the atmosphere, and then, ultimately, into the deep oceans, it will likely have altered the face of the Earth in the process.

So, if the energy crisis of the 1970s did not result from a scarcity of resources in the ground – as was the perceived cause at the time – what was the actual

Table 7.1 World primary energy use and reserves, 2001

Source	Primary energy (exajoules, EJ)	Primary energy (10⁹ tonnes of oil equivalent, Gtoe*)	Percentage of total	Proved reserves (10⁹ tonnes of oil equivalent, Gtoe*)	Static reserve-production ratio (years)[a]	Static resource base-production ratio (years)[b]	Dynamic resource base-production ratio (years)[c]
Fossil fuels	332	7.93	79.4	778			
Oil	147	3.51	35.1	143	41	~200	125
Natural gas	91	2.16	21.7	138	64	~400	210
Coal	94	2.26	22.6	566	251	~700	360
Renewables	57	1.37	13.7				
Large hydro	9	0.23	2.3			Renewable	
Traditional biomass	39	0.93	9.3			Renewable	
'New' renewables[d]	9	0.21	2.2			Renewable	
Nuclear	29	0.69	6.9	55			
Nuclear[e]	29	0.69	6.9	55	82[f]	~300 to > 10000[f]	
Total[f]	418	9.99	100.0				

Source: U.N. Development Programme (2004).

Notes:

* 1 toe = 42GJ.

a Based on constant production and static reserves.

b Includes both conventional and unconventional reserves and resources.

c Data refer to the energy use of a business-as-usual scenario—that is, production is dynamic and a function of demand. Thus these ratios are subject to change under different scenarios. Dynamic resource base – production was calculated based on a 2 percent growth rate per year from 2000 to peak production (oil 6.1 Gtoe, gas 6.3 Gtoe, and coal 8.9 Gtoe), followed by a 2 percent decline per year until the resource base is exhausted.

d Includes modern biomass, small hydropower, geothermal energy, wind energy, solar energy, and marine energy. Modern biomass accounts for 6.0 exajoules; 2.9 exajoules comes from all other renewables. "Modern biomass" refers to biomass produced in a sustainable way and used for electricity generation, heat production, and transportation (liquid fuels). It includes wood/forest residues from reforestation and/or sustainable management, rural (animal and agricultural) and urban residues (including solid waste and liquid effluents); it does not include traditional uses of fuelwood in inefficient and pollutant conversion systems.

e Converted from electricity produced to fuels consumed assuming a 33 percent thermal efficiency of power plants.

f Based on once-through uranium fuel cycles excluding thorium and low-concentration uranium from seawater. The uranium resource base is theoretically 60 times larger if fast breeder reactor are used.

cause? What can be learned from this episode that lasted approximately a decade? The energy market turmoil of these years spawned a sub-discipline of natural resource economics – energy economics. It turns out that the findings and consequent belief system of this group of economists are likely to have a major impact on the way climate policy is handled.

Consider the case of a major increase in, say, the price of gasoline. What are the possible causes? Between the point of crude oil production and the gasoline pump, there is a very large number of problems that can occur, none of which have anything to do with the physical amount of resources in the ground. A partial list would include: demand growing more rapidly than supply in an industry where the development of added capacity takes substantial time; monopoly restriction of output to drive up price (e.g. OPEC); scarcity of refinery capacity; scarcity of a key gasoline ingredient (e.g. ethanol); a natural disaster such as a hurricane affecting important production or distribution facilities; political turmoil in key producing areas (revolutions, strikes, etc.); gasoline taxes; and inappropriate government policies. Energy markets are frequently disturbed or shocked by these or similar disturbances. In the 1970s, it so happened that high gasoline prices were primarily triggered by political crises (an embargo and a revolution). Energy economists nevertheless focused on the last item in the list: inappropriate U.S. government policies that served to amplify rather than dampen the disturbances originating in the energy markets. Specifically, energy economists identified price controls in the oil and gas markets as major sources of problems. They can cause physical shortages in the short-run when markets are disturbed and cause chronic shortages in the long-run by encouraging consumption while discouraging supplies. Over the past two and a half decades, the major thrust of energy policy in the U.S., with energy economists as cheerleaders, has been "deregulation," meaning less and less direct interference by the government (including state public utility commissions) in setting the prices of the various forms in which energy is consumed, including electricity. This implies an acceptance of, and increasing emphasis on, market forces in guiding society's energy use into the future.

Environmental economics

This sub-field is largely based on the recognition that certain economic actions have consequences for third parties that are not accounted for by the decision maker ("an externality"). Oftentimes these consequences are negative and they involve damages to environmental quality. Pigou (1920) proposed to account for these by taxing the activity or product causing the negative externality in an amount corresponding to the value of the damage suffered by others. That would penalize the source appropriately and cause the decision-maker to "internalize" the externality. Much later, Coase (1960) argued that, under certain conditions, including well defined property rights, the parties involved (e.g. the polluters and those suffering from pollution) could get together and negotiate an agreement that would be socially "efficient," and it would therefore not be necessary for the government to intervene.[13] Since global warming impacts so many people in so many jurisdictions in different ways, Coase's insights would predict that it is particularly hard for those damaged to organize themselves to define and enforce property rights and to create the overall best resolution. Add two other circumstances compounding the difficulty: first, the obvious observation that those most damaged by global warming belong to future generations and so won't show up at the negotiating table; second, the damage is done to what economists call "a public good," the Earth's climate stability. This is a crucial point requiring some elaboration.

Technically, a public good is one that (a) no-one can be excluded from enjoying and (b) one person's enjoyment of it does not diminish the enjoyment others have from the same good. A public good will never be supplied by the market since non-exclusion means a private supplier is unable to charge those who enjoy it. One of the essential roles of government is therefore to supply or care for public goods. It turns out, however, that for such goods it is a challenge for the government to get people to express themselves honestly about their valuation if they sense that they will be charged accordingly. If, based on deceit, they end up paying less, the impact on the overall supply of the public good may be small, yet the impact on their own budget large. This is the well-known "free-rider" problem. The same incentive to strategic behavior affects the global warming policy negotiations between nation-states. There may even be an incentive to cheat on an agreement once reached, which would be another way to free-ride on the efforts of others.

To an environmental economist, global climate stability is a public good that everybody's well-being depends on and whose care becomes the responsibility of the global community. Caring for this environment creates a flow of avoided future damages, or "benefits." There is also a flow of sacrifices – "costs" – which are mainly in terms of the foregone benefits of continuing to base our energy consumption on inexpensive and abundant fossil fuels, chiefly coal.[14] The basic analytical tool of the environmental economist is cost–benefit analysis, which entails finding the proper balance between these two flows over a period of time. Ideally, this analysis should identify the least costly way to stabilize atmospheric concentrations of greenhouse gases as well as the optimal atmospheric concentration level (and therefore also the optimal global emission path over time). The climate policy should reflect costs and benefits weighing less in the decision the farther into the future they occur. The weight attached to the costs and benefits in each year is determined by the discount rate – the higher the discount rate, the less the future matters to the analysis and the policy. In a later section, implications of this weighing for climate policy will be discussed.

The environmental economist would like to be near the top of the policy-decision pyramid, selecting projects where costs exceed benefits and identifying cost-minimizing policies to implement the project. If enlightened policymakers follow these recommendations, the resulting policies will be "efficient" in the economist's sense. How close is this desired role to reality? A leading environmental economist, Freeman III (2002) reviews U.S. federal government environmental policy from its rapid escalation starting in 1970. In the early stages, economic analysis was practically absent from these policies, but has been an increasing part of federal environmental policy since the 1990s. Nevertheless, federal programs could benefit from even more economic analysis.

> The first and perhaps most important policy implication of this analysis is to emphasize that virtually all environmental policies and programs could be improved by making them more cost-effective, i.e., by finding ways to reduce the costs of attaining given targets.
>
> (Freeman III (2002), p. 143)

The general sense is that such efficiency can best be achieved by using market-based tools (environmental taxes or markets) rather than command and control policies (e.g. emission standards).[15] The U.S. federal government pioneered the use of environmental markets with a "cap-and-trade" system for sulfur dioxide emissions by power plants. This program is widely acclaimed as a success, both in terms of managing current emissions, but also in terms of inducing technological innovations to reduce the cost of emission reductions.

Shared beliefs

The basic economic diagnosis of the climate issue is that it is a case of a negative externality from fossil fuel consumption damaging a global public good. With that starting point, the analysis proceeds to the choice process that generates the externality so as to identify cost-effective mitigation policies. The actual conversation regarding these issues oftentimes takes place in the context of global, dynamic economic models, which are the economic equivalents of global climate models. These integrate knowledge from sub-fields of economics in addition to the two discussed above as well as important relationships and parameters from outside economics.

The overall belief system that guides most economists, including those from the natural resource or the environmental side, is that energy resources are abundant and they should be managed through market-based policies rather than forcing people to adopt particular kinds of behavior. The inclination is to make fuel users experience the true cost of their fuel and let them be free to respond. This freedom should be limited by an overall constraint on total CO_2 emissions defined with reference to the common good. As discussed below, however, the proposed institutional changes that follow from these beliefs come with their own set of limitations and vulnerabilities.

Building cost-effective institutions

One of the guiding principles in the United Nations Framework Convention on Climate Change is cost minimization: "policies and measures to deal with climate change should be cost-effective so as to ensure global benefits at the lowest possible cost" (Article 3). Considering the various professions involved in policy development, the economist can fairly claim to be the king of the cost minimizing analysis. The UNFCC's commitment therefore opens the door wide for economics to play a vital role in climate policy. Most likely, a large number of policies will be developed and implemented ranging from market incentives to detailed regulations of behavior and product characteristics. The focus below is on the candidates for selection as the most important tool for a cost-minimizing policy: a carbon tax and a cap-and-trade system.

The following section starts with a discussion of these two policies, which are more fully explained in the Appendix. The section then considers dynamic features, such as creating political coalitions and commitments, and the potential for rapidly reducing the costs of emission cutbacks. The section concludes with a discussion of equity implications flowing from the two systems and observations on their vulnerabilities.

Carbon taxes versus cap-and-trade programs

Suppose policymakers, in some ideal world, have somehow decided on a target concentration level for warming gases in the atmosphere and a corresponding series of worldwide, annual targets for emissions. To most economists, the gold standard for a cost-efficient policy to reach these targets would be a corresponding time sequence of tax rates on carbon emissions applied uniformly across the world. Think of the tax as being collected from fossil fuel producers at all production sites and ignore the practical problems of doing so. The Appendix outlines how the carbon tax would impact the fossil energy market in a typical year and the corresponding cost-minimizing adjustment process. The key points are that the carbon tax reduces fossil fuel energy consumption and therefore emissions while leading to:

1   those who place the highest value on fossil fuels continuing to be served by those with the lowest costs;
2   the uniform carbon tax giving the same cost signal to all market participants and to cause the cost (including the tax) of the last unit produced to be the same for all producers ("the equimarginal principle" is satisfied); and
3   those who reduce fossil fuel consumption pursuing alternative opportunities as contained in the Kaya (1990) identity, motivated by profit and utility maximization.

Jointly, these imply that the social sacrifice from climate policy is minimized.

The adjustment process to a carbon tax is consistent with the economists' notion that the government should get out of the way. Market participants are given "where and how" flexibility to accomplish the job as inexpensively as possible. Beyond that, the appeal of the carbon tax consists in its simplicity, combined with its powerful transformative effects. It may thus be considered the "gold standard" for climate policy.

As demonstrated in the Appendix, one of the fundamental principles of climate policy is that a carbon tax and a cap-and-trade program are theoretically equivalent approaches in an idealized, timeless framework without uncertainty. Whether one starts with a carbon tax or a fixed number of permits with resale allowed, the economic analysis ends up with the same cost-minimizing results. Both policy tools are based on the market mechanism by allowing utility- and profit-maximizing agents in the markets to move the economy over to a targeted, lower carbon emission path. Ignoring information and implementation challenges, cost-effective climate policy is, in principle, easy. Simply legislate the right carbon tax rate or issue the right volume of emission permits with resale allowed.[16]

Looking at the real world policy choices, the momentum is clearly behind the more complicated cap-and-trade system and not the simple carbon tax. The countries in the European Union now have a relatively active and growing cap-and-trade system; there is a functioning, voluntary trade system in the U.S.; and several New England states have been developing such a system for years. Most recently, the state of California has expressed an interest in such a system, and in linking it to a similar system elsewhere.[17] The question that naturally arises is: if the two are equivalent and economists appear to have a preference for a carbon tax, why do policymakers seem to prefer the more complicated cap-and-trade system?[18]

The choice of primary policy instrument: dynamic efficiency

Current emission reduction policies were not designed by detached economists. They arose in a particular historical context due to individual countries negotiating country-specific emission cutbacks or by particular jurisdictions, such as California, making independent commitments. Under the Kyoto Protocol, the average cutback aims to be 5 percent below 1990 emissions for the time period 2008–2012. The advantages of an open and transparent permit market rather than a carbon tax in this context are that:

1   it gives better assurance that the agreed-on emission targets are actually reached by the deadline; and
2   it helps integrate emission reduction efforts in a cost minimizing way across the various countries and jurisdictions that participate.

Numerous studies have shown that there can be a dramatic reduction in emission abatement costs when larger areas and a greater range of countries are integrated into a single cap-and-trade market.[19] Moreover, policymakers have shied away from taxes because of voter opposition, which is particularly strong in the U.S. Paraphrasing one participant in the California negotiations over its recently enacted policy: "Tax is a toxic word in politics, so we made every effort to avoid it in the negotiations."

An additional historical circumstance is that, by the year 2004, it became apparent that without Russia ratifying the Kyoto Protocol, it would not have gone into effect due to inadequate participation. With emissions substantially below Kyoto targets, the prospect that Russia would be able to sell its large surplus of emission units into the E.U. cap-and-trade market probably played a major role in the country's decision to join and thereby allow the Treaty to take effect. Under that logic: no cap-and-trade market, no Russian ratification, no Kyoto Treaty implementation, and a therefore a great policy fiasco which could have set back climate policy by years.

Beyond the historical context, there is a further, profound consequence that follows from a cap-and-trade program: it creates a functioning commodity market in emission permits with open access beyond emitters and initial permit holders. The vision is that an entirely new industry will emerge dedicated to carbon emission cutbacks. Industry participants will not need to deal directly with CO_2 emitters, but can sell their product, CO_2 emission reductions, into an impersonal and transparent market with a single, known price. The resources this industry brings to the task and the solutions that emerge will be major determinants of the success of climate policy in terms of bringing down costs rapidly. They may identify projects that reduce emissions anywhere in the world, most likely under the Kyoto Protocol's Clean Development Mechanism. For example, a zero-emission electricity-generating facility built in a poor country could sell electricity into the local market *and* sell the corresponding emission permits into the cap-and-trade market. These emission credits will be in addition to those supplied by the government.

Quite possibly, this commodity market may develop standard derivative products (options and futures) with the associated opportunities for hedging strategies. If everything goes right, the cap-and-trade program could place carbon emission reduction units within the general family of commodities traded in international, financial markets. Being thus placed, the newly created industry may gain easier access to the economic resources available in these markets. A significant example in that regard is that one of the premier U.S. investment bankers, Morgan Stanley, declared in late 2006 that it is committing $3 billion to emission cutback projects and trading over the next five years.[20]

This emerging commodity market is nevertheless a curious market in that the supply side contains two types of participants: a government that "produces" permits through its legislative or executive branch and private suppliers who engage in projects to "produce" emission reductions to sell into the market. Are these credible suppliers? What games may they play to the detriment of other participants and to undermine the overall intent of the cap-and-trade program?

The challenge to the government as a supplier of permits is to formulate credible emission targets and thereby a predictable supply, for example those contained in the Kyoto Protocol. Within these overall targets, the government also needs to be predictable about how many permits will be given to the particular CO_2-emitting industries that are included in the market. A serious violation of this condition recently occurred in the European carbon market. About one-half of the global warming emissions in Europe comes from electric generation utilities and a handful of other, energy-intensive industries. These are also allowed to trade in the E.U. carbon market. In April and May 2006, it became evident that individual E.U. countries had unexpectedly allocated many emission permits to these industrial sectors, which shifted the balance of supply and demand dramatically. As a result, the price per unit fell by about one-half. Such governance causes shocks to the market and raises the risk to market participants, undermining the long-run dynamic efficiency of the cap-and-trade market.

The private suppliers offer emission reductions, i.e. a negative quantity. It is tempting to call these "nega-carbons." The product is both invisible and standardized, and its actual production needs to be inferred and certified somehow. A major challenge for the cap-and-trade system is to create a set of institutions and a process that can credibly certify carbon emission cutbacks relative to some benchmark derived from standardized, transparent, and enforceable criteria. Quite likely, this will lead to another industry or layer of bureaucracy focused on carbon emission reduction certification. On the other side of the market, there needs to be a similar process for ensuring that emission permit holders stay within their permitted limits. The considerable costs of this support industry, basically aimed at detecting and punishing cheating in order keep the market credible, should be considered part of the cost of carbon cutbacks under a cap-and-trade program.

Based on these considerations, a cap-and-trade program can be seen largely as a choice to get climate policy started in a given political context and with a cost-minimizing policy tool. The program also has the potential to bring down mitigation costs by unleashing a commodity market in emission reduction units which may attract significant resources and boost energy research and development spending.

Aside from the dynamic efficiency, who wins and who loses when policy-makers choose a cap-and-trade program over a carbon tax?

The choice of primary policy tool: fairness

The fundamental intra-generational equity issue raised by the choice of a cap-and-trade program concerns who receives the property right to the atmosphere's ability to absorb carbon: the public at large or historical users. With a tax system, the rights are implicitly assigned to the public in the taxing jurisdiction with the government receiving tax revenue for its use. With a cap-and-trade program, the property right is typically assigned for free to historical users, who may either sell it or use it. Considering the volume of overall emissions in participating countries, the high marginal cost of emission cutbacks reported in numerous studies, and the prospects for increasing emission cutbacks in the future, the potential value of these emission permits in total is simply enormous, perhaps in the trillions of dollars.[21,22]

A safe bet is that the choice of policy – whether a carbon tax or cap-and-trade – is not only motivated by the dynamic efficiency of the policy, but also related to who wins and who loses.

Using standard economic notions of surplus, the Appendix discusses the distribution of costs from climate policy under three scenarios: business as usual;

a carbon tax; and a cap-and-trade system. Not surprisingly, the BAU is the preferred policy seen from the narrow self-interest of fossil fuel market participants. The carbon tax is potentially a huge source of tax revenue for the general public, captured from producers and buyers in the fossil fuel markets. Lastly, the cap-and-trade program, with free allocation of emission permits, produces no public revenue and is largely paid for by fossil fuel producers. Large users (electric utilities and energy-intensive industrial sectors) who receive the permits, by contrast, may lose or win from the scheme. Although they will most likely end up losing as compared to BAU, it is nevertheless apparent that the cap-and-trade system, as practiced in the E.U. for example, serves to protect the values of assets in industries that are heavy users of fossil fuels. The free allocation of permits probably slows down retirement of their capital equipment and may delay the transitioning to a lower carbon emission path. It furthermore helps prevent industry flight to areas without a climate policy and serves to generate less opposition from the group of large CO_2-emitters and the customers they serve.

From a dynamic perspective, the cap-and-trade program may also bring down the cost of mitigation over time more rapidly than a carbon tax, even including the costs of establishing and running a credible commodity market in emission permits. If that turns out to be the case, then the timeless analysis becomes misleading. The value of emission rights may then shrink rapidly and the policy leads to lower costs for society as a whole as compared to a carbon tax. If one has faith in the power of international capital markets to mobilize economic resources, including human talent, to go to work on the climate issue, then rapid cost reductions would be the implied prediction. It is noteworthy in this context that venture capital is increasingly being steered towards the energy and environment arenas.[23]

Cost effectiveness and politics

Current climate policy is largely shaped by the need to build international coalitions and to get domestic support from affected groups, including fossil fuel end-users. In this situation, it is significant that the chosen primary policy tool is from the economist's short list of those that are cost-effective, and which natural resource and environmental economists can both embrace. In fact, the choice of a cap-and-trade program reflects the increasing adoption of market-based policy tools to address social challenges, which is consistent with what most economists would advocate.

The issue of who actually pays the costs will likely become increasingly controversial as climate policy escalates and the general public becomes more sophisticated. In that regard, it will be tempting to think of the value created by issuing property rights to the atmosphere as creating a huge slush fund. The uses of this slush fund will lead to major fairness controversies in climate policy and potential erosion of public support. A particularly toxic combination would be questions of fairness combined with doubts about the proper functioning of the cap-and-trade market, especially regarding trade of emissions permits internationally. Fortunately, there is a large amount of flexibility in the cap-and-trade program, allowing the negotiation of compromises along at least four dimensions:

1 the portions of permits allocated by auction versus those granted free of charge;
2 the set of fossil fuel end-users subject to the program;
3 the set of countries to include; and
4 setting a maximum price for the emission permit at which some public entity would be willing to sell an unlimited amount.

Compromising along any of these four dimensions need not undermine the dynamic efficiency of the cap-and-trade program. In that regard, the biggest threat to a functioning climate policy is the risk of participants in the cap-and-trade program cheating: governments by supplying excessive permits; private suppliers deceiving the market about emission reductions; and buyers (fossil fuel end-users) not staying within their permit limits. In order to assure that neither of these destroys the market, an elaborate regulatory system needs to be created. It is the opinion of this author that the ability of this regulatory system to maintain an efficient and credible market is the Achilles heel of current climate policy.

Finding the best mitigation path

The preceding section focused on mitigation costs and how to minimize them, but what about mitigation benefits? These should be estimated to find the right extent and timing of mitigation efforts. The reality of current climate science, however, is that it has not yet reached the level where it is meaningful to define an ultimate stabilization target for the atmospheric concentration of warming gases and a corresponding series of annual emission targets. The flavor of current policy is therefore one of doing what seems right given what is known and to revise course based on new data and knowledge. In the language of the emerging literature, the challenge is to make the optimal sequence of decisions conditional on what is revealed about climate mitigation costs and benefits over time.

The argument made in this section focuses on the role economics can play in this process. It starts with pointing out two areas of inadequacy (assessing values and coping with the long time perspective) that contribute to the difficulties of defining the optimal level and timing of mitigation. It finishes with a set of observations about how economics can contribute to decision making within a sustainability framework in a situation with large scientific uncertainty and major risks to the human ecology.

Challenge: finding willingness and ability to pay

As policymakers are well aware, the major current challenge to climate policy is to get started in the first place. This is straightforward to understand from an economic perspective. Recall that climate stability – a global public good – is threatened by an economic externality and take into account the long time-lags involved. Then consider the people involved. The threat is caused partly by the actions of people who are no longer alive, partly by those who are alive, and, under the BAU scenario, will be tremendously aggravated by those yet to be born. None of them have had or will have a narrow economic interest in caring about the damages they cause. These damages will, overwhelmingly, be suffered by people who are not yet alive. Initial mitigation costs will be carried by people who are not likely to experience much, if any, of the direct economic benefits. Furthermore, they live in jurisdictions which, when negotiating with other jurisdictions, have an economic incentive to understate the mitigation benefits to its citizens' and to cheat on mitigation policy agreements they may enter into. From a policy development point of view, it just couldn't get much worse. Global warming truly is "an inconvenient truth" (Gore, 1996).

So, who will step forward to carry the initial costs?

One of the guiding principles of the United Nations Framework Convention on Climate Change is the notion of "common and differentiated responsibilities." The U.N. makes a distinction between rich and poor countries and assigns greater responsibility for climate policy to rich countries. Obligations to pay mitigation costs are thereby tied to income and wealth, and thus ability to pay. This does not, however, necessarily correspond to citizens' willingness to pay. Those who are expected to pay the bill tend to live in democratic societies where they can vote their refusal. If so, the sovereign states in which they live could opt out of international agreements aimed at emission reductions, as the U.S. has done.

There are early signs of major controversies over the issue of who pays. The Kyoto Protocol, as now implemented, basically divides countries into three groups: rich countries that plan to implement the agreed upon emissions restraints, rich countries that are not implementing the restraints (e.g. the U.S. and Australia), and poor countries without emission reduction obligations (e.g. China and India). To the U.S., one of the sticky points has been that poor countries do not participate in climate policy in a meaningful way, yet emissions from these countries are expected to dominate global emissions starting about the middle of this century. Furthermore, the cheapest emission cutbacks are likely found in poor countries and should therefore be exploited before more expensive sources in rich countries.[24]

Political issues aside, the notion of "common and differential responsibilities" raises some interesting general questions about the relationship between income and people's willingness to pay for environmental quality. In economics, this issue is sometimes addressed through a device called the environmental Kuznets curve.[25] This curve depicts a relationship between pollution and income as measured by the GDP such that pollution first rises, reaches a peak and then declines as economic development progresses and GDP increases. If true, it implies increased willingness to pay for environmental improvements beyond some critical economic development point. There is some evidence to the effect that the curve applies to some countries and to some local and regional pollutants, but to the best of the author's present knowledge, it has never been applied to the global environment. Accordingly, there is no empirical, economic study to support the notion that people's willingness to pay for improvements in the global environment increases with income. The absence of studies does not mean, however, that high income people and countries are not willing.

Despite these difficulties, the reality is that many countries, jurisdictions, and even private companies have started either laying the groundwork for emission cutbacks or actually started the cutbacks, some under the Kyoto protocol and some independently. It is well known, however, that the current projects, as stand-alone projects, hardly matter to global climate in, say, the year 2100. Consider, for example, that the effect of the Kyoto Protocol, if continued beyond 2012 and through to the end of the century, would push back the global temperature increase by only six years, and at very high costs to the parties involved (Lomborg, 1998, p. 302). Furthermore, the U.K. probably has the most aggressive climate policy in the world, yet it accounts for only 2 percent of annual global emissions of warming gases. The state of California with about the same emission level, has independently adopted a climate policy.[26] Despite the small impacts, these places are willing to carry the costs to help coalition-building. If successful, the current mitigation costs incurred by these countries may be more than offset by reductions in future adaptation costs. There is, however, the chance that the coalition-building efforts will fail, free-riding will be pervasive, and the incurred mitigation costs will therefore largely have been wasted. In that case, the "coalition of the willing" would have been better off using their resources on later adaptation to higher temperatures rather than early mitigation. Country specific climate policy is therefore a social investment subject to high risk. Playing it safe seems like an attractive strategic option which, nevertheless, has not been chosen by the countries that go first.[27,28]

Economic analysis of the coalition-building effort tends to be dominated by assumptions about narrow self-interest and strategic decision-making, leading one to skepticism that a climate-policy coalition is sustainable if it even gets underway in the first place. Starting with the Kyoto parties, such a coalition is being built however, and it seems to be expanding as more countries, states, and cities are drawn into the effort. One wonders whether the economists' standard models are missing something here. Contrary to models based on narrow self-interest, the world is actually full of examples of people donating money and effort to causes where the direct benefits to themselves are small or non-existent. In environmental economics, such "non-use" values are referred to as "option values," such as when the environment is preserved for possible future enjoyment; "existence values" are when there is no plan to ever enjoy the preserved resource, yet knowledge of its unspoiled existence yields pleasure; "bequest value" is when there is pleasure from passing on undamaged nature to future generations; and "stewardship value" is pleasure from preserving nature for all living species.[29] An example of how these values can come into play in a political situation is the perennial, intense debate in the U.S. Congress over oil exploration and development in Alaska's Arctic National Wildlife Refuge.

As one climbs the ladder of decreasing self-interest towards altruism, one enters the realm of religion and spirituality. Not surprisingly, the major religions of the world have something to say about environmental protection in general and global warming in particular. U.S. Catholic bishops, for example, have expressed that "if we harm the atmosphere, we dishonor our Creator and the gift of creation."[30]

It would seem that these altruistic values, however one classifies them, would play a particularly strong role when it comes to protecting the global environment. If people have non-use values associated with particular environmental features or amenities, then the non-use value of protecting the global environment should be equal to, or greater than, the sum of *all* the non-use values of *all* individual features which are threatened by global environmental degradation. These could add up to a considerable amount and be an important motivation and force in climate policy.

The challenge to economics in this situation is that global warming is an issue where the tension between the two sides – narrow self-interest and associated strategic behavior on the one hand, and altruistic values on the other – is particularly strong. This establishes a strong barrier to reaching a consensus about optimal extent and timing of mitigation. Three further concerns are: first, in trying to understand the situation and propose policy, economists may overstate the importance of selfish values and understate the unselfish ones out of analytical habit; second, climate policy conflicts may end up being particularly intense because of the polarization between those who emphasize use-values and those who emphasize non-use values; third, the choice of policy tools to manage emissions will be heavily influenced by the need to build initial coalitions and thereafter to expand and sustain these for the long haul.

Challenge: the timescale

Climate policies incur early costs by reducing emissions while expecting later benefits in the form of reduced environmental damages. Analysis and evaluation of this type of social investment is the classic problem in environmental economics. The solution should be the emission path over time, which maximizes the difference between late benefits and early costs while accounting for the fact that society has limited resources to pursue multiple good causes. Disregard for the moment how to calculate these costs and benefits, and focus on the method for comparing late benefits to early costs. As is well known, economists use a discounting technique whereby benefits experienced farther and farther into the future have less and less value to the current decision maker, so they carry less and less weight in the decision. The choice of discount rate becomes critical to the decision of whether or not to invest. For private decision makers, the appropriate discount rate is simply the per-dollar cost of financing the project, in the simplest case the interest rate applicable to a bank loan to fund the project. For environmental projects, where the government is the decision maker, should the discount rate, by analogy, simply be the interest rate applicable to government loans?

The relevant debate over which discount rate to use in public policy is not new in economics, but the climate policy debate serves to intensify it.[31] In this context, some non-economists argue that the discount rate should be zero, thus attaching equal weight to all costs and benefits in all time periods from here to infinity. This strikes the economist as irrational since it implies that climate mitigation would become the financial equivalent of a black hole in the sense that it might lay claim to all of society's investment funds and thereby leave all other good causes unfunded. Future generations will benefit from climate mitigation investment as well as other investments made by the present generation. These competing investments may include such projects as housing, education, health care, infrastructure, business equipment, and research and development. These investments are the sources of economic growth that benefit future generations. The discount rate debate is essentially about the degree to which mitigation investments should be given priority over non-mitigation investments.

Among economists, those at the low discount rate end – perhaps near 1 percent – argue that it should be some small positive number to adjust for two circumstances: that people usually have a preference for current consumption compared to later consumption and that future incomes will likely be higher and thus additional consumption will be valued less. At the high end – perhaps up to about 5 percent – other economist argue that the rate should be equal to some estimate of the government's cost of borrowing money as observed in the financial markets.[32]

As mentioned earlier, typical climate policy analyses run for 100 years, with some economists arguing for a longer time period of up to 300 years. Two inter-related dilemmas follow from this long time perspective. The first is that balancing costs and benefits by discounting implies that events beyond a certain time period become irrelevant; the higher the discount rate, the more quickly comes the point of irrelevance. Second, within a given time-horizon, the conclusion of the analysis is very sensitive to the interest rate choice. These two points are illustrated in Figure 7.3 and Table 7.2.

As shown in Figure 7.3, at a 5 percent discount rate, the value of $1 million today is equivalent to $7000 in 100 years, and is worth nothing 300 years from now. Even with an unusually low 1 percent rate, present values are cut to one-third a century from now, and one-twentieth three centuries from now. The problem that follows from the figure is that the economic future beyond 100 to 300 years, depending on which discount rate one uses, practically vanishes. Whichever positive interest rate one uses, after some time period, the future as well as future generations do not matter to current decision makers. This implication is one that many people will object to because of the implied indifference towards the well-being of future generations. Naturally, they will look for ways to supplement the economic analysis with alternative frameworks.

Table 7.2 illustrates the impact of the choice of discount rate for present values at two points in time, 50 years and 100 years from now. It answers the following question: if society invests $1 million in climate mitigation today at the given interest rate and if, hypothetically, all the benefits show up in a single

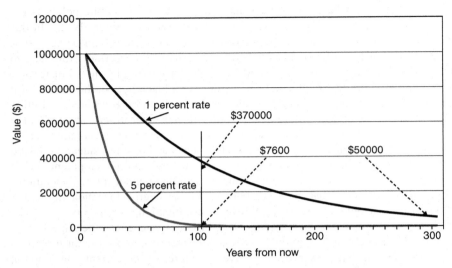

Figure 7.3 Present value of $1 million to be received at different times in the future, at 5 and 1 percent discount rates.

year in the future, 50 or 100 years from now, how large must the benefit be to make it worth the current mitigation costs? Alternatively, the entries in the table can be thought of as the value to which $1 million would grow in a bank account earning the indicated interest rate for the given number of years. The point of the table is to show how rapidly the marginal benefit must increase as the chosen discount rate increases percent for percent. At 50 years, marginal benefits must increase by a factor of 1.6 to make up for a 1 percent increase in the interest rate. Put a different way, if the applied discount rate increases from 1 to 2 percent, the benefit of the marginal investment must increase by 64 percent to make it worthwhile. At 100 years, the increase is by a factor of about 2.6 – or 160 percent – for every 1 percent increase in the interest rate. These numbers indicate the very large sensitivity of marginal benefits – and thus the policy choices and optimal emission path – to small changes in the discount rate.

The reality is that one cannot derive a unique and appropriate discount rate for mitigation investments from economic theory. Absent a theoretically founded consensus among economists, it is therefore more appropriate to speak of a reasonable range, perhaps as low as 1 percent to as high as 5 percent. Since results are very sensitive to the choice within this range, economic analysis based on standard discounting becomes a very rough tool for defining the optimal emission path. It furthermore seems predictable that economists whose opinion is that society should move relatively quickly to mitigate climate change are likely to argue for a low discount rate, while those with the opposite opinion will likely argue for a high discount rate. Knowing or suspecting this, non-economists will supplement the economic analysis with other concepts and approaches. This serves to undermine the power of cost–benefit analysis in climate management.

Table 7.2 Present-value equivalents

Discount rate (%)	Future value of $1 million after 50 years	Ratio*	Future value of $1 million after 100 years	Ratio*
0	$1,000,000		$1,000,000	
1	$1,644,632	1.64	$2,704,814	2.70
2	$2,691,588	1.64	$7,244,646	2.68
3	$4,383,906	1.63	$19,218,632	2.65
4	$7,106,683	1.62	$50,504,948	2.63
5	$11,467,400	1.61	$131,501,258	2.60

Note
* Calculated as the ratio between a given present value and the present value with a 1 percent lower discount rate.

There is, however, a way to leave the discount rate controversy out of the economic analysis while still providing meaningful input into the decision-making process. The most common way is to estimate GDP growth (or the growth of private consumption) under various mitigation scenarios. Since resources used for mitigation are not used to fuel GDP growth, the implication is that more mitigation means slower GDP growth. This makes explicit the opportunity cost of mitigation efforts (calculated as GDP-loss) while not valuing and discounting benefits. A separate accounting for benefits, including use of indicators of the state of the human ecology and social justice, could be done within a sustainability framework, as discussed in the following section.

Challenge: scientific uncertainty and risk

At this time, the causes of global warming appear to be well-known and accepted within the scientific community. There is, however, still great uncertainty about its consequences since important parameters (e.g. climate sensitivity) are not known precisely. There is, furthermore, uncertainty about the conditions needed to trigger catastrophic events, the most well-known being the melting of the Greenland and Antarctic ice sheets. This would submerge low lying land areas in sea water as the water level rises perhaps hundreds of feet. Combined with other, simultaneous changes related to global warming, this would, indeed, qualify as vast and dangerous changes in the human ecology.

These scientific uncertainties carry over to the economic analysis. With analogies to financial models, it is, in principle, possible to build cost–benefit analysis on considerable uncertainty as long as one is able to identify and value possible outcomes and characterize their likelihood with a probability distribution. Even if a probability distribution can be developed for, say, the melting of ice sheets under given emission scenarios, it is still unclear how one would value avoidance of a global catastrophe.

Citing a series of scientific uncertainties, the IPCC draws the following, clear conclusion:

> the benefits of different greenhouse gas reduction actions, including actions to stabilize greenhouse gas concentrations at selected levels, are incompletely characterized and cannot be compared directly to mitigation costs for the purpose of estimating the net economic effects of mitigation.
>
> (IPCC, 2001a, p. 104)

As a result, the reality of current climate policy is that it is obviously not conducted by a careful comparison of economic costs and benefits. This does not mean, however, that economics has become irrelevant. What has happened instead is that economic analysis has become one of several ways to probe the long term consequences of global warming within a more comprehensive framework centered on the notion of sustainable development.

Within the United Nations context, the stated purpose of climate intervention is to avoid "*dangerous* anthropogenic interference with the climate system" (UNFCCC, 1992, article 2, emphasis added). This suggests the use of physical/biological indicators rather than economic indicators, to decide on the optimal emission sequence. The Kyoto Protocol sets an emission limit for participating countries for the years 2008–2012 without reference to costs and benefits. The IPCC, the primary source of data and analysis to guide global climate policy, is quite explicit about the recommended decision framework. For the IPCC, the key term to judge benefits is the notion of "sustainable development," defined in the IPCC (2001a, p. 386) in the same way as in the World Commission on Environment and Development (1987) as "development that meets the needs of the present without compromising the ability of future generations to meet their own needs." The most general, pure notion of sustainability integrates three sets of values: economic well-being; social justice; and environmental quality in a limitless time perspective. In the climate context, the power of the beautiful notion of sustainability is that it recognizes the interdependence between these core values in a global system that is subject to a threat of its own making. The weakness, however, is that it is not clear how to make the notion operational in an actual decision-making setting. For example, some may argue that there are trade-offs between the core values; others that environmental quality is just a means to realizing the other two values. In particular situations, controversies may arise over the criteria to judge the degree to which the values are realized. As a result, uses of the sustainability notion runs the risk of being arbitrary. One way to avoid arbitrariness is to bring together people from various professions and affected constituencies to resolve, in an open discourse, how to implement the notion of sustainability with reference to a particular issue. If so, the sustainability notion may become a framework for discussions to clarify common values and priorities and to develop appropriate ways to protect and enhance those values. This is, of course, a general, although imperfect, description of what happens within the U.N. context with the IPCC as the lead analytical entity on climate issues.[33]

By contrast, economists would like to think of the social cost–benefit analysis as being the one appropriate decision framework for social investments such as climate mitigation. When properly done – by economists, of course – the social cost–benefit analysis assures that resources are channeled into the uses where they yield the highest return to society. For the reasons explained in the section above, this ambition is not achievable with mitigation. The question arises of what can be said in general about when a cost–benefit analysis is appropriate and when it should yield to a more comprehensive sustainability analysis. Is there an appropriate division of labor between the two? Figure 7.4 seeks to answer that question.

Starting in the left column of Figure 7.4, the cost–benefit analysis assumes that the decision maker has limited resources available within a time period, and that these can be allocated to alternative uses or substitutes. Trade-offs exist between these, so it becomes a question of what proportion of resources are allocated to the various end-uses so as to maximize the overall benefit. In such a setting, it suffices to use a single value criterion (present value) to make a decision as long as costs and benefits are properly defined, i.e. all externalities and non-market values are accounted for, and as long as the discount rate fairly accounts for the return to the same resources in alternative uses. It makes the analysis easier if the project is simple and separable from other projects in the sense of standing or falling on its own merits, and that the risk is low, particularly the risk of events that can be catastrophic to the decision maker. Similarly, it makes the decision easier if the question of who benefits and who loses is irrelevant to the decision, perhaps because the gains from the project can be used to compensate those who lose or because it is uncontroversial who the beneficiaries are.

Stated this way, cost–benefit analysis is simply the economic way of thinking that is at the core of economic models of human behavior. It is also a common

Cost–benefit analysis: ⟷ Sustainability analysis:

Cost–benefit analysis:	Sustainability analysis:
• Substitutes exist	• No substitutes
• Trade-offs	• Constraints
• Maximize	• Protect
• Single value decision critereon	• Multiple criteria
• Seperateness	• Wholeness
• Partial system adjustment; change	• Whole system health or survival; integrity
• Low or no risk of catastrophic events	• Risk of catastrophic events alarming
• Short term	• Long term
• Simplicity	• Complexity
• Justice separable from efficiency	• Justice and efficiency inseparable

As the decision situation is increasingly better described by the items on the right, cost–benefit analysis loses power. Similarly, sustainability analysis loses power from right to left.

Figure 7.4 The power of decision frameworks: cost–benefit versus sustainability.

way for people, private companies, and public agencies to evaluate projects, either implicitly or explicitly. If they do not, an economist could advise them that they can likely improve their situation by adopting a cost–benefit framework.

As the conditions in the left column are increasingly violated – as they are with global warming – cost–benefit analysis loses its power. In the extreme, the characteristics of the decision-setting can become like those in the right column. If there is a cause – a dominant cause – that *must* be funded as a precondition for protecting all other good causes, then there are no substitution possibilities. In effect, the freedom to pursue other projects becomes constrained by the need to protect this dominant good cause to the degree necessary. The level of investment, as judged by multiple criteria or sustainability criteria, becomes that necessary to protect the survival, wholeness, and integrity of the dominant cause. It makes the decision to commit funds to this cause easier if there is a sense that failure to do so could lead to catastrophes, particularly when there is major uncertainty brought about by complexity combined with a long time perspective. Adding to the motivation to fund the cause would be if failure to do so leads to controversial fairness issues.[34]

Described this way, the decision-setting in the right column seems to capture some of the essence of the global warming mitigation project. But it also captures the nature of other projects that societies pursue without carefully weighing long-term costs and benefits. The sustainability analysis seems appropriate when an entire system is threatened, e.g. to commit to military defense, especially in times of war when the social system is threatened from the outside. But the social system also has vital subsystems that are intensely resource consuming, such as that dedicated to socializing the young and the legal system to maintain order and justice. The social discourse about dedicating resources to these systems is better described within a sustainability framework than as an application of cost–benefit thinking.

If the economic way of thinking – cost–benefit thinking – is just one of many ways to grapple with resource allocation in some settings – especially those conforming to the left column in Figure 7.4 – what is the most productive role economists can play?

When it comes to environmental policy, including climate policy, cost–benefit analysis should be seen as a contribution to getting productive negotiations started, not as a way to end them.[35] Its main virtue is the systematic accounting for all the positive and negative circumstances that are relevant to the decision and to thus guide the discussion towards a better solution. It furthermore provides a framework for discussing what is lost or gained if the conclusions of the analysis are not followed. It thereby brings into view more clearly what is at stake. As discussed above, the analysis comes with shortcomings and different economists applying it to the same issue may therefore reach widely different conclusions, for example Lomborg (2004) versus Stern (2006). A major virtue of the analysis, however, is that it forces those who apply it to make explicit their assumptions within a well-established, systematic framework. The debate about these assumptions may then play an essential role in guiding policymakers, perhaps as they are compared to broader criteria for sustainability.

Conclusions

The debate over whether or not global warming is happening and whether humans are the cause has basically ended. The focus of the debate is now on the extent and timing of mitigation and the inevitable questions: who pays? How? When? How much? At the time of writing, these questions are at the top of the European policy agenda and are moving towards the same level in the U.S. It seems safe to predict that as comprehensive policies are launched, the lives of individual people will be disrupted as the energy system is transformed.

Some people will experience global warming policy as a nuisance leading to just another expense. Others may be motivated to ask basic questions about their way of life and make major lifestyle changes. Most will probably be somewhere between. The impacts on individual lives may be small, for example, if it turns out that carbon capture and storage is inexpensive and safe; an enzyme or microbe is discovered which can easily make the sugars in switch grass fermentable; nuclear fusion becomes practical and economical as a power source; or some other good-luck technology scenario plays itself out. Alternatively, adopted policies may become very expensive and call for significant sacrifices. Most economic studies of mitigation policy suggest that costs are about 1 percent of GDP for feasible stabilization scenarios (near 550 ppm CO_2 atmospheric concentration). Since people in developed countries are likely to carry most of the burden, the implied cost for people in those countries may about 2 percent, which is equivalent to setting back developed country GDP growth by about one year. On the face of it, and given the various disaster scenarios that can gain momentum and become irreversible without mitigation, this sacrifice probably seems small to most people. That may render the entire discussion above about using economics to define an appropriate emission path uninteresting. The cost–benefit analysis may be so overwhelmingly in favor of large and early mitigation that it is a no-brainer. Certainly, that's the position taken in Stern (2006). On the other hand, the economists in Lomborg (2004) reach the opposite conclusion and claims there are better causes.[36]

At the human ecology system level, the fundamental challenge is to transform the energy system, hopefully by peaceful means and in a way that minimizes costs. Fossil fuels have served the historical role of freeing human dependence on muscle power and are inextricably linked to the leap in human welfare that has followed the industrial revolution. The dark side of this new dependence is, however, increasingly shaping the lives of people around the globe as well as the human ecology in general: local and regional pollution are already major killers while global warming is emerging as an even more vicious threat, and there are major dangers associated with competition for global fossil fuel resources in a world where nuclear weapons proliferate.

When confronted with this dark side and all the ingrained reasons why it exists and gets worse year by year, it is easy to become pessimistic. This chapter may offer additional and, perhaps, more clever reasons to be even more pessimistic, notably the diagnosis of the problem as an externality affecting a global public good with tremendous time lags. The purpose, however, was not to create more pessimism, but simply to point out how the *existing* institutional framework channels our resources and behavior and thereby creates the problem. The cleverness, if any, consists in framing the problem the right way – institutional failure on a grand scale – so that new ways of doing things can be developed and implemented.

Economics is often called the "dismal" science because of its practitioners' inclination to point out the best course of action, and then immediately spoiling it by pointing out the benefits of the course *not* taken. Even so, economists are generally not cynics. To the contrary, from the birth of modern economics with Adam Smith's *Wealth of Nations*, the primary mission has been to unlock the tremendous potential power contained in the social organization to address the vital needs of humankind. The global warming process is a case of the social organization appropriate to earlier conditions now failing the human specie and our other friends in nature. As sketched in this chapter, the solution must therefore be to rearrange the present social organization to align it with the long-term needs of the species populating the earth. Economics offers a peaceful and cost-effective way to accomplish that. The alternatives to the economist's way seem truly dismal.

Appendix

The basic analytical framework

The economic diagnosis of the climate problem is that it is a market failure and therefore that market behavior needs to be re-channeled by means of new incentives and institutions. Below, the basic analytical perspective reflecting this view is outlined.

The carbon tax benchmark

Suppose policymakers, in some ideal world, have somehow decided on a target concentration level for global warming gases in the atmosphere and a corresponding series of worldwide, annual targets for CO_2 emissions. To most economists, the gold standard for a cost-efficient policy to reach these targets would be a corresponding time sequence of tax rates on carbon emissions applied uniformly across the world and corresponding to the damage done by these emissions. Think of the tax as being collected from fossil fuel producers at all production sites and ignore all practical problems, including imperfect information. Figure 7.A1 illustrates the partial equilibrium analysis of the situation in the global energy market in a typical year.[37]

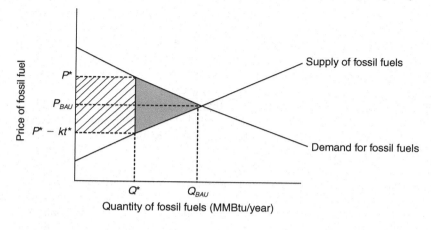

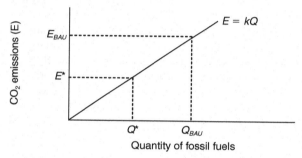

Figure 7.A1 The fossil fuel market and the corresponding CO2 emissions.

For simplicity, combine the three fossil fuel markets (coal, oil, and natural gas) into one market by constructing a typical fossil fuel energy unit containing, for example, one million British Thermal Units (MMBtu). Let the three fossil fuels have constant proportions in this composite energy unit and let these proportions remain fixed as total energy use changes. Furthermore, let consumption of a typical unit of energy emit a fixed amount of carbon, say k units, and let carbon emissions expand in proportion k to energy use. The initial situation is shown in Figure 7.A1, the top frame showing the initial equilibrium solution under the business as usual scenario with the corresponding price (P_{BAU}), the level of energy use (Q_{BAU}), and – in the lower frame – the level of emissions, E_{BAU}.[38]

Next, suppose the best level of global emissions in the selected year is identified as E^* associated with fossil energy use Q^*, in fact, $E^* = k \cdot Q^*$. Consider the optimal tax rate t^* per unit of carbon and let it be collected from energy producers by an amount kt^* dollars per unit of fossil energy. The tax drives a wedge between what buyers pay and what sellers receive, and it reduces the quantity traded in the market. The new situation in the market is that buyers now pay P^*, sellers receive the net price $P^* - kt^*$, supply equals demand at Q^*, and the optimal emission level E^* is reached. Sellers unambiguously receive less revenue since both the net price and the fossil fuel quantity have been reduced. This implies that some demand has shifted out of the fossil fuel market and shows up elsewhere in the economic system. The Kaya identity (1990) indicates where to look for the adjustments that will take place: a reduction in GDP, in the energy intensity of GDP, and the carbon intensity of energy.

The economist's belief system implies that this adjustment process should not be managed by the government through detailed regulation and enforcement. Observe first that, in the energy market, only those willing to pay P^* or above will consume fossil energy and only producers accepting $P^* - kt^*$ will produce and sell. Those who place the highest value on the fossil fuels will therefore continue to use them while their demand will be satisfied by the lowest cost producers. Outside the fossil fuel market, utility and profit maximizing market participants will find the economically most desirable substitutes among the possibilities indicated by the Kaya identity. By assumption in this model, the tax rate, t^*, is the same in all countries and to all decision makers so that everyone faces the same uniform cost signal. As a result, cutbacks in fossil fuel consumption would be such that the cost of the last unit consumed would be the same in all countries and all industries. Technically, this means that "the equimarginal principle" applies, which is a condition for cost minimization. Given target levels for atmospheric concentration of warming gases and a corresponding series of emission levels, the uniform global carbon tax provides "how, when, and where" flexibility to reallocate global economic resources in a way that minimizes overall social costs. This policy tool is therefore consistent with the basic belief system of natural resource and environmental economists, and the intent of the UNFCCC. It may thus be considered the "gold standard" for climate policy.

The cap-and-trade alternative

There is another reason why the lower frame in Figure 7.A1 is crucial to climate policy. As already observed, if t^* is imposed on the fossil fuel industry, the result is a cutback to E^*.[39] But there is an alternative way to create the same solution. Rather than initiating the economic changes by legislating t^*, one can instead cap emission levels at E^* by allocating a corresponding number of "emission rights" to fossil fuel users and let them trade these "emission rights" within a "cap-and-trade" program. Given the absolute constraint on emissions, the program would force fossil fuel consumption back to Q^* from Q_{BAU} and price would go to P^*, as with the t^* policy. To see why this would happen, start at the initial equilibrium point in the top frame of Figure 7.A1 and keep in mind: (a) that each unit of fossil energy releases k units of emission; and (b) a unit of energy cannot be used without k emission permits. Now, let the issuing body allocate $kQ^* = E^*$ emission permits. In the initial market equilibrium at P_{BAU} and Q_{BAU} there is more demand for energy than there is emission permits. Those with a desire to consume fossil fuel, but without sufficient emission permits, will now create a demand for the permits and its price starts going up. As it does, the cost of energy consumption to the consumer, which is the sum of the per-unit energy price and the emission permit costs, starts going up. Only when the permit price reaches t^* (the permit cost per unit of energy is kt^*), is there equality between the actual emissions from fossil fuel use and the number of emissions permits. Units of energy consumed beyond that are illegal. This leads to exactly the same price and quantity solution as under a tax system.

Under a cap-and-trade program, what is the corresponding adjustment process *outside* the energy market? It is the same as described with the tax strategy: The elements in the Kaya identity are adjusted in the same way by utility-maximizing final buyers and profit-maximizing firms seeking substitutes for fossil fuels.

The costs and benefits of climate policy

How does one find the cost of climate policy? Consider the carbon tax benchmark. Carbon taxes are a cost to energy suppliers, but they are not a cost to society as a whole since their use creates offsetting benefits. In this hypothetical case, poor countries could, for example, receive a portion of the tax revenue in order to motivate their participation in the climate policy, other portions could be used to fund research and development of non-fossil fuel resources, reduce inefficiencies in the tax system by reducing other taxes, etc.

The true cost of climate policy to society is the foregone benefit of using cheap and abundant fossil fuels and instead using the substitutes indicated by the Kaya identity.[40] The social cost of this foregone opportunity is commonly measured in a way that is illustrated by the vertical difference between the supply and demand schedules in the upper graph in Figure 7.A1. For any given unit, this cost equals the difference between the highest price the buyer is willing to pay and the lowest price at which the seller is willing to sell. To find the total loss from all foregone units of fossil fuel consumption, start the tax rate at t^* and allow it to gradually shrink to zero. As this happens, quantity increases from Q^* to Q_{BAU}. In effect, the hypothetically shrinking tax rate traces out the shaded triangle in the upper frame of Figure 7.A1. It is a triangle in that figure because the supply and demand schedules have been drawn as straight lines. So, here is an important insight regarding climate policy: the cost of climate policy using a given, uniform carbon tax rate can be approximated as kt^* multiplied by the estimated reduction in fossil fuel consumption, ΔQ, divided by two, i.e. ($\Delta Q \cdot kt^*/2$). This corresponds to the shaded area in the upper frame of Figure 7.A1.

More interesting, however, is the relationship between *emission* reductions and costs. To find this, draw a graph with emission reductions along the horizontal axes and the tax rate along the vertical axis. Under the BAU scenario, the tax rate is zero and cutbacks are zero, thus the economy is at the origin. If the tax rate is set equal to t^*, the cutbacks will be E_{BAU} minus E^*, or ΔE, as shown in Figure 7.A2. Draw a line from the origin through the point (ΔE, t^*). The shaded triangle in Figure 7.A2 will be the same area as the shaded triangle in Figure 7.A1 because:

$$\text{social cost} = (\Delta Q \cdot kt^*/2) = (\Delta E \cdot t^*/2) \text{ since } \Delta Q \cdot k = \Delta E$$

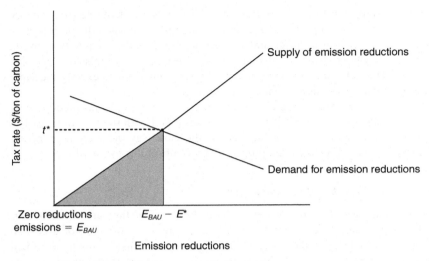

Figure 7.A2 Emission reductions supply and demand.

The importance of this exercise is that it generates society's marginal cost schedule for emission reductions. It turns out that the carbon tax rate equals the marginal cost per unit of emission reduction. Of crucial importance to climate policy is: how rapidly is the marginal cost schedule rising? In terms of costs, how easy or difficult is it to get emission cutbacks? This marginal cost schedule is also the economy's supply schedule of emission cutbacks. At any cost level per unit of carbon emission (in the present case in the form of a tax), it shows how people in the economy would cut back and pursue the Kaya alternatives instead.

Hypothetically, one could also derive a demand schedule for carbon cutbacks, as illustrated in Figure 7.A2. This demand schedule would account for all the market valued and non-market valued damages done from here to eternity by emissions in the present period. In fact, the demand schedule would show the benefits of avoiding those damages as emission reductions increase. A major argument in an earlier section of this chapter is that it is not possible to value these damages reliably given the current state of knowledge, tools, and decision criteria relevant to climate policy formulation. As a result, the current practice in those countries that do have climate policy is to define emission targets and thereby require a certain level of emission reductions. Nevertheless, Figure 7.A2 shows that supply and demand for emission reductions are analytically meaningful concepts and that there is a price that will clear this market. This price can either be a carbon tax or the price established in the cap-and-trade market.

Fairness: who carries the burden of climate policy?

Building on Figure 7.A1, distributional impacts of the two policies are shown in Figure 7.A3. All the graphs in Figure 7.A3 repeat the top graph in Figure 7.A1, and labels have therefore been minimized to avoid confusion. The exhibits illustrate that with market exchange, every transaction yields a benefit to both the buyer and the seller. The economic notion of surplus is based on the difference between what buyers are maximally willing to pay in a range of purchases and the minimum price at which suppliers are willing to sell the product in that range. Each row of graphs in Figure 7.A3 shows a policy scenario. By adding up gray areas in the graphs from left to right, the sum is the total surplus under the policy scenario of that row. Without government interference – the BAU scenario in the top row – buyers capture the area above the equilibrium price line and sellers capture the area below. Think of the buy side as consisting of final users of fossil fuels. It the case of commercial and industrial users, they are likely to have the opportunity to pass any cost increases on to the buyers of the products they make and sell. Thus the cost increases originating in the fossil fuel industry are likely to be spread widely in the economy. On the sell side, think of the players as producers of fossil fuels, many of which have costs substantially below market prices.

Now, impose a carbon tax. The immediate effect is to raise price, reduce quantity, and reduce the surplus (compare the total surplus in the first to the second row in Figure 7.A3). This loss of surplus is, presumably, more than offset by benign climate impacts as market participants pursue substitutes. Out of what remains, the general public takes a big bite through taxes, leaving both buyers and sellers worse off.

Next, consider the cap-and-trade policy in the bottom row. More specifically, let the system be of the European type, which presently includes large source-emitters of CO_2 (electric utilities; cement, iron, and steel producers; and others).

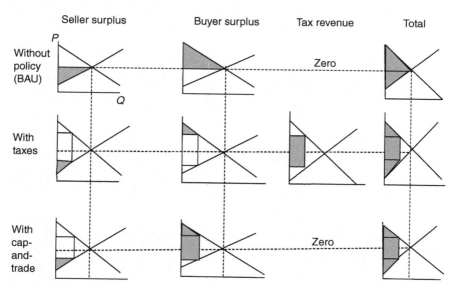

Figure 7.A3 Fossil fuel market surplus under three policy scenarios.

These buyers of fossil fuels are allocated emission permits based on historical use. In this simple model, the fossil fuel industry loses by the same amount as under a tax policy and the general public receives no tax revenue. The large CO_2 emitters, having captured the newly created private-property right, get both the shaded square and triangle in the bottom row. Not surprisingly, cap-and-trade is far superior to a carbon tax to large emitters.

With the assumptions made in this simple model, there is even the possibility that the cap-and-trade program yields *more* surplus to permit receivers relative to the case of no climate policy. Compare the buyer surplus in the top row to the one in the bottom row. Under cap-and-trade, the buyer has lost surplus because of the quantity reduction but gained because of the price decrease. If the price decrease is relatively high compared to the quantity decrease, there is a possibility that the cap-and-trade program translates to *increased* profits for the large end-users. However, this scenario seems unlikely in the real world, given the relatively small size of end-users now subject to cap-and-trade in the international fossil fuel markets and therefore a likely small price decrease. It nevertheless underscores how cap-and-trade serves to protect the values of assets in industries that are heavy users of fossil fuels. The free allocation of permits probably slows down retirement of their capital equipment and may delay the transitioning to a lower carbon emission path. It furthermore helps prevent industry flight to areas without a climate policy and serves to generate less opposition from the group of large CO_2 emitters and the customers they serve. It should be noted, however, that the conclusions drawn from the timeless framework in Figure 7.A3 may be misleading if the cap-and-trade system brings down costs more rapidly over time than does the carbon tax system.

Notes

1 This ambition is, of course, not new. A prominent contribution, for example, is Clark (1989) who provides a general framework for understanding the exchanges between the human and the natural world and a corresponding research program. This book sees this effort from the point of view of economics.

2 This is the main theme of the current bestseller by Diamond (2005), *Collapse: How Societies Choose to Fail or Succeed*. An economist's perspective on Diamond's framework can be found in Page (2005).

3 United Nations Framework Convention on Climate Change (1992), Article 2.

4 Kyoto Protocol To the United Nations Framework Convention On Climate Change (1997).

5 The U.S. federal government position, essentially based on voluntary emission reductions, is presently being challenged in the nation's Supreme Court and a ruling is expected in mid-2007 (*Massachusetts* v. *EPA, 05–1120*).

6 The question of the limits of economics in climate policy is hardly trivial. Consider, for example, Lomborg (2004) bringing together a panel of world-class economists to use cost–benefit analysis to allocate a large, fixed sum of money across ten carefully selected world problems. Climate policy ended up as the lowest priority, i.e. the poorest social investment among those considered. By contrast, the Stern Review (Stern, 2006), using a modified cost–benefit framework, argues that the global community should waste no time to take aggressive action.

7   The common reference is the IPCC's Third Assessment Report (2001a, b, c, d) downloadable at www.ipcc.ch. The fourth assessment report is expected in late 2007. A widely read, more popular reference is Flannery (2005), which emphasizes the science background. Dessler and Parson (2006) cover the science background and is also a good primer on the economics and politics of the issue. A recent book focusing on the economics of the issue and intended for a wide audience is Jaccard (2005).

8   In this brief chapter, numerous simplifications have been made, one being focusing on CO_2 from burning fossil fuels while ignoring CO_2 from other sources (e.g. deforestation) and the five other warming gases listed in the Kyoto Protocol. CO_2 from energy use accounts for two-thirds of greenhouse gas emissions, their use is growing rapidly and there are huge fossil fuel resources available (IPCC, 2001a, pp. 314–316). Thus the climate future seems overwhelmingly dominated by what happens to fossil fuel consumption.

9   The Kaya identity can be written as:

$$CO_2 = GDP \times (EN/ GDP) \times (CO_2 / EN),$$

EN refers to total energy use. Note that the expression collapses to an identity after canceling terms. The growth form of the identity is used in Figure 7.2. Also, observe that if EN is cancelled in the last two terms and the identity is written in growth form, it becomes: percent ΔCO_2 = percent ΔGDP + percent $\Delta(CO_2/GDP)$. The countries adhering to the Kyoto Protocol are targeting emissions, the left side of the identity, whereas the U.S. policy at the federal level targets only the carbon intensity of GDP – the second term on the right – and seeks to lower it. The U.S. approach therefore allows CO_2 emissions to increase in a growing economy. President Bush's climate policy is available at www.whitehouse.gov/news/releases/2002/02/climatechange.html

10 The U.S. Energy Information Administration is one of several sources that provides annual updates on the energy markets and their prospects at www.eia.doe.gov/oiaf/forecasting.html. The United Nations Development Programme (2004) contains a good inventory of the various energy sources.

11 By a sub-discipline of economics is meant a relatively well defined topical area of research and teaching practiced by a subset of economists organized into one or more professional organizations and with one or more journal outlets for their research. Although economists tend to share a common approach to analysis and a corresponding set of analytical tools, different sub-disciplines tend to emphasize different tools appropriate to their area. Within such a group, a dominant perspective on their area may emerge. This perspective, shared by many but not necessarily all, is taken to be "the beliefs" of the economists practicing the specialty.

12 There is an important link between how one views natural resource scarcity and global warming. The greater the scarcity of fossil fuels, the less global warming is a problem over the long haul. It is precisely because economists believe in fossil fuel abundance that global warming has become a high-priority issue in the profession.

13 This is a simplified statement of the famous "Coase Theorem." Needless to say, the distribution of benefits under the socially efficient solution would depend on who the property rights are assigned to.

14 It may be possible to continue to burn fossil fuels and still avoid global warming if the CO_2 is captured and stored in a safe manner in the ground or in the oceans.

15 See for example Ellerman (1999). This article is also a clear statement of how the views of energy economists and environmental economists have converged when it comes to defining the appropriate role of government.

16 When choosing a policy in the real world, it is not possible to ignore uncertainty, political feasibility, and other important conditions. Weitzman (1974), for example, triggered a debate about the choice of a carbon tax versus cap-and-trade in a world where marginal mitigation costs and the benefits of mitigation are not known. With

uncertainty, it turns out that the best policy choice depends on the relative steepness of marginal abatement costs as compared to marginal benefits. When arguing about the shapes of these curves, it also turns out to matter whether one takes a long-run perspective or a short-run perspective. Add to this that the flexibility of the policy-maker to change the policy instrument (whether taxes or the emission quota) as new information about costs and benefits is received is also important to the choice of policy instrument. This chapter circumvents this debate and asserts that the actual choice of primary policy instruments so far has largely been determined by political feasibility and other dynamic considerations, as argued in what follows.

17 For a recent, comprehensive review of the European Union emission trading system, see Stowell (2005). Web site references for these initiatives are, respectively, www.europeanclimateexchange.com/index_flash.php; www.chicagoclimatex.com/; www.rggi.org/calendar.htm. California's policy can be found at www.climatechange.ca.gov. The global carbon market was valued at $21.5 billion in the first nine months of 2006, up from about $11 billion for all of 2005, mostly in the E.U. market (*Wall Street Journal*, October 26, 2006)

18 The claim about economists is based on casual observation, not on a formal survey. Gregg Mankiew, for example, observes in his blog that most economists he knows would reject the Kyoto Protocol and accept a modest carbon tax. See blog at www.gregmankiw.blogspot.com/2006/06/kyoto-carbon-and-al-gore.html

19 See for example the series of articles in *The Energy Journal* 1999 special issue entitled *The Costs of the Kyoto Protocol: A Multi-Model Evaluation.*

20 It should also be noted here that there is no reason why individuals and organizations should not be able to buy emission permits to either offset their own carbon footprint or to simply increase emission cutbacks over and above that determined by the government. Reportedly, there are now about 20 websites in the U.S. where people can buy emission permits to offset, for example, the carbon emissions of an airplane trip.

21 There is an interesting social justice issue here about what is meant by historical users. Fossil fuel consumers have obviously used, and overused, the atmosphere's ability to absorb carbon, so there might be a historical right in that. The other extreme argument, and a more reasonable one from a fairness perspective, is that people in general's enjoyment of a stable climate predates the historical rights of carbon emitters and that emission permits should therefore be equally distributed across the world's population.

22 As demonstrated in the Appendix, for a given emission cutback, marginal cost equals the tax rate equals the price of the emission right in the cap-and-trade market. As discussed later in the text, auctioning of permits as well as hybrid systems that combine features of the cap-and-trade program with a tax system are possible.

23 Total world venture capital financing was nearing $32 billion in the year 2006, a healthy increase driven by "... the growing allure of new technologies that conserve energy and protect the environment." See "VC funding may top $32 Billion. Recovery from dot-com bust continues with more money flowing into startups" in *San Francisco Chronicle*, December 12, 2006, available at www.sfgate.com. It should be noted here that a portion of the venture capital investment in clean energy is probably motivated by the high energy prices that prevailed before and during the year 2006. The perspective of the leading clean energy venture capitalist can be found in "Kleiner's Green Investment Machine," *Wall Street Journal*, December 13, 2006.

24 In the Protocol, there is a way to include poor country emissions into the global reduction effort. The so called "Clean Development Mechanism" under the Protocol allows emission reducing projects in poor countries to offset emissions in rich countries. This mechanism presents an interesting business opportunity for companies who undertake such projects with the aim of selling emission credits on the E.U. Climate Exchange. There is, however, an elaborate approval mechanism for such

projects. It is unclear how important this mechanism will be in the overall emission reduction effort.

25   For a review of this literature, see Dasgupta *et al.* (2002).

26   California's newly adopted policy is at www.climatechange.ca.gov

27   There is an analogy here to the famous "Prisoners' Dilemma" in game theory. Suppose two parties are competing in a strategic game where the payoff to one party depends on the strategy chosen by the other. In some specifications of this game, there is an incentive for the two to pick a safe (or "dominant") strategy that causes an inferior overall solution. Such a solution can be avoided in the real world through means that include credible and enforceable contracts, repeated interaction or interaction in other contexts.

28   It should be noted here that the Kyoto emission targets have been adopted as law by the Eurpean Union and are thus legally binding to the member states (decision no. 280/2004/EC of the European Parliament and of the Council of February 11, 2004 concerning a mechanism for monitoring EC greenhouse gas emissions and for implementing the Kyoto Protocol).

29   These values are discussed in most textbooks on Environmental Economics, see for example Field and Field (2002).

30   See U.S. Catholic Bishops at www.usccb.org/sdwp/international/globalclimate.htm. A gateway to the positions of the major religions of the world when it comes to environmental and global warming issues can be found at www.pbs.org/moyers/moyersonamerica/green/sites.html

31   A recent, good introduction to this issue in the climate context is the series of papers on this issue in Lomborg, (2004).

32   Economic analyses of climate policy are typically conducted in real dollars, so interest rates should be considered real rates.

33   It turns out that two-thirds of the 385 scientists and others credited as authors and expert reviewers of the IPCC's third assessment report (IPCC, 2001a, b, c, d) are from Europe and North America (IPCC, 2001a, pp. 356–364). Bangladesh, possibly the country most at risk for global warming consequences, was represented by one expert. These numbers are first and foremost a reminder of the tragically unequal distribution of knowledge and expertise between rich and poor countries. They also indicate that the ideal situation of a truly representative decision body guided by value-neutral experts is impossible to attain in reality. The second reminder is therefore that we live in a world where we often have to settle for second-best solutions.

34   One could make the argument that adaptation is a substitute for mitigation and that one can be traded off for the other. There are two main problems with this argument. First, it is very unclear what the trade-off is given the uncertain impacts on the human ecology under BAU and other scenarios and therefore what people ultimately would need to adapt to. Second, there is a serious equity issue that may render the trade-off irrelevant. This has to do with the fact that, most likely, those paying for mitigation live in the world's most affluent countries and those most harmed by absence of mitigation are those – now and in the future – living in the poorest countries of the world.

35   This notion of the role of cost–benefit analysis is reminiscent of an observation made by John M. Keynes: "The theory of economics does not furnish a body of settled conclusions immediately applicable to policy. It is a method rather than a doctrine, an apparatus of the mind, a technique which helps its possessor to draw correct conclusions."

36   Lomborg's response to the Stern Review is that it is "selective and its conclusions flawed." See Bjørn Lomborg's "Stern Review," *Wall Street Journal*, November 2, 2006.

37   The basic model used in this section is similar to that of Weyant and Hill (1999), who use it to discuss the notion of costs contained in models that seek to arrive at

quantitative estimates of climate policy costs. In this section, the model is used to explain the nature of cost-minimizing policy approaches.

38   The partial equilibrium approach used in this Appendix relies on a series of simplifications; one is that the feedback effects on the energy market from overall economic adjustments are ignored as are the impacts on the economy of spending the revenues from the carbon tax. The aggregation of the three fossil fuels in constant proportions into one market ignores that they are not likely to expand in the same proportions as total energy use expands. Furthermore, a carbon tax is likely to change the ratio in which they are consumed. In particular, a carbon tax is likely to favor natural gas over coal in electricity consumption since coal contains almost twice as much carbon per unit of energy as compared to natural gas. The IPCC (2001a, p. 318) sees such substitution of natural gas for coal as a promising way of reducing carbon emissions.

39   In the lower frame of Figure 7.A1, the emission cutback along the horizontal axis is $(Q_{BAU} - E^*)$ since the origin with zero cutbacks corresponds to Q_{BAU}.

40   This statement ignores policy administrative costs, which should be a part of policy analysis, but often isn't.

References

Cambell, C.J. (1997) *The Coming Oil Crisis*, Brentwood, U.K.: Multi-Science Publishing Company and Petroconsultants S.A.

Clark, William C. (1989) "The Human Ecology of Global Change," *International Social Science Journal*, XLI (3): 316–321, 323–345.

Coase, Ronald H. (1960) "The Problem of Social Cost," *Journal of Law and Economics*, 3: 1–44.

Dasgupta, S., Laplante, B., Wang, H., and Wheeler, D. (2002) "Confronting the Environmental Kuznets Curve," *The Journal of Economic Perspectives*, 16 (1): 147–168.

Dessler, Andrew E. and Parson, Edward A. (2006) *The Science and Politics of Global Warming: A Guide to the Debate*, New York: Cambridge University Press.

Diamond, Jared (2005) *Collapse: How Societies Choose to Fail or Succeed*, New York: Viking Penguin.

Ellerman, A. Danny (1999) "The Next Restructuring: Environmental Regulation," *The Energy Journal*, 20 (1): 141–147.

Field, Barry C. and Field, Martha K. (2002) *Environmental Economics: An Introduction*, 3rd edn, New York: McGraw-Hill.

Flannery, Tim (2005) *The Weather Makers*, New York: Atlantic Monthly Press.

Freeman III, A. Myrick (2002) "Environmental Policy Since Earth Day I: What Have We Gained?" *The Journal of Economic Perspectives*, 16 (1): 125–146.

Gore, Al (1996) *An Inconvenient Truth: The Planetary Emergency of Global Warming and What We Can Do About It*, Emmaus, PA: Rodale Books.

Hotelling, Harold (1931) "The Economics of Exhaustible Resources," *Journal of Political Economy*, 39: 137–175.

IPCC (Intergovernmental Panel on Climate Change) (2001a) *Climate Change 2001: Synthesis Report*, Cambridge: Cambridge University Press.

IPCC (2001b) *Climate Change 2001: Mitigation*, Cambridge: Cambridge University Press.

IPCC (2001c) *Climate Change 2001: The Scientific Basis*, Cambridge: Cambridge University Press.

IPCC (2001d) *Climate Change 2001: Impacts, Adaptation, and Vulnerability*, Cambridge: Cambridge University Press.

Jaccard, Mark (2005) *Sustainable Fossil Fuels*. New York: Cambridge University Press.

Kaya, Y. (1990) Impact of Carbon Dioxide Emission Control on GNP Growth: Interpretation of Proposed Scenarios. Paper presented to the IPCC Energy and Industry Subgroup, Response Strategies Working Group, Paris (mimeo).

Krautkraemer, J. (1998) "Non-renewable Resource Scarcity," *Journal of Economic Literature*, 36 (4): 2065–2107.

Lomborg, B. (1998) *The Skeptical Environmentalist: Measuring the Real State of the World*, Cambridge: Cambridge University Press.

Lomborg, B. (ed.) (2004) *Global Crises, Global Solutions*, Cambridge: Cambridge University Press.

Meadows, Donella H., Meadows, Dennis L., Randers, Jorgen, Behrens III, William W. (1972) *The Limits to Growth*, New York: Potomac Associates.

Meadows, Donella H., Randers, Jorgen, Meadows, Dennis L. (2004) *The Limits to Growth: The 30-Year Update*, Vermont: Chelsea Green Publishing Company.

Page, Scott E. (2005) "Are We Collapsing? A Review of Jared Diamond's Collapse: How Societies Choose to Fail or Succeed," Journal of Economics Literature, XLIII (4): 1049–1062.

Pigou, A. (1920) *The Economics of Welfare*, London: Macmillan.

Simon, Julian (1996) *The Ultimate Resource 2*, Princeton: Princeton University Press.

Stern, Sir Nicholas (2006) Stern Review on the Economics of Climate Change. Final report to the U.K. Prime Minister and the Chancellor of the Exchequer. Online, available at: www.hm-treasury.gov.uk/independent_reviews/stern_review_economics_climate_change/sternreview_index.cfm

Stowell, Deborah (2005). *Climate Trading: Development of Greenhouse Gas Markets*, New York: Palmgrave Macmillan.

United Nations Development Programme (2004) *World Energy Assessment Overview: 2004 Update*. Online, available at www.undp.org/energy/weaover2004.htm

Weitzman, M. (1974) "Prices vs. Quantities," *Review of Economic Studies*, 41 (4): 477–491.

Weyant, John P. and Hill, Jennifer (1999) "Introduction and Overview," *The Costs of the Kyoto Protocol, the Energy Journal*, special edition: 1–24.

World Commission on Environment and Development (1987) *Our Common Future*, New York: Oxford University Press.

8 Re-adjusting what we know with what we imagine

Antonio Cassella

Introduction

We have lost sight of the belief systems and social agreements that animated and organized human groups in the lush and mysterious environment that gave rise to *homo sapiens* more than 100,000 years ago. Today, most of us are facing increasing estrangement from a natural world that is vanishing both in visible reality and in our memory. There are grounds for our unease. The increasing potential for social strife; shortages of food, water, and energy; loss of biodiversity; and catastrophic climate change tells us that civilization as we know it is unsustainable. In his quest for ideas on the sustainability of our human ecology, the author examines the prospects up to the year 2060 under the envelope of two mutually exclusive scenarios, referred to as "drifts." One drift is what the author calls the Siege of Troy, in which the gap between the "haves" and the "have-nots" becomes socially intolerable; and the other drift is Chimæra, in which attempts at making wealth and health available to everyone will accelerate global warming and the depletion of the biosphere.

In the author's framework, when we opt for either drift we empower the logical side of the mind (the first attention) – which tries to conserve known reality by choosing what we believe is right (order) over what we deem wrong (chaos). Because each drift eventually becomes a trap, however, we need to go beyond the influence of the first attention. We also need to empower our creative side (the second attention) – which unleashes our fantasy the very instant we embrace mutually exclusive tenets (as with the Siege of Troy and Chimæra) simultaneously. Unfortunately, the first and the second attention destroy each other when we use the tension between reality and fantasy for one-sided gain. By contrast, they become complementary (the third attention), unveiling a new horizon of sustainable human ecology, when we lean on that tension in order to co-create the world with others.

In the last three centuries, the advance of science and technology has enabled us to achieve a comfortable average per-capita wealth (by and large, in the developed countries), reproduce explosively (mostly, in the less-developed countries), live longer, and invade most ecological niches.

At present, however, we are finding that there are physical and cultural limitations to our senseless appropriation of Nature's resources. Most people are challenged by both the emptiness that comes with the loss of ancestral traditions and the difficulty to adapt to cultural and technological changes. To make things worse, ominous signs at a global level are warning us that unless we re-adjust our ways of being, our children – and we as well – will experience the end of the Age of Plenty.

We learn from Roy Allen (Chapter 9) that we should gain from our willingness to choose our ways of being, instead of being chosen by them. In fact, according to Allen:

> a mentally healthy person, as well as a healthy human ecology, might need to find appropriate balance, tolerance, and hierarchy between various ways of being ... [The] sustainability of human ecology requires reconciliation between them rather than destructive competition between them.

This chapter introduces the play of cognitive dynamics that may lead us to re-adjust our ways of being in favor of a sustainable human ecology. The findings offered here were made possible by linking two scenarios of the global prospects up to 2060 with the author's research on why autistic individuals fail to adapt to changes of context.

Listing a few concerns will introduce the reader to the challenge of becoming an actor in the world scene rather than a hunter or a victim:

- If fertility rates remain above two children per family in the less-developed countries, by 2060 the world's population could swell to 10–13 billion. The number of people affected by poverty, meager literacy, reduced legal rights, and unsteady health – which at present amounts to about 1.2 billion[1] – will double.
- Over the last 400 million years, the background extinction rate in the biota has been one species every four years. Nowadays, the yearly background extinction rate – 200 and up – may cut biodiversity in half by the end of the twenty-first century.[2]
- Worldwide, the per-capita yield of grains, proteins, and water continues to be unsatisfactory. While the have-nots starve, the haves consume excessive amounts of junk food that is rich in calories and toxins but stripped of essential micronutrients.
- The combination of high fossil-energy consumption, low energy efficiency, and the destruction of tropical forests is accelerating global warming. If we do not try to arrest it now, new patterns of oceanic currents,[3] the melting of the polar caps and the permafrost,[4] and the surfacing of methane clathrates[5] or of hydrogen sulfide from the oceans[6] could bring on catastrophic climate change.
- Humanity as a whole has lost track of its critical mind-set and underlying social value: the co-creation of the world. That loss is producing ineffective local and global governance, runaway consumerism, destructive fundamentalism, and the proliferation of weapons of mass destruction (WMD).

To help us think of the kind of ethics and cognitive approaches for sharing control with other human beings, social groups, and species, the author examines the listed concerns through two mutually exclusive drifts (described briefly below – also see Appendix A) – inflexible visions that, tantalizing though they may seem, cannot be allowed to remain, for each one strengthens the possibility of apocalypse.

1   The first, inertia-driven drift is called the Siege of Troy. It represents the continuation of today's seemingly unjust world, in which the widening gap between the haves and the have-nots wreaks social havoc.

2   The second, the utopian Chimæra, in which the process of making every human being wealthy and healthy will accelerate global warming, the mass extinction underway, and the depletion of Earth's resources.

If poor countries reached the standard of living and the technological edge that rich countries enjoy (Chimæra), the biota would collapse under adverse climate change. If, however, inequalities in wealth and health deepen, the people left behind may unleash an unstoppable assault on civilization (the Siege of Troy). In sum, *neither the utopia of a common wealth (Chimæra) nor the survival of the fittest (the Siege of Troy) is a permissible solution.*

Although each drift by itself is a bad choice, choosing both simultaneously may lead us to viewing the path to a new cycle of growth. Choosing both drifts at the same time is a metaphor for the prospect of learning from both a new way of growing with others and especially with the natural world. In other words, if we can withstand with sobriety, serenity, and unselfishness, the unsettling tension generated by this confrontation between diametrically opposed interpretations of the future, we will arrive at undreamed-of solutions.

Confrontations are generated by the fact that what is order for someone (for example, the view attached to the Siege of Troy) may be chaos for someone else (for instance, the view inherent in Chimæra).

From there, this author calls the first attention the primacy of known order in the mind of an individual or in the minds of the members of a group (for example, consider the authoritative legitimacy of the shared meaning of the words listed in the *American Dictionary of the English Language* edited by Noah Webster).[7] The first attention is necessary, for without the conservation of shared order we cannot grow; and yet it is insufficient, because there comes a time in which new problems invite us to seek new solutions. Arriving at new patterns, however, calls for dealing creatively with a confrontation in which the familiar order we are attached to is challenged by an opposite view (chaos). (For instance, that is the way by which a few known words fade away and new ones are created.)

Novel harmony arrives only when we make use of what the author calls second attention, the paradoxical ability to reconcile seemingly irreconcilable interpretations (among many examples: when we embrace the Siege of Troy and Chimæra at the same time; when we posit mutually exclusive hypotheses before undertaking an experiment; when we play with ill-assorted meanings in understanding a pun; when we amuse spectators by pretending to be someone else in the stage of a theater, or when we lean on irony so as to make our point in a spontaneous dialogue).

The cognitive power of the second attention can save us against all odds. Nevertheless, if we try to enslave it so as to exploit the world unilaterally (as in deceiving others), in the end, its power will backfire. That is why we need to reach the third attention, or the quantum jump by which the altruistic deployment of our second attention will lead us to a sustainable world.

The author was able to take a glimpse of the mysterious interplay of these three cognitive dynamics from the experimental finding that autistic individuals conserve the rigid first attention, whereas the second attention, or the flexible facet of social intelligence, is severely impaired in them.[8]

In the first place, empirical experiments suggest that the first attention (the autistic, or logical, side of the mind, the cognition that is intact among autistics) is driven by a perfection-oriented systems dynamic (to be called sequence), which, by virtue of its inflexible nature, is forced to reject change. When we side with the order inherent in perfect control (for example, by obeying the law or by pronouncing correctly the words we use) as opposed to the chaos that attaches to imperfect control (for example, by jailing the person who breaks the law or by rejecting the illegitimate pronunciation of a foreign person), we follow sequence, the cognitive force that compels us to conserve the world we trust and to keep everything the same.

In addition to standing at the root of our cognitive capacity for sharing with all members of our group the central meaning and the correct pronunciation of familiar words, the first attention helps us center our mind in a single and unambiguous idea and purpose (in the author's view, that feat would make *sequence* the dynamic behind the cognitive style of "hedgehogs" – see Snyder, this volume).

In the second place, it is worth observing that unity of thought and purpose becomes very dangerous when we are mistaken (recall the defeat of the seemingly invincible Nazi war machine under the joint chiefs' blind obedience to Hitler's arrogance and inflexible whims). In the end, the lack of a critical attitude will make us socially unfit.

The author corroborated the fact that autistic individuals owe their social limitations to the impairment of the second attention – our artistic, or creative, side. The research on the cognitive limitations inherent in autism suggests that the second attention is regulated by a less-than-perfect systems dynamic (to be called simultaneity). By embracing order and chaos at the same time, simultaneity allows us to re-adjust the familiar world guarded by sequence (and that places simultaneity behind the cognitive style of "foxes" – again, see Snyder, this volume.)

Because what is order in the view of our first attention is chaos to the first attention of our opponents, there is always a need for arbitration (for instance, before finding a defendant innocent or guilty, a balanced jury will lean on their second attention in listening to both the order viewed by the prosecutor and the opposite order viewed by the defense lawyer. Also, the mediation of a balanced referee is needed in a soccer match because what is perfect order to the players and fans of a team is imperfect chaos to the opposite side, and vice versa.)

In the creative process, sequence (or the confrontation between alleged perfection and alleged imperfection) is insufficient, and yet it is necessary, for new harmonies emerge only from differences of interpretation. Now, because unmanageable confrontation is uncreative, and even destructive, we need to value – but only to a point – the logic, repetition, and sameness (order) imposed on us by the first attention. If we do not re-adjust our autistic side in time, its proclivity to view any kind of difference as chaos will seek to destroy whatever stands in its way (this is the agenda of terrorists and of authoritarian leaders as well).

Things may change for the better only when a mediator chooses order and chaos at the same time (again, in the example offered above on a soccer match, an impartial referee will not favor one team [order] over the other [chaos], for he is supposed to favor both teams simultaneously – which is equivalent to "moving" to and fro between them at infinite speed). In an individual, mediation between opposite tenets or goals is managed by our creative side – a feat we attach to people endowed with self-criticism.[9]

The conservation of the familiar reality sought by our first attention and the rejuvenating imagination brought into being by our second attention seem to be at odds with each other, to the point that bigots too often confuse flexibility and novelty with chaos. Again, viewing simultaneity as chaos only is a serious mistake, for the second attention embraces both order and chaos at the same time.

Thus, we may re-adjust the authoritarian saying "whoever is not with me is against me" by thinking that "only the person who is and is not with me can help me create something new and grow with me." Consequently, we may view the mystical legacy of our ancestors in the belief that *a new, sustainable world arises only out of our appreciation of the views of our opponents and the reconciliation of opposite views in our own minds.*

Unless simultaneity and sequence empower each other in a balanced way (the third attention), a global involution may occur. Proof of the divisiveness that can follow the stifling or the misuse of simultaneity can be found in the *Book of Judges* (12:4–6). We read there that the men of Gilead slaughtered their own brothers, the men of Ephraim. Ironically (to us), the Gileadites recognized the Ephraimites by their inability to pronounce "correctly" the term *shibboleth* (the Ephraimites pronounced it *sibboleth* – to the Gileadites, *shibboleth* was order and *sibboleth* was chaos; the reverse was true for the Ephraimites).

Today, the destructive confrontation between order and chaos continues unabated. Perhaps a principal cause of various global challenges owes to the fact that many of us have replaced the works of creative imagination with a narrow interpretation of scientific knowledge and the law, and with a literal reading of sacred texts. In particular, we have lost sight of the value that sustains social systems: the co-creation of the world with all the players in the field. In the end, the disuse and, especially, the misuse of the creative power attached to the second attention may derail the progress of civilization.

We can avoid the potential havoc introduced by global warming and ideological confrontations if we recognize that we have become too disruptive toward the natural and the social world. In the thirteenth century, Saint Francis wrote:

> May Thou be praised my Lord, for brother Wind,
> and for the air, and for cloudy, clear, and every weather
> by which You sustain Your creatures ...
> ... May Thou be praised, my Lord for those who forgive for
> the sake of Thy love,
> And endure infirmity and tribulation ...

At this point, redirecting the awesome power of simultaneity is vital. Thus, a key way out of global warming or social strife and into a new cycle of growth is placing hatred and selfishness between parentheses and convincing ourselves and our children of the beauty, elegance, social worth, and sustainability inherent in ways of being that understand nature and strangers.

Before undertaking a massive intervention in re-educating our minds and our children, however, we need to review the conditions that may transform the predicaments presented in the Siege of Troy and Chimæra into blessings. That entails:

1   consciously separating the role to conserve known reality (the first attention) from the role to change it by way of our imagination (the second attention); and
2   empowering both the autistic and the creative side of our minds within the mantle of the third attention.

If we *go* into the unknown with the purpose of re-adjusting what we know with what we imagine for the good of ourselves, our opponents, and other species, we will *come back* to a sustainable world.

The next five sections introduce the challenges inherent in each drift.

Population growth

As Table 8.1 shows, at the end of the second millennium the average denizen of countries with advanced economies (AE)[10] enjoyed an income that was 35 times larger and consumed 11 times more energy than his or her counterpart in sub-Saharan Africa and South Asia, the poorest regions within the population-driven countries (PDC).[11]

World population has swollen by about ten times since the seventeenth century, from about half-a-billion to about six-and-a-half billion. This increase is due to dramatic improvements in health care, nutrition, and the exploitation of the Earth's once abundant – and now dwindling – low-cost and high-quality

Table 8.1 Per-capita income and energy consumption in the AE compered with sub-Saharan Africa and southern Asia at the turn of the twentieth century

	GDP*/capita ($2005/year)	Energy/capita (Boe per year)
Advanced Economies (AE)	35,000	33
	35 times	**11 times**
Sub-Saharan Africa and southern Asia	1,000	3

fossil-energy resources. But it is not all good news. For instance, a paradoxical consequence of the uneven diffusion of science, technology, and free trade is both the quest for more riches and longer life in the AE and the inescapable poverty and shorter span of life in the PDC.

Today, more than half of the world population is below the age of 20 and lives in the PDC. In many of these countries, corrupt and authoritarian governments, inadequate education, scarce financial resources, misinformation, and a fertility rate above two children per family have led to a pervasive destitution. By contrast, the affluence found in the AE goes hand in hand with a replacement fertility rate (less than two children per family).

Unrestrained fertility will result in unalleviated misery, famine, social unrest, and pollution. If, however, the new fertility rate were put in place immediately, the population could be kept constant at the present level.[12] Still, environmental and social limitations will prevent most countries in the PDC from either maintaining a high fertility rate or reducing it to the replacement rate. Thus – provided that abrupt climatic changes, pandemics, and wars based on the use of WMD are averted – world population may grow to between ten and 13 billion by the year 2060.[13] (See also Appendix B.)

The higher estimate (13 billion) of the growth of the population corresponds to a Siege of Troy view, in tandem with the stagnation of per-capita income in the PDC. And the lower figure (ten billion) corresponds to Chimæra, following the assumption that increasing the wealth of poor countries and social justice may bring world population and social unrest under some degree of control.

At present, we fail to understand that the effort to increase wealth is as bad a handicap as the growth of the population. As a consequence, either looming social strife (the Siege of Troy) or environmental mayhem resulting from the deep exploitation of Earth's resources (Chimæra) may lead to a drastic reduction in world population and the biota. The next section explores the projected consequences of the growth in the number of the poor (the Siege of Troy) and of the rich (Chimæra).

The increase of poverty and affluence

About one-sixth of the world's population suffers from multiple deprivations such as malnutrition, poor health, lack of housing and education, unemployment, reduced access to informational services, and few opportunities to assert their social, legal, and political rights. These deficiencies affect mostly children, women, the handicapped, and the elderly.

The hypothetical Siege of Troy drift (Figure 8.1) assumes that during the next 50 years the rate of economic growth will be roughly equal to the rate of growth of the population in the PDC (see Appendix B). According to Edward Parker,[14] the consequence of such an outcome is that the number of individuals trapped in abject poverty will double in the second half of the twenty-first century. Indeed, in 50 years the average denizen in the AE would continue enjoying a wealth about 16 times higher than that of the average denizen of the PDC (Figure 8.1).

The growing ranks of the poor create difficult challenges. What can be done to boost wealth and health in the PDC? For most countries, education is the answer. Still, their governments in general are unwilling or unable to improve literacy rates; besides, we have become blind to what makes true social education. In the countries left behind, the money and human resources needed for tackling poverty, famine, and educational neglect are nowhere to be seen. Ironically, there seems to be no shortage of capital for buying expensive weaponry.

Within both the AE and the PDC, corrupt, weak, or authoritarian governments rule nations and sectors plagued by a lack of creative ideas and social values. As a consequence, most people to whom democracy is an alien construct will be unable to overcome their social and technological disadvantages. Thus, the conflicts that a drift like the Siege of Troy would bring point to a standstill in the material progress we have enjoyed in the last three centuries, and even to an involution.

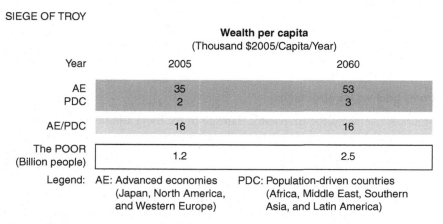

SIEGE OF TROY

Year	**Wealth per capita** (Thousand $2005/Capita/Year)	
	2005	2060
AE	35	53
PDC	2	3
AE/PDC	16	16
The POOR (Billion people)	1.2	2.5

Legend: AE: Advanced economies (Japan, North America, and Western Europe) PDC: Population-driven countries (Africa, Middle East, Southern Asia, and Latin America)

Figure 8.1 Siege of Troy: growth of the poor.

CHIMÆRA

Wealth per capita
(Thousand $2005/Capita/Year)

Year	2005	2060
AE	35	117
PDC	2	51
AE/PDC	16	2.3
The POOR (Billion people)	1.2	0.6

Legend: AE: Advanced economies   PDC: Population-driven countries

Figure 8.2 Chimæra: growth of the rich.

In the PDC, the economy grows faster than in the AE, *but the population more than doubles* (see Appendix B); wealth per capita per year stagnates, *and the number of the poor increases from 1.2 billion to approximately 2.5 billion.*

At this point, it is fitting to consider the Chimæra drift, the world seen through rose-colored glasses (Figure 8.2).

The Chimæric point of view (inspired by Parker's "High Road to Rome" scenario[15]) assumes that in the PDC the economy would grow at about 6 percent per year over a span of 55 years. It also assumes that the growth of the population of the PDC in this drift will reach six billion in 2060 – two and a half billion people less than in the Siege of Troy. The assumption here is that in the PDC every person will enjoy a better life if the rate of growth of the population drops while economic growth remains very high (as with China). For example, Chimæra would improve the lot of the 500 million people who now drink water contaminated with fecal matter. Indeed, a good measure of progress would be the availability of quality food and water for every human being on Earth. This utopian drift would create a sizable middle-class worldwide.

In the PDC, the economy grows considerably faster than in the AE, *while population growth lessens* (see Appendix B); wealth per capita grows more than 20 times the level of 2005, *and the number of the poor decreases.*

The next section deals with the difficulty of increasing water and food supplies.

Food and water shortages

Figure 8.3 sums up the irreparable damage to the biota and the dire social consequences of the over-exploitation of our collectively owned resources – the commons of the Earth.

Since 1996, Brown[16] warned against assuming that world grain production in the long term will match the inter-annual growth that took place between 1950 and 1990 for a mean of 2.5 percent. Several factors support the hypothesis of unstable food supplies coupled with rising and volatile prices in the first half of the twenty-first century.

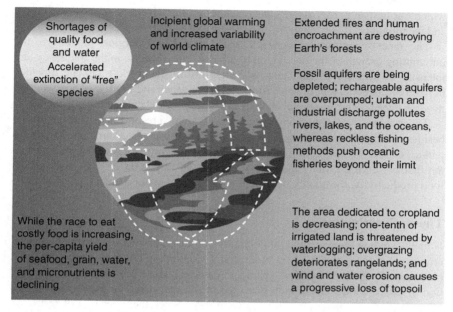

Shortages of quality food and water

Accelerated extinction of "free" species

Incipient global warming and increased variability of world climate

Extended fires and human encroachment are destroying Earth's forests

Fossil aquifers are being depleted; rechargeable aquifers are overpumped; urban and industrial discharge pollutes rivers, lakes, and the oceans, whereas reckless fishing methods push oceanic fisheries beyond their limit

While the race to eat costly food is increasing, the per-capita yield of seafood, grain, water, and micronutrients is declining

The area dedicated to cropland is decreasing; one-tenth of irrigated land is threatened by waterlogging; overgrazing deteriorates rangelands; and wind and water erosion causes a progressive loss of topsoil

Figure 8.3 The deterioration of the commons of the Earth.

Rangelands are deteriorating due to overgrazing and a pervasive draught that can be attributed to global warming;[17] one-tenth of irrigated lands is threatened by waterlogging (an unwelcome rise in the water table), increased salinity, and decreased moisture; non-renewable fossil aquifers, generated millions years ago, are being depleted; refillable aquifers are overpumped; and many rivers fail to wet croplands or reach their historical estuaries due to urban and industrial demand.

Without water, fertilizers cannot be used effectively. And even with adequate water supplies, there are limits to plants' capacity to absorb nutrients. Furthermore, as Lento[18] reported, the increased use of pesticides to protect genetically uniform plant populations will continue to lower their natural resistance to environmental threats. A decrease in the number of beneficial insects, a growing number of insect pests, the degraded quality of organic matter in soil, the progressive loss of topsoil to wind and water erosion, water and air pollution may offset the yield gains of the second half of the twentieth century.

The irresponsible over-exploitation of collectively owned resources (the commons of the Earth) causes the irreversible involution of the biota.

Consider now the effect of an increasing population as a denominator in obtaining per-capita yields of grain, seafood, and water. Per-capita yields were already declining during the 1990s.[19] In the Chimæra drift, this problem is magnified by humanity's race to consume foods that contain a lot of calories per unit volume (for example, ice cream). Nowadays, nutrition is far removed from the micronutrient-centered diet of vegetables, fruits, and occasionally animal protein, which our human predecessors consumed before the advent of sophisticated tools and techniques.[20]

The race to increase affluence in the AE and in emerging economies, the unremitting growth of the population in the PDC, the increase in the frequency and intensity of heat waves, and unusual variability in the world's climate unveil a horizon of disruptions in the provision of quality water and food. It is possible that in a few decades starvation will stalk us in proportions unheard of in human history.

The reckless overexploitation of collectively owned resources is overwhelming: besides leading to the scarcity of food and water resources, shortsighted thinking will accelerate the destruction of the world's biodiversity. We seem to have forgotten that preserving a rich biodiversity is essential to raising or even maintaining food productivity, the quality of air and water, and even our mental equilibrium.

The sixth extinction

Notwithstanding Darwin and Lyell's theory of gradual progression, there have been erratic changes in the world's biodiversity. According to paleoanthropologists' observations, about 500 million years ago random chance brought about the selection of the 33 fundamental body plans (or phyla) that make up extant animal life, whereas about 70 phyla mysteriously vanished.[21] Since then, because of restricted ecological opportunities, major extinctions have not affected phyla. However, variety in the biota has come up through speciation – the rise of diverse species from invariant phyla.

Within Darwin's theory of evolution, the dance of rigid need and random chance – reflected in the free rise of a variety of species (five to 100 million) (chaos) within unchanged phyla (order) – is the aftermath of five major extinctions, from the end of the Ordovician (440 million years ago) to the end of the Cretaceous (65 million years ago).[22]

In Leakey and Lewin's view, a circle of predation (by which each link becomes hunter and prey simultaneously) prevented domination by a few species before the emergence of humans. The fact is that in relation to our prey – most species on Earth – we have become so powerful that hunting has lost its meaning. In particular, as Gould[23] asserted, our genome has acquired a generalist power among the Earth's species, with the capacity to dominate in all regions, including the fragile tropical habitats and dry lands that favor biodiversity.

Natural biodiversity reached a peak about fifteen thousand years ago, just before our capacity for deception led us to the eradication of big game and, indirectly, of the saber-toothed tiger. That feat shows that since prehistoric times we have been viewing non-human, undomesticated, and free-ranging species as our prey and competitors rather than as invaluable partners. Today too many farmers continue encroaching on unspoiled forests, while we lose fertile land, pastures, and water resources to poisonous urban and industrial development. The end result will be that free or natural biodiversity will soon cease to have a place in the sun. That is very bad news! For example, by destroying forests we will end up relying solely on the genes attached to a few wild varieties preserved in "gene banks." The consequence is that 50 percent of our food supplies could suddenly vanish (Figure 8.4).

Mature ecological communities with mutually dependent species react as a whole against an invading species.[24] Yet they easily fall prey to the "Humpty-Dumpty" effect: once we break down an ecosystem, we cannot restore it to its original state (Figure 8.4).

During the past 400 million years, *the average background extinction rate amounted to one species every four years.*[25] According to Leakey and Lewin, *despite the fact that the present yearly extinction rate – 200 and up – is at least one thousand times above background values, annual rates of 5,000 to 100,000 species may come to pass by the end of the century.*

Undomesticated plants are important for other reasons. Beyond the assessment that 35,000 species of plants may be edible, and that essential drugs could be obtained from wild plants,[26] what counts is that our environment, including the atmosphere, is a biological rather than a physical product. Certainly, all forms of life are integrated in a balanced ecosystem.[27]

We are as lethal to biodiversity as the large asteroid that hit the Earth 65 million years ago. In the view of Leakey and Lewin, as many as 50 percent of the world's species might be lost by the end of the twenty-first century because of our reckless infringement on tropical ecosystems. To that, we may add the development of pervasive climate change – also the work of human beings.[28]

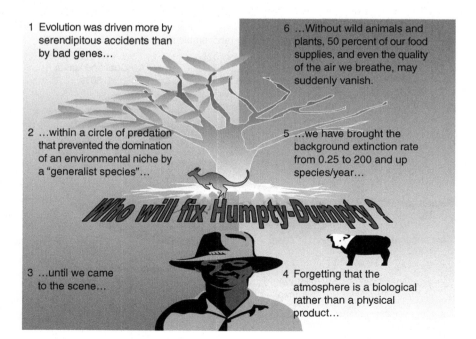

Figure 8.4 The effects of human encroachment on biodiversity.

The present mass extinction of animals and plants – the sixth major extinction on Earth – is caused by the reckless assault of humans on "free" species (that is, undomesticated forms of life that do not need our control in order to survive). A growing population and its need for food, water, space, and energy are causing a precipitous decline in the number of free species (symbolized by the kangaroo in Figure 8.4) in favor of enslaved, engineered ones (exemplified by the bovine in Figure 8.4).

Among the factors that disrupt natural speciation, lies our thirst for energy resources.

The myth of green energy

Fossil fuel is still abundant, totaling between 60 and 70 trillion BOE (barrels of oil equivalent),[29] but low-cost, high-quality conventional oil and natural gas make up only about 8 percent of the total (Figure 8.5).

According to Kunstler,[30] the peak production of low-cost, high-quality oil and gas is being reached during the first decade of the twenty-first century.

The author[31] places the peak as being by the end of the second decade.

In the marginal economic growth of the Siege of Troy drift, world energy consumption grows moderately, from about 205 million BOE per day in 2005 to about 220 million BOE per day by the year 2060 as the consequence of increased energy efficiency in general and stagnant economic growth in the PDC. Figure 8.6 shows that the already reduced per-capita consumption of energy in the PDC

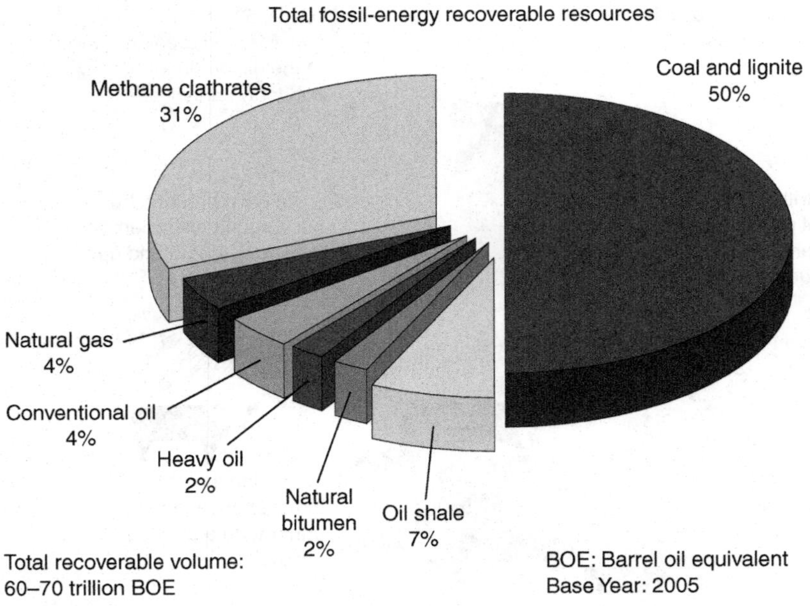

Total fossil-energy recoverable resources

Methane clathrates
31%

Coal and lignite
50%

Natural gas
4%

Conventional oil
4%

Heavy oil
2%

Natural bitumen
2%

Oil shale
7%

Total recoverable volume:
60–70 trillion BOE

BOE: Barrel oil equivalent
Base Year: 2005

Figure 8.5 An assessment of fossil-fuel resources.

SIEGE OF TROY

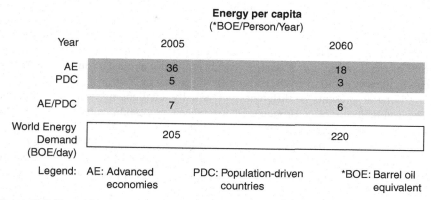

Energy per capita
(*BOE/Person/Year)

Year	2005	2060
AE	36	18
PDC	5	3
AE/PDC	7	6
World Energy Demand (BOE/day)	205	220

Legend: AE: Advanced economies   PDC: Population-driven countries   *BOE: Barrel oil equivalent

Figure 8.6 Siege of Troy: growth in per-capita and world energy consumption.

would decrease from five BOE per year in 2005 to three BOE per year in 2060 – the combined effect of lower energy intensity and increased poverty.[32]

In the PDC, the per-capita energy consumption decreases as a combined effect of improved efficiency and, especially, the growth in the number of the poor.

In the AE, the consumption of energy per capita would decrease by about 50 percent, from 36 BOE per year in 2005 to about 18 BOE per year in 2060. This drop would be due to a decrease in energy intensity (see Appendix B) within a context of increased wealth. In sum, the Siege of Troy suggests that in the second half of the twenty-first century, the average person in the AE would still consume about six times more energy than his or her counterpart in the PDC.

By contrast, in Chimæra (Figure 8.7), the consumption of energy per capita in the PDC would increase from five BOE per year in 2005 to 28 BOE per capita in 2060 – higher than the corresponding value for that year (23 BOE) in the AE.

CHIMÆRA

Energy per capita
(*BOE/Person/Year)

Year	2005	2060
AE	36	23
PDC	5	28
AE/PDC	7	0.8
World Energy Demand (BOE/day)	205	910

Legend: AE: Advanced economies   PDC: Population-driven countries   *BOE: Barrel oil equivalent

Figure 8.7 Chimæra: growth in per-capita and world energy consumption.

The rise of energy per capita in the PDC would be the consequence of accelerated economic growth and lower population increase (see Appendix B).

The utopian dream of closing the gap between rich and poor countries (as shown in Figure 8.2) leads to a considerable increase in the per-capita energy consumed in the PDC (from five to 28 BOE per year), as well as a four- to five-fold increase in the use of energy worldwide (from about 205 million BOE per day in the present to over 900 million BOE per day in 2060).

Chimæra presents a different, yet equally challenging, set of problems. The implications of a pronounced growth in per-capita consumption in the PDC are staggering. By 2060, the world's energy demand would reach about 900 million BOE per day – over four times the level of 2005. Energy consumption would double even if the per-capita income in the PDC reached only $8,000 per year – about one-quarter of what the average person in the AE earns now.

Certainly, as energy consumption increases, we can use more renewable, or green energy, uranium, and even spent nuclear fuel that could be reprocessed in breeder reactors. Thus, the author posits that the impact of global warming, the social disruptions caused by our reckless lifestyle, and the prospect of very high oil prices (above $100/Barrel or $4/gal at the pump in the U.S.A.) may compel the AE to decrease their energy intensity and their addiction to conventional fossil fuels produced by unreliable sources while increasing the use of nuclear and green energy.

Nonetheless, limiting the use of fossil fuels is unlikely within Chimæra.

Figure 8.8 emphasizes the fact that in order to produce over 900 million BOE of energy by the year 2060 we will need to increase the production of both fossil fuels and green energy. Chimæra would require an enormous amount of renewable energy, which would swell from about 15 million BOE now to more than 200 million BOE per day in 2060. Is that possible?

Fossil fuels will be the backbone of any energy strategy in the twenty-first century. Over time, renewable energy might become the main source; still, this change may not necessarily be more beneficial to biodiversity than fossil energy.

At an oil price above $25 per barrel of Brent, green energy is quite affordable and will continue to compete well with other sources of energy. The reason is that the actual cost of oil in the Northern Hemisphere is above the value shown by market transactions. In particular, the military cost of protecting unreliable oil sources – which this author sets at about $30/barrel at present – may not decline in the future. Before switching contentedly to green energy, however, we should remember that the oil and coal we use today derive from the competition for space that occurred millions of years ago.

Today, fossil fuels – the remains of organisms that lived several million years ago – do not compete for space with free species. Green energy does. In essence, we should pay more attention to the fact that renewable energy facilities require the use of fossil fuels to start up and more space per unit of output than do fossil fuels. Thus, we cannot easily assume that in all cases green energy is friendlier to biodiversity than are fossil fuels.

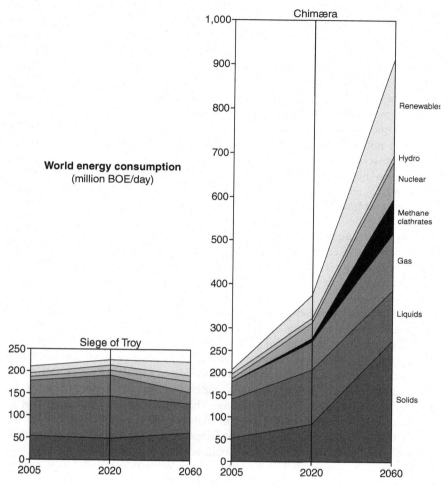

Figure 8.8 Energy surplus by source, 2005–2060.

In any case, there is no doubt that increasing the consumption of fossil energy in the world three-fold will exact a heavy price on the environment. In more detail, citing research by Kump, Pavlov, and Arthur,[33] Ward[34] stated that major extinctions in the past cannot be attributed solely to the impact of large asteroids on our planet. In Ward's view, global warming associated with an increase of carbon dioxide in the atmosphere above 1,000 parts per million (ppm) in the Permian period (about 250 million years ago), may have caused ocean anoxia (by elevating the interface that separates sulfur bacteria from oxygen breathers in the deep), the massive release of hydrogen sulfide into the atmosphere, the destruction of the ozone layer, and the death of most oxygen-based life on Earth. Can such a situation revisit Earth in the near future?

Temperature increases in the range of 1.1–6.2°C are expected by the end of the twenty-first century.[35] This forecast is in line with the quantity of carbon dioxide released in the Siege of Troy drift (at about 2.5 ppm/year in the period 2005–2060). In the Siege of Troy, the concentration of CO_2 in the atmosphere – now about 380 ppm – would not increase above 560 ppm in 2060. And that is not too bad, for Socolow and Pacala observed that an atmospheric concentration of CO_2 above 560 ppm, double the pre-industrial value, is "a level widely regarded as capable of triggering severe climate changes."[36]

Consequently, whether the Siege of Troy included carbon capture and storage (CCS) or not, we may conclude that social havoc is the main concern at the center of that drift.

Now, an aggressive CCS plan would be more difficult to implement at the levels of CO_2 released in Chimæra (9 ppm/year or more in 2060). In fact, recall that Asbjorn Moseidjord (Chapter 7) observes that

> The challenge to economics … is that global warming is an issue where the tension between the two sides – narrow self-interest and associated strategic behavior on the one hand, and altruistic values on the other – is particularly strong.

In Chimæra, the difficulty of scaling the production of energy to very high levels is compounded by the strong possibility that the melting of the polar caps and the permafrost would introduce large quantities of CO_2 and methane into the atmosphere.[37] Furthermore, Flannery reported that positive feedback loops (for example, the collapse of the Amazon rain forests and the massive release of methane from the ice-methane crystals (clathrates) trapped on the bottom of the oceans) could intensify global warming. Therefore, one may envisage that in Chimæra the concentration of CO_2 will increase above 1,000 ppm around the end of the twenty-first century. If that happened – *and we cannot allow it to happen* – the major part of the biota could be choked to death by the reduction of oxygen in the oceans and in the atmosphere. We may conclude, then, that in Chimæra the main concern is climatic havoc.

The perception of injustice within the have-nots in the Siege of Troy and the dire consequences of increasing wealth in Chimæra lead this author to join Roy Allen's view in positing that the sustainability of our human ecology rests in reconciling our ways of being into a new blend – particularly, one that would lead us into more altruistic uses of our flexible imagination.

The next section explores the impact that marrying new technologies with a better knowledge of the cognitive roots of creative intelligence may have on redefining social practices and interspecies relations.

Toward human-level artificial intelligence (HLAI)

The low-cost transfer of information may offer the poor and the unskilled the productivity tools they would need to navigate modern society. A brighter future offered to us through the spread of low-cost information-processing technologies was detected a decade ago.[38] The expanding global network of voice communication and data transfer by satellites and the worldwide web will negate the need to build costly infrastructures in developing countries. Voice communication on a global basis and high-volume data transfer to any location in the world will become increasingly affordable.

The opportunities are as limitless as our imagination. However, we are in need of two breakthroughs.

1 The first involves PSIT (proximal-senses information transmission). This means expanding speed-of-light communication from the digital transmission of texts that can be read by our remote senses (sight, hearing) (e.g. TV, radio) to a transmission that can be read by our proximal senses (touch, smell, taste) as well, as if the sender and the far-away recipient of the intended stimuli shared the same locality.

2 The second breakthrough is the creation of human-level artificial intelligence (HLAI). In fact, if we uncovered the cognitive roots of spontaneous discourse, language differences would become less of a barrier to communication. The design of software capable of translating metaphors from one language to another can emerge only from HLAI.

Both breakthroughs might increase the role of the second attention – for better or for worse. For example,

- PSIT and HLAI could eliminate obstacles to the free flow of work and information worldwide and accelerate the growth of virtual immigration (the capacity for working in foreign countries without leaving the homeland);
- virtual universities, virtual governments, and virtual communities could prosper anywhere; and
- the *need for travel* would be reduced considerably.

If all this became true, the competition for space with free species would lessen and, at first glance, global sustainability would be enhanced.

What is missing from the rosy scenario described above is the fact that digital computationalism – the technological basis of artificial intelligence (AI) – is at a stalemate. The main reason is that the "frame problem" (or the capacity for adapting to context, which is damaged in autism) has not been solved yet (the situation proves that present approaches to AI are essentially autistic-like).

Hard reality shows us that we have not succeeded in modeling the brain of the simplest animal. For instance, we have no idea of the organization behind the 300 neurons and the 7,000 synapses in the brain of the nematode *C. Elegans*.[39] Because the number of synapses in the human cortex alone is 100 billion times larger than that in *C. Elegans*, we may conclude that, unless we uncover the roots of the cognitive limitations of autistic individuals, the probability is very low that we will stumble upon or work out the ways of the systems dynamic behind our capacity to adapt to context. In sum, Kassan reports that "after 50 years of pursuing human-level artificial intelligence (HLAI), we have nothing but promises and failures."

The diffusion of technological advances and, especially, of HLAI – should we arrive at the key of our intellectual acuteness – will occur at great peril to us, unless we uncover the mystery behind the third attention (the cognitive balance between our zeal to conserve the familiar world and our eagerness to change it *with the free cooperation of others*). To begin with, even if the world had 1,000 times fewer people, the misuse of technology could eradicate our civilization and Earth's biodiversity in the blink of an eye.

Hence this author emphasizes the importance of understanding the role of the third attention in reconciling our physical, cognitive, and social growth with Nature's growth. That is the charter of the next section.

The meeting of the self and the other

Science and technology have enhanced our dominance over a natural world viewed as a never-ending source of material and biological resources. We resist the notion that the animals and plants we force to satisfy our whims and appetite could become our allies in the process of re-creating and sustaining both the natural and the social world. Still, understanding the ways of the third attention or the harmony that gives rise to natural systems and social values may reverse the trend of involution that pervades the entire biota.

We cannot manipulate our genetic inheritance to breathe carbon dioxide and eat plankton; nor is it possible to re-create eras of greater biodiversity, low population levels, and abundant physical resources. Given the need to go forward, fostering the capacity for co-creation in our children may introduce changes for the better. Thus we can only hope that new teaching methods may guide us toward a sustainable transformation of the world. Paradoxically, history shows that the teachings we seek were given to us at least 26 centuries ago.

At that time, the Chinese sage Lao Tzu praised flexibility as the Way to co-creation:

> All creatures, grass and trees, alive
> Are plastic but are pliant too,
> And dead, are friable and dry ...
> Unbending rigor is the mate of death,
> And yielding softness, company of life ...
> The strong and mighty topple from their place;
> The soft and yielding rise above them all.

Unfortunately, our fondness for total control and bureaucracy shows that we have always paid more attention to the need for order and obedience to authority preached by Confucius (ancient writers report that although Lao Tzu and Confucius met, they never came to an understanding). And yet, this author posits that we could reach the third attention, or enlightenment, if we favored both Confucius's bent for respecting authority and tradition (the first attention) and Lao Tzu's altruistic deployment of the second attention.

The second attention can be very amusing, as a good pun shows; and yet it can be excruciating. For example, Hamlet's "to be or not to be" reflects the agony of his patience. If he were only mad, he would kill his murderous uncle (Claudius) after the wild accusations of a ghost; and if he were only autistic (and thus blind to the possibility that King Claudius killed his father), he would merrily marry his fiancée, Ophelia. Paradoxically, in the very end he finds the truth (that is, he reaches the third attention) because, within his doubts and hopes, he is autistic (for he obeys the order embraced by the first attention) and mad (for he also obeys the chaos rejected by the first attention) at the same time (the second attention).

Hamlet's tragedy is that he finds the truth too late. Fortunately, it is not too late for us. Unlike Hamlet, we hope that if we act with decisiveness and sobriety, the truth will meet us in time; and our civilization will unfold in the end as in a comedy. Only when humor and patience come together can we trick our first attention into becoming the guardian of a re-adjusted familiar reality. At that point, sequence and simultaneity become complementary; which can be wonderful, for their complementarity leads to the creation and development of our best works and of all that exists.

Sustainable growth occurs only when the self meets the other; that is, when we care for the other as much as we care for the self. That is impeccability – the core social value we received untold ages ago.

When it is deployed impeccably, the second attention paves the Way explored by Lao Tzu. The Way, in which the self and the other meet, is entered when we lean on sobriety in order to control the excessive fear, self-importance, anger, ambition, and greed that separate the order that is recognized by the familiar self from the chaos that is attributed to the unfamiliar other.

After all, order and chaos seek to replace each other. That is why they belong to the same cognitive dynamic – *sequence*. Indeed, the price of vanquishing the fear of chaos is giving one's absolute allegiance to order. Because those with a fundamentalist faith in perfect order cannot tolerate criticism, authoritarian leaders and their deceived or deceitful accomplices are compelled to control whomever or whatever stands in their path.

People imprisoned by their desire to achieve total control over others cannot see or will co-creation anymore. In their view, the second attention's extraordinary power to conceive must be used to deceive. By subduing simultaneity into the rigidity that sequence seeks, they clearly see and will the destruction of their alleged opponents, for they are not willing to depend on chance in writing their stories. Believing that imprecise, or less-than-perfect, control – a byproduct of ambiguity – will destroy their clarity of mind and reintroduce fear, rigid people go to extremes to avoid change. Thus, to extremists that value only order as opposed to chaos, the desire to maintain permanence or to control change gives rise to a need to victimize the other.

By contrast, in free systems people co-create their stories with others. Only by valuing other persons and other species as much as we value ourselves can we narrate stories in which similarity (order) meets difference (chaos).

Social groups and all biological webs in general derive their sustenance from the act of welcoming parts that are similar to each other and different from each other at the same time. Because the human self too is a collection of parts similar to and different from one another, growth in any individual or in any system reflects the complementarity between the similarities guarded by the first attention and the differences that are reconciled by the second attention.

The first attention – the offshoot of sequence – is essential. Indeed, would anyone wish to live in a world that did not offer some kind of repetitive order? Is there a human being – or any animal for that matter – that is not terrified by the absolute isolation inherent in unknowable chaos? Still, the first attention is insufficient, for we need the second attention – the offshoot of simultaneity – in order to adapt to change.

But as wonderful as it is, the second attention also is insufficient. We may enter with hope the world of the unknown (Figure 8.9) that mediates between the known (order) and the unknowable (chaos), but we cannot be gone for too short or too long a while. In the end we must come back "home" – hopefully, with a gift that will change it in unforeseen ways.

For sure, if we are unwilling or unable to come back to the attitude of reconciliation by which we care for the social and natural environment that sustains our illusion of permanence, then, we risk losing ourselves in the chaos of the unknowable – that is, we risk becoming prey to madness.

Now, because the first attention is the guardian of any consensus about reality,

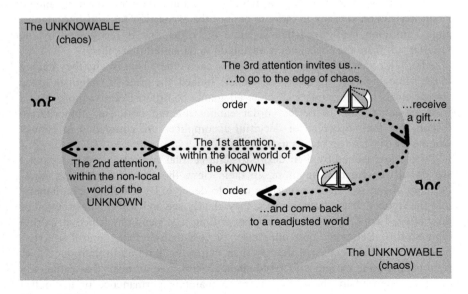

Figure 8.9 To go and to come back.

we cannot easily persuade it to place within parentheses the legitimacy of a known meaning with the purpose of re-adjusting the familiar world. In the view of the rigid-minded first attention, the moment we place a known meaning between parentheses (the works of the second attention), we negate reality – and thus enter the realm of chaos. By contrast, and by default, autistics tell us only a strong creative side can build the bridge through which we may persuade our logical side – within the world of familiar order – into accepting the alleged chaos introduced by unfamiliar interpretations – the only ones that may refresh reality.

The hope of sustainable growth begins when we place the known between parentheses and enter the unknown that lies between order and chaos. Our anguish becomes more and more intense while we travel toward the edge of unknowable chaos. Still, two good things may happen to us:

1 In the non-locality that "lies" beyond space and time we may envision harmonies never seen before; and
2 in time other travelers may find our unexpected views intriguing, elegant, nice, or supportive of their dreams and growth in some way. That is the point at which we come back to a renewed "home."

Paradoxically, a new agreement necessarily emerges from an initial disagreement and, sooner or later, ends up being challenged by an opposite view – a situation that may lead to further renovation (as with the advance of science). Growth arises when we re-adjust the reality guarded by sequence through the imagination freed by simultaneity; and *growth becomes sustainable when our imagination joins the imagination of others so as to co-create the world with them.*

Concluding remarks: the slaying of the dragon and the return of Quetzalcoatl

Most of us will agree on the fact that our human ecology cannot be sustained unless we reverse global warming within the next 50 years. In the short term, whether by mandate or through the generation of economic incentives, we should try to reach state-of-the-art energy efficiencies in the production, transportation, and consumption of all kinds of fuels. Further, if we boost the production of non-carbon fuels, remove carbon from CO_2 fumes at the same rate that the economy grows, and regenerate tropical forests, we will revive the atmosphere and the free biodiversity that created it in eons past.

Making true the dreams highlighted in the previous paragraph seems very necessary; and yet, it is insufficient. For one reason, our reckless lifestyle will not change much unless we renew our belief systems and social agreements.

As it goes, the ways of being that drive us do not make sense in the light of the challenges we are facing now. Hence, they will make less sense by 2060. Embracing the Siege of Troy and Chimæra simultaneously tells us that either selfishness or the idealistic belief in equality of wealth, instead of making our refuge (as some may believe now), will make our prison, and finally, our grave.

In other words, when we unfold the global implications brought by Chimæra – as enticing as such a drift may seem to us – we see that it reflects the delusional aim of a lifestyle based on the high consumption of energy and costly foods. In this drift, because global warming cannot be easily reversed, unprecedented upheavals in climate may accelerate the mass extinction *underway* in the biota. Chimæra does not recognize the limitations imposed by the need to preserve the biota. Hence, this drift should not be allowed to spread out.

As to the Siege of Troy, even if some of us would like to continue enjoying a comfortable life, the social strife inherent in this drift compels us to reject it. In fact, the Siege of Troy shows that the consumption of energy and high-quality food and water cannot be limited to a few countries and social sectors. Increasing the number of the poor to more than two billion by 2060 would be without precedent in human history. Ultimately, the political tensions inherent in this drift will enhance the possibility of pervasive havoc.

With either drift, most species would be threatened by enslavement or extinction, and neither life nor civilization could continue evolving. In other words, if our creative power is applied solely to the advancement of technology and to the exploitation of natural resources so as to maintain a status quo that will continue breeding social injustice (the Siege of Troy) or making gratification available to all (Chimæra), much of bio- and cultural diversity on Earth will be destroyed.

Where can we find the solution to our dilemma, then?

Empowering the second attention so as to accelerate the discovery of new technological tools may come to our rescue. Perhaps we will master the speed-of-light information-transmission technologies that can be read by proximal senses (PSIT technologies); and perhaps we will arrive at building robots endowed with all the knowledge we have developed so far, the capacity for instantaneous translation from any language to another, and especially the ability to display an "independent," socially-inclined, human-level artificial intelligence (HLAI).

Within economic growth, favoring mental over physical movement – a trend that has been growing geometrically since Tezla and Marconi invented the radio – should help. However, the portentous feat of arriving at PSIT and HLAI might become counterproductive unless we come to terms with the fact that the second attention is marvelous and dangerous at the same time.

The conservative guardians of social order in any society have always feared the power of disruption associated with the second attention. That is why they have always tried to stifle it. For example, in the Middle Ages pious characters feared dragons – mythical creatures endowed with both the body of a serpent and the wings of a bird. Certainly the image of Saint George slaying a dragon appealed in the past to devout believers in the established legitimacy. And yet, getting rid of the second attention kills the hope of devising a new way to sustainability when unforeseen change knocks at the door.

Moreover, the myth of the return of the "Plumed-Serpent" (or "Quetzal-coatl") in Mesoamerican cultures – a metaphor for the explorer who returns home from the unknown with the gift of a new vision of the social and the natural world – suggests that sustainable solutions rest on regaining the enlightened social consciousness (the third attention) that gave rise to *homo sapiens*. That myth implies that the third attention will enlighten us – as it did our ancestors – the instant we persuade the two facets of our mind (the first attention and the second attention) to empower each other.

Ironically, although we have advanced far in many fields (for example, science and technology), we have been unable to get reacquainted with the subtle works of the third attention in the co-creation of the social and the natural environment. Fortunately, because autistic individuals are socially impaired, they can show us the Way to the third attention if we explore and understand their predicament: holding onto a sterile first attention abandoned by the creativeness of the second attention. Paradoxically, because autistics cannot deal with the ambiguity inherent in fantasy and social nuances, they can help us reconcile our ways of being between themselves and with those of others in the world of doubt and hope that reaches to the edge of incomprehensible chaos.

At the edge of chaos we may find that the sustainability of our human ecology will come when we acquire the power to control power. Upon achieving that goal, human beings will wake up to the resonating set of ways of being in which – and by which – physical resources and non-human species, populations, belief systems, and social agreements are reconciled and deployed toward the co-creation of the world.

Saint Francis of Assisi realized that truth when he said:

> May thou be praised, my Lord, for our sister mother Earth, who sustains and guides us, and produces various fruits with colored flowers and greens.

Saint Francis' works invite us to avoid becoming the prey of ways of being in the like of excessive fear, self-pity, self-importance, arrogance, anger, hatred, greed, or ambition; to resist the desire to control others; and to nurture our minds and the minds of our children by understanding, seeking, and displaying altruism, humility, motherly love, serenity, sobriety, and responsibility.

Under the light of a natural, humane, altruistic, and thus social, education, girls and boys may find out that there is a common denominator to the ways of being that make a good mother and Mother Nature: the realization that the only way to keep control is to share it.

Appendix A: definitions of key concepts

On the growth of the global economy and energy in the period 2005–2060

AE

Advanced economies. Economies driven by high creativity, industrial growth, and a low population growth (lower than two children per family).

CPE AND EX-CPE

Centrally planned economies and former centrally planned economies. Essentially, the former Soviet Union, Eastern Europe, and China. Notice that within the CPE, some countries (e.g. Eastern Europe and China) are catching up with the AE.

PDC

Population-driven countries. Economies driven by the relentless exploitation of natural resources, destruction of forests, low competitiveness and creativity, and high population growth (more than two children per family).

GDP AND GDP/CAPITA

Gross domestic product. The market value of the final goods and services produced within a country in a given period of time. That value over the number of inhabitants results in the GDP per capita.

BOE

Barrel oil equivalent. The caloric content in any source of energy when measured as the equivalent of a barrel of Brent oil.

On the scenarios or drifts reviewed in this chapter

DRIFT

A possible, yet reckless current to the future. Either of the two drifts described here may be viewed as Order or Chaos.

THE SIEGE OF TROY

The drift in which the consumption of energy and high-quality food and water is limited to a few countries and social sectors. The loss of faith in social values and the destruction of tropical forests make this drift undesirable.

CHIMÆRA

The utopian drift in which a lifestyle based on the irresponsible consumption of energy and costly foods is offered to all. The acceleration of global warming, the depletion of Earth's resources, and the extinction rate of free species also make this drift undesirable.

On social and political issues

DEMOCRACY

The way by which we are able to place between parentheses our own and others' beliefs in order to find new avenues of growth. It is equivalent to embracing at the same time order (the beliefs that the logical side of our minds totally trust) and chaos (the beliefs of our opponents or, simply, the beliefs we do not trust). In a democracy, people listen to the divergent views of others before trying to control them. And that allows the parts of a system to lean on one another's strengths in order to co-create their world.

DUALISM (CONFRONTATION)

Any situation in which order opposes chaos.

FUNDAMENTALISM

The predilection for order as seen in the literal or univocal interpretation of sacred texts, the predominance of patriarchy, and the establishment of a rigid hierarchy.

On the cognitive system that allows human beings to conserve reality (the system spared in autism)[40]

SEQUENCE, OR PERFECT CONTROL (ORDER) AS OPPOSED TO IMPERFECT CONTROL (CHAOS)

The direct systems dynamics that seeks order – that is, the certainty offered by rigid measurement and direct observation, 100 percent probability of existence, the unaltered repetition of a pattern or of a visible form, the respect for tradition, the reliance on authority, a unique central meaning for each word in the dictionary, and so on. Without the order sought by sequence, the world lacks meaning. That is why, under the command of sequence, we are compelled to reject chaos.

Chaos may be taken as zero percent probability of existence, the impossibility of repeating a pattern or a measurement, the other that seeks to rob us of our place in the sun, the obstacles we find on our way, anything we cannot comprehend, anything we cannot recognize, our opponent in a match or in a war, and so on.

In a confrontation, what is order to one side is chaos to the opposite side. That is why order and chaos will forever seek to replace each other. Under the sway of sequence, there is no way that opposite parts may reach an agreement, co-create the world, or grow. Confrontations driven by sequence will end in suicide, the victory of the strongest side, or mutual destruction.

Sequence drives the first attention, or the logical (or autistic) side of the mind.

THE FIRST ATTENTION, OR THE LOGICAL SIDE OF THE MIND

The cognitive system by which we are able to assign only one, repetitive meaning to an event, sign, object, and so on, and by which we believe that we can do only one thing at a time.

Some examples of the doings of the first attention are:

> our immutable features and names; our habits; the known way to our home, school, or work; the unalterable sequence of past events; the literal meaning of what we have read; the rules of syntax; the most familiar meaning (semantics) and the correct pronunciation of known words; the characteristics of any repetitive process; the bulk of scientific knowledge that allows us to predict what will happen; the laws of our country and the rigidity of the officers that enforce them; the definition of the borders with neighboring countries and the decided will and loyalty of the army that must guard those borders from illegitimate change; the autoimmune system that protects our bodies from the chaotic intrusion of hostile bacteria; and so on.

> (Cassella *et al.*, in press)

On the cognitive system that allows human beings to re-create reality (the system impaired in autism)[41]

SIMULTANEITY, OR LESS-THAN-PERFECT CONTROL

The inverse systems dynamics by which we are able to embrace opposite or ill-assorted tenets at the same time. We may use the infinite speed of simultaneity so as to re-create with others the known world or to destroy it for good.

Simultaneity drives the cognitive system impaired in autism: the second attention, or the creative side of the mind.

THE SECOND ATTENTION OR THE CREATIVE SIDE OF THE MIND.

The cognitive capacity that frees our imagination.

Some examples of the not-doings of the second attention are: our understanding and our devising a pun; the use of irony, metaphor, and allegory in literature; the correct use of personal pronouns; any kind of modulation between utter certainty (the known or order) and dire uncertainty (the unknowable or chaos); the use of the word "maybe" in any spontaneous discourse; the paradoxical plots that make mesmerizing detective stories; fascinating movie scripts or addicting soap operas; and the adoption of mutually incompatible hypotheses before designing a scientific experiment.

The rise of the second attention may be observed experimentally in babies at the age of three to four months.

On the Balance between the Conservation and the Renovation of Reality

THE THIRD ATTENTION

The serendipitous understanding and planning that arises when the first attention and the second attention empower each other. The third attention is responsible for acts in which we co-create the world with other human beings and other species.

Appendix B: the growth of world population, economy, and energy demand (2005–2060)

Table 8.A1 Global population growth 2005–2060

Economic zone		Population 2005 million	Siege of Troy Population 2060 million	Chimaera Population 2060 million
North America	A	330	379	351
Western Europe		504	621	575
Pacific		201	248	230
Advanced economies		*1,035*	*1,248*	*1,157*
Eastern Europe	B	106	131	121
Former Soviet Union		313	386	358
China and others		1,430	2,592	2,125
CPE and EX-CPE		*1,849*	*3,108*	*2,604*
Latin America	C	577	1,253	961
North Africa and Middle East		360	797	611
South-Eastern Asia-Pacific		569	1,256	964
PDC 1		*1,506*	*3,306*	*2,536*
Africa sub-Sahara	D	594	1,578	1,114
South Asia		1,480	3,978	2,810
PDC 2		*2,074*	*5,556*	*3,925*
Advanced economies	A	1,035	1,248	1,157
Population-driven countries	C+D	3,580	8,861	6,461
World		6,469	13,218	10,222

Table 8.A2 Global GDP growth in Siege of Troy

Economic zone		2005 billion $	2060 billion $	2020 % 05–20	2060 % 20–60
North America	A	13,990	24,549	1.5	1.0
Western Europe		15,821	25,208	1.5	1.0
Pacific		7,067	12,067	1.5	1.0
Advanced economies		*36,878*	*61,824*	*1.5*	*1.0*
Eastern Europe	B	1,186	2,605	2.5	1.5
Former Soviet Union		3,029	8,215	2.5	1.5
China and others		3,494	12,451	4.0	2.5
CPE and EX-CPE		*7,709*	*23,271*	*3.0*	*1.9*
Latin America	C	3,029	10,160	3	2
North Africa and Middle East		1,749	5,430	2.8	1.8
South Eastern Asia-Pacific		3,192	11,990	2.8	2.3
PDC 1		*7,970*	*27,580*	*2.9*	*2.1*
Africa sub-Sahara	D	662	1,365	3.0	2.0
South Asia		1,616	3,730	2.6	1.6
PDC 2		*2,278*	*5,094*	*2.7*	*1.7*
Advanced economies	A	36,878	61,824	1.5	1.0
Population-driven countries	C+D	10,246	32,674	2.8	2.0
World		54,835	117,769	2.0	1.4

Table 8.A3 Global GDP growth in Chimæra

Economic zone		2005 billion $	2060 billion $	2020 % 05–20	2060 % 20–60
North America	A	13,990	43,042	2	2
Western Europe		15,821	58,189	3	2
AE Pacific		7,067	26,555	4	2
Advanced economies		*36,878*	*127,786*	*3*	*2*
Eastern Europe	B	1,186	10,010	7	3
Former Soviet Union		3,029	19,050	5	3
China and others		3,494	141,829	7	7
CPE and EX-CPE		*7,709*	*183,318*	*6*	*5*
Latin America	C	3,029	52,701	6	5
North Africa and Middle East		1,749	31,610	8	5
South Eastern Asia-Pacific		3,192	76,208	8	5
PDC 1		*7,970*	*160,518*	*7*	*5*

(Continued)

Table 8.A3 Continued

Economic zone		2005 billion $	2060 billion $	2020 % 05–20	2060 % 20–60
Africa sub-Sahara	D	662	42,011	8	8
South Asia		1,616	104,694	8	8
PDC 2		2,278	146,706	8	8
Advanced economies	A	36,878	127,786	3	2
Population-driven countries	C+D	10,248	307,224	7	6
World		54,835	617,328	5	4

Table 8.A4 Global GDP per capita ($2005/capita)

Economic zone		2005 thousand $	Chimaera 2060 thousand $	Siege OF 2060 troy thousand $
North America	A	46	130	69
Western Europe		28	107	43
AE Pacific		20	72	30
Advanced economies		35	117	53
Eastern Europe	B	10	88	21
Former Soviet Union		14	90	31
China and others		2	71	5
CPE and EX-CPE		4	74	9
North Africa and Middle East	C	4	55	6
South Eastern Asia-Pacific		4	84	7
PDC 1		4	67	7
Africa sub-Sahara	D	1	40	1
South Asia		1	40	1
PDC 2		1	40	1
Advanced economies	A	35	117	53
Population-driven countries	C+D	2	50	3
World		8	64	9

Table 8.A5 Global energy demand

Economic zone		2005 MMBOE/D	Chimaera 2060 MMBOE/D	Siege of troy 2060 MMBOE/D
North America	A	47.3	31.0	30.6
Western Europe		30.2	26.6	19.7
Pacific		15.0	15.4	9.7
Advanced economies		*92.5*	*73.0*	*60.0*
Eastern Europe	B	6.1	9.7	5.9
Former Soviet Union		29.4	37.9	28.4
CPE of Asia		30.2	290.7	57.6
CPE and EX-CPE		*65.6*	*338.3*	*91.9*
Latin America	C	10.0	53.5	14.8
North Africa and Middle East		11.4	57.3	15.3
South Eastern Asia-Pacific		9.3	66.9	14.1
PDC 1		*30.7*	*177.7*	*44.3*
Africa sub-Sahara	D	6.9	141.3	10.4
South Asia		10.2	181.7	12.9
PDC 2		*17.1*	*323.0*	*23.3*
Advanced economies	A	92.5	73.0	60.0
Population-driven countries	C+D	47.8	500.7	67.6
World		205.9	912.0	219.5

Table 8.A6 Global energy intensity (Boe/1,000$, 2005)

Economic zone		2005 BOED/1,000$	Chimaera 2060 BOED/1,000$	Siege of troy 2060 BOED/1,000$
North America		3.4	0.7	1.2
Western Europe		2.1	0.4	0.7
Pacific		2.2	0.5	0.8
Advanced economies	A	*2.6*	*0.5*	*0.9*
Eastern Europe		5.8	0.9	2.1
Former Soviet Union		6.5	1.2	2.4
CPE of Asia		11.0	1.9	4.4
CPE and EX-CPE	B	*7.9*	*1.8*	*3.3*
Latin America		3.6	0.9	1.5
North Africa and Middle East		7.7	1.7	3.4

(*Continued*)

Table 8.A6 Continued

Economic zone		2005 BOED/1000$	Chimaera 2060 BOED/1000$	Siege of troy 2060 BOED/1000$
South Eastern Asia-Pacific		4.0	0.8	1.6
PDC 1	*C*	*4.6*	*1.1*	*1.9*
Africa sub-Sahara		16.5	3.2	7.2
South Asia		7.2	1.6	3.2
PDC 2	*D*	*9.4*	*2.1*	*4.3*
Advanced economies	A	2.6	0.5	0.9
Population-driven countries	C+D	5.7	1.5	2.4
World		4.0	1.4	1.8

Table 8.A7 Global energy per capita

Economic zone		2005 BPY/person	Chimaera 2060 BPY/person	Siege of Troy 2060 BPY/person
North America	A	56	32	30
Western Europe		22	17	12
Pacific		27	25	14
Advanced economies		*33*	*23*	*18*
Eastern Europe	B	21	30	16
Former Soviet Union		34	39	27
CPE of Asia		7	50	8
CPE and EX-CPE		*13*	*47*	*11*
Latin America	C	6	20	4
North Africa and Middle East		11	34	7
South Eastern Asia-Pacific		6	25	4
PDC 1		*7*	*26*	*5*
Africa sub-Sahara	D	4	46	2
South Asia		2	24	1
PDC 2		*3*	*30*	*2*
Advanced economies	A	33	23	18
Population-driven countries	C+D	5	28	3
World		11	33	6

Notes

1 The number of the poor in the world is debatable. The author's estimate is used as a basis toward analyzing potential variations in the next 50 years.
2 Leakey and Lewin, 1995.
3 Coppock, 1998.
4 Flannery, 2005.
5 Ibid.
6 Ward, 2006; Kump, Pavlov, and Arthur, 2005.
7 For more examples of the world of the first attention, see Appendix A.
8 Cassella, 1997, 2000, 2002a, 2002b, 2002c; Cassella, *et al.*, in press.
9 That is why autistic-like leaders driven by sequence cannot easily admit they have made a mistake. Paradoxically, when in danger, many voters are enticed by a self-assured, heavenly enlightened – and in the end, reckless – leader, while they reject cautious flip-floppers, who are eager to change their minds if they realized they have made a mistake.
10 Essentially, the countries that make up the OECD (see Appendix B).
11 Mainly the developing countries, with the exclusion of former centrally planned economies (Russia, China, Eastern Europe, North Korean, and Cuba – see Appendix B).
12 Nebel and Wright, 1996.
13 Cassella, 1998.
14 Parker, 1993.
15 More precisely, Edward Parker (1993) posited that only a rate of economic growth of 10 percent and up during at least 20 years – as is happening in China – would allow for some wealth to trickle down to the poor.
16 Brown, 1996.
17 Flannery, 2005.
18 Lento, 1998.
19 Brown, 1996.
20 Burke and Ornstein, 1995.
21 Leakey and Lewin, 1995.
22 Ibid.
23 Gould, 1996.
24 Leakey and Lewin, 1995.
25 Ibid.
26 Ibid.
27 Capra, 1996.
28 Flannery, 2005.
29 The assessment includes about 30 trillion BOE of methane clathrates trapped at the bottom of the oceans.
30 Kunstler, 2005.
31 Cassella, 1998.
32 Notice that energy intensity in BOE per $1,000 of incremental wealth decreases when energy efficiency goes up, meaning that we use less energy to create goods worth $1,000.
33 Kump *et al.*, 2005.
34 Ward, 2006.
35 IPCC-WG1 (2007).
36 Socolow and Pacala, 2006, pp. 53–57.
37 Flannery, 2005, pp. 196–200.
38 Dertouzos, 1997.
39 Kassan, 2006, pp. 30–39.
40 The definitions in this section are taken from Cassella *et al.*, in press.
41 Ibid.

Bibliography

Brower, M. (1992) *Cool Energy.* Cambridge, MA: MIT Press.

Brown, L. (1996) *Tough Choices.* New York: Norton.

Burke, J., and Ornstein R. (1995) *The Axemaker's Gift.* New York: G.P. Putnam's Sons.

Capra, F. (1996) *The Web of Life.* New York: Doubleday.

Cassella, A. (1997) Self-Other Differentiation and Self-Other Integration from the Perspectives of Language Development and Autism. Master's thesis, Cambridge, MA: Harvard University.

Cassella, A. (1998) *Lifestyle and Energy Use in the Next century: An Eco-Systemic and Cognitive View.* Petróleos de Venezuela S.A., Planning Vice-Presidency, Caracas.

Cassella, A. (2000) Fundamentos cognitivos y semióticos de la creatividad: Aportes del Autismo. Doctoral Thesis approved for publication, UNESR, Caracas, Venezuela.

Cassella, A. (2002a) *El Desarrollo de la inteligencia social: Aportes del autismo.* Maracaibo: Ediluz.

Cassella, A. (2002b) *The Flameless Fire: From Autism to Creative Intelligence.* Quincy, MA: LogosResearch.

Cassella, A. (2002c) *Creativity at the crossroads of life and death: Autism and Logos.* 1st edn. Quincy, MA: LogosResearch.

Cassella, A., Cassella, G., and Uribe, L. (in press) *The Power of the Third Point.* Melbourne, FL: LogosResearch.

Castaneda, C. (1987) *The Power of Silence: Further Lessons from Don Juan.* New York: Simon and Schuster.

Coppock, R. (1998) Implementing the Kyoto Protocol. *Issues in Science and Technology,* 14 (3): 66–74.

Dertouzos, M. (1997) *What Will Be.* New York: HarperCollins.

Flannery, T. (2005) *The Weather Makers.* New York: Grave Press.

Gell-Mann, M. (1994) *The Quark and the Jaguar.* New York: Freeman.

Gould, S.J. (1996) *Full House.* New York: Harmony Books.

Horgan, J. (1997) *The End of Science.* New York: Helix Press.

Intergovernmental Panel on Climate Change (2001) *Climate Change 2001: Synthesis Report.* Cambridge: Oxford University Press.

IPCC-WG1 (International Panel on Climate Change) (2007) *Fourth Assessment Report: Climate Change 2007. Summary for Policy Makers. A Report of Working Group I.* IPCC-WMO.

Kassan, P. (2006) The Futile Quest for Artificial Intelligence. *Skeptic,* 12 (2): 30–39.

Kump, L.R., Pavlov, A., and Arthur, M.A. (2005). Massive Release of Hydrogen Sulfide to the Surface Ocean and Atmosphere during Intervals of Oceanic Anoxia. *Geology,* 33 (5): 397–400.

Kunstler, J.H. (2005) *The Long Emergency: Surviving the End of Oil, Climate Change, and Other Converging Catastrophes of the Twenty-First Century.* New York: Grove Press.

Leakey, R. and Lewin, R. (1995) *The Sixth Extinction.* New York: Anchor Books.

Lento, R. (1998) A Greener Revolution. *Issues in Science and Technology,* 14 (3): 5–7.

Lynch, M. (1996) *International Petroleum Price, Supply and Demand Projections through 2020.* Gas Research Institute.

Nebel, J.B. and Wright, R.T. (1996) *Environmental Science.* Upper Saddle River, NJ: Prentice-Hall.

Padrón Guillén, J. (1996) *Análisis del Discurso e Investigación Social.* Caracas: UNESR.

Parker, E. (1993) *Objectif: 10 percent de Croissance.* Paris: Criterion.

Pinker, S. (1994) *The Language Instinct*. New York: Harper Perennial.

Rimland, B. (1964) *Infantile Autism: The Syndrome and its Implications for a Neural Theory of Behavior*. Englewood Cliffs, NJ: Prentice-Hall.

Sabini, J. (1995) *Social Psychology*. New York: Norton.

Safina, C. (1998) Scorched-Earth Fishing. *Issues in Science and Technology*, 14 (3): 33–36.

Samuelson, R.J. (1997) Dancing around a Dilemma. *Washington Post*, 15 July.

Socolow R.H. and Pacala, S.W. (2006) A Plan to Keep Carbon in Check. *Scientific American*, 295 (3): 50–57.

Ward, D.W. (2006) Impact from the Deep. *Scientific American*, 295 (4): 64–71.

World Energy Council. (1998) *Summary of the Conference*.

9 "Ways of being" in the economic system

Roy E. Allen

Introduction

A decade ago, the author wrote an account of world economic history that identified and tracked the role of various "ways of being" that have been influential in this historical process. Various "gods" from Greek mythology were used to represent ways of being, and other ways of being were also identified and named (Allen, 1997, reviewed in *Ecological Economics*, 1998). These "gods," or "ways of being," are found to be important components of the economic system. As per the human ecology approach to economics outlined in Chapter 1, the reader should note that the humanities – literature which is typically excluded from economic analysis – is thus formally included.

As organized in Figure 9.1, four basic structural conditions in the human ecology are belief systems (ways of organizing alleged truths and convictions), social agreements, physical environments and resources, and human populations. (see Chapter 1). From these four structural conditions other structural conditions emerge, such as "ways of being." As shown in Figure 9.1, the author would define a "way of being" as a bundle of faiths, beliefs, social behaviors, personality traits, and physical energies, which is similar to the notion of a god in Greek mythology. Ways of being can change and co-evolve along with belief systems, social agreements, human populations, and physical environments and resources. Ways of being are thus derived from each of these four structural components of the human ecology, as opposed to ideologies (systems of ideas and ideals, often used to support an agenda), mythologies, and other examples of one structural component – belief systems.

In contemporary usage, "ways of being" are somewhat broader than what people call "cultural types" or "personality types," because they also include "physical energies" – just as many of the Greek gods not only represent aspects of human mind and spirit, but also partnered those intangibles with more tangible physical and material forces (e.g. Zeus's patriarchal cultural order was associated with the most aggressive, competitive energies and even "lightening bolt" enforcement characteristics).

The ways of being (gods) in the author's pantheon include: Chaos – various powers leading toward random inertness; Gaia – that which nurtures and sustains

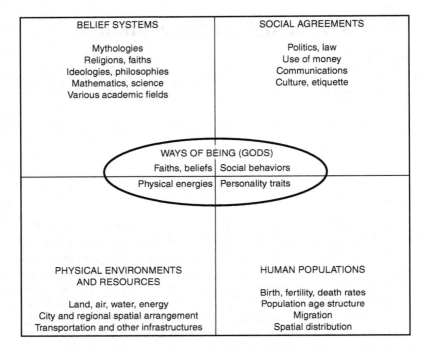

Figure 9.1 Ways of being (gods) as structural conditions of the human ecology.

the living earth; Zeus – aggressive, competitive, expansionist powers, pre-modern, patriarchal discipline; Trinity – integrative, cooperative, contractionist tendencies, unconditional love, mercy, compassion, that which is idealized (but not necessarily practiced) within most monotheistic religion; Cybor – modern, innovative, scientific, rational, moderate-individualism tendencies; and Buro – modern, hierarchically-organized, communitarian-disciplined tendencies (Table 9.1). The author's work includes other ways of being besides these six, but for the purposes of this book these six are emphasized.

Table 9.1 Examples of ways of being (gods) within the global economy

Chaos	Various powers leading toward random inertness
Gaia	That which nurtures and sustains the living earth
Zeus	Aggressive, competitive, expansionist powers
	Pre-modern, patriarchal discipline
Trinity	Integrative, cooperative, contractionist tendencies
	Unconditional love, mercy, compassion
	That which is idealized (but not necessarily practiced) within most monotheistic religion
Cybor	Modern, innovative, scientific, rational, moderate-individualism tendencies
Buro	Modern, hierarchically-organized, communitarian-disciplined tendencies

Figure 9.2 shows how these gods relate to each other in a cosmological diagram called a *mandala*, which means "circle" in Sanskrit. In religion and psychology, mandalas are drawn, modeled, or danced, and they usually contain a pattern within the circle such as a cross or star. Mandalas typically represent elements or forces which tend to fall apart or oppose each other. By organizing seemingly irreconcilable forces on opposite sides of the circle or in concentric rings, there is an attempt to "find the center" or "find unity" – an attempt to overcome or even better, "live with" conflict and ambiguity, which is related to the religious path toward enlightenment or God and the psychological attempt to overcome dissociation or disorientation (Storr, 1983, pp. 235–8). As discussed by Cassella in Chapter 8, *dissociation or disorientation from each other and from the natural world are two fundamental problems faced by people across the global human ecology.* A well-known mandala in the Hindu religion shows "cosmogenesis" (Smith, 1994, p. 23) whereby the universe evolves from dense matter into more ethereal spheres. Mandalas can thus represent various evolutionary or time-based processes as well as timeless or static processes.

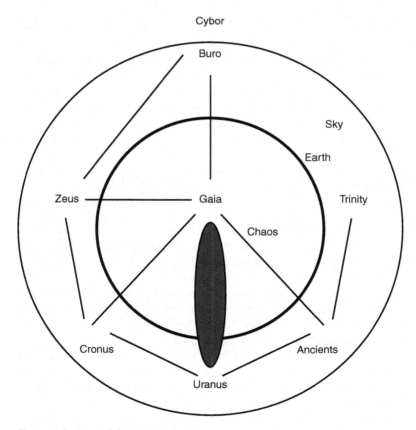

Figure 9.2 A mandala for the human ecology.

Similar to cosmogenesis, Figure 9.2 shows how some ways of being (or gods such as Gaia and Chaos) are more "earth-centered," or oriented toward dense matter and physical processes (empirical, tangible processes would be emphasized), and some gods, such as Trinity and Cybor, are more "sky-based" and transcendent of physical processes (processes of mind, spirit, and social values would be emphasized). Earth gods are located more to the center of the concentric figure, and sky gods are located more to the periphery. To the author Gaia and Chaos represent the most primary processes in the human ecology from which other processes are allowed (in this sense the author is more of an empiricist than a transcendentalist); therefore they, especially Gaia, are located in the center of the mandala to give coherence or balance to the other ways of being.[1]

The author's use of a wide plurality of ways of being as interactive agents is similar to the perspective of Carl Jung, who wrote:

> The truth is that we do not enjoy masterless freedom; we are continually threatened by psychic factors which, in the guise of "natural phenomena," may take possession of us at any moment. The withdrawal of metaphysical projections [such as gods, is a bad idea because it] leaves us almost defenseless in the face of this happening, for we immediately identify with every impulse instead of giving it the name of the "other," which would at least hold it at arm's length and prevent it from storming the citadel of the ego. "Principalities and powers" are always with us; we have no need to create them even if we could. It is merely incumbent on us to *choose* the master we wish to serve, so that his service shall be our safeguard against being mastered by the "other" whom we have not chosen. We do not *create* "God," we "choose" him.
>
> (Storr, 1983, p. 246)

The author recognizes that many different pantheons are possible, including the one in which there is only one God or one enlightenment. For readers inclined toward monotheism, the author would reference the life work of the neo-Calvinistic philosopher Herman Dooyeweerd. Similar to the author's "gods," Dooyeweerd posits four "ground motives" or "cosmonomic ideas." There is the "Christian religious motive" (similar to the author's Trinity), and three apostate motives: "the motive of Greek matter and form" (similar to the author's Chaos and Gaia); "the Scholastic motive of nature and grace" (a synthesis of the Christian and Greek motives); and "the Humanistic motive of nature and liberty" (similar to the author's Cybor and Buro, becoming important in the modern age).

The life work of the "eco-theologian" Father Thomas Berry identifies these same basic historical shifts in what he calls "religious orientations" or "mediations" – for example, the shift from a dominant "divine-human mediation" in the Scholastic Middle Ages to a dominant "inter-human mediation" in the modern age. Berry identifies, and advocates, a current shift toward a more "earth-human mediation," which would elevate Gaia within a pantheon of religious orientations.

Thus, the author's pantheon need not be inconsistent with monotheistic traditions. As discussed at the end of this chapter, it is left to the reader to determine hierarchy within the pantheon (which to Dooyeweerd is Trinity, and to Berry seems to be Trinity and Gaia), and out of determinations of hierarchy, notions of good versus bad, and freedom can be derived. Once again, the author's framework is proposed to help all perspectives communicate effectively and jointly understand the recent history of civilization, reconcile destructive opposition between cultures, increase our understanding of good versus bad, political and moral freedom, etc.

As stated by Dooyeweerd:

> These fundamental motives are the true motive forces which have dominated the evolution of Western scientific and philosophical thought. Each of them has established a community among those who have started from it. And the religious motive as hidden motive force of his spiritual community dominates the thinker all the more if he is unconscious of it. The thinker, indeed, can fashion this motive according to his individual view, but the motive itself is supra-individual.
>
> (Dooyeweerd, 1953, Vol. 1, p. 61)

Thus, the author has a suggestion for scientific and academic groups, political and business leaders, and all others who advance their theories and agendas in the economic system.

Please, provide your audience with a self-assessment of your underlying belief system, personality traits, and ways of being, including an assessment of the social dynamics through which you obtain compensation and status and through which your institution is maintained. In the context of Donald Snyder's Figure 3.2, what are your prior beliefs about economic globalization, and what is your evidence for those beliefs? In the context of a pantheon of gods such as Table 9.2, which gods do you worship in what balance? When your audience has this information, then there is less chance of misunderstanding and dysfunctional behavior. The alternative is that someone, as per Donald Snyder or this author, might do the assessment for you.

Reconciling opposition between ways of being

How might this pantheon of ways of being be used to better understand the global economic and social system, including what is necessary to sustain it? In this section, reconciling opposition (understanding how the gods relate to each other) is discussed; in the following section, hierarchy (understanding which ways of being are dominant) is discussed; and in the final section, based on these notions of reconciling opposition and hierarchy, notions of good versus bad and freedom are developed – all with application to the sustainability of what we know and value in the global system.

Reconciling opposition is fundamental to the human condition – a basic principle in the author's framework is that we commonly think in terms of opposites or contrasts: male versus female, order versus disorder, true versus false, good versus bad, individualism versus communitarianism, power-worship versus love-worship, etc. Furthermore, the dualities might inter-penetrate or balance each other and then produce unities. In Hegel's terms, thesis and antithesis can lead to synthesis, which then becomes a new thesis. The new thesis might then find or provoke a new antithesis. In mythological terms, mother and father join to produce a child, which maintains some qualities of both parents, while having new qualities as well. The child grows up, sometimes deposing one or both parents or consorting with one, or possibly finding a new consort from outside the family. Conflicts arise outside the family as well as inside. Some theses and some gods are "immortal," i.e. humans "know them forever," and some die out. If balance or integration between gods is not allowed, destructive things can happen. If powerful gods do not cooperate, there may be war – either within the human psyche, or in the world. The following are some examples that are relevant to the purposes of this book.

Chaos and Gaia

The most basic duality in the author's pantheon is provided by Chaos and Gaia: various powers leading toward random inert disorder (Chaos), versus that which nurtures and sustains the orderly chemical and temperature conditions of life on earth (Gaia). Chaos, or "the void," nevertheless provides the material basis from which life springs forward – the creative void (Chaos) versus the creative impulse (Gaia).

In the earliest mythologies, these dualities are worked out. In Hesiod's *Theogony:*

> Chaos was born first and after came Gaia
> the broad breasted, the firm seat of all
> the immortals who hold the peaks of snowy Olympus,
> and the misty Tartarus in the depths of broad-pathed earth ...

> [The pre-Athenian Greeks] perceived a correlation between the processes of the Earth and those of the female, and this connection was frequently expressed with sexual imagery. ... So the conceptualizations of Gaia, even from the earliest expressions, were a celebration of the elemental power of the female. [They] viewed all life as coming from the womb of the Earth Mother, into which all beings were received at the end of life.
>
> (Spretnak, 1987, p. 69)

> The Olympians [such as Zeus] may be seen as human writ large, in whom we can recognize ourselves; whereas to be taken over by Gaia is to be over-whelmed by a clearly extra-human force, to be taken out of ourselves.
>
> (Downing, 1987, p. 146)

In the author's mythology, Chaos and Gaia represent the most basic duality – "the mother and father of all." Somehow, to the author, all other human challenges and debates are played out in the context of whether "orderly and sustainable life" is possible in otherwise chaotic and harsh conditions. As discussed next, if Chaos and Gaia are understood as inseparable partners, then it is easier to understand why the Gaia Hypothesis and the Chaos Revolution were both named and popularized simultaneously in the 1970s.

It was Nobel laureate William Golding who suggested to James Lovelock that he name his new scientific theories after Gaia. In 1972, after a period of "conversion" to Gaia, Lovelock published his Gaia Hypothesis.

> Lovelock claims to have wrestled between poetry and professional propriety, but ultimately his frustration with the madness of the planet's chaotic system transformed to awe over the method behind it all. ... The living planet, he proposed, not only maintained the unstable combination of gases on which it depended for its very existence, but Gaia somehow had determined to do so. The goddess of the Earth, in Lovelock's earliest formulations, had a mind and a will of her own and could plan ahead, intentionally controlling her own environment. ... Fundamentally the Gaia Hypothesis finds the Earth to be more like a life form than an inanimate sphere, adjusting to internal and external changes much as an organism might react to threats and opportunities in the environment.
>
> (Joseph, 1990, p. 30)

Lynn Margulis, renowned microbiologist, advanced the Gaia Hypothesis with Lovelock, by arguing that Gaia uses even the tiniest biological organisms as a controlling influence in her global system. And in between the microbiology of Margulis and the atmospheric science of Lovelock, many fields of science have been "unpredictably infected by Gaia-orientation." And from its rebirth in the scientific community, Gaia worship has captured the popular imagination. Festivals, films, books, workshops, and various other rites and rituals honoring the goddess have proliferated. From sources ranging from Merlin Stone's books to Ted Turner's cable TV network programs on Gaia, most people now know of Gaia. In the language of Thomas Kuhn as per *The Structure of Scientific Revolutions*, a transcendental, sociological "paradigm shift" had occurred. *And, for many, "global sustainability" was equated with Gaia worship.*

Increased attention to Gaia was made possible by increased awareness of her inseparable partner, Chaos. Lovelock's "frustration with the madness of the planet's chaotic system" was what "transformed to awe over the method behind it all." Similarly, Margulis's understanding of the symbiosis and cooperation between all life on Earth, including the smallest microbes, is understood to be a self-sustaining order only in contrast to what otherwise would be a chaotic and life-hostile environment. In his book *Chaos, Gaia, Eros*, Chaos pioneer Ralph Abraham claims that:

> The mythic struggle between Chaos and Order [Gaia] is the emotional motor driving (and resisting) the Scientific Revolution now in progress. ... In the

1970s the mathematical waves of chaos theory crashed on the beaches of the sciences. First struck, in 1971, was fluid dynamics, an event occasioned by the proposal of Ruelle and Takens to model turbulence in fluids with a chaotic attractor. Then, in 1975, population dynamics was given a chaotic mathematical model. Rapidly, the other physical and biological sciences followed suit. Recently, the earth sciences, social sciences, and even psycho-analysis, have fallen into the new paradigm of chaos.

(Abraham, 1994, p. 124)

The meaning of chaos to Abraham, James Gleick, and other chaos pioneers is "a dynamical [capable of motion or change] system that is neither static [capable of a stationary state] nor periodic [returns to the same state over and over]" (Ibid., p. 235). Chaos would thus be a system which is continually changing, but never appears to change back into what it was. The chaotic pattern infinitely unfolds itself in a sequence called a trajectory, or time series. And the most common name given to one of these infinitely unfolding patterns is "fractal." Compared to lines, circles, and more traditionally identified patterns, "fractals came to stand for a way of describing, calculating, and thinking about shapes that are irregular and fragmented, jagged and broken up" (Gleick, 1987, pp. 113–14). An example of a chaotic fractal pattern in Gaia's living systems is the way that trees grow into the air, rivers "branch out" in a watershed, and blood vessels "branch out" through a creature – a pattern that allows the efficient flow of fluid and nutrients to sustain life as Gaia works her magic on Chaos' inert elements.

Cybor

The way of being (god) called Cybor by the author – modern, innovative, scient-ific, rational, moderate-individualism tendencies – in the author's framework grew out of the scientific and industrial revolutions of the 1700s and 1800s. The eighteenth century Enlightenment was characterized by a new rationalism, and the new economic relations treated land, labor, and capital as commodities which could be increasingly disembedded from older social relations by the force of the money economy and the pursuit of profit (Karl Polanyi's *The Great Transformation*). In *The Theory of Moral Sentiments* and *The Wealth of Nations*, Adam Smith identified and advocated this way of being as appropriate to the new market capitalism. What the author calls "moderate-individualism" in this way of being is consistent with Smith's new emphasis on liberty and restrained (as opposed to heroic, warlike, Zeusian) individualism as per Smith's profit-seeking "prudent man" in *Moral Sentiments*.

The Theory of Moral Sentiments is thus, in its largest focus, a book about the socialization of men and women who have emerged from the straitjacket of a traditional [pre-modern] often dogmatic social order, and must create a work-able system of morality and social order in a new condition of "perfect" liberty.

(Heilbroner, 1986, p. 62)

As discussed next, this way of being, called Cybor by the author, is named because, in the current period, these tendencies have encouraged "cybernetics," "cyborgs," and "cyberspace."

The scientist Norbert Wiener helped the allies in World War II with air defense systems against Hitler's (Zeusian) *blitzkrieg* (lightning war). Immediately after the war, he established the field of cybernetics:

> The group of scientists about Dr. Rosenblueth and myself had already become aware of the essential unity of the set of problems centering about communication, control, and statistical mechanics, whether in the machine or in living tissue. ... We have decided to call the entire field of control and communication theory, whether in the machine or in the animal, by the name *cybernetics*, which we form from the Greek *steersman*. ... Although the term cybernetics does not date further back than the summer of 1947, we shall find it convenient to use in referring to earlier epochs of the development of the field. ... If I were to choose a patron saint for cybernetics out of the history of science, I should have to choose Leibniz ... the *calculus ratiocinator* of Leibniz contains the germs of the *machina ratiocinatriz*, the reasoning machine ... the same intellectual impulse which has led to the development of mathematical logic has at the same time led to the ideal or actual mechanization of processes of thought.
>
> (Wiener, 1948, p. 11)

The term cyborg was coined by two scientists to mean a "cybernetic organism." The term premiered in "Cyborgs and Space," an article by Manfred Clynes with Nathan S. Kline published in the September 1960 issue of *Astronautics*. Clynes would later say about the genesis of cyborgs:

> The main idea was to liberate man from constraints as he flies into space – that's a kind of freedom – but it seemed necessary to give him the bodily freedom to exist in another part of the universe without the constraints that having evolved on earth made him subject to. For example, the level of gravitation that is here, the oxygen, the atmosphere. And some of the other things that have conditioned the physiology of man to be what it is.... In other words man has now become conscious enough of the way he was built physiologically, and here, I emphasize physiologically, that he could now supplement the homeostasis with which he evolved... so as to supplement it by his own imagination and through his own creativity. In such a way as to make it possible to exist, qua man, as man, not changing his nature, his human nature that evolved here. Not to change that but to simply allow him to make use of his faculties, without having to waste his energies on adjusting the living functions necessary for the maintenance of life. They become unconscious, automatic rather, the way they are here. You don't have to constantly adjust your blood pressure, for example.
>
> (Gray, 1995, p. 47)

Kline, director of the research facility at Rockland State Hospital in New York, was interested in the application of drugs for the treatment of mental patients. Clynes was the chief research scientist in the Dynamic Simulation Laboratory at Rockland State Hospital, and they based their 1960 article on a paper that they gave to the Psychophysiological Aspects of Space Flight Symposium sponsored by the U.S. Air Force School of Aviation Medicine in San Antonio, Texas.

> Enraptured with cybernetics, [in their 1960 article] they thought of cyborgs as "self-regulating man-machine systems". ... Space-bound cyborgs were like miniaturized, self-contained Gaias. One of Clynes and Kline's first cyborgs, a kind of pilot project for Gaia-Man, was our standard white laboratory rat implanted with an osmotic pump designed to inject chemicals continuously to modify and regulate homeostatic states. The rodent's picture was featured in the article that named its ontological cyborg condition. The snapshot belongs in Man's family album.
>
> (Haraway, 1995, p. xv)

In the 1980s, scientists provided people with even more powerful means to socialize their cyborg selves: personal computers. For those who cannot be (heroic Zeusian) astronauts and break free from Gaia's organic conditions into outer space, computers allow people to contrive their own (moderate-individualism) "virtual realities" in a transcendental inner space. In William Gibson's *Neuromancer*, "cyberspace" is the name given to the intangible place inside these new computers where people communicate and "live." The protagonist, Case:

> who'd lived for the bodiless exultation of cyberspace...still dreamed of cyberspace ... and he'd cry for it, cry in his sleep, and wake alone in the dark, curled in his capsule in some coffin hotel, his hands clawed into the bedslab, temperfoam bunched between his fingers, trying to reach the console that wasn't there. ... He'd operated on an almost permanent adrenaline high, a byproduct of youth and proficiency, jacked into a custom cyberspace deck that projected his disembodied consciousness into the consensual hallucination that was the matrix. ... The body was meat.
>
> (Gibson, 1984, pp. 4–6)

In the cyberspace literature, Descartes' disembodied human mind as per the rationalism of the Enlightenment ("I think, therefore I am") prevails over the human body-machine and the natural world of Gaia; so too the "cyberpunk" culture refers to the human body as "meat" which can be left behind when one "jacks" into cyberspace. Meat typically carries a negative connotation relative to the pure consciousness that can be obtained in the virtual realities of cyberspace.

Cybor, Gaia, and Chaos

It is not a coincidence that the Gaia Hypothesis and the Chaos revolution occurred in the wake of advances in (Cybor's) "cybernetics," the study of control and communications systems; "cyborgs," organisms with scientifically implanted or connected controlling devices; and "cyberspace," the electronic places "inside the computer" where information is communicated and controlled.

On November 9, 1967, the "cyborgian" Apollo 4 astronauts sent back to Earth the famous first U.S. picture of the whole Earth. Because of the advances in cybernetics and cyborgs which allowed astronautics, Gaia's beauty was revealed to humans as never before, and the picture influenced Lovelock and other Gaia revivalists. Lovelock's book, *Gaia: A New Look at Life on Earth*, uses cybernetics as the scientific basis for the recognition of Gaia.

Gaia-consciousness was also awakened by the nuclear arms race. Cybernetic modeling of a nuclear exchange, and the nuclear winter which might descend on Gaia and destroy her life and fertility, prompted greater respect and love for mother earth.

Gaia-worship was advanced in the global environmental movement, which blossomed in the early 1970s. Science and technology, while allowing unprecedented economic success, also heightened awareness of *The Limits to Growth* (Meadow *et al.*, 1972, revised 2004). This influential book by the Club of Rome correlated resource availability, industrial output, pollution, food supplies, population growth, and other variables in various scenarios, some of which were quite disturbing. In the U.S., unprecedented economic success could support expensive environmental initiatives – environmentalism was in many ways a "full-stomach phenomenon." The U.S. Clean Air Act was passed in 1970, the Clean Water Act in 1972, and the National Environmental Policy Act (NEPA) began requiring environmental impact analyses of big economic development projects. In the following 30 years, carbon monoxides and sulfur dioxides would be reduced by one-third in U.S. cities, particulate pollutants would be reduced by two-thirds, atmospheric lead by 97 percent, and even the Great Lakes would be revived.

Concurrently, the information technology and computer revolution allows many chaotic systems to be identified and even generated with mathematical equations. Technology-enhanced humans, with new cyberspace computing and graphics capability, brought attention to Chaos during the same years that cyborgian astronauts and other technology-enhanced scientists brought attention to Gaia.

But whenever chaotic patterns seem to be fully predictable in nature, more careful scrutiny with cyborgian science finds random anomalies which shatter the full predictability hypothesis. Humans thus increasingly realize that it is impossible to be conscious of complete order or complete disorder without the presence of the other. "Dischaos" would be defined as a "state of inadequate chaos, the result of an obsession with order," just as "disorder" would be defined as a "state of inadequate order, the result of an obsession with chaos" (Abraham, 1994, p. 235).

Thus, the forces of Cybor, Gaia, and Chaos have inter-penetrated in various dialectics, which have in turn led to new political and social priorities and legislations. In the Introduction to E.F. Schumacher's classic text on ethics and values in the world ecology, *Small is Beautiful* (1974), Theodore Roszak writes:

> How strange that this renewed interest in ancient ways of livelihood and community should reappear even as our operations researchers begin to conceive their most ambitious dreams of cybernated glory. And yet how appropriate. For if there is to be a humanly tolerable world on this dark side of the emergent technocratic world-system, it will surely have to flower from this still fragile renaissance of organic husbandry, communal households, and do-it-yourself technics whose first faint outlines we can trace through the pages of publications like the *Whole Earth Catalog*, the *Mother Earth News*. ...

Scientists struggle to understand and "fix" imbalances between Cybor, Gaia, and Chaos; and political and social communities try to decide what environmental efforts to support based upon the evidence. Those who have "dreams of cybernated glory" are optimistic that technological fixes in the free market economic system will solve problems and allow Gaian life to thrive. Those who are less inclined toward this Cybor-worship fear that we are creating "a more humanly [in]tolerable world on the dark side of the emergent technocratic world-system." The latter group, inclined more toward Gaia-worship, have advocated "thinking globally" but "acting locally" to preserve mother earth.

For example, following on the work of M. King Hubbert, Colin Campbell and others have come to prominence for the view, supported by a massive data base, that global crude oil production will be dropping by 2013 at the latest (Campbell, 2002). In popularizing this position, they provide Gaia-worshippers with a strong argument that we need to start conserving oil now in order to sustain the human ecology in the future – it is suicide to excessively exploit our Earth Mother. After articles in *Scientific American* and *The National Interest*, Campbell attracted a response by the influential columnist George Will, who asserted the belief that technology and individual entrepreneurship in the free-market capitalist system will save us from a coming oil crisis – a pure Cybor view that was also supported by Daniel Yergin in the March/April 1998 issue of *Foreign Affairs*. Yet who is right, and can the two sides reconcile their mythic belief systems sufficiently to clarify what the true risks are?

Based upon the degree of Gaia-worship versus Cybor-worship versus worship for other gods, various political and economic efforts develop a predictable ideological bias. For example, the pro-Gaia editorial agenda of various environmental groups tends to be in opposition to the pro-Cybor agenda of various business groups. *What is sometimes less obvious is the ideological agenda of various scientific and academic societies.* The more "objective" research efforts nevertheless tend to support certain paradigms and seek certain kinds of funding from less objective sources. And, scientists and academics do tend to worship Buro – to a certain degree they value the hierarchically-organized, communitarian-disciplined methods of favor and disfavor in their professional societies, refereed journals, conferences,

University and research departments, etc. When Buro-worship is strong, innovative objectivity that goes against the beliefs of the group may be discouraged.

Might a more Gaia-worshipping society, compared to a more Cybor-worshipping society, predict population growth differently, based upon different myths regarding: the inevitability of orgiastic life propagating itself; the degree of "free will" that people might use to rationally choose less children based upon economic considerations, environmental stress, etc.? Or, might a more Gaia-worshipping group assess climate change differently? If research funding comes from private or public sources that grew out of the Gaian environmental movement of the 1970s, then dangers to Gaia might be exaggerated in order to secure greater institutional support for her study and protection. On the other hand, if institutional support is threaded with industrial market-capitalist ideologies, which advocate fossil-fuel based economic growth as a primary value in the human ecology, then the risks of global warming may be minimized in order to protect this value-system and way of life from high taxes or quotas on fossil fuel use. Even when a bureaucratic research agenda is objectively "right," bureaucracies might have the bullish group discipline of Buro, and new evidence or anomalies which inevitably pop up to challenge the belief-paradigm or *raison d'etre* of the bureau may be censored.

The author thus returns to his suggestion for the scientific and academic groups which advance their theories with regard to various political-economic or environmental-economic crises: these groups should provide their audience with a self-assessment of the underlying belief systems, personality traits, and "ways of being" of their group, including an assessment of the social dynamics through which funding and status is obtained and institutional order is maintained. In the context of a pantheon of ways of being such as the author's, which gods are worshipped and in what balance? When an audience has this information, then there is less chance of misunderstanding and dysfunctional behavior based upon ideological false consciousness or hidden agendas.

The Chaos way of being has been embraced by many people, such as Michael Bakunin, the dominant founder of nineteenth-century anarchism. Born into Russian nobility, he renounced his privileges in protest of Czarist oppression, and joined rebellions against the upper class in Dresden, Paris, Austria, and elsewhere. As described by Richard Wagner, a fellow participant in the 1849 Dresden uprising, "everything about him was colossal, and he was full of a primitive exuberance and strength" (Carr, 1961, p. 196). Furthermore:

> this man was born not under an ordinary star but under a comet ... Bukunin's handwriting was as chaotic as his other traits ... [his major work, *God and the State*, has] a lack of proportion; moreover it breaks off abruptly: we have searched in vain to discover the end of the manuscript.
> (Bakunin, 1970, pp. v, x, 6)

Chaos – various powers leading toward random inertness – is embedded in the way of being of many counter-cultural or revolutionary groups which strive to wreck havoc in the established order. One example is the more aggressive vein of the extreme anti-globalization movement discussed by Donald Snyder in Chapter 3. In milder form, Joseph Schumpeter and others have argued that "creative destruction" of existing economic structures, recessions, and other "chaos" are necessary so that inefficient or unprogressive structures can be eliminated and new creativity allowed – the "creative void" aspect of Chaos can be seen as a healthy, necessary part of the evolutionary process, or "species approach" as discussed by Modelski in Chapter 2.

Zeus, Buro, and Cybor

In the author's framework, Zeus, Cybor, and Buro each represent different authority systems at play in the human ecology, each of which advances its power by exploiting the energy and life allowed to it by Chaos and Gaia. Recall from Chapter 1, one definition of human ecology "is simply the human proclivity to expand the use of physical substances and to convert these substances into resources (to transform Nature into Culture, for better or worse" (Bennett, 1996). Thus, Zeus, Cybor, and Buro can be thought of as dominant ways of being at play in this process.

Of these three, Zeus is the earlier, pre-modern patriarch. The Zeusian way of being enforces strict discipline, with violence if necessary, through family-based models of organization. Organized crime networks are generally Zeusian, with their "gold, goons, and guns." Many corporations, especially older male-dominated ones, have Zeusian organizational structure, with arbitrary "cloak and dagger" hierarchies enforced by the "good old boys." Zeus's aggressive, competitive, expansionist, power-seeking and heroism has been worshipped by most political and military regimes at one time or another. Zeus inspires the adventurer, military hero, and sportsman, typically young men, to achieve superiority over rival forces. Zeus-worshippers try to overcome their rivals without much concern for restraint or mercy, and the victory belongs to Caesar, the King, the Czar, or the Fuehrer, i.e. the patriarch.

When defeat is near, the Zeusian-patriarch may suffer a denial-syndrome, decision-paralysis, or even choose "death with honor" for himself and his patriarchal clan, because the admission of defeat is demoralizing and antithesis to the aggressive competitive, expansionist Zeusian character. Examples include the inability of Hitler to surrender, the Japanese tradition of hara-kiri, and the relentless expansion of certain corporations to gain market share at the expense of profits or even sustainability. Virtually every empire has suffered terrible setbacks because of the illogical Zeusian "empire-overreach" phase. For the Zeusian character, the driving force is often expansion of the powerful clan, or bust. Admitting that one has been wrong, or a failure, is a terrible loss of face and is therefore usually avoided except maybe at the chaotic end of the reign of power.

In the wake of the 1997 Asian financial crisis, and in the search for organizational explanations, various Zeusian belief-structures, personality traits, and ways of being were exposed. Terms like "crony capitalism," "nepotism," "decision-paralysis," "gridlock," "inflexible institutions," "corruption" are used to describe the human ecology at the top of Asia's regimes.

> "To expect integrity or honesty in a politician is like trying to buy fish at a produce market," a blunt Minister for Justice (and former Tokyo police chief) once remarked. Elite officials, qualified by stiff examinations and bound by school and college ties, were long held in awe, almost like a quasi-priesthood of the national religion, Shinto. Until the present crisis these officials ran Japan much as they collectively saw fit. ... Japanese stockbrokers, functionally descended from the traders who bribed the shoguns' officials and gambled on rice futures, were tacitly allowed to make secret deals with favored clients and to trade on their own account – or, to speak plainly, to rig the markets for their political and business friends.
>
> (Sayle, 1998, pp. 87–8)

As another example, what some analysts did not understand was the degree to which these types of Zeusian corporatist networks, with their patriarchal discipline, seized power in the former Soviet Union during the transitionary 1980s and 1990s under the smokescreen of market capitalist ideology (which is supported by Cybor-ideology), or communism (which is supported by Buro-ideology).

Many heads of state in the modern world, Zeusian by position and motivation, choose denial and every other possible means to save face, rather than admitting that they were wrong, and changing policies appropriately for the benefit of the public. An example relevant to this book is the strong Zeusian interest in the use of oil-revenues to fund the political-economic expansionist power at the top of OPEC countries. Admitting that oil revenues might diminish, and admitting that alternative political-economic regimes might have to be established, might come hard for OPEC leaders. It may also be hard for Zeusian leaders to form an oligarchy and strengthen OPEC – by nature and ideology they might resist sharing power.

Also, in the U.S. and other nations that depend on oil as the fuel-basis for the economy, key decision makers also have a vested interest in oil ideology, and changing ideology to a fuel-switching ideology will not come easily. Perhaps this Zeusian ideology-momentum, especially if it infects the supporting bullish bureaucracies (an alliance between Zeus and Buro) can be called "the Titanic effect." In Greek mythology, myth after myth identifies these kinds of "hubris" which inevitably lead to "nemesis." Whether the fossil-fuel using momentum of the entire world economy is just this kind of Titanic-hubris is discussed by Moseidjord and Cassella in Chapters 7 and 8, and likely it is a "Chimæra" drift as titled by Cassella that risks climate catastrophe and loss of biological diversity.

Most fascist regimes are obvious examples of Zeus-worship. However, the patriarch that is being honored with hubris may also be a nation, or team, or cluster of idolized symbols, such as "the glory that is Rome," the business corporation, the local sports club, or even "lady liberty" that harks back to the "patriarch" of Athens, Athena. In Greek mythology, Athena was born from Zeus's head and thus has Zeusian-male as well as female qualities. She is a crafty goddess of war as well as the patroness of Athenian democracy.

A regime is a practical system of management and control, the Realpolitik of power, as opposed to idealistic or theoretical politics. Thus, a political system could be communist or democratic in theory, but more fascist or Zeusian in practice. For example, not long after Pericles' funeral oration in praise of democracy, the Athenians sent an expedition against the island of Melos, and the famous Melian dialogue occurred as written by Thucydides. In this dialogue and its aftermath, the Athenians demonstrated the difference between their beuiling rhetoric of democracy, and their Zeusian quest for power.

Parallels between ancient Athens and the U.S. are easy to make. Both idealize democracy, but both have Zeusian elements. Like Athens, the early history of the U.S. tolerated slavery and only male patriarchs could vote. Both regimes repressed and at times slaughtered what they called "inferior" or "foreign" indigenous populations as they expanded and consolidated their empire.

Cybor and Buro are ways of being which are derived from (i.e. "sons of") the Zeusian way of being; thus they also represent aggressive, competitive, expansionist, power-seeking systems, but they use more modern methods, ideologies, and regime rules. For example, as discussed in the previous section, Cybor represents a more moderate individualism compared to Zeus' more heroic individualism. Military-adventurer-sportsman heroes are more Zeusian "in your face" individuals – aggressive business entrepreneurs and other individuals who mask their competitiveness are more "Cyborian."

The way of being called Buro by the author – modern, hierarchically-organized, communitarian-disciplined tendencies – in the author's framework co-evolved with the Cybor way of being in the 1700s and 1800s (i.e. Cybor and Buro are "fraternal twins" and represented next to each other in Figure 9.2). This period was not only characterized by new rationalism, innovative scientism, and new notions of liberty (Cybor's doing), but it was also a time when powerful, modern, secular nation-states were built at the expense of more traditional political-economic regimes such as the Holy Roman Empire, which formally ended in 1806 with the renunciation of title by Francis II (in the author's mythology, the Holy Roman Empire combined the older ways of being of Zeus and Trinity in "uneasy alliance"). The modern nation-state has a hierarchical-organized structure, but it developed with an increased civic concern for the dignity and welfare of the population at large, which the author would call communitarian-disciplined (rather than Zeusian patriarchical or hierarchical-disciplined).

In the author's framework, the Buro way of being is named because of the modern bureaucracies which formed along with the modern nation-state, and because of what it is like to work in a modern "office," for which the German word is *büro*. When these types of organizations become too domineering and pervasive, as per Orwell's *1984*, then "big brother is watching us." In the author's framework, of the twins Cybor and Buro, Buro is the "big brother" who inherited some of Zeus's aggressive-controlling tendencies. The Cybor way of being, with its emphasis on high-tech cybernetic systems and management of information flow, can in some cases also be aggressive-controlling over human activity, but the control mechanisms are more masked so that the way of being maintains at least an ideology of individualism. The life work of Michel Foucault sorts out these distinctions, as per "Foucaultian surveillance" of the individual by social mechanisms which might restrict freedom.

When people define their heroism or ideals in organizational terms, wherein an overriding goal is to serve the modern nation-state or Party or bureaucracy, therein is worship of Buro. The writings of Karl Marx as per *The Communist Manifesto* and *Capital* helped to establish this way of being, and it is embedded in most socialist and communist ideology and political movements. Based upon the writings of Marx and others, Lenin inspired the ideology that the Party was the hero – not its charismatic leader. When he became aware that he was being made into a demi-god, he asked one of his aides in the Council of People's Commissars:

> What is this? How could one permit it? ... They write that I'm such and such, exaggerate everything, call me a genius, a special kind of man. Why, this is horrible. ... All our lives we have carried on an ideological struggle against the glorification of personality, of the individual. We long ago solved the question of heroes.
>
> (Tucker, 1975, p. 1)

For Lenin and other Buro-worshippers, the modern professional Party was meant to be the guiding light toward greater destiny, not the personality of its leader. Describing Lenin, Ken Jowitt writes:

> The fact that Lenin possessed personal charisma is not as significant as the way in which he defined charisma and related it to the organization he created. As an individual, he combined forceful charismatic certainty with a genuine and persistent emphasis on empirical and impersonal modes of investigation and interaction. His party was created (so to speak) in his own image. And that image was distinctive in its novel recasting of elements – heroism, arbitrariness, and absolute certainty, along with impersonal discipline, planning, and empirical investigation.
>
> (Jowitt, 1992, p. 7)

Lenin also had some of the Cybor way of being, displaying "persistent emphasis on empirical and impersonal modes of investigation and interaction." But, in the late 1920s and early 1930s, Leninism reverted to the more Zeusian "cult of Stalin," and the U.S.S.R. sacrificed some of its Cyborian, intelligent empirical precision as well as some of its Buroian communitarianism. Stalin's rhetoric maintained Lenin's wish that "the Party cadres decide everything," but Stalin's reality soon meant that the cult of Stalin must decide most things. Lenin had warned of this: his will requested that Stalin not succeed him. By the late 1930s, Stalin had purged the Communist Party of his personal opponents and collectivized the peasants under the authority of his cadres.

Zeus and Trinity

In the author's framework, Zeus represents the aggressive, competitive, expansionist, power-seeking and heroic patriarchal tendencies and authority systems. In sharp contrast, Trinity is that which is idealized, but not necessarily practiced, in most monotheistic religions – integrative, cooperative, contractionist tendencies, unconditional love, mercy, and compassion. Trinity is what is *idealized*, but not always *practiced* in most monotheistic religion – giving, sharing, a martyred hero of *love* rather than the pagan hero of *conquering*. Perhaps nowhere is this distinction made better than by Dostoyevsky in *The Brother's Karamazov*, when Ivan gives his parable, "The Grand Inquisitor." When the Lord appears in front of the Grand Inquisitor, He is condemned to burn at the stake because He represents just about everything that the Zeusian Spanish Inquisition is not; and after "listening intently" and "looking gently" at the Inquisitor, "He suddenly approached the old man in silence and softly kissed him on his bloodless aged lips. That was all his answer."

Trinity's qualities – integrative, cooperative, and contractionist – are more stereotypically feminine, especially when combined with the "motherly" principles of unconditional love, mercy, and compassion. Zeus then represents the opposing stereotyped masculine qualities – aggressive, competitive, expansionist – especially when combined with the "fatherly" principles of conditional love as based on achievements and proper moral codes of justice. In Figure 9.2, Trinity and Zeus are thus located on opposite sides of the mandala to represent extreme opposition.

If a worshipper, nation, or group embraces Trinity in ideology, but accepts Zeusian codes of conduct in practice, then, in the author's mythology, it can be said "to be worshipping both Zeus and Trinity." The type of joint worship is usually not sustainable as the two realms inter-penetrate and clash with each other – in this case, mistaken ideology or false consciousness is revealed. The "two-self individual" nation or group may even experience hysteria or schizophrenia or some such loss of function or harmony. To the degree that there is unsustainable hypocrisy, Trinity and Zeus would have an uneasy alliance.

However, in the author's framework there are both Zeus and Trinity qualities in most people and groups; most of us are subject to various balances between the aggressive power-seeking and the integrative loving. To avoid loss of function or loss of harmony in the individual psyche, and to avoid another Spanish Inquisition or Holocaust, humans need to find sustainable ways to reconcile the opposition between Zeus and Trinity; we need to find ways that Trinity can restrain Zeus instead of having to "go away into the dark alleys of the town" (as the Lord does at the end of "The Grand Inquisitor"). In the author's view, these forces must be kept in balance in order to prevent a destructive excess of the aggressive, competitive, expansionist way of being.

Cybor and Buro, and other ways of being that can be aggressive, also need to be restrained by opposing forces for the same reasons. Otherwise, there will be war both inside the psyche and within the world system. Much of the violence and tragedy in the world seems to be driven by a craving to throw our psyche into allegiance with one aggressive impulse or "community of worship" at the expense of another. As the Grand Inquisitor states pessimistically:

> This craving for community of worship is the chief misery of every man individually and of all humanity from the beginning of time. For the sake of common worship they've slain each other with the sword. They have set up gods and challenged one another, "Put away your gods and come and worship ours, or we will kill you and your gods!" And so it will be to the end of the world, even when gods disappear from the earth; they will fall down before idols just the same.

Hierarchy (which ways of being are "dominant?")

A basic principle in the author's framework is the notion of a hierarchical order in the ways of being of people. Some belief systems and ways of being are more autonomous and controlling, and some are more embedded and constrained. As stated by E.F. Schumacher:

> Without the recognition of "Levels of Being" or "Grades of Significance" we cannot make the world intelligible to ourselves nor have we the slightest possibility to define our own position, the position of man, in the scheme of the universe. ... Maybe it is man's task – or simply, if you like, man's happiness – to attain a higher degree of realization of his potentialities, a higher level of being or "grade of significance" than that which comes to him "naturally": we cannot even study this possibility except by recognizing the existence of a hierarchical structure.
>
> (Schumacher, 1973, p. 89)

Over time, we choose to elevate some ways of being over others. One historical epoch may be distinguished from another by its change of gods. For example, in the author's mythology, the Modernism that came with the Enlightenment of the seventeenth and eighteenth centuries was the beginning of the age of Cybor and Buro as they began their rise to dominate the more ancient ways of Zeus and Trinity. This new age questioned older, established beliefs; it emphasized the free use of reason, scientific empiricism, and the innovations of the Industrial Revolution (Cybor's doing). Also, powerful, secular nation-states and modern bureaucracies were formed at the expense of the Holy Roman Empire, and there was a predominant civic concern for the dignity and welfare of the population (Buro's doing).

In the author's framework, the new dominant god is Cybor in terms of the cluster of patriarchal authority values and accompanying personality types and ways of being. This dominance plays itself out in the world system, ever since the Cybor way of being and its market capitalism dominated the Buro way of being and its command communism at the end of the Cold War. Cybor is now the more autonomous and controlling patriarch, and the other patriarchs are more embedded and constrained. However, Cybor's political-economic-social system, and the ways of his worshippers, depend upon the material resources and life-energies allowed by Gaia and Chaos. As discussed earlier, under "Cybor, Gaia, and Chaos," certain balances between these three are required, and the author would also say that Cybor, Chaos, and Gaia are dominant.

In the Hegelian dialectics which move civilization along, it may be that Cybor does not remain the dominant patriarch; it may be that his worshippers eventually turn to other gods. Hierarchy can also be thought of in terms of which belief systems, personality traits, and ways of being maintain themselves as more fundamental, and more sacred over the history of civilization. To the author, as discussed previously, Chaos and Gaia represent the most basic duality from which the other gods rise and fall. Until the sun is gone and the world is reclaimed by Chaos, it is likely that Gaia will nurture life forward. To the author, Gaia can thus be thought of as the most influential god, because she is the closest to organic-life-being as well as the mother of all. Of course, most monotheistic religions elevate Trinity over the other gods and give Him dominion over Gaia's life.

Various Hegelian theses and antitheses have led to the synthesis called Cybor. But, Cybor may not become immortal as an unchanging element in new theses which will inevitably come. Instead, he may be overthrown by existing gods; or he may find a partner with whom to generate offspring, and the offspring may overthrow him as, in Greek mythological terms, the Oedipal cycle turns once again. Instead of thesis-antithesis-synthesis, the process may end with inert prosthesis.

Good versus bad, and freedom

The ways of being that are discussed in this chapter are not meant to be the most complete pantheon; just some examples from the author's research for the purposes of this book. The organized collection of ways of being used here bundle together, as gods in a pantheon, various faiths, beliefs, personality traits, social behaviors, and physical energies. In the modern human ecology, these gods might help us identify what we worship, and what religions we have. "Worship" and "religion" are difficult words. In this chapter the author is allowing these words to have their broad secular meaning as well as their sacred or spiritual meaning. "Worship" in the *New Webster's Dictionary* can be "reverence; submissive respect; loving or admiring devotion" as well as "paying divine honors to the Supreme Being."

For example, worshipping Cybor means reverence and submissive respect for the beliefs, personality traits, and ways of being consistent with the innovative, scientific, rational, moderate-individualism tendencies that, to one degree or another, are in all of us. Worshipping Trinity means reverence and submissive respect for the beliefs, personality traits, and ways of being consistent with the giving, sharing, martyred-hero, unconditional love tendencies that, to one degree or another, are in all of us. When we worship Cybor, Trinity, or other gods in the author's pantheon, we are showing reverence and respect for certain aspects of ourselves. As quoted from Jung earlier:

principalities and powers are always with us; we have no need to create them even if we could. It is merely incumbent on us to choose the master we wish to serve, so that his service shall be our safeguard against being mastered by the "other" whom we have not chosen.

Given these definitions, "good versus bad" can be defined with the following types of schemes: "Good" ways of being are consistent with gods W, X, Y, etc. arranged in hierarchy Z; "bad" would be a hierarchy which is incompatible with Z. For example, a Christian might define "good" to be when Trinity dominates the pantheon and "bad" to be when Zeus or Buro (or any other god) dominates, or a communist might define "good" to be when Buro dominates and "bad" to be when Cybor or Trinity (or any other god) dominates.

Somebody else might define "good" to be when Christian and communist can "get along" so that neither claims the religious high ground; what is then required is that Trinity-worship and Buro-worship are reconciled somehow. A synthesized new "good" might then arise out of an historical dialectic which once had communism as an antithesis of Christianity. This example is working itself out in Russia, as the monotheistic religious practices and ideals are revived along with the Communist Party. Likewise, when the Pope visited Fidel Castro in Cuba in January 1998, there were various reconciling speeches. A synthesis of communism and Christianity in the former Soviet Union would also have to sort out the role of Zeus and Cybor. Zeusian religion supports organized crime based upon strict familial models of patriarchal discipline and aggression, and Cyborian religion supports individualistic market capitalism with all of its trappings, and both are powerful forces now at play in the former Soviet Union that threaten both Christian and communist traditions.

All of this patriarchal rivalry between potentially dominant sky gods Zeus, Trinity, Cybor, and Buro takes place in context with the organic conditions of life and death as represented by earth gods Gaia and Chaos. In the author's framework, all of these ways of being are present. In 1990, Valentin Fallin, head of the international department of the Communist Party of the U.S.S.R., conceded in "submissive respect" for Gaia and Chaos: "If we don't release funds from military expenditure to fight for the ecology, in ten years we will have no world worth fighting over."

Having constructed a framework whereby all of these religions and gods are inside all of us, and all of them are at play in the world in various hierarchies, the author is often asked, "What about free will?" In fact, the author would venture to say that the dichotomy between free will and determinism, or freedom and interference, is one of the most important dichotomies *in current mythic structures.* In the modern period of history, perhaps this dichotomy has become more important than the dichotomy between skeptical empiricism and transcendental idealism. Dooyeweerd (1953) identifies this dichotomy-shift – he argues that the dominant ground motive is now the humanistic motive of nature and liberty. Moving from the pre-modern to the modern period of history, humans would thus be compelled more by notions of liberty and less by notions of grace.

In the modern period, "will" is usually related to emotive "impulse" and "desire" as well as the more rational "power to make conscious choices." In the author's framework, emotive desires which are related to the creative impulse and various sexual and sensual energies are Gaian forces. The more egotistical "will to power" is the spirit of Zeus which is inherited by his sons Cybor and Buro. The rational power to make conscious choices is a more recently cultivated phenomenon in human history, and since the European Enlightenment it has been mostly Cybor's domain. Thus, Cybor-worshippers usually combine "will to power" with "will to exercise rational decisionmaking capabilities." The notable Zeusian Cybor-worshipper in this sense was Nietzsche, for whom "will to power" deserved recognition as the fundamental driver in human psychology. In this context, Nietzsche's famous quote "God is dead" means "Trinity-worship has declined; don't expect much from Trinity or you will have false consciousness, because Zeusian energies and Cyborian processing of these energies dominate." Nietzsche did not have much respect for Buro's communitarian restrictions, and Nietzsche was conscious of the gloomy psychological and social risks of excessive Zeus–Cybor worship when he realized that "nihilism stands at the door," i.e. "Chaos looms large" under these conditions.

Bertrand Russell is famous for his quote that "Freedom in general may be defined as the absence of obstacles to the realization of desires," but very few philosophical or social thinkers have defended freedom in this sense. In many Eastern religions, desires, especially egotistical desires, are "bad," and should be minimized rather than satisfied. In Western traditions, desires tend to be "good" as long as they are not socially destructive (destructive of Buro's civil societies, Trinity's religious communities, or Cybor's market capitalist arrangements, etc.).

In popular culture today, the strong emotive will which bubbles up in the form of impulse or desire is more likely to be accepted as a god exercising powers beyond our control, as compared to the more rational will which we use to make conscious choices. However, the author would accept this latter *capability* to make rational choices as a god, and in the "age of reason" he associates this capability with the Cybor way of being. However, *the actual choices which we make, which the Cybor-capability facilitate, may not have to be consistent with Cybor-worship.* As Cybor might tell Gaia:

> I gained worshippers by helping them develop this choice-making consciousness, and I do not fear it. If a man chooses to help Gaia nurture and sustain life. ... If a man chooses to seek glories and power and honor Zeus ... that is also fine with me.

Despite the common belief in Cybor's neutrality, i.e. the so-called value-free objectivity of rational, scientific, moderate-individualism tendencies, the author would instead identify this way of being as just another cultural "god" or "norm" which has arisen in a long historical value-selection process. Furthermore, the author would argue that this way of being contains "a system of faith, thought, and practice that offers people a frame of orientation and forms of worship" – one definition of religion used in this essay. And, as in most cultures which need some coherence around norms to survive, there is non-neutral value-ridden conformity, even in the (ironical) statement "we are all individuals." Kenneth Boulding advanced this position in his Presidential address to the American Economic Association in 1968:

> Science is a human learning process which arises in certain subcultures in human society and not in others, and a subculture as we have seen is a group of people defined by the acceptance of certain common values, that is, an ethic which permits extensive communication among them. The scientific subculture...is characterized by a strong common value system. A high value, for instance, is placed on veracity, on curiosity, on measurement, on quantification, on careful observation and experiment, and on objectivity. Without this common value structure the epistemological process of science would not have arisen; indeed it did not arise in certain societies where conditions might otherwise have been favorable but where some essential common values of the scientific subculture may be in some disrepute.
>
> (Boulding, 1968, p. 2)

Does faith in "moral freedom" or objectivity, ironically, reflect certain deep-seated religious commitments to Cybor or other gods? Might we be more constrained than we think with regard to moral freedom? Jung advances this position:

> Not only is "freedom of the will" an incalculable problem philosophically, it is also a misnomer in the practical sense, for we seldom find anybody who is not influenced and indeed dominated by desires, habits, impulses, prejudices, resentments, and by every conceivable kind of complex. All these natural facts function exactly like an Olympus full of deities who want to be propitiated, served, feared and worshipped, not only by the individual owner of this assorted pantheon, but by everybody in his vicinity. Bondage and possession are synonymous. Always, therefore, there is something in the psyche that takes possession and limits or suppresses our moral freedom. In order to hide this undeniable but exceedingly unpleasant fact from ourselves and at the same time pay lip-service to freedom, we have got accustomed to saying apotropaically, "I *have* such and such a desire or habit or feeling of resentment," instead of the more veracious "such and such a desire or habit or feeling of resentment has me." The latter formulation would certainly rob us even of the illusion of freedom. But I ask myself whether this would not be better in the end than fuddling ourselves with words. The truth is that we do not enjoy masterless freedom...
>
> (Storr, 1983, p. 246)

The author is less inclined than Jung to treat freedom as an ideological illusion or false consciousness. It is a helpful word as contrasted with determinism or intervention by others. The author's *will* to create this mythology was partly directed by his conscious wish to help himself and others be greater masters of their own pantheons. The author is the "individual owner of this assorted pantheon" but he does not believe that it is the only pantheon; furthermore even if it was the only pantheon, he believes that the free individual has great discretion to choose among its gods. Also, the author hopes that his pantheon might help clarify the meaning, if not the causes of political freedom and moral freedom as discussed next.

Political freedom and democracy

Many people have a strong, passionate, *religious* faith in the protection of political freedom, as per the U.S. *Declaration of Independence*: "We hold these truths to be *self-evident*, that all men are created equal, that they are *endowed* by their *Creator* with certain *unalienable* Rights, that among these are Life, Liberty and the pursuit of Happiness" [italics added].

To the author, this quote from the *Declaration of Independence* is quite consistent with Jung's rhetoric when Jung writes (as quoted previously):

> principalities and powers are always with us [i.e. there are *self-evident truths* that should carry the weight of law]; we have no need to create them even if we could [i.e. we are *endowed* by our *Creator* with them and thus cannot be *alienated* from them]. It is merely incumbent on us to choose the master we wish to serve, so that his service shall be our safeguard against being mastered by the "other" whom we have not chosen [i.e. we have the right to commit treason and fight against the King of Great Britain and armies whom we have not chosen in order to serve *our* cause of life, liberty, and the pursuit of happiness].

In the author's mythology, the modern version of political freedom, in the context of democracy, flows out of the British, American, and French Revolutions as Cybor and Buro wrestle power away from Zeus and other Ancients. These modern democracies were based just as much on Buro's civil societies and effective bureaus as they were based on Cybor's clever economics and individualism. Working together as young twins against the other gods, Cybor and Buro combined their strengths. Their modern methods built a powerful and united England in the seventeenth century. Young England thrived because it integrated Cybor's individualism with Buro's collectivism, because it combined the efficiencies of entrepreneurial markets and self-interests with the responsibility to the group's common, civic values. *The free, i.e. conscious rational, choices of the individual might be more fully realized if they are consistent with the will of the group, and vice versa.*

As Cybor-worship and Buro-worship expanded widely beyond England in the nineteenth century, it inspired belief in this kind of democracy, whereby the notion of liberty for individuals was combined with the notion of justice for all.

The twins, together, inspired J.S. Mill, Rousseau, and others to find the link between liberty and national identity, to claim that only an integrated nation can sustain a republican constitution. Thus, the first half of the nineteenth century gave rise to liberal nation-states with the pluralism of the twins in England, America, Canada, and to a lesser extent in France (the French Revolution, after getting rid of the Zeusian King, gained a Zeusian Emperor Napoleon).

The pluralism of the twins, which combined political freedom for citizens with the parochial identity of the nation, minority rights with majority rule, had not yet spread into the communities of Zeus and other Ancients by the late nineteenth century. Italy, Germany, Greece, and the Balkans, in Eric Hobsbawm's words, had "mutated [nationalism] from a concept associated with liberalism and the left, into a chauvinist, imperialist and xenophobic movement of the right" (Hobsbawm, 1992, p. 121) – not a bad description of Zeus-worship.

In redesigning West Germany, Japan, and other nations immediately after World War II, aggressive national economic policies were combined with the liberties and incentives of individuals to seek efficiency in the marketplace. In West Germany, many of the modern welfare state traditions that had begun with Bismarck in the 1870s were improved, including a substantial public sector budget and employment, which supported research, occupational training, and social welfare protection of citizens. The major private banks, the government, the German Bundesbank, and German corporations worked together, and subsidies and tax incentives were designed to promote economic efficiency in balance with social justice. Similarly, in Japan after World War II, state paternalism supported the industrial and financial bureaus with research and trade promotion, while also providing the communitarian values within which the market incentive system and U.S. technology could thrive. Cybernetic systems and cyberspace management techniques, in both private and public offices, constitute a major part of the modern political economy, i.e. the systems of Cybor are combined with the communitarian offices of Buro.

Thus, in the author's mythology, "reverence; submissive respect; loving or admiring devotion" i.e. worship for the type of political freedom contained in modern democracies means "worship of Cybor and Buro working together." As always, other gods give context, but typically there is "separation of church and state" so that the modern Cybor–Buro secular-state regime can protect itself from older gods who are relegated to "churches."

There are different clusters of values underlying modern democracy versus modern free-market capitalism. With minor variations, believing in democracy means worshipping Cybor and Buro together, whereas believing in free-market capitalism means worshipping Cybor alone. Modern democracy may survive (survive Chaos) to the degree that Buro's civic communities can be maintained, and to the degree that Zeusian elements can be minimized in order to avoid "a chauvinist, imperialist and xenophobic movement of the right." These points are well argued by Lester Thurow in *The Future of Capitalism* and by Benjamin Barber in *Jihad Vs. McWorld.*

The balance between gods that is necessary for sustainable democracy is also defined by the most basic duality in the author's pantheon: the balance between Chaos (various powers leading toward random inert disorder) and Gaia (that which nurtures and sustains the orderly conditions of life). Along these lines, it has been argued by Antonio Cassella that:

> Democracy thrives by courting legitimacy and illegitimacy, order and chaos, at the same time. … Democracy seeks to avoid both the sterile ORDER inherent in a dictatorship and revolutionary CHAOS in which traditional ORDER is lost for good. … Without the balanced handling of virtual confrontations, DEMOCRACY vanishes into strict ORDER or unremitting CHAOS. By contrast, within DEMOCRACY, ORDER and CHAOS work together, for our spirits are eager to "see" contrasting opinions at the same time, choose new worlds (patterns, rules, processes, words, etc.), and finally guard them against unfair change. In sum, we gain a lot by understanding and appreciating the creativity inherent in the coming together of different interpretations of reality. If we become blind to the advantages of virtual confrontation, we may end up experiencing the extreme, brutal suffering brought about by either imposed LEGITIMACY or chaotic ILLEGITIMACY.
>
> (Cassella, 2006)

Moral freedom

So finally, this chapter addresses the question of how to live. Those people who are interested in this question, in the question of moral freedom, are concerned with the principles of good and bad conduct and character, and with the ability of the individual and the group to make choices in this regard. This book does not intend to tell people how to live, but it attempts to provide knowledge which can help people with their decisions, especially economic decisions, in the human ecology. Specifically, in the author's interpretation, this book intends to prevail against a kind of fatalistic and confused determinism that prevails in the postmodern age. The editorial line of this book seems to be that knowledge need not be so disjointed; so that real world problems, whether in material conditions or human systems, can be sorted out; so that people can learn by comparing theoretical predictions to empirical observation; so that humans can define desirable and feasible changes and be effective problem solvers and beneficial agents in history; so that progress toward various human ideals is possible, etc.

As an attempt to help in this regard, this chapter has provided a framework and a pantheon of various ways of being. Hopefully this scheme has allowed the reader to "hold at arms length" and contemplate various belief systems, character traits, and ways of being which exist in the economic system, and which drive civilization along its course. Hopefully, clustering together various "powers and principalities" as gods is a useful way to reduce the massive chaotic flux of fragmented and haphazardly-turning knowledge. Maybe relegating Chaos to an appropriate place in the pantheon, and holding him and other gods at arms length increases our ability to live with these gods. In Jung's terms, a god is then less able to "storm the citadel of the ego" because we are more aware of the presence of "balancing gods." Once conscious of a fuller pantheon around us, we might be better able to choose a god or be less dysfunctional when a god has chosen us.

In the current age, with its stress on liberty, individualism, scientism, and other Cybor-worship as per the author's mythology, many essays on ethics take cultural norms as exogenous starting points of the analysis. With Cybor now the dominant god, many people seem loath to construct a hierarchy among cultural norms, because such a hierarchy would challenge these Cybor-notions. In the author's framework, this non-hierarchical ideology is somewhat superficial and even false-consciousness when it claims to be culture-neutral or god-neutral, because in fact it elevates Cybor-culture and Cybor-ethics above the culture and ethics of the other gods.

In other words, the author would like to raise the possibility that we (either as individuals or organizations) cannot escape hierarchy, and if we cannot, then it is important to develop frameworks or pantheons that help us choose between our gods. When Cybor, like the other gods, is held at arms length, then essays on ethics become essays on deep mythic structures. And, when we develop greater consciousness of the deep mythic structures, we might be less dysfunctional when Cybor or another god chooses us. This argument seems especially relevant in the globalizing human ecology as different cultures increasingly clash – especially as the modern Cybor way of being spreads rapidly in global society and pervades previously more isolated and traditional cultures.

It is also the author's hope that his pantheon helps clarify and therefore expose certain kinds of destructive hidden agendas and false ideologies. For example, Zeus-worshippers might wreak less havoc if they are exposed as power-seeking Zeus-worshippers and balanced-out by Trinity-worshippers or Gaia-worshippers or others. Cybor-worshippers might not be able to justify so much righteous neutrality if they are better understood as Cybor-worshippers, Buro-worshippers might be prevented from too much irrational and destructive bullish stampeding, and so on.

Of course the author's pantheon does not perfectly represent what is going on in the world. The media of representation cannot always negotiate successfully between subjective human consciousness and the objective conditions in our environment. Despite his attempt to induct Cybor and Buro into the historic pantheon, the author would not presume to have created two gods, but at the very most to have named two gods that have been around for at least 400 years. The reader is encouraged to construct his own pantheon, but like the author's it will be human-made and finite, and thus limited. In Jung's words:

> Though our choice characterizes and defines "God," it is always man-made, and the definition it gives is therefore finite and imperfect. (Even the idea of perfection does not posit perfection.) The definition is an image, but this image does not raise the unknown fact it designates into the realm of

intelligibility, otherwise we would be entitled to say that we had created a God. The "master" we choose is not identical with the image we project of him in time and space. He goes on working as before, like an unknown quantity in the depths of the psyche.

(Storr, 1983, pp. 246–7)

These things having been said, the author supports freedom of conscience to create a pantheon. There are many existing mythologies that might be helpful in this process, going back at least as far as *The Epic of Gilgamesh*, which is at least 1,500 years older than Homer's *Illiad* and *Odyssey.*

Joseph Campbell, perhaps the world's foremost authority on comparative mythology, found many reccurring myths and gods that seem immortal enough that they should be included in most mythologies. Yet we change, and the world changes, and new mythologies are necessary to orient ourselves. The author's sense is that the new gods Cybor and Buro have been born from Gaia. Campbell, less than two years before his death in 1987, had the following exchange with Bill Moyers:

MOYERS: Scientists are beginning to talk quite openly about the Gaia principle.

CAMPBELL: There you are, the whole planet as an organism.

MOYERS: Mother Earth. Will new myths come from this image?

CAMPBELL: Well something might. ... And the only myth that is going to be worth thinking about in the immediate future is one that is talking about the planet, not the city, not these people, but the planet, and everybody on it. That's my main thought for what the future myth is going to be. And what it will have to deal with will be exactly what all myths have dealt with – the maturation of the individual, from dependency through adulthood, through maturity, and then to the exit; and then how to relate to this society and how to relate this society to the world of nature and the cosmos. That's what the myths have all talked about, and what this one's got to talk about. But the society that it's got to talk about is the society of the planet. And until that gets going, you don't have anything.

(Campbell, 1988, p. 32)

In closing this book, the author would like to break with the more formal, Cyborian academic tradition, and wish the reader: "vaya con los dioses." Going with various gods, or at least recognizing the various ways of being at play in the global human ecology, and finding one's place in such a pantheon, may be necessary for the task at hand: to better understand and sustain what we know and value.

Note

1 The dashed lines between gods in Figure 9.2 represent "inter-penetration" or "dialectic," which means the ability of the two gods to: (a) change each other; or (b) define

each other in meaningful contrast. And, as per Greek mythology, starting with Gaia and Chaos, (c) one god is created from the other(s). In mythological terms, Figure 9.2 is a family tree with the polygamous Gaia in the center, and in each case the dashed lines go between parent and offspring. In this mythology, Chaos and Gaia are the father and mother of gods, respectively, and their first offspring is Uranus (sky) who is generated from the void at the bottom of the figure. New gods are then generated, and the historical succession proceeds from the bottom of the figure to the top of the figure. In philosophical terms, the dialectical relation between thesis and antithesis results in a synthesis which becomes a new thesis.

Moving from the archaic bottom of Figure 9.2 to the modern top of Figure 9.2, a more modern "sky god" is generated from a more archaic sky god (father) as well as Gaia (mother). It would be somewhat misleading to call the axis going from the bottom to the top of the figure the time axis, because chronological time was an early transcendental construct, generated by the titan Cronus in Greek mythology. Cronus is in the lower portion of the figure, and shares the same (horizontal) archaic status as other Ancient gods that are not discussed in this chapter.

Figure 9.2 and the author's pantheon are consistent with Greek mythology, except that the author "updates" Greek mythology by adding Trinity (similar to the way of being that is idealized in most monotheistic religion) and Cybor and Buro (the author's creations) to the classical Greek pantheon. In the author's mythology, Cybor and Buro were generated from Zeus and Gaia, and they contain some properties of Gaia and Zeus while also possessing modern attributes that stand in meaningful contrast to Gaia and Zeus. The modern age can be considered as the top half of the figure, and the pre-modern age is the bottom half. Therefore, Cybor and Buro are the only two entirely modern-age gods. Zeus, Gaia, and Trinity are neutral with regard to modern versus archaic distinctions.

In the Western traditions of Greek mythology, represented on the left side of Figure 9.2, inter-penetration or dialectic between Gaia and Uranus first produces Cronus. Cronus eventually replaces Uranus and becomes the dominant Western sky god, and then dialectic between Cronus and Gaia (actually Gaia's byform Rhea) produces Zeus. The process repeats as Zeus eventually dominates Cronus. In the author's update of Greek mythology, Zeus consorts with Gaia to produce the twins Cybor and Buro. Shown at the top of the figure, Cybor and Buro are the current dominant sky gods over Gaia, with Cybor even more transcendent than Buro. Cybor and Buro, while arising out of more Western traditions, now have considerable dominance in the East as well as the West, and therefore they are horizontally centered in Figure 9.2. New ways of being in the human ecology thus arise from old ways, and they now spread globally.

In Eastern traditions, represented on the right side of Figure 9.2, various Ancients are generated from Gaia and Uranus. Then, from these Ancients, Trinity is generated. In the author's view, Trinity is the one sky god that was not directly generated from Gaia (no dashed line from Trinity to Gaia). In the author's mythology, the ever-fertile, sensuous earthy-orgiastic Gaia did not play an important *direct* role in generating the god Trinity that is idealized in most monotheistic religion. Instead, Gaia's presence in Trinity comes more *indirectly* in the second generation through other Ancients from Eastern as well as Western traditions. There is also no strong dialectic between Trinity and any other god after the Ancients – no other dashed lines – indicating that Trinity has largely broken free from processes of dialectic and historical change.

Bibliography

Abraham, Ralph (1994), *Chaos, Gaia, Eros: A Chaos Pioneer Uncovers the Three Great Streams of History*, HarperCollins Publishers (New York).

Allen, Roy E. (1997), *Cybor and Gaia: The New World Order*, Global Outlook Publishing (Oakland, California).

Bakunin, Michael, (1970), *God and the State*, Dover Publications, Inc. (New York).

Barber, Benjamin (1995), *Jihad Vs. McWorld*, Times Books (New York).

Baudrillard, Jean (1975), *The Mirror of Production*, trans. Mark Poster, Telos Press (St. Louis).

Bennett, John W. (1996), *Human Ecology as Human Behavior: Essays in Environmental and Developmental Anthropology*, Transaction Publishers (New Brunswick).

Berry, Thomas (1988), *The Dream of the Earth*, Sierra Club Books (San Francisco).

Bonaparte, Napoleon (1812), "Reponse a l'adresse du Conseil d'Etat," in Kennedy, Emmet (1978), *Destutt de Tracy and the Origins of "Ideology,"* American Philosophical Society (Philadelphia), p. 215.

Boulding, Kenneth E. (1969), "Economics as a Moral Science," *American Economic Review*, 59 (1): 1–12.

Campbell, Colin J. (2002), *Forecasting Global Oil Supply, 2000–2050*, Hubbert Center Newsletter #2002/03, M. King Hubbert Center, Colorado School of Mines, Golden, Colorado, U.S.

Campbell, Joseph (1988), *The Power of Myth*, edited by Betty Sue Flowers, Doubleday (New York).

Carr, E.H. (1961), *Michael Bakunin*, Vintage Books (New York).

Cassella, Antonio (2006), *On Democracy*. Online, available at: www.logosresearch.net/files/Democracy.pdf.

D'Alessandro, K.C. (1988), "Technophilia: Cyberpunk and Cinema," paper delivered at the Society for Cinema Studies Conference, Bozeman, Montana, July.

Dahrendorf, Ralf (1990), *Reflections on the Revolution in Europe*, Chatto and Windus (London) and Random House (New York).

de Saussure, Ferdinand (1916), *Course in General Linguistics*, trans. Roy Harris, La Salle (Open Court).

Descartes, Rene, (1960) *Discourse on Method and Meditations*, trans L.J. Lafleur, Bobbs-Merrill (Indianapolis).

Dooyeweerd, Herman (1953), *A New Critique of Theoretical Thought*, Uitgeverij H.J. Paris (Amsterdam) and The Presbyterian and Reformed Publishing Company (Philadelphia).

Downing, Christine (1987), *The Goddess: Mythological Images of the Feminine*, Crossroad Publishing Company (New York).

Ecological Economics 27 (1998), pp. 330–1, Book Review of *Cybor and Gaia: The New World Order*, by Roy E. Allen.

Edinger, Edward F. (1994), *The Eternal Drama: The Inner Meaning of Greek Mythology*, Shambhala Publications (Boston, MA).

Freud, Sigmund (1950) *Totem and Taboo: Some Points of Agreement between the Mental Lives of Savages and Neurotics*, trans. James Strachey, W.W. Norton (London).

Fromm, Erich (1976), *To Have or To Be?* Continuum Publishing Company (New York).

Gibson, W. (1984), *Neuromancer*, Ace Books (New York).

Gleick, James (1987), *Chaos, Making a New Science*, Penguin Books (New York).

Gray, Hables C. (ed.) (1995), "An Interview With Manfred Clynes," in *The Cyborg Handbook*, Routledge (New York and London).

Haraway, D.J. (1995), "Cyborgs and Symbionts: Living Together in the New World Order," in *The Cyborg Handbook*, Routledge (New York and London).

Hawkes, David (1996), *Ideology*, Routledge (London and New York).

Hegel, Georg Wilhelm Friedrich (1807), *Phenomenology of Spirit*, trans. A.V. Miller (1977), Clarendon Press (Oxford).

Heilbroner, Robert, (ed.) (1986), *The Essential Adam Smith*, W.W. Norton & Company (New York).

Hesiod (1953) *Theogony*, trans. by N.O. Brown, Macmillian Publishing Co. (New York).

Hobsbawm, Eric (1992), *Nations and Nationalism Since 1780*, Cambridge University Press (Cambridge).

Hughes, J. Donald (1986), "Mother Gaia: An Ancient View of Earth," in proceedings of Is the Earth a Living Organism? symposium at Amherst College, Audubon Expedition Institute (Spring).

Joseph, Lawrence E. (1990), *Gaia: The Growth of an Idea*, St. Martin's Press (New York).

Jowitt, Ken (1992), *New World Disorder: The Leninist Extinction*, University of California Press (Berkeley).

Kuhn, Thomas (1970), *The Structure of Scientific Revolutions*, 2nd edn, University of Chicago Press (Chicago).

Lovelock, James (1979), *Gaia: A New Look at Life on Earth*, Oxford University Press (Oxford).

Meadow, Donella H. *et al.* (1972), *The Limits to Growth: A Report For The Club Of Rome's Project On The Predicament of Mankind*, Universe Books (New York).

Milbrath, Lester (1989), *Envisioning a Sustainable Society*, State University of New York Press (New York).

Peck, M.S. (1983), *People of the Lie: The Hope For Healing Human Evil*, Touchstone, Simon and Schuster (New York).

Polanyi, Karl (1944), *The Great Transformation*, Octagon Books (New York).

Robins, Kevin, and Les Levidow (1995), "Socializing the Cyborg: The Gulf War and Beyond," in *The Cyborg Handbook*, Routledge (New York and London).

Sayle, Murray (1998), "The Social Contradictions of Japanese Capitalism," *The Atlantic Monthly*, 281: 84–94.

Schumacher, E.F. (1973), *Small is Beautiful*, Harper & Row Publishers (New York).

Smith, Huston (1994), *The Illustrated World's Religions: A Guide To Our Wisdom Traditions*, Harper Collins (San Francisco).

Sobchack, Vivian (1985), "The Virginity of Astronauts," in *Shadows of the Magic Lamp: Fantasy and Science Fiction in Film*, (ed.) George Slusser and Eric S. Rabkin, Southern Illinois University Press (Carbondale).

Spretnak, Charlene (1987), "Knowing Gaia," *ReVision: The Journal of Consciousness and Change*, 9 (2): 69–73.

Springer, C. (1996), *Electronic Eros: Bodies and Desire in the Postindustrial Age*, University of Texas Press (Austin, TX).

Sterling, B. (1991), "CATscan: Cyber-Superstition," *Science Fiction Eye 8* (Winter).

Stone, Merlin (1979), *Ancient Mirrors of Womanhood: Our Goddess and Heroine Heritage*, New Sibylline Books (New York).

Storr, Anthony, (ed.) (1983), *The Essential Jung*, MJF Books (New York).

Swimme, Brian and Thomas Berry (1992), *The Universe Story*, Harper Collins (San Francisco).

Thucydides (1954), *The Peloponnesian War*, trans. Rex Warner, Penguin Books (New York).

Thurow, Lester C. (1996), *The Future of Capitalism: How Today's Economic Forces Shape Tomorrow's World*, Penguin Books (New York).

Tucker, Robert C. (ed.) (1975), *The Lenin Anthology*, Norton (New York).

Wiener, Norbert (1948), *Cybernetics: Or Control and Communication in the Animal and the Machine*, M.I.T. Press (Cambridge, MA).

Wilson, Edward O. (1998), "The Biological Basis of Morality," *The Atlantic Monthly*, 281: 53–70.

Wilson, Edward O. (1993), "Is Humanity Suicidal?" *New York Times Magazine* (May 30).

Zizek, Slavoj (1993), *Tarrying With the Negative: Kant, Hegel, and the Critique of Ideology*, Duke University Press (Durham).

Zizek, Slavoj (1989), *The Sublime Object of Ideology*, Verso (New York).

Index

Abraham, Ralph 271–272
absolute inequality 76–77
Acevedo, Carlos 125
AE (advanced economies) 236, *236*, 254
affluence 237–238
agrarian economies: Nepal 105
agrarian reform 103–104, 108
agricultural productivity 105–106
aid dependency: Nepal 107, 108, 110, 113
Aisbett, Emma 79–80, 84
America *see* U.S.A.
American credit unions 74
anarchism: and globalization 62–65, 87
ancien régime see France (*ancien régime*)
ancient era 29
anti-globalization groups 52–53
anti-globalization protests 50
arbitration 233–234
Arnould, Ambroise Marie 172, 178–179
Arrow, K.J. 119
Asian Development Bank 114
Asian financial crisis 278–279
Athena 279–280
Atlantic economy 32, 36
atmospheric concentrations **191**
Australia: emissions restraints 208
autistic individuals 233

Bakunin, Michael 277
Baran, Paul 57
Barber, Benjamin 289
BAU benchmark scenario 193, 194, 205–206
Bayseian belief updating 87–89
belief systems: anarchists 62–65; and economic globalization 52–69; economic nationalists 65–69; free-market 55–56; and globalization 12–13; and land reform 97–102; localists

60–62, 64–65; Marxian tradition 56–60; mercantilism 163–164; neoclassical 55–56; as a structural condition 6, **7**, 8, 9; and wealth 154
Bennet, John W. 3
Berlin, Isaiah 83
Berry, Father Thomas 268
Bhagwati, Jagdish 49, 74
Bhardan, Pranab 65
biodiversity 240–242
Boulding, Kenneth 6, 287
Bourguignon, Francois 69
Braudel, Fernand 34
Brazil: absolute inequality 77
Bretton Woods system 158
Britain: Industrial Revolution 33; K-waves data 36, 37, 39; *see also* U.K.
Bronze Age 29
Brown, Brendan 153
Brown, Daniel E. 3
Brown, L. 238
Buchanan, Patrick 66, 67
Buro 100, 266, **267**, 268, 276–278, 280–283, 285, 288–289, 291, 292
Business As Usual (BAU) benchmark scenario *see* BAU benchmark scenario
Business Cycles 23

Campbell, C.J. 197, 276
Campbell, Joseph 292
"cap-and-trade" system 201, 202–207, 220–221
capital inflow: USA 143–144
capitalism 53, 152, 154
carbon emissions **191**, 192–193
carbon tax benchmark 218–220
carbon tax program 202–207
"casino capitalism" 154
Cassella, Antonio 290

change: of world economy 22–27
Chaos 265–266, **267**, 268, 270–272, 284, 290
Chaos Revolution 271, 275–278
Charlton, Andrew 50, 81
Chimæra drift 232, 238, 239, 243–244, 246, 252, 254, *258–259*
China: early trading 32, 36; income growth statistics 78; and trade liberalization 71
CHIPS (Clearing House Interbank Payments System) 145
chryshedonism 174–177
Churchill, Winston 84
"churning" 91*n*77
civil war 103, 111
Clark, Gregory 15
classical era 29
Clean Development Mechanism 204, 226*n*24
Clearing House Interbank Payments System (CHIPS) *see* CHIPS
Clément, P. 178
climate change: altruistic values 209–210; "cap-and-trade" system 201, 202–207, 220–221; carbon tax benchmark 218–220; causes 231; and Chimæra 252; coalition-building 209; consequences 213; cost–benefit analysis 213–217; environmental economics 199–201, 209; IPCC (Intergovernmental Panel on Climate Change) 189–190; Kyoto Protocol 190; mitigation costs payment 207–210; natural resource economics 196–199; policies 194–195, 201–207, 221–224; process of 190–193; timescale 210–213
cliometricians 163
Clynes, Manfred 273, 274
co-action 24–26
co-evolution 24–27
CO_2 emissions **191**, 192–193
Coase, Ronald H. 199
cognitive styles 81–84
Colbert, Jean-Baptiste 177–178
Colombo House 170
colonial trade 163–164
colonialism 58, 60
command economy 29–30
common heritage resources 61–62
commons of the Earth 238–239
communications industry 40–44
computer technology: and productivity 41
Confucius 248
consumerism 231

consumption spending 152–153
Conway, Patrick 50
corruption 103, 109
"cosmogenesis" 267
"cosmonomic ideas" 268
cotton textile industry 33
country case studies 79
"coupled oscillators" 26–27
credit unions 74
Cromwell, Oliver 87
currencies 147
cybernetics 273, 274, 275
cyberspace 274
Cybor 266, **267**, 268, 272–277, 280–281, 282, 283–284, 286, 288–289, 291
cyborgs 273, 274, 275

Daly, Herman 17
David, Paul 41
de Gaulle, Charles 158
debt crisis: Latin America 149
debt-repudiation crises 154
Declaration of Independence 288
Deininger, Klaus 99
democracy 108–109, 255, 288–290
dependency theorists 57
developing countries 69–78
development: globalization and 69–78
"development industry" 113–114
"distress sales" 107, 122
dollar: role of 147, 150
Dollar, David 77
dollar devaluation 158
dollar havens 153, 159
domestic prosperity 166
Dooyeweerd, Herman 268, 269, 285
Dosi, Giovanni 23
Dostoyevsky, Fyodor 282
Downing, Christine 270
drifts 230, 232; *see also* Chimæra drift; Siege of Troy drift
dual tenancy 119–120
dualism (confrontation) 255
duality: Chaos and Gaia 270–272, 290
Dutch-French trade 177–178
Dutch Republic: K-waves data 39

ecological economics 4
economic evolution 22–27
economic globalization 31–37
economic growth: and financial liberalization 73–75; and trade openness 71–73; USA 159–160
economic history, world 28–32

economic nationalists: and globalization 65–69
economic policies: Nepal 108–109
economic wealth 154
economics: definition 4
electronic funds transfer systems 145–146
Elliott *et al.* 53, 62, 63
emission permits 204–205, 206
emission trading systems *see* "cap-and-trade" system
energy consumption 242–246; and income *236*
energy demand *260*
energy economics 199
energy intensity *260–261*
energy markets 196–199
energy per capita *261*
energy surplus **245**
energy use *198*
England 164
the Enlightenment 283, 286
environmental economics 195, 199–201, 209
environmental Kuznets curve 208–209
Epstein, Barbara 58
E.U. Climate Exchange 226*n*24
E.U. (European Union): "cap-and-trade" system 203, 204, 206; Kyoto emission targets 227*n*28
evolution: of world economy 22–27
evolutionary approach 22–28
"evolutionary theory" 120
Evolutionary Theory of Economic Change, An 23
exchange rates 77–78
exploitation 58, 59
extinction rate 231, 240–242, 245

Fallin, Valentin 285
Fedwire 145
fertility rates 231, 236
fiat money systems 150
financial crises 74, 147–150, 278–279
financial liberalization 73–75, 109, 148
financial markets: developments in 145–147
first attention 232, 233, 234, 250–251, 256
Fischer, David Hackett 32
"flat Earth economists" 197
flow of funds 145–146
food shortages 238–240
foreign aid 113
former Soviet Union 279, 285; *see also* Russia

fossil fuel 242–246
Foucault, Michael 281
Foucaultian surveillance 281
fox–hedgehog metaphors 233
fractals 272
France (*ancien régime*): chryshedonism 174–177; economic growth (eighteenth century) 166–168; external trade 177–182; labor reserves 168–169; market participation 169–174; mercantilist trade policies 177–182; monetary capital 171–174; monetary system 176–177; overview 164; population 167–169; producers 171; quality control 171; traders 170–171
Franco-Dutch trade 177–178
Frank, Andre Gunder 36
free-market belief system 55–56
"free-rider" problem: global warming policy negotiations 200
free will: and determinism dichotomy 285–288
freedom 285–292
Freeman, Christopher 23, 41, 73
Freeman III, A. Myrick 200–201
Friedman, Milton 83
fundamentalism 231, 255
Fundamentals of Human Ecology 3

Gaia 100–101, 265–266, **267**, 268, 270–272, 284, 290
Gaia Hypothesis 271, 275–277
GDP per capita *259*
GDP-productivity 151–152
General Systems Theory 6
Germany: K-waves data 36
Gibson, William 274
GIRO credit transfer 145–146
Gleick, James 272
global climate models 191
global economic evolution 31–37
global political leadership: and K-waves 37–40
global sustainability: policy responses for 161
global warming *see* climate change
global warming stability: "free-rider" problem 200
globalization: attitudes to 53–55; and belief systems 52–69; complexity of 79–80; controversy over 78–86; debate about 50; and development 69–78; economic 49–50; and economic nationalists 65–69; and human ecology

globalization *continued*
   approach 50–52; ideologies 53–55; and
   inequality 75–78; and poverty reduction
   75–78; uncertainty about 47–48
globalization activists 62–65
Golding, William 271
good *versus* bad 285
Gould, S.J. 240
governance 231
government failure 56, 59, 81, 92n98
Grameen Bank 74
Grantham, George W. 168
Gray, Hables C. 273
green energy 244
greenhouse gas concentrations 193; *see
   also* climate change
Greenspan, Alan 41, 83, 150
Griffin *et al.* 117
"ground motives" 268
group inequality 111–112

Haidar, Jörg 66
Haraway, D.J. 274
Harberger, Arnold 71
Hardin, Garritt 62
hedgehog–fox metaphors 83–84, 233
Hegel, G.W.F. 270
Heilbroner, Robert 272
heritage resources 61–62
Hicks, John 28, 29
hierarchy 283–284, 291
history: world economy 28–32
HLAI (human-level artificial intelligence)
   247–248, 252
Hobsbawm, Eric 289
Hopkins, Sheila 32
horizontal inequality 76
Hotelling, Harold 196
Hubbert, M. King 276
human ecology: and climate change
   193–195; definition 6, 7; elements of
   51–52; structural overview 4–10; as a
   term 3–4
Human Ecology: Problems and Solutions
   3
*Human Ecology as Human Behavior:
   Essays in Environmental and
   Developmental Anthropology* 3
human ecology framework: Nepal 111
human-level artificial intelligence (HLAI)
   see HLAI
human populations 6–7, 8, 9, 12, 21
"Humpty-Dumpty" effect 241
Huygens, Christiaan 26

ideologies: of globalization 53–55
IMF (International Monetary Fund) 61, 87
IMF study 74
imperialism 57, 58
income: and energy consumption *236*
income distribution 75–78
India: absolute inequality 77
Industrial Revolution 33, 283
inequality 75–78
inflation 159
information age 33, 40–43
information industries 40–43, 152
information transfer 246–247
innovation 33–36, 151
institutions 21–22
Intergovernmental Panel on Climate
   Change (IPCC) *see* IPCC
International Monetary Fund (IMF) *see*
   IMF
Internet 41, 42
IPCC (Intergovernmental Panel on Climate
   Change) 189–190, 214
Italy: global economic evolution 32, 36

Japan: Cybor and Buro 289; electronics
   companies 42; information industries 43
Japanese yen 153
Joseph, Lawrence E. 271
Jowitt, Ken 281
Jung, Karl 268, 284–285, 287, 288,
   291–292
junk food 231

K-waves 23, 24, 26, 27, 32–40
Kanbur, Ravi 53, 80–81
Kaya identity 192
Keynes, John Maynard 60, 84
Kline, Nathan S. 273, 274
knowledge capital **173**
Kondratieff, Nikolai 33
Kondratieff-waves *see* K-waves
Kormondy, Edward J. 3
Kraay, Aart 77
Krautkraemer, J. 197
Krugman, Paul 50
Kuhn, Thomas 271
Kump *et al.* 245
Kunstler, J.H. 242
Kyoto Protocol 190, 203–204, 208, 209,
   214

land: demand for 103–104
land distribution 103
land ownership: Nepal 108

land reform: and belief systems 97–102;
    Nepal 104–108, 112, 115–125; and rural
    poor 98
land sales 107
Landes, David 36
landlessness 111, 116
Lands Act (1964): Nepal 120–123
Lao Tzu 248
Latin America: debt crisis 149
leadership, global political: and K-waves
    37–40
Leakey, R. 240, 241
Lenin, Vladimir 57, 281
Lento, R. 239
LePen, Jean Marie 66
Lewin, R. 240, 241
liberalization: of finance 73–75; of trade
    71–73, 81
liberty *see* freedom
limit-cycle oscillators 27
liquidity discount 158–159
localists 60–62, 64–65, 73–74, 87
location: of computer industries 41–42;
    and innovation 35, 36–37
Lomborg, B. 197, 216, 217, 224n6
Lovelock, James 271
Lucas–Phelps model 176

McNeill, William 30
mandalas 267
Manji, Ambreena 121
Maoist insurgency 111, 112–113; Nepal 98
Maoists 100, 102, 103, 104–105, 114–115
Margulis, Lyn 271
market-assisted land reform 105, 117–118
market economy 29–30
market exchange rates 77–78
market failure 56, 59, 81, 92n98
market systems 30
Marx, Karl 53, 56–57, 281
Marxism 56–60, 73, 87
Marxists 63, 104, 154
Meadows *et al.* 194, 197
mediation 234
Mensch, Gerhard 23
mercantilism 16, 67, 68–69, 157–158,
    163–164
mercantilist trade policies: *ancien régime*
    177–182
"merchant capital" 172–174
Mexican peso 147
micro-finance 109
microprocessors 42
Milanovic, Branko 60, 62

Mill, J.S. 174
Mishkin, F.S. 150
misrepresentation 80–81
Modelski, George 151
monetary capital 171–174, **173**
monetary wealth 144, 155–157, 165
money: as capital 174–177
"money-mercantilism" 16, 69, 144,
    155–160
moral freedom 290–292
moral philosophy: and economics 11–12
Moyers, Bill 292
multinational corporations 62

National Environmental Policy Act
    (NEPA) *see* NEPA
nationalism 57, 58, 65–69, 87
natural resource economics 195, 196–199
natural resource markets 196–199
Navigation Acts-type trade policies 164
Nelson, Richard 23
neoclassical belief system 55–56, 99–100,
    163–164, 175
neoclassical theory 91n57
neoliberalism 87
NEPA (National Environmental Policy
    Act) 275
Nepal: agrarian reform 103; agricultural
    productivity 105–106, 116–117; aid
    dependency 107, 108, 110, 113;
    corruption 109; current legislation
    117–123; democracy 108–109;
    "development industry" 113–114; early
    land reforms 115–117; economic
    policies 108–109; economic situation
    102–103; elites 108; financial
    liberalization 109; group inequality
    111–112; land reform 102, 104–108,
    112, 115–125; Lands Act (1964)
    120–123; Maoist insurgency 98, 111,
    112–113; market-assisted land reform
    117–118; micro-finance 109; NGOs
    108–109, 114, 115; poverty 110;
    tenancy 117–120; trade deficit 109;
    trade liberalization 109
Nepalese Tarai 106, 115, 116
NGOs 54–55, 114, 115
Nietzsche, Friedrich 286
Nitzan, Jonathan 156
Norgaard, Richard B. 4
North, Douglass 7, 12, 21

ocean anoxia 245
offshore financial markets 153, 155

OPEC countries 279
"option values" 209
organizations 7, 21–22
oscillators 26–27

Palen, Ronan 153
Parker, Edward 237
payment systems 146
PDCs (population-driven countries)
    235–236, 254
Perez, Carlotta 23
Phelps-Brown, Henry 32
physical environments and resources 7, **8**,
    9, 12, 21
Pigou, A. 199
Platteau, Jean-Philippe 121
Polanyi, Karl 15
political freedom 288–290
political leadership: and K-waves 37–40
population 231
population-driven countries (PDCs) *see*
    PDCs
population growth 235–236, *257*
Portugal: global trading 32; K-waves data
    39, 40
poverty 69–78, 98, 231, 237–238
poverty reduction 75–78, 80, 108
precious metals 157, 166, 174, 176–177,
    179–180
price revolutions 32
Pringle, J.W.S. 26
prior beliefs 80, 84–85, 87–89
productivity 151–152
productivity paradox 41
property ownership 152
property rights 118
protectionism 66–67, 80–81
protests 50
Proudhon, Pierre-Joseph 63
PSIT (proximal-senses information
    transmission) 247, 252
public goods 200
pulse coupling 27
purchasing power parity (PPP) exchange
    rates 77–78

quasi-moneys 147–148, 153

ratio inequality 76–77
Ravallion, Martin 75–77
Reagan, Ronald 160
reconciling opposition 269–278
redistribution: income 70–71; land
    104–105

regression studies 79
relative inequality 76–77
reputation capital 172
Rhodes, Cecil 58–59
Rodrik, Dani 67–68, 72
Roszak, Theodore 276
rubles 147–148
rural poverty 98
Russell, Bertrand 286
Russia 147–148, 203–204; *see also* former
    Soviet Union

Sachs, Jeffrey 59
Saint Francis 235, 253
Sala-I-Martin, Xavier 78
Sayle, Murray 279
Scheve, Kenneth 55
Schumacher, E.F. 276, 283
Schumpeter, Joseph 23, 33, 34, 151, 278
second attention 233, 234, 249, 250, 256
Sen, Amartya 49
sequence 233, 234, 249, 255
sharecropping 118, 119
short-term finance 74
Siege of Troy drift 232, 237–238,
    242–243, 246, 252, 254, *258*
Silk Roads 30, *31*, 36
Simon, Julian 197
simultaneity 233, 234, 235, 256
Slaughter, Matthew 55
small-farmer productivity theory 106–107,
    117
Smith, Adam 272
social agreements 6, 7, 8, 9, 12, 21, 154
social capital 172, **173**
socialism 53
Soddy, Frederick 154
soft-currencies 147–148, 153
software 42
Solomon, Elinor Harris 146
Soros, George 74
South Korea: electronics companies 42
Soviet Union, former 279, 285; *see also*
    Russia
Spain: global trading 32
specialization 55, 56–57
Spretnak, Charlene 270
Stalin, Joseph 281
starvation 231
"steady state" economy 17
Stern, Sir Nicholas 216, 217
Stern Review 224*n*6
Stiglitz, Joseph 50, 74, 81
Storr, Anthony 268, 287, 291–292

structural conditions 6–10, 21
sub-Saharan Africa: income and energy consumption *236*; Marxian-based theories 58
subsidarity, principle of 61
sustainability 194, 214, **215**, 216, 249, 251; definition 11
sustainable development: definition 17
Swiss banks 153
synchronization 26–27

tax havens 153
tenancy 117–120, 122
tenurial reforms 105
Tetlock, Philip 78, 81–84, 85
Thai baht 147
Thatcher, Margaret 160
Theory of Economic Development 23
third attention 233, 234, 248–249, 253, 257
Thompson, William R. 32, 35, 41, 151
Thurow, Lester 289
titling 120
trade liberalization: Nepal 109
trade openness 71–73, 81
"tragedy of the commons" 62, 67, 111
transaction 166
Trinity 266, **267**, 268–269, 280, 282, 283, 284–286, 291
Tucker, Robert 281

U.K. (United Kingdom): climate policy 209; *see also* Britain
U.N. (United Nations) 190
United Nations Environment Programme 189–190
United Nations Framework Convention on Climate Change 17–18, 190, 201–202, 208, 214
U.S. Treasury 80–81
U.S.A.: and ancient Athens 280; "cap-and-trade" system 201, 203; capital inflow 143–144; consumption spending 152–153; credit unions 74; *Declaration of Independence* 288; economic growth 159–160; emissions restraints 208; financial crises 150; global trading 32;

information industries 42–44; K-waves data 36, 37, 39, 40; and Kyoto Protocol 189–190; money mercantilism 155–160; and Nepal 113
USAID 114

Van Duijn, J.J. 33
Veblen, Thorstein 156, 157
venture capital: and energy 206
vertical inequality 76
virtual money 146
voice communication 247

Wade, Robert Hunter 75, 77–78, 80–81
Wagner, Richard 277
Ward, D.W. 245
water shortages 238–240
"ways of being": definition 187–188, 265; examples 265–266
wealth: human ecology understanding of 150–155
wealth-productivity 151–152
weapons of mass destruction (WMD) *see* WMD
Wells, H.G. 4–5, 50–51, 97
West Germany 289
Wiener, Norbert 273
"will to power" 286
Winter, Sidney 23
WMD (weapons of mass destruction) 231
World Bank 61, 107, 120
World Brain 5
World Commission on Environment and Development 214
World Development Report 2000 80–81
world economic history 28–32
world market 30
World Meteorological Organization 189–190
world poverty 75; *see also* poverty
world reserve currency 147, 150
world-systems theory 58
World Wide Web 41, 42
worship 284–285
W.T.O. (World Trade Organization) 61

Zeus 100, 265–266, **267**, 278–280, 282